Handbook
for the
Revised
Common
Lectionary

D0506508

Handbook
for the
Revised
Common
Lectionary

Peter C. Bower
editor

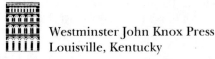

Westminster John Knox Press
Louisville, Kentucky

Appreciation is expressed to *Societas Liturgica* for permission to adapt portions of an article published in its journal *Studia Liturgica* 21, no. 1 (1991), "*Common Lectionary:* Origins, Assumptions and Issues," by Horace T. Allen, Jr., and to the Alcuin Club and the Contributors for permission to adapt portions of a chapter of its *Festschrift* in honor of Canon Donald Gray titled "Preaching and Lectionary," by Horace T. Allen, Jr., published by The Canterbury Press, Norwich, England, 1995.

Book design by Jennifer K. Cox
Cover design by Vickie Arrowood

First edition

Published by Westminster John Knox Press
Louisville, Kentucky

This book is printed on acid-free paper that meets the American National Standards Institute Z39.48 standard. ∞

PRINTED IN THE UNITED STATES OF AMERICA

99 00 01 02 03 04 05 — 10 9 8 7 6 5 4 3 2

Library of Congress Cataloging-in-Publication Data

Handbook for the Revised common lectionary / Peter C. Bower, editor. —
   1st ed.
       p.   cm.
   Includes bibliographical references and index.
   ISBN 0-664-25657-0 (alk. paper)
   1. Presbyterian Church (U.S.A.)—Liturgy.   2. Common lectionary
(1992)   3. Presbyterian Church—United States—Liturgy.   4. Lectionary
preaching—Presbyterian Church (U.S.A.)   I. Bower, Peter C.   II. Common
lectionary (1992)
BX8969.5.H36   1996
264′.34—dc20   96-2441

In memory of *Robert Eugene*
a quiet leader

*"Listen, children, to a father's instruction,
and be attentive, that you may gain insight;
for I give you good precepts."*
PROVERBS 4:1–2

CONTENTS

....

PREFACE

....

In 1990 the Presbyterian Church (U.S.A.) published a new *Presbyterian Hymnal* and, in 1993, *The Psalter: Psalms and Canticles for Singing*. In 1992 the Consultation on Common Texts (CCT) printed its Revised Common Lectionary (*RCL*). These three resources generated the congregations' need for this worship planning resource.

This handbook is modeled on the earlier handbooks to the lectionary and the common lectionary (published in 1980 and 1987), but this book includes as primary resources the *Presbyterian Hymnal* (1990) and the *Psalter*. Similar in format to its predecessors, this volume provides materials for every Sunday of the year as well as midweek festival days. Its particular features include:

1. Brief notes on each of the three biblical texts (Peter C. Bower)
2. Anthems evoked by the biblical texts (Lucile L. Hair)
3. Musical settings for the psalm appointed for the day (Sally Watkins Gant)
4. Organ music for the day (Robert E. Stigall)
5. Hymns for the day (Peter C. Bower)

These resources should provide practical help to pastors, musicians, and worship committees.

This volume provides additional helps by economizing on duplicate entries. That is, identical lections assigned to the same day in all three years (for example, Christmas Eve/Day, Epiphany of the Lord, Easter Vigil) are labeled as (ABC). Notes on these lections and their suggested anthems, psalm readings, organ music, and hymns are printed in full *only* in Year A and cross-referenced in Years B and C. This arrangement provides readers one combined listing for all the liturgical suggestions for that day for all three years rather than arbitrarily dividing these resources across three separate entries.

The number of each Sunday in Ordinary Time is given within brackets in the heading. Also, it may be worth noting here that Year A begins on the First Sunday of Advent in 1998, 2001, 2004. Year B begins on the First Sunday of Advent in 1996, 1999, 2002. Year C begins on the First Sunday of Advent in 1997, 2000, 2003, and so forth.

An insightful and provocative Introduction by Horace T. Allen, Jr., addresses the ecumenical acceptance of the Revised Common Lectionary, its historical and ecumenical origins, and the implications of careful and disciplined homiletical use of the lectionary as laid out in this handbook.

Deep appreciation is expressed here for each of the persons who labored out of love to make this handbook possible. Thanks are given to Horace T. Allen, Jr., Sally Watkins Gant, Lucile L. Hair, and Robert E. Stigall. In researching, writing, editing, and *tirelessly* proofreading each of their contributions, they assured that this handbook in its totality would truly evidence the adage that the whole is greater than the sum of its parts.

A servant of Christ who painstakingly keyed entries into computers, suggested countless new and improved ways to make this handbook user-friendly, and proofread again and again is Molly M. Macaulay, elder of the Drayton Avenue Presbyterian Church in Ferndale, Michigan.

Each of us will derive the greatest thanks from worship planners and leaders when they use these resources as a means to give scripture a central place in the church's worship. Perhaps the current Presbyterian Church's Directory for Worship puts it best: "Lectionaries offered by the church ensure a broad range of readings as well as consistency and connection with the universal church. Using lectionaries . . . is helpful in seeking to hear the full message of God's Word" (W–2.2003; W–5.3003).

CONTRIBUTORS

....

HORACE T. ALLEN, JR., serves as Associate Professor of Worship at the School of Theology, Boston University, co-chair of the English Language Liturgical Consultation, and a member of the Consultation on Common Texts and the Task Force on Revision of the Common Lectionary. He developed *A Handbook for the Lectionary* (Philadelphia: Geneva Press, 1980).

PETER C. BOWER, former Editor of *Reformed Liturgy & Music* (for fourteen years), serves as Stated Supply of Northside Presbyterian Church in Ann Arbor, Michigan. He also served as the editor and principal writer of *Handbook for the Common Lectionary* (Philadelphia: Geneva Press, 1987).

SALLY WATKINS GANT serves as Director of Music at Shallowford Presbyterian Church, Lewisville, North Carolina, and Director of Education and Special Programs at the Museum of Early Southern Decorative Arts, Winston-Salem, North Carolina.

LUCILE L. HAIR serves as Director of Music at the University Presbyterian Church, Baton Rouge, Louisiana.

ROBERT E. STIGALL serves as Director of Music at Myers Park Presbyterian Church, Charlotte, North Carolina. He also serves as Lecturer in Music and College Organist at Queens College, Charlotte.

ABBREVIATIONS

....

Psalm Resources

ANMP	*A New Metrical Psalter*
APS	*A Psalm Sampler*
CC	*Cantor/Congregation Series*
CS/PFTCY	*Celebration Series (Psalms for the Church Year)*
DP/SLR	*Daily Prayer.* Supplemental Liturgical Resource 5
GG	*The Gelineau Gradual: Responsorial Psalms from the Lectionary for Mass for the Sundays and Principal Feasts of the Liturgical Year*
GGP	*The Grail Gelineau Psalter: 150 Psalms and 18 Canticles*
GPI	*Grail Psalms: The Psalms*
H82	*The Hymnal* (1982)
HB55	*The Hymnbook* (1955)
HL33	*The Hymnal* (1933)
MFTII	*Music from Taizé II*
PH87	*The Psalter Hymnal* (1987)
PH90	*The Presbyterian Hymnal: Hymns, Psalms, and Spiritual Songs* (1990)
PP	*Psalm Praise*
PR&T	*Psalm Refrains and Tones for the Common Lectionary*
PS93	*The Psalter: Psalms and Canticles for Singing* (1993)
10P	*Ten Psalms*
20P&3C	*Twenty Psalms and Three Canticles*
24P&1C	*Twenty-four Psalms and One Canticle*
30P&2C	*Thirty Psalms and Two Canticles*
RCL	*Revised Common Lectionary*
RITL	*Rejoice in the Lord: A Hymn Companion to the Scriptures*
SPJP	*Singing Psalms of Joy and Praise*
SOI	*Songs of Israel: Seasonal Responsorial Psalms for the Entire Year*
TIP/PSCY	*The Ionian Psalter: Fifteen Psalms for the Seasons of the Church Year*
TIP/MTYL	*The Ionian Psalter: Music for the Three Year Lectionary of the Book of Common Prayer*
WIII	*Worship III*
WB72	*The Worshipbook: Services and Hymns* (1972)

Anthems

(E)	Easy
(ME)	Medium-Easy
(M)	Medium
(MD)	Medium-Difficult
(D)	Difficult

Tunes

C.M.	Common Meter (8.6.8.6)
C.M.D.	Common Meter Double
L.M.	Long Meter (8.8.8.8)
L.M.D.	Long Meter Double
S.M.	Short Meter (6.6.8.6)
S.M.D.	Short Meter Double

Other

alt.	altered (hymn text); alternate (reading)
CL	*Common Lectionary* (1983)
NRSV	New Revised Standard Version
RCL	*Revised Common Lectionary* (1992)
st(s)	stanza(s)

RESOURCES
FOR THE PSALM SETTINGS

....

ANMP   *A New Metrical Psalter.* Christopher L. Webber. Texts
              only with suggested hymn tunes. Published by The
              Church Hymnal Corporation, 800 Second Avenue,
              New York, NY 10017.

APS   *A Psalm Sampler.* A sampling of metrical and responsor-
              ial psalms for use by congregations, small groups,
              families, and individuals, in retreat settings and in
              judicatory worship. 1986. The Office of Worship.
              Westminster Press.

CC   *Cantor/Congregation Series.* Through-composed respon-
              sorial psalms of varying difficulty. Some scored for
              optional instruments. Various composers. Published
              by G.I.A. Publications, 7404 South Mason Avenue,
              Chicago, IL 60638.

CS/PFTCY   *Celebration Series (Psalms for the Church Year).* Volume 1,
              Volume 2, Volume 3. Celebration Series is marked
              by "contemporary folk-style sounds." Various com-
              posers. Published by G.I.A. Publications, 7404 South
              Mason Avenue, Chicago, IL 60638.

DP/SLR   *Daily Prayer* Supplemental Liturgical Resource 5. The
              Office of Worship, Presbyterian Church (U.S.A).
              Published by Westminster Press, 1985. Available
              from Westminster John Knox Press, 100 Witherspoon
              Street, Louisville, KY 40202-1396.

GG   *The Gelineau Gradual: Responsorial Psalms from the Lec-
              tionary for Mass for the Sundays and Principal Feasts of the
              Liturgical Year.* Published by G.I.A. Publications, 7404
              South Mason Avenue, Chicago, IL 60638.

GGP   *The Grail Gelineau Psalter: 150 Psalms and 18 Canticles.*
              Compiled and edited by J. Robert Carroll. Complete
              edition. G-1703. Available from G.I.A. Publications,
              7404 South Mason Avenue, Chicago, IL 60638.

GPI   *Grail Psalms: The Psalms.* An inclusive-language version
              based on the Grail translation from the Hebrew.

Available from G.I.A. Publications, 7404 South Mason Avenue, Chicago, IL 60638.

GTHR *Gather.* A collection of contemporary folk style hymns, songs and psalms. 1988. Robert J. Batastini, General Editor. Published by G.I.A. Publications, 7404 South Mason Avenue, Chicago, IL 60638.

H82 *The Hymnal 1982.* According to the use of The Episcopal Church. The Church Hymnal Corporation, 800 Second Avenue, New York, NY 10017.

HB55 *The Hymnbook* (1955). Published by Presbyterian Church in the United States, The United Presbyterian Church in the U.S.A., and the Reformed Church in America. Out of print.

HL33 *The Hymnal* (1933). Published by the Presbyterian Church in the United States of America.

MFTII *Music from Taizé II.* A second volume in the published collection of music from the community of Taizé. Edited by Brother Robert. Published by G.I.A. Publications (G-2778), 7404 South Mason Avenue, Chicago, IL 60638.

PH87 *The Psalter Hymnal 1987.* CRC Publications, 2850 Kalamazoo Avenue, SE, Grand Rapids, MI 49560. Includes metrical settings for all 150 psalms.

PH90 *The Presbyterian Hymnal: Hymns, Psalms, and Spiritual Songs* (1990). Published by Westminster John Knox Press, 100 Witherspoon Street, Louisville, KY 40402-1396.

PP *Psalm Praise.* G.I.A. Publications, 7404 South Mason Avenue, Chicago, IL 60638.

PR&T *Psalm Refrains and Tones for the Common Lectionary* with Inclusive Language for God and People. Hal H. Hopson. Hope Publishing Company, Carol Stream, IL 60188.

PS93 *The Psalter: Psalms and Canticles for Singing* (1993). Published by Westminster John Knox Press, 100 Witherspoon Street, Louisville, KY 40402-1396.

10P *Ten Psalms.* Hal H. Hopson. HH-3030. Hope Publishing Company, Carol Stream, IL 60188.

20P&3C *Twenty Psalms and Three Canticles.* Joseph Gelineau. G-1476. G.I.A. Publications, 7404 South Mason Avenue, Chicago, IL 60638.

24P&1C *Twenty-four Psalms and One Canticle.* Joseph Gelineau. G-1424. G.I.A. Publications, 7404 South Mason Avenue, Chicago, IL 60638.

30P&2C   *Thirty Psalms and Two Canticles.* Joseph Gelineau. G-1430. G.I.A. Publications, 7404 South Mason Avenue, Chicago, IL 60638.

RITL   *Rejoice in the Lord: A Hymn Companion to the Scriptures.* Edited by Erik Routley. Wm. B. Eerdmans Publishing Company, 255 Jefferson Avenue, SE, Grand Rapids, MI 49503.

SPJP   *Singing Psalms of Joy and Praise.* Fred R. Anderson. Philadelphia: Westminster Press, 1986.

SOI   *Songs of Israel: Seasonal Responsorial Psalms for the Entire Year.* Volumes 1 and 2. C. Alexander Peloquin. G.I.A. Publications, 7404 South Mason Avenue, Chicago, IL 60638.

TIP/PSCY   *The Ionian Psalter: Fifteen Psalms for the Seasons of the Church Year.* Peter R. Hallock. PS-801. Ionian Arts, Inc., P.O. Box 259, Mercer Island, WA 98040-0259.

TIP/MTYL   *The Ionian Psalter: Music for the Three Year Lectionary of the Book of Common Prayer.* Peter R. Hallock. PS-801. Ionian Arts, Inc., P.O. Box 259, Mercer Island, WA 98040-0259. A complete three-year cycle of the psalms for the lectionary of the *Book of Common Prayer* (1977), consisting of antiphons for congregation and verses for choir in a modified Anglican form.

WIII   *Worship III.* Published by G.I.A. Publications, 7404 South Mason Avenue, Chicago, IL 60638.

WB72   *The Worshipbook: Services and Hymns* (1972). Published by Westminster Press. Available from Westminster John Knox Press, 100 Witherspoon Street, Louisville, KY 40202-1396.

Introduction:
Preaching in a Christian Context

Horace T. Allen, Jr.

Preaching in Protestant America, and indeed in much of the English-speaking world, has entered a new era. The uniqueness of this era is rooted in two fairly recent developments. The first is the development of a broadly based consensus to be found in contemporary worship books and directories for worship concerning the use of the historically normative weekly celebration of both Word *and* Sacrament on the Lord's Day. This early Christian assumption that the Lord's Day was always to be observed by both spoken *and* enacted proclamation of the Word of God, as the only appropriate way to participate in the presence of the risen Lord, has mysteriously eluded Christian praxis. On the one hand, many traditions, East and West, allowed the sacramental ceremonies to overwhelm and upstage the reading and preaching of the Word, in mass and liturgy, and on the other hand, reforming and evangelical preoccupations were content to relegate sacraments and sacramentals to the sidelines of infrequent and incidental liturgical embellishments.

Happily, one of the fruits of a century-old movement for liturgical renewal in many churches, Catholic and Protestant, has resulted in a widespread commitment to restoring this balance to the weekly worship of Christians. In this way the subjectivity of personal speech—the sermon or homily—is balanced by the objectivity of ecclesial sacrament(s). And the historical witness to the Christ-event—the sacrament—is balanced by the contemporaneous witness to the Spirit-given presence of Christ in proclamation and preaching. And within the Word sequence this same balance is achieved by the combination of systematic use of scripture week by week (known as "lectionary") and the pastorally and personally crafted sermon. Equally, within the sacramental sequence, this balance is found in the combination of eucharistic praying, which is biblically and theologically resonant, and corporate participation in spoken and sung acclamations. This is coupled with an emphasis on more frequent sharing of both bread and wine by the whole community, which might be facilitated by concurrent song and mobility on the part of the congregation. Further, even in traditions where the celebration of the Sacrament of the Lord's Table is not yet a weekly event, these same new worship books and directories for worship propose a liturgical structure that follows the sermon with congregational actions such as profession of faith, corporate and sometimes spontaneous intercessions ("Prayers of the People"), offering of monetary gifts, the exchange of Peace, and a concluding general prayer of thanksgiving completed by the Lord's Prayer (this alternate to a sacramental conclusion being classically known as "Ante-Communion").

These ecumenical developments provide preaching with a completely new context. No longer will it be possible or acceptable to abandon the

1

sermon on "Communion Sunday" for a modest nonexegetical "Communion meditation." Nor will an impromptu assemblage of topical, pastoral, congregational, or devotional reflections suffice as an exegetical homily on the lessons for the day. Further, the sermon or homily (synonymous terms having nothing to do with the length of the oration) will have always to take account of the fact that it is not in itself the climactic event of worship but simply the opening up of the mystery of the Lord's Day assembly, which is finally constituted in its "sacrifice of praise and thanksgiving," normatively over bread and cup. Thus the sermon "textualizes" the sacramental or nonsacramental Thanksgiving, and the Thanksgiving "con-text-ualizes" the sermon and its scripture.

The second and more recent development that is shaping this new era of preaching is the appearance in the last few decades of a new and also ecumenical consensus regarding the liturgical use of scripture, the written Word. Here too a vast shift in theory and practice has taken place. Preachers, both Catholic and Protestant, especially in the English-speaking world, now find themselves in the presence of an ecumenically acceptable system, or "lectionary," for determining the choice and arrangement of scripture for the Sunday celebration. Although some churches are quite accustomed to the use of a lectionary, many are not, and even those that are have never considered the possibility that others might also be using the *same* set of readings, Lord's Day by Lord's Day, which will include readings from both biblical Testaments.

Thus scripture, as well as a concluding act of thanksgiving, becomes the operative context of Christian preaching. It is not the other way around; nor is it now simply a matter of personal or denominational choice. Because of the consonance, coherence, and interdependence of the universal Roman Catholic Lectionary (*Ordo Lectionum Missae,* 1969),[1] with its derivatives in Anglican, Lutheran, and Presbyterian books in the 1970s, to say nothing of its second- and third-generation ecumenical adaptations in the *Common Lectionary* (1983)[2] and the *Revised Common Lectionary* (1992),[3] preachers throughout Australia, New Zealand, Canada, South Africa, Korea, Great Britain, and the United States are now being confronted and challenged by virtually the same biblical texts each week. There has not been such wide agreement on readings since the breakup of Western Catholicism in and after the sixteenth century.

Because of the particular principles of selection underlying this three-year ecumenical lectionary system, which will be analyzed later in this Introduction, it is now the case that the preacher who uses this system will have to be far more biblically sophisticated and responsible than heretofore in at least two ways: (1) The extensive use of "continuous reading" week to week (so-called *lectio continua,* which characterizes more than half the Sundays of the entire year) requires a careful attention to the

---

1. Sacred Congregation for Divine Worship, *Ordo Lectionum Missae* (Rome: Vatican Polyglot Press, 25 May 1969).
2. Consultation on Common Texts, *Common Lectionary: The Lectionary Proposed by the Consultation on Common Texts* (New York: Church Hymnal Corporation, 1983).
3. Consultation on Common Texts, *The Revised Common Lectionary* (Nashville: Abingdon Press, 1992).

overall unity of biblical books and their theological assumptions, as opposed to the reading of random selections week to week from various books of the Bible in a kind of "oracular" nonsequence. (2) The relation of the scripture readings to certain festivals and seasons and their interrelationships (so-called *lectio selecta,* which occupies the remaining Sundays of the year) requires more careful attention to the theological and pastoral assumptions of the classic weekly and annual Christian calendars than is manifested in such dubious assumptions as Lord's-Day-as-"Sabbath," Advent-as-Christmas, Lent-as-penitential, Pentecost-as-"birthday of the church," and Holy Week as a literalist, historicist drama.

Conceivably, the new contextualization by scripture of the sermon will result in preaching that is more biblically informed and seasonally grounded, and less hortatory and moralistic. Perhaps such preaching can fill the "gap" between a somewhat free-wheeling homiletic, which only occasionally takes the scriptures seriously, and the opposite and equally *unserious* literalism, which simply says "The Bible says." In this way the classic Protestant traditions might discover (to their surprise?) an appealing and effective response to both conservative and charismatic challenges.

This new style of preaching requires an analysis from both sides: sacramental and liturgical, on the one hand, and ecumenical and biblical on the other. For both Catholic and Protestant preachers, this may well be uncharted territory. The purpose of this introduction is to provide something of a road map of that territory for such preachers, lest by the use of this handbook they simply plunge into the lectionary as a quick and handy way to choose Sunday's scriptures, without realizing that it will only worsen their preaching if they fail to grasp the underlying assumptions and principles of selection of liturgical and calendrical contexts. The broad extent of that terrain may be indicated by six important assumptions that should underlie the careful and disciplined homiletical use of the *Revised Common Lectionary* as laid out in this handbook. They are as follows:

1. Sunday as sequential, making possible narrative preaching rather than disconnected hits or misses.
2. Scripture as its own context, due to the *lectio continua* principle and the respect necessary for various literary genres as found in the Bible.
3. Scripture as governing the liturgical calendar, especially in the festal seasons of Advent—Christmas Day—Epiphany, and Lent—Easter Day—Pentecost.
4. The preacher as "obedient" to the text rather than choosing it for his or her own purposes.
5. Preaching as a more participatory experience within the parish, in terms of a richer integration of musical and educational programs, and more participatory ecumenically, in terms of local mutual study across denominational lines.
6. Integration of the sermon into the whole liturgy for the day, and particularly in relation to the celebration of sacraments and pastoral offices such as weddings, funerals, care of the sick, and vocational and faith decisions.

Before proceeding to a discussion of these six assumptions inherent in the proper and effective use of the *Revised Common Lectionary*, I will provide a brief sketch of the historical and ecumenical origins of this lectionary system. First, note that in using the word *lectionary* to describe this system of scriptural passages ("pericopes") we are opting for a narrow use of that word, since its primary reference has always been to the liturgical *book* from which Sunday's lessons have been read publicly (as distinct from the more Protestant use of a complete "pulpit" Bible). In this narrower sense, therefore, it could be said that all preachers use a lectionary, the only questions being: Who put it together, preacher or church? and, What, if any, are the operative principles by which it has been put together? Thus, the *Revised Common Lectionary*, being a table, not a book of readings, does not address wider issues of choice of translations, or generic language, or troublesome historical problems such as possible anti-Semitism, except insofar as its choice of lessons might seem to indicate an editorial bias concerning such problems.

Another prefatory comment is in order that refers to any and all lectionary systems (or nonsystems). It is particularly important here in that this handbook is deliberately intended to serve the preacher, who is probably also the principal liturgical planner for the worshiping community. The use of the scriptures in public worship is a multilayered and multi-mannered experience. Any good service of worship will use scriptural material all through the event—in hymns, anthems, prayers, sentences, and symbols, as well as in the readings and sermon. This testifies to the fact that the homiletical use of a lectionary is not its only use. Scripture functions—as it should, in a variety of ways—liturgically. Nor can it be said that these functions are always complementary or of equal significance. This, for instance, is the simple answer to the often-asked question, Why should a given lesson be read on a given Sunday if it is not to be the subject matter for preaching? Thus one might list the following six ways in which the scriptures, especially as ordered by a lectionary table, function liturgically. This listing is not necessarily in order of importance, but it may relate to the historical development of lectionaries.

1. Full and catechetical
2. Preaching
3. Ecclesiastical feasts, festivals, and seasons
4. Cultural, climatic, seasonal, and ethnic
5. Liturgical and doxological
6. Historical and ecumenical witness

It is now appropriate to turn to the origins and purposes of the production of the *Revised Common Lectionary*, a process that, as an ecumenical undertaking, began with the publication by the Roman Catholic Church in 1969 of its "Order of Readings at Mass" (*Ordo Lectionum Missae*). This singular event in ecumenical history was the direct result of a directive of the Second Vatican Council:

The treasures of the Bible are to be opened up more lavishly, so that a richer share in God's word may be provided for the faithful. In this way a more representative portion of holy Scripture will be read to the people in the course of a prescribed number of years.[4]

In this way the Council, with its first deliverance, *Sacrosanctum Concilium* (4 December 1963), took into the life of the Roman Church the principal concern of the sixteenth-century Reformers regarding the central place of the Bible in the worship of the Catholic Church.

This Roman lectionary proposes three readings for each Lord's Day over a three-year cycle. In addition, a psalm is provided for use following the Old Testament pericope. This table is now in universal use in that church. A supplemental second edition was published in 1981 that in no way altered the 1969 pattern but simply supplemented it and more amply rehearsed its rationale. This 1969 table was almost instantly taken up by a number of other churches, as I described in my Introduction to the 1983 publication of the *Common Lectionary* (hereinafter designated as *CL*):

> The wisdom embodied in the work of *Coetus XI* (the Roman working group which produced the *Ordo*), now in universal use in the churches that follow the Roman rite, has been attested by a completely unexpected and salutary development, particularly in North America, but also in other parts of the world. That is the appropriation of the Roman Lectionary by more than a few Protestant and Anglican churches. This process began with the publication in 1970 of an edition thereof in *The Worshipbook,* a service book and hymnal jointly produced by three Presbyterian churches in the United States. Shortly thereafter the Episcopal and Lutheran churches included it in preliminary studies which resulted in its inclusion in the *Draft Proposed Book of Common Prayer,* and also in the *Lutheran Book of Worship.* In the meantime the United Methodist Church in the U.S.A. made an edition available in 1976 and the Disciples of Christ as well as the United Church of Christ in the U.S.A. adopted for voluntary use the Presbyterian version. These developments were materially assisted by the publication of a consensus edition in pamphlet form by the ecumenical Consultation on Church Union, representing (at that time) nine Protestant denominations seeking fuller unity. In Canada the United Church has undertaken experimental use of the three-year lectionary in a number of parishes, and the Anglican Church has published a pamphlet (1980) making it available.[5]

4. Vatican Council II, "Constitution on the Liturgy," *Sacrosanctum Concilium* (4 December 1963), trans. International Commission on English in the Liturgy, *Documents on the Liturgy, 1963–1979: Conciliar, Papal and Curial Texts* (Collegeville, Minn.: Liturgical Press, 1982), para. 51.
5. Consultation on Common Texts (1992), p. 8.

This proliferation of edited versions of the original Roman table was ecumenically encouraging but also dismaying. No less than five subtly varied forms of the Roman table came into circulation. Worse, the method of calculation of which lessons to use on the Sundays after Pentecost differed among them. Attempts of local clergy to meet together for sermon planning were plagued by this diversity, and published materials for homiletical work were confronted by multiple options. Increasingly, the cry went up for some standardization of the situation.

An ecumenical body that had been in existence since 1964, the Consultation on Common Texts (of North America), moved into the discussion by convening a meeting of representatives of some thirteen churches from Canada and the United States, in Washington, D.C., March 28–31, 1978. Chairing the meeting was the Rev. Prof. Massey H. Shepherd, Jr., of the Episcopal Church. Also in attendance were Fr. Gaston Fontaine, Secretary of *Coetus XI,* and the Rev. Prof. James F. White of the United Methodist Church, then President of the North American Academy of Liturgy. This writer was present as well.

There was general agreement on the excellence of the Roman table and the desirability of greater uniformity in its use. Minutes of the meeting also record agreement that a consensus table of readings should be drawn up for recommendation to the churches and that, in particular, the Old Testament selections needed revision

> in order to provide readings that are more completely representative of the Hebrew Bible and not simply prophetic or typological; this includes the possibility of aligning the Old Testament passage with the New Testament selection rather than with the Gospel.[6]

As a result of this action, the Consultation on Common Texts, which I chaired at the time, set up a working group, the North American Committee on Calendar and Lectionary, presided over by the Rev. Dr. Lewis A. Briner, a minister of the United Presbyterian Church who had been instrumental in the inclusion of the Roman *Ordo* in his church's *Worshipbook: Services* (1970).[7] Membership on the Committee included pastors and scholars from the Roman Catholic, Episcopal, Presbyterian, Lutheran, and United Methodist churches. The committee met twice annually and generally worked by delegating given portions of the lectionary to designated members. Its working principles were as follows:

1. The basic calendar and structure of three readings presupposed by the Roman Lectionary are assumed.
2. The Gospel pericopes are assumed with only minor textual

---

6. "Minutes of the Consultation on Common Texts," Washington, D.C., 28–31 March 1978.
7. The Joint Committee on Worship for the Cumberland Presbyterian Church, Presbyterian Church in the United States, and the United Presbyterian Church in the United States of America, *The Worshipbook: Services* (Philadelphia: Westminster Press, 1970).

rearrangement to accommodate churches which use a Bible for liturgical use rather than a lectionary.

3. The New Testament pericopes are largely accepted with some lengthening of pericopes and minor textual rearrangement to include contextual material such as apostolic and personal greetings and local ecclesial issues.

4. The typological choice of Old Testament pericopes has been addressed in that this has been the area of most serious criticism of the lectionary from Catholic and Protestant scholars and pastors. In response, the Committee has proposed a revision of the Roman table for a number of Sundays "of the year" in each of the three cycles. The lessons are still typologically controlled by the Gospel, but in a broader way than Sunday by Sunday, in order to make possible semi-continuous reading of some significant Old Testament narratives.[8]

The finished work of this committee was published in 1983 as the Consultation's "proposal." After it had gone through a full testing of twice through the entire three-year cycle, the Consultation set up a Lectionary Task Force which, after soliciting evaluations of *CL* from a wide spread of churches, pastors, and biblical and liturgical scholars, recommended a revision to be published by the Consultation, now in print since 1992 as *Revised Common Lectionary* (hereinafter designated as *RCL*).

During this time a new international liturgical group was formed, initially to work on a revision of common liturgical texts that had been published in a booklet in 1975 by the International Consultation on English Texts (which then disbanded). This booklet was titled *Prayers We Have in Common*.[9] Thus in Boston, Massachusetts, in 1985 the English Language Liturgical Consultation (ELLC) came into existence to take another look at these texts, its member bodies then being the Consultation on Common Texts, the International Consultation on English in the Liturgy (Roman Catholic), the Australian Consultation on Liturgy, the British Joint Liturgical Group, and the Liturgical Committee of the South African Church Unity Commission. Very soon this body entered into collaboration with the North American Consultation with regard to the revision of *CL*, and it has since taken responsibility for the promotion of wider use for *RCL*.

As reported at the meeting of the English Language Liturgical Consultation (ELLC) in Ireland (August 1995), *RCL* is now in official or alternate use in North America by Episcopal/Anglican, Presbyterian, Reformed, Lutheran, United Methodist, and Disciples denominations as well as countless local churches such as Baptist, Mennonite, and Unitarian. In Great Britain, it is used not only by "established" churches, the Church of England and the Church of Scotland, but also by a number of

8. Horace T. Allen, Jr., "Address to *Societas Liturgica*," mimeographed (Paris, 25 August 1981).
9. International Consultation on English Texts, *Prayers We Have in Common*, 2d rev. ed. (Philadelphia: Fortress Press, 1975).

other denominations, as in North America. The same is true in Australia, New Zealand, and South Africa. There is also growing use of *RCL* by Presbyterian churches in Korea. Except for the latter instance, all of this is occurring in the English-speaking world. However, at a meeting of the scholarly body *Societas Liturgica* in Ireland in August 1995, no less than sixty people attended a seminar on the subject (fully one quarter of the total attendance at *Societas*), many of whom were from non-English-speaking countries.

At the same time, the English Language Liturgical Consultation (ELLC) has already made presentations of this work to the Faith and Order Commission of the World Council of Churches in Geneva, Switzerland, and to the Congregation on Divine Worship and Sacraments at the Vatican. Thus it seems assured that *RCL* will continue on its way toward becoming, along with its Roman antecedent, a universally agreed-upon instrumentality for the liturgical use of the holy scriptures. That in itself should suggest to its readers that it may be one of the most important, if also unexpected, expressions of genuine ecumenicity of our time. And for Protestants, what more significant sign of unity could there be, short of intercommunion, than fellowship each Lord's Day, on a worldwide basis, around the scriptures as they are appointed to be read?

Certain of the major structural features and hermeneutical assumptions of *RCL* need identifying in order to appreciate how its use varies from season to season.

1. *RCL* is meant for the weekly Lord's Day celebration (normatively eucharistic). For that reason the Gospel lesson is always, in one way or another, the "controlling" lesson. These readings are almost invariably the same as the Roman table.

2. *RCL* assumes the classic Western calendar consisting principally of the Sundays and seasons related to (a) Christmas, i.e., Advent—Christmas—Epiphany/Baptism of the Lord, and (b) Easter/*Pascha*, i.e., Lent—Holy Week—Easter—Pentecost/Trinity. On these Sundays all three lessons are thematically related, as is the Psalm for the day, which is always paired with the Old Testament lesson and should, therefore, immediately follow it as an act of sung praise.

3. *RCL* regards the Lord's Day as a festival in its own right and, therefore, sees the Sundays "after Epiphany" and "after Pentecost" not as seasons as such, but as a single sequence of Lord's Day celebrations. On these 33 or 34 Lord's Days (known in the Roman calendar as "*Dominicae per annum*," "Sundays of the Year," or "Ordinary Time") the Synoptic Gospels are read in a continuous (*lectio continua*) fashion (being interrupted only for the Lent-Easter season, although some of the Gospel lessons during that time are drawn from the year's Gospel, i.e., Year A—Matthew, Year B—Mark, Year C—Luke). In this way, these

narrative writings are respected and read as such. In the same way, on these Sundays of Ordinary Time, most of the Pauline, "catholic," and Johannine Epistles are read over the entire three years (which means, of course, that there will be no necessary thematic connection with the Gospel for the day). This too is largely parallel with the Roman table. However, the Old Testament set in Ordinary Time ("after Pentecost" only, since the number of Sundays after Epiphany varies from year to year) does diverge from the Roman selections in that its week-by-week typological principle of selection has been broadened to govern only the Old Testament *books* to be read each year rather than choosing each Sunday's *pericopes* to relate to the Gospel. The use of these books is narrative or semicontinuous. Thus in Matthew's year (A) the Old Testament material is drawn from the Patriarchal and Mosaic narratives in the Pentateuch; in Mark's year (B) the Old Testament material is drawn from the Davidic narrative in the historical books; and in Luke's year (C) the Old Testament material includes the Elijah-Elisha sequence from the historical books and selections from the entire prophetic canon. Toward the end of the post-Pentecost Sundays, Wisdom literature is introduced; and immediately preceding Advent, because of its ancient reference to the Second Coming rather than to Christmas, apocalyptic material is used.

4. *RCL* employs the Fourth Gospel (John), not in Ordinary Time, since its literary structure is less chronological narrative than seasonal and liturgical, but rather on the Sundays around Christmas and Easter. John 6, however, is used in the course of the Markan year, if only because Mark is the shortest of the Gospels.

5. *RCL* does not read from the Old Testament during the Sundays of Easter, so as not to force the unique event of the resurrection upon Old Testament material, and also in order to make use of the book of Acts, which provides the church with its most primitive witness to the resurrection, that is, the coming into being of the church. The theologian and biblical scholar Joseph Sittler once remarked to me, "The *events* narrated in the book of Acts precede the *accounts* of the resurrection in the four gospels."

6. In Ordinary Time (after Pentecost), the choice of Psalms diverges from the Roman table in order to relate to the changed Old Testament passages. As always, therefore, they should be sung immediately following that passage.

The question, then, is basically this: How might the use of *Revised Common Lectionary* significantly alter and enhance the sort of preaching that has long characterized churches unused to the provision of such guidance for preachers? To a lesser or different extent, the question also pertains to churches such as Lutheran, Episcopal, and Roman, in that the structure of *RCL* as just sketched differs significantly from the systems used in those communions prior to 1969. Six areas of homiletical practice may be described.

Sunday as Sequential-Narrative Preaching

Perhaps the single most revolutionary result of using *RCL,* for churches that have never used a lectionary *and* for churches whose lectionaries were based in the Western, Latin tradition, will be the experience of Sunday as the occasion for a sequence of biblical passages. It could be said that the history of lectionaries in the Western church has been a gradual shift from *lectio continua* (as in the synagogue and the early Roman church) to *lectio selecta.* The continuing occasion for this shift was calendrical, in that the Sunday calendar came to include more annual dates, in contrast to the earlier pattern (of the first four centuries) wherein the *Pascha* (Easter) was the only annual festival (and only after the Council of Nicaea did it always occur on the Lord's Day). To this may perhaps be added Epiphany in the East (because it has a fixed date, it too occurred only occasionally on the Lord's Day), and Christmas (as of sometime in the fourth century, but also with a fixed date). Thus, as the sixteenth-century Reformers perceived, the principal recurring festival of the church was, in fact, the weekly Lord's Day. Hence there was no reason to interrupt the continuous reading of "the memoirs of the apostles or the writings of the prophets."[10] It was only as the annual calendar became more elaborate in the cycles of Sundays around Christmas and Pascha that the *continua* pattern was interrupted by a *selecta* principle. This had probably been done even in the synagogue on Sabbaths proximate to the *Pascha* and the High Holy Days insofar as these festivals were celebrated at the beginning of the Christian Era.

As the first millennium of the church drew to its close, other calendrical cycles had imposed their own "selected" pericopes on the Sunday sequence such as sanctoral, theological, and Marian festivals. Thus by the time of the Reformation of the sixteenth century continuous reading had virtually disappeared, and even had it not, the linguistic barrier (of Latin) would have rendered it unintelligible. Further, the celebration of Mass—which might have secured the uniqueness of the Lord's Day festival, having become a daily event—was insufficient to suggest to the faithful that the Lord's Day, as a recurring weekly event, formed its own calendar with a combination of proper (changing) and ordinary (fixed) elements having to do with the regular *anamnesis* or remembrance of the death and resurrection of the Lord. The increasing secularization of the Lord's Day, and the increase in the number of holy days, only reinforced the loss of that day as a continuing sequence of christological celebrations.

---

10. Justin Martyr, *First Apology* LXVII (c. 155), quoted by James F. White, *Documents of Christian Worship* (Louisville, Ky.: Westminster/John Knox Press, 1992), p. 101.

It was probably John Calvin, with his extensive knowledge of the early Fathers, who most clearly understood the symmetry among

1. the Lord's Day as the primary Christian festival,
2. the Lord's Supper, and
3. the continuous reading of scripture on that day.

Thus Calvin's reading and preaching of the scriptures on the Lord's Day in Geneva reverted to *lectio continua*, being interrupted only by the annual festivals of Christmas, Easter, and Pentecost. Indeed, when thwarted in his attempts to recover a weekly eucharistic celebration or even a monthly schedule, he turned to those great festivals as the eucharistic days, a strategy that even his own ecclesial descendants in Scotland and North America have never understood, as witnessed by their strict quarterly (or, as now, monthly) pattern. Strangely, the continuous practice of scripture reading, until very recently under the impact of *RCL*, also disappeared, even though it was recommended by the Puritan anti–Prayer Book *Directory for Worship* of the Westminster Assembly (1645).

With the publication by the Holy See of the 1969 Roman lectionary, the Western rite at last returned to this principle in large measure. Thus the Synoptic Gospels are read in their entirety (except for some parallel passages) week by week, year by year, the lectionary resorting to a *selecta* pattern only for the festal seasons around Christmas and Easter. Thus also the Pauline, Johannine, and Pastoral Epistles are read in the same way during Ordinary Time, post-Pentecost. And with *RCL* (and *Common Lectionary*) the *continua* principle was applied to the First Reading in Ordinary Time, post-Pentecost. This departure from the Roman original has created the greatest controversy. That is why *RCL* provides an alternative set of Old Testament pericopes for this period in the year that more nearly accords with the Roman typological system, as found also in the U.S.A. Lutheran and Episcopal books. However, it has been announced in the English Language Liturgical Consultation (ELLC) that in the United States both the Evangelical Lutheran Church in America and the Episcopal Church have officially approved *RCL* as an option or alternative to the tables now printed in their book, although the Lutheran Church recommends the typological option for the Sundays post-Pentecost.

But what does this recovery of *lectio continua* mean for peaching? It is interesting that the most important points apply equally to traditional lectionary-using churches and to those that have not done so until this past decade, since the *continua* pattern was absent from even those lectionaries. This recovery requires that the preacher, as well as the hearers, needs to think about a Sunday-to-Sunday sequence of pericopes. Put another way, the scriptural context for Sunday's sermon (certainly in Ordinary Time) is "horizontally" determined rather than "vertically," which is to say that on those Sundays there will not be a predetermined "theme" linking all three readings, but each of them will relate to the relative readings on the Sunday before and the Sunday following. The consonance of lessons is week-to-week rather than lesson-to-lesson on a given Sunday, though the latter will be true on the Sundays of the festal seasons. This makes quite ironic the often-heard complaint that "lectionary preaching" does not provide opportunity for "series" sermons, since the *continua* principle builds that possibility into the heart of proclamation. The difference from the popular assumption is that the "series" sermons are embedded in the scriptures themselves rather than in some artificial construct such as "Great Personages in the Bible," "The Apostles' Creed in Paul's Letters," and so forth.

This places the preacher and people in a new relationship to the recurring Lord's Day. It assumes a fairly stable and regular congregation, and means that both preacher and people must undertake through the week the kind of preparation for the Lord's Day that may well, as a side effect, bring back to Protestant homes the daily scrutiny of the scriptures, so long lost. For the preacher, it certainly necessitates a more careful study of biblical books in use than was ever the case when one skipped around in one's favorite books each week. My students are counseled each year in Advent, or shortly before, to purchase and familiarize themselves with the latest and best commentaries on the Gospel for the year to come. The same could be said for the Epistles to be read after Pentecost. Further, it is to be hoped that by the end of each year of the three-year cycle the congregation itself will have a fairly clear picture of the unique characteristics of the Synoptic Gospel for that year.

This is not meant to turn the Lord's Day celebration into a liturgical Bible study session, as some have feared. It is simply to include in one's preaching, as the basis for sermons and homilies, the sort of contextualization that is essential to understanding the pericopes.

What is equally difficult for many preachers to accept is the above-mentioned fact that for fully half the calendar year, the three readings for the day may well have no thematic coherence. Even the most sophisticated series of lectionary commentaries find it tempting to find some sort of interrelationship among the three (and some would say four, because they fail to grasp the unique function of the Psalm for the day as a sung response to the First Reading). What is worse is that—whether guided by these commentaries or their own traditional concept of preaching—some preachers, realizing there is no inner relationship thematically, will preach three rather brief and simplistic sermonettes. Evidence of this sort of assumption often surfaces with the question, Why, if one is not going to use all three lessons in the homily, are the ones not to be used read at all? In certain traditions the assumption has been that one reads only from the scriptures for the purpose of preaching. This is why it is important to recall that there are other quite important reasons to proclaim the scriptures in the liturgical assembly. Surely such an assumption reveals a kind of Protestant "priestcraft" that is thoroughly inappropriate precisely in that tradition. One recalls a line from a much-loved hymn of William Cowper: "God is His own interpreter, and He will make it plain."

There is a way to work with this seeming problem, especially in Ordinary Time, and that is to preface all readings by the briefest kind of lead-in ("*incipit*"), whereby the community is reminded of the textual context of each lesson, whether or not it is to be used homiletically. This handbook provides such material. Care should be taken that the *incipit* be both brief and merely contextualizing, not homiletical.

Thus, we can posit the proposition that *RCL*, properly used, will require of the preacher a new level of biblical background, and of the people a new level of concentration that will carry over from one Sunday to the next. We need not belabor the deeper implications of this as a theologically suggestive description of the character of the liturgical assembly as the principal place for continuing catechesis and deepening in faith wherein the ever-changing biblical material, in sequence, is paired with the ever-the-same liturgy and eucharistic celebration. And there certainly lies here a completely new agenda for that currently so shaky and undefined institution called the church school or adult education.

Scripture as Its Own Context

This point is closely related to the previous one. The particular matter that needs attention here has to do with the questions of literary genre and the formation of the various books of the Bible in relation to their communities and the canonization process. Here we are taking aboard at least two fairly recent schools of biblical study: the "canon criticism" school, which addresses the historical process by which given Christian communities formed and canonized their books, and the "literary historical" school, which reads the scriptures in terms of their relationship to known literary forms of their times.

These two schools of thought are actually describing the formation of the canonical books as "lectionaries in the making." The goal of these two schools of study is to provide us with a sensitivity as to how given books were formed, in the context of their particular communities and of literary conventions of their own times. Just so, the goal of Roman and common lectionaries is to provide contemporary communities with a form of proclamation that takes account, on a weekly basis, of these factors in order to re-form those historic communities for the present day, the homily being the operative literary form. In this regard one thinks of the suggestive small book of Raymond E. Brown, *The Churches the Apostles Left Behind,*[11] or James A. Sanders's *Torah and Canon,*[12] *Canon and Community,*[13] and *God Has a Story Too.*[14]

These schools of biblical criticism return the study and proclamation of the scriptures to their original communal, ecclesial context in prospect—just as the use of a lectionary whose basis is largely *continua* and whose *selecta* Sundays relate to the community's recurring annual festivals, does the same in retrospect. Moreover, with scripture as its own context ("interpreter," as in Cowper's hymn), the liturgical assembly is constantly being introduced to what the late Karl Barth called "The Strange New World within the Bible." As he put it: "Within the Bible there is a

---

11. Raymond E. Brown, *The Churches the Apostles Left Behind* (New York: Paulist Press, 1989).
12. James A. Sanders, *Torah and Canon* (Philadelphia: Fortress Press, 1972).
13. Sanders, *Canon and Community* (Philadelphia: Fortress Press, 1984).
14. Sanders, *God Has a Story Too: Sermons in Context* (Philadelphia: Fortress Press, 1979).

strange, new world, the world of God. . . ." And again, "There is a river in the Bible that carries us away, once we have entrusted our destiny to it—away from ourselves to the sea."[15] Here too we discover a powerful symmetry between the Liturgy of the Word and the Liturgy of the Table, between the spoken language of scripture and sermon and the prayed and gestured language of the Table, between the "two tables." Barth observes in another place, his *Church Dogmatics*, that "proclamation [is] in the form of preaching and sacrament . . ." and also that scripture is "not so much an historical monument as rather a Church document, proclamation in writing."[16]

In this regard it is possible to think of the homily itself as a particular literary form, closely related to the community within which it occurs. A sermon need not always be hortatory, or didactic, or narrative, though it well may be, depending on the scriptural material for the day. A sermon may be lyrical, poetic, hymnic, euchological (prayerful), or meditative as well. One has only to dip into the homilies of the ancient Fathers to discover this, and it is interesting to find that they were often, if not always, working with a *continua* principle. That, of course, is the reason that *RCL* reads books such as Epistles, Synoptic Gospels, Acts, and Old Testament history in a continuous or semicontinuous way, whereas the Fourth Gospel is used in a selected way in relationship to the Christian calendar, just as it seems to be organized in relationship to the Jewish calendar.

At a time when the world of the Bible is increasingly "strange," both because of increasing biblical illiteracy and because of the increasingly secular and even violent character of contemporary society, the preacher must be able to find a way for the people of God to enter into the world of God. And a preacher, Catholic or Protestant, who works carefully with such a lectionary system as we now have, will find that the "world of God" just might make more sense than the "worlds in collision" of our times, which seem always to be either exploding or imploding. As Luther's hymn proclaims, "That word above all earthly powers, no thanks to them, abideth. . . . God's truth abideth still: His kingdom is forever."

Lectionary and Calendar

We now turn our attention to the guidance that *RCL* provides for the preacher in those festal seasons where the principle of selection is not *continua* but *selecta*: Advent—Christmas (including Epiphany and First Sunday after Epiphany), and Lent—Easter (including Pentecost and Trinity). Once again we must take note of the different "directions" from which preachers in various traditions will come to *RCL*. Clergy of the so-called "liturgical churches," such as the Roman Catholic, Lutheran, and Anglican, will be quite used to the consonance of season and lectionary,

---

15. Karl Barth, *The Word of God and the Word of Man*, trans. Douglas Horton (London: Hodder & Stoughton, 1928), p. 34.

16. Karl Barth, *Church Dogmatics*, I/1: *The Doctrine of the Word of God*, trans. G. T. Thomson (Edinburgh: T. & T. Clark, 1936), p. 114.

even though the lections chosen may well require certain changes in their traditional understanding of these seasons. On the other hand, clergy of the so-called "free churches" have either paid no attention to the classic annual calendar or (and this is of considerable importance) have begun to celebrate these cycles of Christmas and Easter simply as seasons, without regard to the regulatory authority of a lectionary. Curiously, this has been the pattern in many North American Protestant communities. Thus these seasons of Advent–Christmas–Epiphany and Lent–Easter–Pentecost have come to be observed without proper attention to the way in which classical Western lectionaries have *defined their meaning*. On the face of it, this is a strange and even contradictory way for Protestants to shape their worship, that is, by reference to a set of seasons without regard to the way in which biblical selections for those seasons define them. This has resulted in all manner of anomalies such as the Fourth Sunday of Advent being designated "Christmas Sunday," although its Gospel pericope is properly that of the Annunciation, not the Birth. In one church's Ministers' Daily Diary, the Sunday after Christmas was designated "The Fifth Sunday in Advent." At Epiphany, the Magi often displace the Baptism of the Lord, depending on where in the week January 6 occurs. In the Paschal cycle, a penitential mood has pervaded all the Lenten Sundays in spite of the fact that those Sundays are not even counted as part of Lent in that they, with their Gospels, anticipate Easter, not Good Friday (a misunderstanding which was not altogether absent from the more liturgical churches, and which has only been corrected even there by the Gospels and related pericopes for Lent in the Roman and Common tables). Also, among the Free Churches, there was little sense for the *season* of Easter—the Great Fifty Days—and as a result, Pentecost was a detached, free-standing festival that became "the birthday of the church" (as though Christ had not called his church into being at the moment of the calling of the Twelve).

With the emerging use of *RCL*, however, preachers were jolted into a redefinition of much of the festal times *on the basis* of the biblical pericopes. This is a curious twist, in that a Catholic-derived biblical system was needed to call Protestant preaching to a more evangelical use of the classic calendar. Thus it suddenly became clear that Advent had to do not with the first coming but with the second, and this happened at precisely the moment when North American Protestantism began the now nearly universal practice of lighting candles each Sunday of Advent in anticipation of Christmas. Thus the service on First Advent begins with the solemn declaration, by lighting the first of the Advent candles, that Christmas is only four weeks away, but then at the reading of the Gospel for the day the congregation hears quite another message: "Watch and pray, for no one knows the day or the hour." This confusion is further compounded by the cultural pressure to begin singing Christmas carols as early as that First Sunday in Advent, such that one even hears references to "this Christmas season." And of course, when the Twelve Days of Christmas are beginning on December 25, the worshiping community, like its surrounding culture, has already become tired of the whole thing and shows little interest in further festivity, except perhaps for welcoming the Magi at Epiphany (a Roman innovation of a much earlier date).

The same corrective has been administered concerning the Sundays in Lent by virtue of the biblical plan of Roman and Common lectionaries that anticipates Easter rather than Good Friday. A further revision of Protestant homiletical tradition is suggested by these lectionary systems at the newly designated Passion/Palm Sunday, which calls for the reading of the entire Passion narrative from the year's Gospel, rather than simply the Triumphal Entry, which has been the practice in nonliturgical churches that could not have known that the entry liturgy of palms was simply an elaboration of the opening procession and introit for that day's Eucharist. The unfortunate result of ignoring the Passion on that Sunday is leaving it to the days of Holy Week (which are increasingly poorly attended and celebrated in sometimes embarrassingly literalistic and dramatic fashion), so that the preacher never has an opportunity to preach the Passion, and the congregation proceeds from "Palm Sunday," a sort of little Easter, to Easter itself, never having heard the proclamation of the death of the Lord, except possibly at an evening Eucharist on Maundy Thursday, which, in turn, has the unhappy effect of limiting sacramental piety and devotion to the death of Jesus with determinedly little reference to his resurrection. Finally, the pericopes for the Sundays after Easter now remind the most careless preacher that the Resurrection celebration does not end with Easter Day but, in fact, begins with it.

Thus it has come about that this ecumenical lectionary system has at last reminded the universal church that it is the Bible that shapes the calendar with its preaching, and not the calendar that shapes the preaching. For those who have eyes to see and ears to hear, this is the clear message of Thomas Talley's magisterial study *The Origins of the Liturgical Year*.[17] It is precisely this mix of continuous and selected biblical pericopes that gives the calendar of the Christian community whatever shape and evangelical significance it is to have.

Preacher and Text

For preachers from ecclesial traditions that have never prescribed a lectionary, the current situation requires a totally new way of thinking of their relation to the biblical texts. This new way is in a direction that would seem to be axiomatic for Protestants but that in fact has certainly not been. Thus the preacher now no longer chooses the preaching texts; they choose the preacher. The way this is most often expressed is the complaint that "There's nothing about these texts that 'turns me on.'" To express this situation in a more sophisticated way, one might observe that for the preacher to live with the luxury of choosing the weekly preaching texts is to run the grave risk of reducing the canon of Holy

---

17. Thomas J. Talley, *The Origins of the Liturgical Year* (New York: Pueblo Publishing Co., 1986).

Scripture to those books and pericopes that are congenial with the preacher's own theological preoccupations, or worse, with the limitations of the preacher's seminary study of the Bible. Most preachers who take on the responsibility of working consistently with the lectionary soon become painfully aware of how little of the canon they were using when the principle of selection was entirely their own interests and favorite passages. But underlying this reality, of course, is the larger and more significant theological issue of the inspiration of Holy Scripture. In Calvinism, this has been expressed by the doctrinal affirmation that the scriptures only become "the Word of God" by virtue of the "inward testimony of the Holy Spirit." Nevertheless, the assumption even of the Calvinist tradition is that the entire canon is "the Word of God" and, therefore, fit for preaching. This was part of the argument with Luther as to whether a given book, such as James, could be dismissed because of perceived theological inadequacy. This too is what informs the discussion of how the so-called apocryphal books may be used in Christian worship. *RCL* has had, for this reason, to supply alternate readings wherever the Roman system uses them.

Aside from these heavy theological matters, there is also the much more ordinary and human reality that a particular preacher might or might not feel able to deal with certain pericopes or combinations thereof, particularly in the context of civil, congregational, or personal happenings. At such moments a responsible pastor or preacher will want to exercise the freedom of the ministry of Word and Sacrament to make other choices, and certainly to edit the pericopes as given in the table. This necessarily uncovers a more problematic side to the otherwise laudable practice of placing oneself, as preacher, at the disposal of the lectionary table, under the guidance of the Holy Spirit. That is the danger that one might abandon altogether any creative energy in making the lectionary's choices one's own. This can result either in a careless and forced attempt to define a common theme, even when such does not exist, as in the Sundays after Pentecost, or as mentioned above, a lifeless and perfunctory series of three (or four!) brief comments on the texts of the day—all too easy in these days of multiple books and monthly mail-services of lectionary aids to preaching. This is why lectionary preaching requires that the preacher plan well ahead as to which of the biblical sequences are to be followed, after Pentecost, for instance. It is also doubly important that the preacher have a minimal understanding of the lectionary's own principles and plan, in order that the selections made by the lectionary may be clear to the preacher well before the sermon is planned. It is perhaps even more important that the preacher then bring his or her own critical facilities to bear on any given Sunday's selections, deciding whether and how the lectionary's choices might have to be amended or edited as publicly read, for pastoral or homiletical reasons. Thus, although the use of a lectionary can be of vital assistance to the preacher, one must guard against a certain homiletical laziness because the principal choices for the sermon have already been made. It could be said that the preacher is using the lectionary well only when the sermonic work is harder than when the preacher was choosing the texts week by week.

Preaching as Participatory

Perhaps one of the most important possibilities at the parish level that the use of *RCL* provides (and this is not altogether different from using any other lectionary system) is that it becomes possible to invite the parish community to enter into a regular discipline, along with its preacher, of study and preparation for Sunday's Liturgy of the Word. As was not possible in a time when the preacher chose the texts on a week-by-week basis, often sometime during the week just before their use, it is now possible to alert the congregation in advance (at least at the previous week's service) as to what the lessons will be on the following Sunday. This in turn suggests that regular lectionary study groups might be convened wherein the pastor can work in advance with the faithful to prepare the homily. This could also be conjoined with training sessions for lay readers, for it is often the case that only when one takes the time to proclaim the pericopes out loud that many of their subtleties and nuances begin to appear.

Another aspect of parish participation, already hinted at, has to do with the proper integration of various elements of the parish liturgy and life, such as music and Christian education, which is part of the purpose of this handbook. Use of *RCL* makes possible what churches that have long had their own systems have always known, namely, that it is possible for the parish musician(s) to plan ahead regarding choral and instrumental music, as well as hymns, that will relate to the biblical texts for the day. With the publication of *RCL,* a vast publishing activity has developed to point the way for such integration on a weekly basis. Composers of hymns and anthems freely confess that the appearance of this lectionary has provided them with an entire agenda, never before experienced in churches with a long tradition of hymn singing.

In the same way, use of a lectionary opens an entirely new vista for Christian educators and curricula, as well as wider adult education programs. These programs need no longer be tangential or even totally unrelated to the liturgical and homiletical life of the community, but rather may be supportive thereof.

Another way in which preaching may become more participatory has to do with the particular way in which *RCL* already has been so widely accepted ecumenically. One continues to hear of wider and wider use of this system not only in the English-speaking world but also in other language groups where, because of the intimate relationship between the universal Roman lectionary and *RCL,* the possibility of such cooperation already exists. This means that throughout the world many churches in hundreds of thousands of local situations are reading the same scriptures on the Lord's Day. This has already resulted in the formation of clerical lectionary study groups throughout the world, especially in those places where ecumenical cooperation is an accepted and acceptable experience. One might be allowed the vision that as separated ecclesial communities begin to participate *together* in the weekly homiletical study of the Holy Scriptures, the Lord's high priestly prayer is coming to fruition: "I have given them your word. . . . Sanctify them in the truth; your word is truth . . . that they all may be one" (John 17:14, 17, 21).

The Liturgical and Sacramental Context for Preaching

The question of unity around the Word leads most naturally to that other side of Christian worship, historically understood, the sacramental. This is not the place to discuss either the historical issues involved or the pros and cons of weekly eucharistic worship. We have noted the extraordinary agreement at this point represented by so many recent official service books and prayer books being produced by practically all of the churches that are also adopting *RCL*. This conjunction of liturgical agendas is not accidental, and one might even say that it is providential. To think of scripture and sacrament as the twin boundaries for preaching is evangelical enough for any Protestant, and it is also clearly the will of the liturgical authority in the Church of Rome. The Vatican Council's *Sacrosanctum Concilium* is witness enough. Thus, at the very moment that Roman clerics are seriously undertaking the preaching task at Mass for almost the first generation in many centuries, their Protestant counterparts are having to undertake preaching as an integral part of a liturgy that does not conclude with that event but moves on, if not to a sacramental celebration then at least, in anticipation of the sacrament, to acts of offering, intercession, and thanksgiving. Any student of communication could alert us to the vast significance of such a structural shift, and if we pay no attention to the meaning of that shift we do violence to the sermon itself and trivialize all that follows. More than one frustrated preacher has observed that this postsermonic sequence seems anticlimactic. The problem, however, is not with the sequence itself but with the use that is made of it, especially in relation to the sermon. For instance: Has the sermon made any reference at all to this concluding thanksgiving? Do the prayers of intercession and thanksgiving, or the exhortation to offering, make any "backward" reference to the content of the sermon? Does the action of offering "take over," thus obliterating the thanksgiving—with an unnecessary "Prayer of Dedication," for instance?

So the thrust of this last implication of lectionary use has to do with the shape of the sermon if it is to be fully integrated into what might be described in a geometric metaphor as the *ellipse* of scripture and sacrament (thanksgiving).

Theologically, we may suggest at least three reasons that underlie such an "elliptical" approach to the structure of Lord's Day worship, which will, in turn, provide us with some guidelines for (to paraphrase Dom Gregory Dix) "the shape of the sermon." The first is to propose that a Word-Sacrament shape is importantly and obviously rooted in the central christological affirmation of Incarnation. If indeed "the Word became flesh, and lived among us . . . full of grace and truth" (John 1:14), then surely the liturgical, communal event of the Word on the Lord's Day demands a concrete, incarnational, fleshly expression in addition to the words of scripture and sermon that presumably speak of the Word. And to understand the proper incarnational character of sacramental worship, either in the Supper or in Baptism, it is essential to recall that, especially in Reformed sacramental theology, the sacramental action is not important because it employs *things* such as water, bread, wine, vessels, and the like. The incarnational expressiveness of the Supper does not rest simply in its use of things as such, but in its use of essential human corporate action such as eating and drinking together in the context of a festive meal, or washing and cleansing as a domestic event. Christianity is not, in its sacramental life, a mystery religion but a Semitic one. Its sacramental roots do not lie in changing natural things into supernatural symbols, but rather in investing the most ordinary and essential human, social activities with covenantal truth. The fact that the central ritual moment in our sacraments is a prayer of thanksgiving over bread and wine, or water, reminds us of the Semitic character of these events, for it recalls for us the central prayer form of the Old Testament, namely, blessing (*barak*). When a Jew blesses God for something, anything, the purpose of the prayer is both to draw the subject of the blessing into the conscious and visible arena of God's mighty acts and gracious presence, and also to seek the continued grace of God in just such ways and means. Thus at the Supper the church thanks God for the life, death, and resurrection of Jesus Christ in the signs of his table fellowship and, more particularly, that fellowship as at the moment of his death and resurrection. The prayer then seeks the Spirit, that all of that grace and blessing be poured out afresh on the gathered community and the whole church. The same might be said of the blessing over water at Baptism. This is why even if the Supper is not being celebrated it may be replaced, proleptically, by a concluding action of offering, intercession, and thanksgiving. Thus to conclude Lord's Day worship, not with a sermon (words) but with a sacrament (thanksgiving) is to witness to the Incarnation, because such an action, such a liturgical structure, concretely refers us to the once-and-for-all actions of Incarnation in the words, flesh, and blood of the Lord of the church.

The second theological commendation of this ellipse of Word and Sacrament as the appropriate and shaping context for Christian preaching has to do with what was at the outset of this introduction referred to as the "objective" character of sacramental worship. Here we must clarify what was meant there (which will also perhaps enrich what was meant by referring to the "subjective" aspect of preaching). Just as preaching is inevitably the activity of one person, so also the sacraments are essentially the activity of a community, however important the presence of a presider might be. That is to say, the objectivity of sacramental worship has to do not simply with things, or fixed texts and ceremonies, but with its being an event in community. Baptism involves one or more baptizand(s), sponsors, congregational assent, and participation. The Supper involves communicants (or, from time to time, noncommunicants) who eat and drink, finally and definitively (1 Cor. 10:21–22 and 1 Cor. 11:27–32) as a sign of mutual covenanting, irrevocably and totally. All of this gives sacramental action the kind of finality (objectivity) which no sermon can or should claim. One can go away from a sermon and discuss whether one liked or agreed with it, or whether one will do anything about it or not. One cannot walk away from Baptism and the Supper that casually. What has been done cannot be taken back or changed. In that sense, the community's action has an objectivity about it that no sermon can claim.

The third theological consideration may be described, perhaps surprisingly, as the political significance of sacraments. Again, one might think that it is the sermon that has political potential, rather than the sacrament. No doubt, sermons may and do address political questions. But such a message and address must labor under precisely the sort of subjectivity and questionableness just described. Consequently, the preacher must be able to ground the message with some clarity in scriptural wisdom, one of the two boundaries of the liturgical sermon. But that is precisely the difficult point to prove. Witness the continuing raging battle over the biblical teaching regarding homosexuality, wherein both sides make fervent appeals to the scriptures. Is it possible, however, that the other boundary, the liturgical, sacramental action, as it refers to the concrete life, death, and resurrection of Jesus, may also provide a basis for making convincing political judgments? Contrary to stereotypical criticism, liturgical concern is not always counterproductive of, or irrelevant to, social change. The Wesleyan revival certainly had its own ethical as well as eucharistic dimensions. For the Oxford Movement in the Church of England it was the same. A. G. Hebert's *Liturgy and Society*[18] is a profound witness to this linkage. And to turn to a very different liturgical milieu, we can certainly adduce the rootage in black preaching and ritual (i.e., song) of the civil rights movement as another instance of this connection.

The formal and structural roots of such a connection are to be found in the parallelism between the corporate, liturgical life of an ecclesial community of commitment and the social, political life of a civic pluralistic community. Herein may lie one of the strategic mistakes of American liberal Protestantism of the 1960s and 1970s. It was largely nonliturgical, individually motivated, and uninterested in ecclesial structures except as a validating support system. The same was not true on the Catholic side, as many of the activists were also liturgical (and ecumenical) reformers. Oddly enough, even though it would seem to be sermons that can raise social and ethical issues, it is Supper-as-love-feast and Baptism-as-initiation that form the kind of intentional communities that, by their cult, become countercultural. That was the experience of the Jewish diaspora synagogue and also of the early Christian eucharistic communities in the face of persecution, martyrdom, and exile. The social, objective, incarnational character of liturgy and sacrament provide concrete, visual, flesh-and-blood paradigms of a community whose order includes justice, repentance, solidarity, and hope. Hence Paul Lehmann can affirm in his formative volume on Christian ethics:

> The penultimate chapter of the biblical story is the story of the eucharistic community in the world. Here is a *laboratory of maturity* in the world which, by the operative (real) presence and power of the Messiah-Redeemer in the midst of his people, and through them of all people, the will to power is broken and displaced by the power to will what God wills. The

---

18. A. G. Hebert, *Liturgy and Society* (London: Faber & Faber Ltd., 1935).

power to will what God wills is the power to be what man has been created and purposed to be. It is the power to be and to stay human, that is, to attain wholeness or maturity. For maturity is the full development in a human being of the power to be truly and fully himself in being related to others who also have the power to be truly and fully themselves. The Christian *koinonia* is the foretaste and the sign in the world that God has always been and is contemporaneously doing what it takes to make and to keep human life human. This is the will of God "as it was in the beginning, is now, and ever shall be, world without end."[19]

What then—if these theological points do commend themselves at all—would be the shape of the sermon? If lectionary and Lord's Supper can be seen together as the two contextualities of the sermon, what will it look like as text? Or, to put the question in a way that has been addressed many times over but, perhaps, not enough in some traditions, What is liturgical preaching?

1. A liturgical sermon will work with the given texts for the day. In this way it will say that the scripture is still the church's primary formation and at the same time, that the liturgy with its sacraments is not an "eccentric" situation that requires everything else to give way. The regular conjunction of scripture and sacrament will give the sermon something of a sacramental authority, and it will give the sacrament the authority and relevance of scripture.

2. A liturgical sermon will always invite all to the Table (or at least to its central action of thanksgiving). Its application will always speak of the Lord's banquet as the gospel enactment in concrete terms. This means that the preacher will always be particularly sensitive to references in the day's lessons to meals, domestic metaphors, and communal allusions such as all those liturgical or paraliturgical references in the opening and closing chapters of the New Testament Epistles. And because many liturgies locate the corporate confession of sin between sermon and sacrament, this means that any and all biblical allusions to this dynamic should probably be picked up and turned in the direction of the Eucharist. In such cases, it is also important that the exchange of the sign of Peace be included in this sequence and instruction, if only because it is so regularly trivialized as an insipid and sub-Christian expression of casual affection and friendliness rather than a serious and costly act of forgiveness and reconciliation.

3. The political and societal dimensions of the scripture lessons will be expressed, if only because of the sacramental/Supper character of the church. If the church is a *polis,* a *societas,* then its integrity as such, by the effectual working of the Word, must become a witness to all those political realities in which all Christians participate. A liturgical sermon that speaks honestly about the fullness of Christ's Table can hardly ignore the

---

19. Paul Louis Lehmann, *Ethics in a Christian Context* (New York: Harper & Row, 1963), p. 101.

hunger and homelessness which are the scandal of our society. A liturgical sermon that leads us into the exchange of signs of peace as a form of forgiveness and reconciliation can hardly draw back from commenting on a national foreign policy that is based on nothing more than competitive geopolitics and international gunrunning. A sermon that points to the Supper's eschatological anticipation can hardly ignore the death-by-boredom (or handguns) assumptions of our youth. A liturgical sermon must be a political statement. Any other kind of sermon, especially if based only in the preacher's private choice of texts, is suspect as simply a personal statement.

4. A liturgical sermon is freed of having to do it all. Like the John the Baptist of the Isenheim altarpiece that Karl Barth so regularly referred to, it has only to point beyond itself to the sacramental feast.

And the basis of all such liturgical connections must be in the prior sacramental event, that of the baptismal initiation (at which and about which one so rarely hears a proper sermon), which in an equally serious and suggestive way provides both the material and formal context for both sermon and Supper.

As a conclusion to this introduction, which has moved from lectionary to sermon and from sermon to sacramental liturgy, we cannot do better than to hear a prophetic voice of the Reformed tradition, speaking in the early 1930s from Scotland—that of George F. MacLeod, founder of the Iona Community and *enfant terrible* of the Church of Scotland for most of the decades of this dying century:

> How weary we are today of theories, of debates and of questions; we must have Certainty or die. The Celtic Church offered the Sacrament of Communion to the faithful every Sunday of the year, that men's eyes might see and their hands might often feel the Certainty of Love. Again to offer it so is not merely to meet "our day," but to rediscover the heritage that our very Reformers sought to present. Such readoption could hardly cause commotion to a Church based so proudly on Holy Writ, which manifestly ordains it; hardly perturb the Church of Calvin and John Knox, both of whom valiantly endeavored for such celebration in place of the infrequency which their youth had known. . . .
>
> Indeed if we would be patient we can discover here the link that saves the chain. For it was a return to the simple primitive Catholic Church which was the desire and purpose of the first Reformers. How many, who today invoke the name of John Knox, really know the things for which he stood?—frequent Communion; read prayers from a liturgy; daily service in the churches; the reciting of the Apostles' Creed in worship; the response of the people to prayers; the offering of praise from the Communion Table; the pronouncing of the Benediction at the Communion Table. How many of these acts today—when they are enacted in a Scottish Church—are called "mere aping of another Church"? And yet they are in

reality the things which John Knox practised in his endeavor to recover for Scotland her ancient primitive Faith.

Perhaps the first Reformers are to be vindicated at last, in coming days, by a return to what they sought. If not (at least if we just drift on) then there is thunder in the air. But it will not be the passing thunder of warring religious sects, but the thunder of materialism, of Atheism, and all manner of un-loveliness.[20]

20. George F. MacLeod, "The Church of Scotland in Quest of Her Youth," in *Scotland in Quest of Her Youth,* ed. David Clegham Thomson (Edinburgh: Oliver & Boyd, 1932), pp. 102–3.

Year A

Christmas Cycle
Season of Advent
FIRST SUNDAY OF ADVENT (A)

Isaiah 2:1–5 A vision of the coming Day of YHWH, when all nations gather at the holiest of places, Mt. Zion, for YHWH's teaching on the true way. Result: universal peace reigns; weapons and soldiers are passé because YHWH judges all disputes.

Anthems
And It Shall Come to Pass, Jean Berger (Augsburg) SATB (D). *Canticle of Peace,* Joseph Clokey (Summy-Birchard) unison (E). *Cantata of Peace,* Daniel Moe (Hope) SATB trumpet (D).

Romans 13:11–14 The *kairos* ("hour") of the second coming of the Lord is dawning. So awake, all believers, and be dressed; "put on Christ" and live as the people of light.

Anthems
Sleepers, Wake! A Voice Astounds Us, J. S. Bach, *PH90* #17, SATB or unison. *Salvation Is Created,* P. Tchesnokoff (J. Fischer) SATTBB (M).

Matthew 24:36–44 All time is in God's hands. No one knows the day and the hour of the Second Coming when the remnant will be "taken" (welcomed). So, people of God, discard your everyday hustle-bustle and be vigilant, be prepared, and wait anxiously for the joy and excitement of the Lord's unknown return.

Anthems
Let Your Eye Be to the Lord, Daniel Moe (Augsburg) SATB (M). *O Mighty God, Our Lord,* Heinrich Schütz (Mercury) 2-part (E).

Psalm 122
1. Metrical: *With Joy I Heard My Friends Exclaim.* Text: *The Psalter,* 1912. Tune: GONFALON ROYAL. *PH90* #235; *RITL* #132.
2. Responsorial: *Psalm 122* (1–7). Text: Grail. Refrain: Hal H. Hopson. Gelineau tone. *PS93* #126.
3. Responsorial: *I Rejoiced When I Heard Them Say.* Text: Grail (see also *GPI,* p. 188 and *GPP,* p. 180). Psalm tone and Gelineau tone: *WIII* #766. For other refrains see *24P&1C,* p. 31 and *GG,* p. 155.
4. Metrical: *With Joy I Heard My Friends Exclaim.* Text: *The Psalter,* 1912. Tune: MORNING SONG. *HB55* #439.

See also *ANMP,* p. 206; *SPJP,* p. 65; *PH87* #122; *PR&T,* pp. 2 & 7.

Anthems
I Was Glad, Peter Hallock (Walton) 2-part choir, congregation. *With Joy I Heard My Friends Exclaim,* Percy C. Buck, *PH90* #235.

Organ Music for the Day
1. WACHET AUF (*Sleepers, Wake! PH90* #17), J. S. Bach (various publishers).
2. *Prelude on* LLANGLOFFAN (*Rejoice! Rejoice, Believers, PH90* #15), David P. Dahl (*The Concordia Hymn Prelude Series,* vol. 30, p. 42, Concordia 97-5745).

Hymns for the Day	HL33	HB55	WB72	PH90
Come, Thou Long-Expected Jesus	113	151	342	1
O Come, O Come, Emmanuel	108	147	489	9
O Lord, How Shall I Meet You?	–	–	–	11
Prepare the Way	–	–	–	13
Jesus Comes with Clouds Descending	–	–	–	6
Today We All Are Called (Isa. 2:4)	–	–	–	434

SECOND SUNDAY OF ADVENT (A)

Isaiah 11:1–10 A vision of a time of justice and of peace. From the stump of the tree of Jesse shall grow a new branch, a new ruler upon whom the Spirit of the Lord rests. Then wolves and lambs shall live together, and a little child shall lead them.

Anthem
Lo, How a Rose E'er Blooming, arr. Roger Wagner (Lawson Gould) SATB divisi (M).

Romans 15:4–13 Christ Jesus is the fulfillment of the Old Testament hope and promise (e.g., Isa. 11:10). So in the same manner of Christ, care for one another and thus live in unity and harmony, glorifying God.

Anthem
Come, Jesus, Holy Son of God, G. F. Handel, arr. Hal H. Hopson (Harold Flammer) 2-part (E).

Matthew 3:1–12 From out of nowhere comes John the Baptist (an Elijah-like forerunner to Jesus), who preaches, "The time of 'the age to come' has drawn near; so turn yourselves to the new age." And all Jerusalem and Judea reorient their lives through baptism, confessing their sins. Now they are all charged with the awesome responsibility of bearing fruit that matches their reorientation to the new age.

Anthem
Advent Message, Martin How (Boosey & Hawkes) 2-part (E).

Psalm 72:1–7, 18–19
1. Metrical: *All Hail to God's Anointed.* Text: James Montgomery, alt. Tune: ROCKPORT. *PH90* #205. (See also *HB55* #146, *H82* #616, and *PH87* #72 to the Tune: GERMAN.)
2. Responsorial: *Justice Shall Flourish in God's Time.* Text: NRSV. Psalm tone: Laurence Bevenot. Refrain: John Schiavone. *PH90* #204.
3. Responsorial: *Psalm 72* (1–14). Text: International Commission on English in the Liturgy, *Book of Common Prayer.* Setting: Howard Hughes. *PS93* #64.
See also *PS93* #65; *CS/PFTCY,* vol. 1, p. 16; *ANMP,* p. 123; *SPJP,* p. 42.

Anthem
All Hail to God's Anointed, T. T. Noble, *PH90* #205, SATB.

Organ Music for the Day
1. VENI EMMANUEL. (*O Come, O Come, Emmanuel, PH90* #9), Leo Sowerby (*Advent to Whitsuntide,* vol. 4, p. 2, Hinrichsen Edition, Ltd. 743b).
2. *Prelude on* WINCHESTER NEW (*On Jordan's Bank the Baptist's Cry, PH90* #10), C. S. Lang (*Twenty Hymn-Tune Preludes,* vol. 2, p. 1, Oxford University Press 375524-6).
3. *Postlude on* BEREDEN VÄG FÖR HERRAN (*Prepare the Way, PH90* #13), Carl E. Rosenquist (*Postludier,* vol. 1, Nordiska, distributed by Magnamusic Baton 1301).

Hymns for the Day	HL33	HB55	WB72	PH90
Hope of the World (Rom. 15:13)	–	291	423	360
Isaiah the Prophet Has Written of Old	–	–	–	337
O Day of Peace (Isa. 11:6–9)	–	–	–	450
O Morning Star, How Fair and Bright	321	415	521	69
On Jordan's Bank the Baptist's Cry (Matt. 3)	–	–	–	10
Wild and Lone the Prophet's Voice	–	–	–	409

THIRD SUNDAY OF ADVENT (A)

Isaiah 35:1–10 The barren desert is going to bloom; therefore, strengthen your weak knees, stand up, and say, "God is coming to save you!" The blind, the deaf, the lame, the dumb—all shall be transformed.

Anthems
Then Shall the Eyes of the Blind Be Opened (recitative) and *He Shall Feed His Flock,* G. F. Handel (*Messiah*—any edition) solo.

James 5:7–10 In the same way that farmers await the harvest of their crops, cultivate patience as you await the coming of the Lord. Yes, the prophets were ill-treated for their proclamations, but they patiently persisted. So faithfully and patiently continue your witness.

Anthem
Thou Shalt Know Him When He Comes, Hal H. Hopson (Harold Flammer) SATB (M).

Matthew 11:2–11 Is Jesus of Nazareth the one who is to come, or should we look for another? "What do you hear and see?" replies Jesus. "The blind, the lame, lepers, the deaf, the poor, and the dead all live as if in the new age. What kind of person did you expect to see—a pietist hobnobbing with the king, or a radical social activist?"

Anthem
Go and Tell John, Lloyd Pfautsch (Hope) SATB (ME).

Psalm 146:5–10
1. Metrical: *I'll Praise My Maker While I've Breath.* Text: Isaac Watts, alt. Tune: OLD 113TH. *PH90* #253. (See also *RITL* #140.)
2. Responsorial: *Psalm 146.* Text: Grail. Refrain: Richard T. Proulx. Gelineau tone. *PS93* #150.

See also *PH90* #254; *PS93* #151 & #152; *ANMP*, p. 228; *SPJP*, p. 73; *PH87* #146; *PR&T*, pp. 2, 7, 69, & 75.

Anthem
With All My Whole Heart, O God, LeJeune-Couper (Mercury) SATB (ME).

or **Luke 1:47–55 (Magnificat)**
See Fourth Sunday of Advent (B), p. 136.

Organ Music for the Day
1. *Prelude on* STUTTGART (*Come, Thou Long-Expected Jesus, PH90* #1), Flor Peeters (*Festal Voluntaries*—Christmas and Epiphany, p. 21, Novello & Co., Ltd. 1399).
2. *Prelude on* HYFRYDOL (*Come, Thou Long-Expected Jesus, PH90* #2), Gordon Young (*Eight Organ Voluntaries on Familiar Hymn Tunes,* p. 26, Theodore Presser Co. 413-41034).
3. *Prelude on* MIT FREUDEN ZART (*Lord Christ, When First You Came to Earth, PH90* #7), Hugo Distler (*Choralvorspiele für den Gottesdienstlichen Gebrauch,* vol. 4, p. 338, Bärenreiter Verlag 5484).

Hymns for the Day	HL33	HB55	WB72	PH90
Creator of the Stars of Night	–	–	348	4
Live Into Hope	–	–	–	332
Lo, How a Rose E'er Blooming	–	162	455	48
Lord Christ, When First You Came	–	–	–	7
The Desert Shall Rejoice (Isa. 35)	–	–	–	18
Let All Mortal Flesh Keep Silence	112	148	449	5

FOURTH SUNDAY OF ADVENT (A)

Isaiah 7:10–16 Isaiah offers the disbelieving King Ahaz of Judah a sign of God's care, but the king piously refuses to test the Lord for a sign. "Well, then," says Isaiah, "the Lord will give you a sign: a young woman shall conceive and bear a son, and shall call his name Immanuel, for God is with God's people."

Anthems
Behold, a Virgin Shall Conceive (recitative) and *O Thou That Tellest Good Tidings to Zion* (air and chorus), G. F. Handel (*Messiah,* any edition) (M).

Romans 1:1–7 Paul identifies himself as a slave of Jesus Christ and as one who has been entrusted and set apart by Christ to proclaim the gospel. Those whom Paul addresses are also called to belong to Christ and to proclaim the good news.

Anthems
O Come, O Come, Emmanuel, arr. George Lynn (Mercury) 2-part mixed voices, organ (E). *From Heaven on High I Come to You,* J. S. Bach (Chantry) SATB (MD).

Matthew 1:18–25 Jesus' conception and birth is fulfillment of Isaiah's prophecy. This Son of David and Son of God, begotten through the Holy Spirit, is named Emmanuel, for God is with God's people.

Anthem
Mary on a Mountain, John Carter (Hinshaw) SATB (M).

Psalm 80:1–7, 17–19
1. Metrical: *O Hear Our Cry, O Lord.* Text: Fred R. Anderson. Tune: VINEYARD HAVEN. *PH90* #206 (text only see *SPJP,* p. 43).
2. Responsorial: *Psalm 80* (1–7). Text: Gary Chamberlain. Setting: Hal H. Hopson. *PS93* #70.
3. Responsorial: *Psalm 80.* Text: Grail. Setting: Howard Hughes. Gelineau tone. *PS93* #71.
4. Metrical: *O Shepherd, Like a Flock You Lead.* Text: L.M., Christopher L. Webber. *ANMP,* p. 127.

See also *CS/PFTCY,* vol. 2, p. 25; *PH87* #80; *WIII* #767; *30P&2C,* p. 23; *PR&T,* pp. 1 & 51.

Anthem
O Hear Our Cry, O Lord, Richard Dirkson, *PH90* #206.

Organ Music for the Day
1. *Organ Prelude on* NUN KOMM, DER HEIDEN HEILAND (*Savior of the Nations, Come, PH90* #14), J. S. Bach and other composers (*The Church Organist's Golden Treasury,* vol. 3, Oliver Ditson Co.).
2. *Prelude on* TRURO (*Lift Up Your Heads, Ye Mighty Gates, PH90* #8), Gerhard Krapf (*Various Hymn Settings,* p. 7, Edwin F. Kalmus 3603).

Hymns for the Day	HL33	HB55	WB72	PH90
O Come, O Come, Emmanuel	108	147	489	9
The Angel Gabriel from Heaven Came	–	–	–	16
To a Maid Engaged to Joseph	–	–	–	19
Watchman, Tell Us (antiphonal)	109	149	617	20
People, Look East	–	–	–	12
Savior of the Nations, Come	–	–	565	14

Season of Christmas
CHRISTMAS EVE/DAY
[DECEMBER 24/25] (ABC)

Isaiah 9:2–7 Darkness reigns everywhere, yet people have seen a great light: the presence of God. All rejoice, as with joy at the harvest, for the rule of darkness will be lifted. A child shall reign as God's representative on earth, and God's light shall shine without end.

Anthems

For Unto Us a Child Is Born, M. Praetorius (G.I.A.) (in 3 chorales) 3 equal voices (M). *For Unto Us a Child Is Born,* G. F. Handel (from *Messiah,* any edition) SATB (D). *Rejoice, O Jerusalem, Behold Thy King Cometh,* Healey Willan (Concordia) SATB (M). *Break Forth, O Beauteous Heavenly Light,* J. S. Bach (many editions) SATB (E) (see also *PH90* #26).

Titus 2:11–14 Jesus, the grace of God, has appeared for the salvation of *all* and has taught us a new way of life. Because we now live in the light of his second coming, we can celebrate his first coming, when he gave himself for us and set us free from all wickedness.

Anthems

Salvation Is Created, Paul Tchesnokoff, arr. Becker (G.I.A.) SATTBB (M). *Of the Father's Love Begotten,* Richard Peek (Carl Fischer) SATB (ME). *Salvation Has Come to Us,* J. S. Bach, arr. Buszin (Schmitt, Hall & McCreary) SATB (ME).

Luke 2:1–14, (15–20) The birth of Jesus in the "city of David," Bethlehem, and the angelic proclamation to shepherds in the same area where David was a shepherd. Gloria in excelsis! The shepherds go to Bethlehem. As they return to their fields, they glorify and praise God for all they have heard and seen. Their listeners are astonished. Mary treasures all these things.

Anthems

Birthday Carol, David Willcocks (Oxford) SATB (ME). *All My Heart This Night Rejoices,* Kenneth Jennings (Augsburg) SATB 2 flutes, optional children (ME). *In Excelsis Gloria,* Flor Peeters (Augsburg) SATB (E). *As on the Night,* Orlando Gibbons (Oxford) SATB (ME).

Psalm 96

1. Metrical: *O Sing a New Song to the Lord.* Text: Charles H. Gabriel, alt. Tune: GONFALON ROYAL. *PH90* #216.
2. Responsorial: *Psalm 96.* Text: *A New Zealand Prayer Book.* Refrain: Clifford W. Howell. Tone: Gregorian V. Harmony, Robert J. Batastini. *PS93* #91.
3. Responsorial: *Psalm 96.* Text: Helen L. Wright. Setting: Hal H. Hopson. *PS93* #92.
4. Metrical: *O Sing a New Song to the Lord.* Text: The Scottish Psalter, 1650, alt. Tune: SONG 67. *HB55* #37; *WB72* #525.

See also *ANMP,* p. 158; *PH87* #96; *PH90* #217; *SPJP,* p. 50; *WIII* #779; *PR&T,* pp. 10 & 13.

Anthems

Psalm 96, Peter Hurd (Augsburg) unison and congregation (E). *Sing to the Lord a New Song,* J. Pachelbel, W. Ehret (Hinshaw) SATB, double chorus or SATB and organ (M). *Sing to the Lord a New Song,* Johann Staden (Concordia) SATB 2 flutes (MD). *O Sing Unto the Lord a New Song,* Peter Aston (Hinshaw) SATB (M). *Advent Carol,* George Brandon (G.I.A.) 2-part or unison (E).

Organ Music for the Day

1. VOM HIMMEL HOCH (*From Heaven Above, PH90* #54), J. S. Bach (various publishers) and Georg Böhm (*Sämtliche Orgelwerke,* p. 106, Breitkopf & Haertel 8087).

2. *Chorale Prelude on* SILENT NIGHT (*Silent Night, Holy Night, PH90* #60), Samuel Barber (G. Schirmer, Inc.).

3. *Prelude on* GREENSLEEVES (*What Child Is This, PH90* #53), Searle Wright (*A Christmas Album for Organ*, p. 105, H.W. Gray Co., Inc. GB 655).

4. STILLE NACHT (*Silent Night, Holy Night*), Gordon Young (*Ten Christmas Organ Voluntaries on Familiar Carols*, p. 18, Theodore Presser Co. 413-41134).

5. *Prelude on* IRBY (*Once in Royal David's City, PH90* #49), Gordon Young (*Merry Carols for Organ*, p. 3, Harold Flammer, Inc. HF-5131), Flor Peeters (*Thirty Short Preludes on Well-Known Hymns*, p. 15, C. F. Peters Corp. 6195).

6. *Prelude on* CAROL (*It Came Upon the Midnight Clear, PH90* #38), Albert D. Schmutz (H. W. Gray Co., Inc. 695).

Hymns for the Day	HL33	HB55	WB72	PH90
Born in the Night, Mary's Child	–	–	312	30
Break Forth, O Beauteous . . . Light (Isa. 9)	–	–	314	26
Hark! The Herald Angels Sing	117	163	411	31
Holy Night, Blessed Night	–	–	–	33
Still, Still, Still	–	–	–	47
Joy to the World!	122	161	444	40
O Come, All Ye Faithful	116	170	486	41
Silent Night	132	154	567	60
The First Nowell	129	156	585	56

CHRISTMAS EVE/DAY: ALTERNATIVE LECTIONS 1
[DECEMBER 24/25] (ABC)

Isaiah 62:6–12 Remind YHWH of the promises and plead unceasingly for their fulfillment. Prepare the way, clear it of any obstacles, for YHWH keeps YHWH's promises. "Behold, your salvation comes."

Anthems
Zion Hears Her Watchmen's Voices, J. S. Bach (Cantata 41, *Sleepers, Wake*, Belwin-Mills), unison male voices, violin, and organ (E). *Today Is Salvation Come*, Raymond Haan (G.I.A.) SATB 4 handbells (E). *Be Joyful, O Daughter of Zion*, Everett Titcomb (Carl Fischer) SATB (M). *Daughters of Zion*, G. F. Handel, arr. Buszin (Schmitt, Hall, & McCreary) (M). *The Noel Carol*, arr. Mary Elizabeth Caldwell (H. W. Gray) SATB also SA, SSA, SAB (ME).

Titus 3:4–7 God our Savior has appeared and has saved us by God's mercy (and not because of any good deeds on our part). Through Jesus Christ our Savior, God has poured out the Holy Spirit on us and transformed us and given us new life in the waters of baptism.

Anthems
Love Came Down at Christmas, H. Schroeder (Concordia) SATB with instruments (E). *Love Came Down at Christmas*, John Rutter (Oxford) SATB (M). *A Boy Was Born*, Lewis Kirby (J. Fischer) SATB (ME). *Rejoice, the Savior Is Born*, Robert Wetzler (AMSI) SATB (M). *Come, Love We God*, Daniel Pinkham (E. C. Shirmer) SATB (MD).

Luke 2:(1–7), 8–20 Jesus is born in the "city of David," Bethlehem, and the angels tell the shepherds in the same area where David was a shepherd. Gloria in excelsis! The shepherds go to Bethlehem. As they return to their fields, they glorify and praise God "for all they had heard and seen." Their listeners are astonished. Mary treasures all these things.

Anthems
Infant Holy, Infant Lowly, Gerre Hancock (H. W. Gray) SATB (M). *On Christmas Night All Christians Sing*, James Melby (Concordia) SATB bells (ME). *He Whom Joyous Shepherds Praised—Quem Pastores*, arr. Gerald Near (Calvary Press) SAB (ME).

Hear the Joyful News (from Cantata number 141) J. S. Bach (Galaxy) SATB or SAAB (MD).

Psalm 97

1. Responsorial: *A Light Will Shine on This Day.* Text: Grail (see also *GPI*, p. 139). Psalm tone and Gelineau tone: *WIII* #780 (see also *GG*, p. 14 for optional refrains).
2. Responsorial: *Psalm 97.* Setting: Hal H. Hopson. *PS93* #93.
3. Metrical: *The Lord Is King, Let Earth Rejoice.* Text: L.M., Christopher L. Webber. *ANMP*, p. 159.
4. Metrical: *Lord, You Reign, the Earth Rejoices.* Text: 8.7.8.7.8.7., Fred R. Anderson. *SPJP*, p. 51.

See also *PH87* #97; *PR&T*, pp. 11 & 13.

Anthems

Shout for Joy, C. Alexander Peloquin (G.I.A.) SATB (optional congregation) (ME). *The Lord Is King O'er Land and Sea,* Heinrich Schütz *(Four Psalms,* Mercury) SATB (ME). *Psalm 97,* Heinrich Schütz (Mercury) SATB (M).

Organ Music for the Day

1. Any of the Noels by d'Aquin, Balbastre, etc. (Kalmus and other publishers).
2. IN DULCI JUBILO (*Good Christian Friends, Rejoice, PH90* #28), Dupré (*A Christmas Album for Organ,* p. 2, H. W. Gray Co., Inc. GB 655).
3. ADESTE FIDELES (*O Come, All Ye Faithful, PH90* #41), Guilmant (*The Organ Music of Alexandre Guilmant,* vol. 1, p. 73, McAfee Music Corp. DM 240).
4. *Chorale Prelude on* ES IST EIN' ROS' (*Lo, How a Rose E'er Blooming, PH90* #48), Johannes Brahms (various publishers), and Jean Pasquet (H. W. Gray Co., Inc. 721).

Hymns for the Day	HL33	HB55	WB72	PH90
Angels We Have Heard on High	–	158	299	23
Infant Holy, Infant Lowly	–	–	–	37
Joyful Christmas Day Is Here	–	–	–	39
Gentle Mary Laid Her Child	453	167	375	27
It Came Upon the Midnight Clear	127	160	438	38
O Little Town of Bethlehem	121	171	511	43, 44
Rise Up, Shepherd, and Follow	–	–	–	50
What Child Is This	–	159	630	53

CHRISTMAS EVE/DAY: ALTERNATIVE LECTIONS 2
[DECEMBER 24/25] (ABC)

Isaiah 52:7–10 A messenger is coming across the mountains. Ascending and descending from one hill to the next, he joyously cries out, "Your God reigns!" Let everyone sing together of the "salvation of God."

Anthems

How Beautiful Upon the Mountains, John Carter (Hinshaw) 2-part mixed (E). *How Beautiful Upon the Mountains,* Daniel Moe (Presser) SAB (M). *How Beautiful Are the Feet of Him,* G. F. Handel (E. C. Schirmer) SATB (E). *Let All Together Praise Our God,* arr. John Ferguson (Concordia) SATB, optional trumpets (M).

Hebrews 1:1–4, (5–12) God has spoken to us through the prophets; now God speaks uniquely to us through the Son, the descending-ascending Savior of all. The true image of God is Christ, whose throne is forever and ever. Christ is of the same flesh and blood as we are, yet greater than all the angels. God's Son is the risen, exalted Christ.

Anthems

Of the Father's Love Begotten, arr. John Erickson (Lorenz) unison, handbells (E). *Of the Father's Love Begotten,* Richard Peek (Carl Fischer) SATB (ME). *Let All the*

Angels of God Worship Him, G. F. Handel (*Messiah,* ed. Watkins Shaw, Novello, or any edition) SATB (M).

John 1:1–14 "In the beginning was the Word, and the Word was with God." All things were made through the Word, and in the Word were life and light. The Word came into the world and to God's own people, but the world rejected the Word as did God's own people. Yet those who received and believed in the Word were given power to announce and to bear witness, as John (the Baptizer) did, to the coming of the Word among us, full of grace and truth.

Anthems

In the Beginning Was the Word, W. J. Reynolds (Kjos) SATB divisi (D). *The Word Became Flesh,* George Brandon (Canyon) unison (E). *And the Word Was Made Flesh,* Hans Leo Hassler (Broude) SSAATTB (MD).

Psalm 98

1. Metrical: *New Songs of Celebration Render.* Text: Erik Routley. Tune: RENDEZ À DIEU. *PH90* #218. See also *RITL* #119, *H82* #413, and *PH87* #98 with text by Dewey Westra.
2. Metrical: *To God Compose a Song of Joy.* Text: Ruth C. Duck. Tune: KEDDY. *PH90* #219.
3. Responsorial: *Psalm 98.* Text: International Commission on English in the Liturgy. Tone: Presbyterian 3. *PS93* #94.
4. Responsorial: *Psalm 98* (1–6). Text: *Book of Common Prayer.* Setting: Peter R. Hallock. *PS93* #95.
5. Metrical: *Sing, Sing a New Song to the Lord God.* Text: Dewey Westra, rev. Tune: GENEVAN 98/118. *PH87* #98.

See also *WIII* #781; *ANMP,* p. 161; *SPJP,* p. 53; *PR&T,* pp. 10, 13.

Anthems

New Songs of Celebration Render, Genevan Psalter Tune, adapted by Erik Routley, arr. Carlton Young (Agape) 2-part optional brass (ME). *Sing to the Lord a New Song,* Donald Busarow (Augsburg) SATB congregation, brass (ME). *Sing to the Lord a New Song,* Samuel Adler (*Ecumenical Praise,* number 10, Agape) SATB, congregation (E). *O Sing Unto the Lord,* Hans Leo Hassler (E. C. Schirmer) SATB (M).

Organ Music for the Day

1. DIVINUM MYSTERIUM (*Of the Father's Love Begotten, PH90* #309), Held (*Six Carol Settings,* p. 6, Concordia 97-4985), and T. Frederick H. Candlyn (*A Christmas Album for Organ,* p. 101, H. W. Gray Co., Inc. GB 655).
2. GO TELL IT ON THE MOUNTAIN (*Go, Tell It on the Mountain, PH90* #29), Manz (*Improvisations for the Christmas Season,* vol. 2, p. 14, Morningstar Music Publishers MSM-10-101).
3. *Fantasia on Joy to the World* (ANTIOCH, *PH90* #40), Emma L. Diemer (*Three Fantasies on Advent/Christmas Hymns,* p. 16, Augsburg 11-9479).
4. *Variations on* ADESTE FIDELES (*O Come, All Ye Faithful, PH90* #41), Marcel Dupré (H. W. Gray Co., Inc. GSTC 982).
5. *Prelude on* MENDELSSOHN (*Hark! The Herald Angels Sing, PH90* #31), Emma L. Diemer (*Carols for Organ,* The Sacred Music Press).

Hymns for the Day	HL33	HB55	WB72	PH90
Angels, from the Realms of Glory	124	168	298	22
Away in a Manger	126	157	–	24, 25
Good Christian Friends, Rejoice	130	165	406	28
O Splendor of God's Glory Bright	32	46	529	474
O Word of God Incarnate (John 1:14)	215	251	532	327
Good Christians All, Rejoice and Sing!	–	–	–	111
Joyful Christmas Day Is Here	–	–	–	39

FIRST SUNDAY AFTER CHRISTMAS DAY (A)

Isaiah 63:7–9 In the context of a lament, these words of thanksgiving recount the Lord's *hesed* ("steadfast love"). God made covenant with Israel and was the deliverer in Israel's exodus. God redeemed Israel through steadfast love. God was present with the people.

Anthem
For God So Loved the World, Heinrich Schütz (*A Second Motet Book,* Concordia) SATB (M).

Hebrews 2:10–18 Jesus was of the same flesh and blood as all human beings. He experienced all that we experience: human existence, temptation, suffering, death. In fact, by suffering and dying he was "made perfect" (brought to completion) as one who totally shared humanity. Thus he became the pioneer of salvation and deliverer of all who fear death.

Anthems
I Know Not How, anonymous American hymn, tune arr. George Brandon (Art Masters) SATB (E). *The Blessed Son of God,* Ralph Vaughan Williams (*Carols for Choirs,* Book 1, Oxford) SATB (MD).

Matthew 2:13–23 Rejection and persecution of Jesus by those in authority begins at birth. But God delivers Jesus through Joseph's obedience to divine commands. When the earthly rulers' clamor for Jesus' death subsides, Joseph again faithfully obeys divine commands and brings the child to the land of Israel, to the district of Galilee, to a city called Nazareth.

Anthems
Coventry Carol, arr. Martin Shaw (*Carols for Choirs,* Book 1, Oxford) SAB original and SATB. *In Bethlehem a Newborn Boy,* Wilbur Held, *PH90* #35.

Psalm 148
1. Metrical: *Let the Whole Creation Cry.* Text: Stopford A. Brooke, 1881. Tune: SALZBURG. Harmony, J. S. Bach. *PH90* #256.
2. Responsorial: *Psalm 148.* Setting: Hal H. Hopson. *PS93* #155.
See also *RITL* #141; *TIP/PSCY* #9; *PH90* #256; *H82* #432.

Anthem
Let the Whole Creation Cry, J. Hintze. Harm., J. S. Bach, *PH90* #256.

Organ Music for the Day
1. *Prelude on* HYFRYDOL (*Love Divine, All Loves Excelling, PH90* #376), Diemer (*Seven Hymn Preludes,* Harold Flammer, Inc. HF-5008) and Near (*Preludes on Four Hymn Tunes,* p. 9, Augsburg 11-828).
2. *Prelude on* FOREST GREEN (*All Beautiful the March of Days, PH90* #292), Gordon Phillips (*Six Carol Preludes,* p. 2, Oxford University Press 375644-7).

Hymns for the Day	HL33	HB55	WB72	PH90
In Bethlehem a Newborn Boy (Matt. 2:13–16)	–	–	–	35
Christ, You Are the Fullness	–	–	–	346
Down to Earth, as a Dove	–	–	–	300
Infant Holy, Infant Lowly	–	–	–	37
In the Bleak Midwinter	–	–	–	36
Once in Royal David's City	454	462	539	49
On This Day Earth Shall Ring	–	–	538	46
O Sleep, Dear Holy Baby (Matt. 2:13–15)	–	–	–	45
'Twas in the Moon of Wintertime	–	–	–	61

HOLY NAME OF JESUS
[JANUARY 1] (ABC)

Numbers 6:22–27 The well-known Aaronic blessing: three simple poetic lines, each petitioning YHWH to move toward the people through the presence of YHWH's protection, favor, and peace. And where the name of YHWH is put upon the people, YHWH is present in blessing.

Anthem
The Lord Bless You and Keep You, J. S. Bach (Concordia) SA or TB (M).

Galatians 4:4–7 When God decided the right time had come, God sent the Son, fully human, to release all those under the law so they might be God's children. Then God sent the Spirit of the Son, who empowered these adopted children to name God as "Abba, Father."

Anthem
Children of the Heavenly King, HB55 #340.

or **Philippians 2:9–13** Part of a primitive christological hymn in which the name bestowed by God upon Jesus is the name "Lord." At the name of Jesus, may all confess him as Lord and live as his people, for God will support us.

Anthems
At the Name of Jesus, R. Vaughan Williams (Oxford) SATB with congregation (E).
At the Name of Jesus, R. Vaughan Williams (G. Schirmer) SATB, SAB, or unison (E).

Luke 2:15–21 Shepherds see what the angel of the Lord announced and thus glorify and praise God for all they have heard and seen. After eight days, the infant is circumcised and named "Jesus" in fulfillment of the angel's command at the annunciation.

Anthems
Magnificat, R. Vaughan Williams (G. Schirmer) SATB, SAB, or unison (E). *Magnificat,* Daniel Moe (Carl Fischer) SATB (MD).

Psalm 8
1. Metrical: *O Lord, Our God, How Excellent.* Text: Fred R. Anderson. Tune: WINCHESTER OLD. *PH90* #162. For text only see *SPJP*, p. 15.
2. Responsorial: *Psalm 8.* Setting: Hal H. Hopson. *PS93* #5.
3. Metrical: *Lord, Our Lord, Thy Glorious Name.* Text: *The Psalter,* 1912, alt. Tune: GOTT SEI DANK DURCH ALLE WELT. *PH90* #163. (See also *RITL* #83 to the Tune: SAVANNAH.)
4. Metrical: *O Lord, Our Lord, in All the Earth.* Text: *The Psalter,* 1912. Tune: DUNFERMLINE. *HB55* #95. (See also *PH87* #8 to the Tune: EVENING PRAISE.)
5. Responsorial: *O Lord, Our God, How Wonderful Your Name in All the Earth.* Text: Grail. Psalm tone and Gelineau tone: *WIII* #861. (See also *WIII* #27; *24P&1C*, p. 4. For text only see *GPI*, p. 8.)
See also *ANMP*, p. 44; *PR&T*, pp. 37 & 52.

Anthem
Lord, How Majestic Is Your Name, Austin Lovelace (Broadman) unison (E).

Organ Music for the Day
1. *Prelude on* CORONATION (*All Hail the Power of Jesus' Name!, PH90* #142), Hal H. Hopson (*Five Preludes on Familiar Hymns,* p. 6, Harold Flammer, Inc. HF-5123).
2. *Prelude on* KING'S WESTON (*At the Name of Jesus, PH90* #148), David Johnson (*Music for Worship; Easy Trios,* p. 30, Augsburg 11-9291).
3. *Chorale Prelude on* GOTT SEI DANK DURCH ALLE WELT (Psalm 8, *PH90* #163), Robert J. Powell (*Eleven Chorale Preludes on Hymn Tunes,* Harold Flammer, Inc. 4430).

4. *Prelude on* WAREHAM (*Great God, We Sing That Mighty Hand, PH90*#265), Emma
   L. Diemer (*Celebration*, Augsburg 11-9097).

Hymns for the Day	*HL33*	*HB55*	*WB72*	*PH90*
All Hail the Power of Jesus' Name!	192	132	285	142, 143
At the Name of Jesus	–	143	–	148
Creator of the Stars of Night	–	–	348	4
Hark! The Herald Angels Sing	117	163	411	31
Here, O Lord, Your Servants Gather	–	–	417	465
May the Lord, Mighty God	–	–	–	596
Christ the Lord Is Risen Today	165	–	330	113
Born in the Night, Mary's Child	–	–	312	30
In Bethlehem a Babe Was Born	–	–	–	34

38

JANUARY 1
[WHEN OBSERVED AS NEW YEAR'S DAY] (ABC)

Ecclesiastes 3:1–13 All time is in God's hands. From birth to death, all humans are in God's hands. No one can discern, much less control, the mysterious purposes of God. So relax and enjoy the gift of life, regardless of how mundane it may seem at times. Abandon your vain search for God, and simply trust God's wisdom.

Anthem
A Time for All Things, Douglas Wagner (Sacred Music) SATB (E).

Revelation 21:1–6a Visions of a new heaven and a new earth are seen. The new Jerusalem descends from God and joins the transformed earth where chaotic waters, tears, mourning, crying, death have all disappeared. Human beings will see God and live in holy fellowship together. Shouts the great voice from the throne, "I make all things new."

Anthems
And I Saw a New Heaven, Edgar Bainton (Novello) SATB (D). *The Old Year Now Has Fled,* Richard Peek (H. W. Gray) SATB (E).

Matthew 25:31–46 A terrifying picture: Christ the judge, seated on a throne, separates the wicked from the righteous. All are judged by Christ's call to love endlessly: feed the hungry and the thirsty, welcome strangers, clothe the naked, visit the sick and the imprisoned. The wicked are shocked at their designation, for they did not see the face of Christ in their neighbors, particularly the lowly. Ironically, the righteous are just as surprised, for all they saw was human need and so responded with love.

Anthems
Come, You Have My Father's Blessing, Walter L. Pelz (Augsburg) SAB (ME). *Enter Not Into Judgment,* Thomas Attwood (H. W. Gray) SATB (E).

Psalm 8
See HOLY NAME OF JESUS [January 1] (ABC) in Year A, p. 36.

Organ Music for the Day
1. *Prelude on* WAREHAM (*Great God, We Sing That Mighty Hand, PH90* #265), Healey Willan (*Ten Hymn Preludes,* vol. 2, p. 3, C. F. Peters Corp. 6012) and C. S. Lang (*Twenty Hymn-Tune Preludes,* vol. 1, p. 15, Oxford University Press 375523-8).
2. *Prelude on* SONG 1 (*O God, We Bear the Imprint of Your Face, PH90* #385), Flor Peeters (*Hymn Preludes for the Liturgical Year,* vol. 24, C. F. Peters Corp. 6424), and Healey Willan (*Thirty-Six Short Preludes and Postludes on Well-Known Hymn Tunes,* vol. 2, C. F. Peters Corp. 6162).
3. *Prelude on* ST. PATRICK'S BREASTPLATE (*O Lord, You Gave Your Servant John, PH90* #431), Leo Sowerby (*Ten Preludes,* H. W. Gray Co., Inc. GB 651).
4. *Prelude on* UNSER HERRSCHER (*Open Now Thy Gates of Beauty, PH90* #489), Walcha (*Choralvorspiele,* vol. 1, p. 20, C. F. Peters Corp. 4850).

Hymns for the Day	HL33	HB55	WB72	PH90
God of Our Life	88	108	395	275
Great God, We Sing That Mighty Hand	470	527	408	265
Immortal, Invisible, God Only Wise	66	85	433	263
Now Thank We All Our God	459	9	481	555
Here, O Our Lord, We See You	352	442	418	520
Of the Father's Love Begotten	–	7	534	309
O God, We Bear the Imprint of Your Face	–	–	–	385
O Lord, You Gave Your Servant (Rev. 21)	–	–	–	431
We Meet You, O Christ (Matt. 25)	–	–	–	311
All Things Bright and Beautiful	–	456	–	267

SECOND SUNDAY AFTER CHRISTMAS DAY (ABC)

Jeremiah 31:7–14 Shout for joy because the Lord has graciously delivered Israel from bondage. The Lord will gather the people (including those dependent upon others) from the ends of the earth, and will shepherd them to flowing streams and reveal a parent's love for the firstborn: Declare to the world: "The Lord has repurchased his flock; he will comfort them and bless them with abundant life."

Anthems
My Shepherd Will Supply My Need, arr. Virgil Thomson (H. W. Gray) SATB (E). *The God of Love,* Jane Marshall (Carl Fischer) SATB (ME). *With a Voice of Singing,* Martin Shaw (G. Schirmer) SATB (M). *We Will Rejoice in Thy Salvation,* G. F. Handel (Belwin) SATB (MD).

Ephesians 1:3–14 Thanks be to you, O God, for blessing our union with Christ by bestowing the gift of the Spirit, and for choosing us as your servants for the purpose of praising your glorious free grace. May the God of our Lord Jesus Christ continually give us discernment regarding our calling and rich inheritance.

Anthems
Sing My Soul, Ned Rorem (C. F. Peters) SATB (MD). *Benedictus,* David McKay Williams (H. W. Gray) unison (E). *Blessed Be the Father,* Paul Christiansen (AMSI) SATB (E). *Messenger to Ephesus,* Eugene Butler (Agape) SATB (M). *Because You Are God's Chosen Ones,* G. Allen Smith (Hope) SATB, flute (E).

John 1:(1–9), 10–18 "In the beginning was the Word, and the Word was with God." All things were made through the Word, and in the Word were life and light. The Word came into the world and to his own people, but the world rejected the Word as did his own people. Yet those who received and believed in the Word were given power to announce and to bear witness, as John (the Baptizer) did, to the coming of the Word among us, full of grace and truth.

Anthems
We Saw His Glory, Erhard Mauersberger (Concordia) 2-part mixed (E). *In the Beginning Was the Word,* William J. Reynolds (Kjos) SATB, divisi (MD). *A Wondrous Mystery,* Lloyd Pfautsch (G. Schirmer) double choir (D). *The Word Became Flesh,* George Brandon (Canyon) unison (E). *In the Beginning Was the Word,* Paul Sjolund (Fred Bock) SATB (M). *The Word Was Made Flesh,* James McCray (Mark Foster) SATB (M). *Let Our Gladness Know No End,* Hermann Schroeder (Concordia) SATB 2 flutes, cello (ME).

Psalm 147:12–20
1. Metrical: *Now Praise the Lord, All Living Saints.* Text: C.M., Fred R. Anderson. Tune: ST. ANNE. *PH90* #255 (see also *SPJP,* p. 74).
2. Responsorial: *Psalm 147* (12–15, 19–20). Setting: Hal H. Hopson. *PS93* #154.
3. Responsorial: *Praise the Lord, Jerusalem.* Text: Grail (see also *GPI,* p. 212). Psalm tone and Gelineau tone: *WIII* #862 (see also *WIII* #78).
4. Metrical: *Worship the Lord, Jerusalem.* Text: C.M., Christopher L. Webber. *ANMP,* p. 232.

See also *PH87* #147; *PR&T,* pp. 10 & 13.

Anthems
I Will Greatly Rejoice in the Lord, Jean Berger (Augsburg) SATB (MD). *O Praise the Lord with Heart and Voice,* Joseph Haydn, arr. Hal H. Hopson (Flammer) SATB (M).

Organ Music for the Day
1. *Chorale Prelude on* ERMUNTRE DICH (*Break Forth, O Beauteous Heavenly Light, PH90* #26), Friedrich W. Marpurg (*Twenty-One Chorale Preludes,* p. 35, Augs-

burg 11-9506), and A.P.F. Boely (*Oeuvres Complètes,* vol. 3, p. 46, Editions Bornemann).

2. *Chorale Prelude on* ST. ANNE (*Now Praise the Lord, PH90* #255), C. Hubert H. Parry (*Seven Chorale Preludes,* Novello & Co., Ltd. 1546).

3. *Prelude on* PUER NOBIS NASCITUR (*O Splendor of God's Glory Bright, PH90* #474), Geoffrey Shaw (*Variations on an Old Carol Tune,* J. B. Cramer & Co., Ltd. APS 479).

Hymns for the Day	*HL33*	*HB55*	*WB72*	*PH90*
Angels, from the Realms of Glory	124	168	298	22
Here, O Lord, Your Servants Gather	–	–	417	465
Holy Night, Blessed Night	-	-	-	33
O Gladsome Light	–	61	494	549
O Word of God Incarnate (John 1:14)	215	251	532	327
Once in Royal David's City	454	462	539	49
Thanks to God Whose Word Was Written	–	–	580	331

Day of Epiphany
EPIPHANY OF THE LORD
[JANUARY 6] (ABC)

Isaiah 60:1–6 Awake, light has overcome the darkness! The glory of the Lord's presence will be reflected in Jerusalem's arising to rebuild the city. Open your eyes and see the caravans from all the nations that shall come of their own free will to your light. Rejoice, for they bring your sons and daughters as well as a multitude of treasures and herds of animals.

Anthems
Arise, Shine, Jane Marshall (H. W. Gray) SATB (ME). *Arise, Shine, for Thy Light Has Come,* K. Jennings (Augsburg) SATB (M). *Surge, Illuminare,* Ned Rorem (Boosey & Hawkes) in English, SATB (MD). *Arise, Shine, for Thy Light Is Come,* Healey Willan (Concordia) SATB (E). *Arise, Shine, for Your Light Has Come,* William Mathias (Oxford) SATB (M).

Ephesians 3:1–12 Paul's vocation is the privilege of making known to the Gentiles God's plan of salvation. And his gospel message is that, through the sheer grace of God, the Gentiles have been included in God's people. Now all the people of God, Jews and Gentiles, share the same promises revealed in Jesus Christ and receive his Spirit to proclaim God's plan of salvation.

Anthems
The Only Son From Heaven, J. S. Bach (*Third Morning Star Book,* Concordia) SATB (ME). *We Saw His Glory,* Erhard Mauersberger (Concordia) 2-part (E). *For Your Light Has Come,* Ronald A. Nelson (Augsburg) SATB (E).

Matthew 2:1–12 Magi from the East come to Jerusalem in search of the King of the Jews. King Herod, out of fear, also wants to know where this threatening challenger can be found. So Herod offers the Magi a deal they can't refuse. But when the Magi arrive in the presence of the child, they fall down on their knees and worship him and give him everything they have. They return home another way, other than through Herod's palace.

Anthems
Epiphany Alleluias, John Weaver (Boosey & Hawkes) SATB (ME). *Brightest and Best,* Paul Sjolund (Hinshaw) 2-part (E). *We Have Seen His Star,* Everett Titcomb (C. Fischer) SATB (E).

Psalm 72:1–7, 10–14
1. Metrical: *All Hail to God's Anointed.* Text: James Montgomery, alt. Tune: ROCK-PORT. *PH90* #205 (see also *HB55* #146, *H82* #616, and *PH87* #72 to the Tune: GERMAN).
2. Responsorial: *Justice Shall Flourish in God's Time.* Text: NRSV. Psalm tone: Laurence Bevenot. Refrain: John Schiavone. *PH90* #204.
3. Responsorial: *Psalm 72* (1–14). Text: International Commission on English in the Liturgy, *Book of Common Prayer.* Setting: Howard Hughes. *PS93* #64.
4. Responsorial: *Psalm 72* (1–19). Text: *Book of Common Prayer.* Music: Peter R. Hallock. *PS93* #65. (See also *TIP/PSCY* #3.)
5. Responsorial: *Every Nation on Earth Will Adore You.* Setting: Marty Haugen. (guitar) *CS/PFTCY,* vol. 1, p. 16.
See also *ANMP,* p. 123; *SPJP,* p. 42; *PR&T,* pp. 14 & 15; *WIII* #784.

Anthems
Psalm for Epiphany, Alexander Peloquin (G.I.A.) SATB (M). *All Hail to God's Anointed,* T. T. Noble, *PH90* #205.

Organ Music for the Day
1. *Chorale Prelude* WIE SCHÖN LEUCHTET (*O Morning Star, How Fair and Bright, PH90* #69), Dietrich Buxtehude (various publishers) and Dupré (*Seventy-Nine Chorales,* p. 88, H. W. Gray Co., Inc. GB 195).

2. *A Nativity Suite* (*We Three Kings of Orient Are, PH90* #66), Wilbur Held (Concordia 97-4461).
3. *Prelude on* PUER NOBIS NASCITUR (*What Star Is This, with Beams So Bright, PH90* #68), Dandrieu (*Organ Literature for the Church Year*, p. 10, Belwin Mills Publishing Corp. DM 00254), and Lebègue (*The Church Organist's Library*, vol. 3, p. 20, McAfee Music Corp. DM 253).
4. *Partita on* PUER NOBIS NASCITUR (*What Star Is This, with Beams So Bright, PH90* #68), Flor Peeters (C. F. Peters Corp. 66746).

Hymns for the Day	HL33	HB55	WB72	PH90
Arise, Your Light Is Come!	–	–	–	411
Brightest and Best	136	175	318	67
Christ Is the World's True Light	–	492	326	–
Christ, Whose Glory Fills the Skies	26	47	332	462, 463
Go, Tell It on the Mountain	–	–	380	29
Joy to the World!	122	161	444	40
We Three Kings of Orient Are	–	176	–	66

Ordinary Time
BAPTISM OF THE LORD
[SUNDAY BETWEEN JANUARY 7 AND 13] [1] (A)

Isaiah 42:1–9 YHWH's chosen servant is officially presented. This servant on whom YHWH's Spirit is placed is to perform the task of bringing forth *mishpat* ("justice") to the nations by his own suffering. YHWH gives this servant as a light to the people who live in darkness.

Anthem
Behold, My Servant, Jack Boyd (Boston Music) SATB (M).

Acts 10:34–43 In his speech to Gentile "God-fearers" at Cornelius's house in Caesarea, Peter recounts how his own life has been transformed by the power of the risen Lord, and says that everyone else (Jews and Gentiles) also can be transformed by that power. God's desire is that all people be joined to Christ, for all have been pardoned.

Anthem
Heavenly Light, A. Kopylow, arr. Wilhousky (Carl Fischer) SATB (E).

Matthew 3:13–17 Jesus is baptized by John the Baptist. Why? According to Jesus' first words in Matthew's Gospel, to fulfill God's will and, therefore, begin to put God's plan into action. And, as Jesus emerges from the water, God's Spirit descends upon him like a dove, and a voice from heaven says, "This is my beloved Son, with whom I am well pleased."

Anthems
This Is My Beloved Son, Knut Nystedt (Concordia) SAB (E). *Carol of the Baptism,* George Brandon (Concordia) SAB or 2-part (ME).

Psalm 29
1. Metrical: *The God of Glory Thunders.* Text: Michael Perry. Setting: Norman Warren. *PH90* #180. (See also *PP* #82.)
2. Responsorial: *Psalm 29.* Setting: Hal H. Hopson. *PS93* #26.
3. Responsorial: *The Lord Will Bless His People with Peace.* Text: Grail (see also *GPI,* p. 35 and *GPP,* p. 44). (See also *24P&1C,* p. 10 for optional refrains.)
See also *ANMP,* p. 66; *SPJP,* p. 29; *PH87* #29; *PR&T,* pp. 17 & 66.

Anthem
Give Unto the Lord, O Ye Mighty, Heinrich Schütz (McAfee Music) unison (ME).

Organ Music for the Day
1. *Prelude on* CAITHNESS (*Christ, When for Us You Were Baptized, PH90* #70), Mead (Willis Music Co. 10909), F. Peeters (*Hymn Preludes for the Liturgical Year*—vol. 18, p. 16, C. F. Peters Corp. 6418), and Healey Willan (*Thirty-Six Short Preludes and Postludes on Well-Known Hymn Tunes,* vol. 1, p. 6, C. F. Peters Corp. 6161).
2. *Prelude on* PLEADING SAVIOR (*Jesus, Our Divine Companion, PH90* #305), Diemer (*Seven Hymn Preludes,* Harold Flammer, Inc. HF-5008).

Hymns for the Day	HL33	HB55	WB72	PH90
Christ, When for Us You Were Baptized	–	–	–	70
Down to Earth, as a Dove	–	–	–	300
Great God, Your Love Has Called Us Here	–	–	–	353
Jesus, Our Divine Companion	–	–	–	305
Lord, When You Came to Jordan	–	–	–	71
When Jesus Came to Jordan	–	–	–	72

SUNDAY BETWEEN JANUARY 14 AND 20 [2] (A)

Isaiah 49:1–7 YHWH's chosen servant summons the nations to hear YHWH's word. The servant publicly announces his prenatal call and his subsequent despondency about performing the task in vain. But now YHWH has expanded the call to be a light to all the nations (Gentiles), in order that "salvation may reach the ends of the earth."

Anthem
Canticle of Trust, Richard Purvis (Sacred Music) SATB (M).

1 Corinthians 1:1–9 The opening greeting and thanksgiving in which Paul thanks God for grace given through Christ Jesus. Therefore, we are enriched by spiritual gifts, particularly in "all speech and all knowledge." God has given us everything we need and will sustain us to the day of the Lord, which brings judgment.

Anthem
Temples of God, Ronald A. Nelson (Augsburg) (E).

John 1:29–42 John (the Baptizer) identifies Jesus as the "Lamb of God" and the preexistent one. When John was baptizing with water, he saw the Spirit descend on Jesus like a dove from heaven, bearing witness that this Jesus is the "Son of God." Therefore, two of John's disciples followed Jesus. "For what are you seeking?" Jesus asks all prospective disciples. They answer, "Where are you staying?" "Come and see," invites Jesus. They go where he goes; follow where he leads; stay where he stays. Result: Andrew announces to his brother, Simon Peter, "We have found the Messiah." Jesus changes Simon's name to Cephas, giving him a new name, a new role, a new self, a new life.

Anthem
Lamb of God, I Look to Thee, W. Bengson (H. W. Gray) children, unison (E).

Psalm 40:1–11
1. Metrical: *I Waited for the Lord My God.* Text: *The Psalter,* 1912. Tune: ABRIDGE. *HB55* #413; *RITL* #100.
2. Responsorial: *Psalm 40:1–11.* Text: Helen L. Wright. Melody: Columba Kelly. Harmony, Samuel Weber. *PS93* #36.

See also *WIII* #868; *GG* #107; *ANMP,* p. 91; *PH87* #40; *PR&T,* pp. 18 & 67.

Anthem
I Waited for the Lord, F. Mendelssohn (G. Schirmer) 2 sopranos and SATB (M).

Organ Music for the Day
1. O GOTT, DU FROMMER GOTT (*O God, Our Faithful God, PH90* #277), settings by J. S. Bach (various publishers), Brahms (*Complete Organ Works,* C. F. Peters Corp.), and Reger (*Organ Book Number 5,* p. 26, Oxford University Press 375847-4).
2. DEO GRACIAS (*O Love, How Deep, PH90* #83), Percy Whitlock (*Six Hymn Preludes,* Oxford University Press 375902).

Hymns for the Day	HL33	HB55	WB72	PH90
All Glory Be to God on High	–	–	283	133
Behold the Lamb of God!	153	–	307	–
Guide Me, O Thou Great Jehovah	104	339	409	281
Like the Murmur of the Dove's Song	–	–	–	314
O Jesus Christ, May Grateful Hymns	–	–	509	424
O Lamb of God Most Holy!	–	585	–	82
On Jordan's Bank (John 1:29–30)	–	–	–	10

SUNDAY BETWEEN JANUARY 21 AND 27 [3] (A)

Isaiah 9:1–4 Darkness is everywhere, yet people have seen a great light—the presence of God. All rejoice, as with joy at the harvest, for the rule of darkness will be lifted.

Anthem
Creator of the Stars of Night, Jeffrey Honore (Augsburg) SATB handbells (M).

1 Corinthians 1:10–18 Discussion, quarreling, disunity reign in the Corinthian church. Rival groups of people line up behind their favorite leader and rely on their own wisdom rather than the power of the cross. This church's life denies the gospel of Jesus Christ in which they all believe. "Thank God," says Paul, "that I am not your Savior."

Anthems
Until We Rest in Thee, Sue Ellen Page (Choristers Guild, Lorenz) children and SATB (E). *Let Us Love One Another,* A. B. Sherman (Sacred Music Press) 2-part (E).

Matthew 4:12–23 Jesus begins his public ministry in fulfillment of the prophecy according to Isaiah 9:1–2. He preaches that the kingdom of heaven is at hand, so turn around and recognize, cooperate with, and celebrate the age to come. Then Jesus begins the process of selecting "disciples." As he casually passes by a lake, Jesus almost randomly issues a call to whomever he sees. No job interview, prior experience, or credentials of any kind are needed—he simply calls them. Result: two pairs of brothers abandon everything and follow immediately.

Anthems
He Comes to Us, Jane Marshall (Carl Fischer) SATB (M). *They Cast Their Nets,* arr. Michael McCabe (Carl Fischer) 2-part (E).

Psalm 27:1, 4–9
1. Metrical: *God Is My Strong Salvation.* Text: James Montgomery. Tune: CHRISTUS, DER IST MEIN LEBEN. *PH90* #179. (See also *HB55* #347, *RITL* #95, and *WB72* #388 to the Tune: WEDLOCK.)
2. Responsorial: *Psalm 27* (1–6). Text: Taizé, alt. Helen L. Wright. Refrain: Jacques Berthier. Tone: Hal H. Hopson. *PS93* #25.
See also *CC* G-2762; *PH87* #27; *ANMP*, p. 63; *SPJP*, p. 26; *WIII* #792 and #852; *PR&T*, pp. 57 & 16, pp. 42 & 50.

Anthem
One Thing I Ask of the Lord, Heinrich Schütz, arr. D. McAfee (Capella Music) 2-part (ME).

Organ Music for the Day
1. *Prelude on* CHRISTUS, DER IST MEIN LEBEN (*God Is My Strong Salvation, PH90* #179), Johann Walther (*The Church Organist's Golden Treasury,* vol. 1, p. 111, Oliver Ditson Co.).
2. *Prelude on* TRURO (*Live Into Hope, PH90* #332), Seth Bingham (*Twelve Hymn Preludes,* H. W. Gray Co., Inc.).

Hymns for the Day	HL33	HB55	WB72	PH90
Break Forth, O Beauteous Heavenly Light (Isa. 9)	–	–	314	26
Creator of the Stars of Night	–	–	348	4
God Is My Strong Salvation	92	347	388	179
Live Into Hope	–	–	–	332
Lord, You Have Come to the Lakeshore	–	–	–	377
The Church's One Foundation	333	437	582	442

46

SUNDAY BETWEEN JANUARY 28 AND FEBRUARY 3 [4] (A)

Micah 6:1–8 YHWH summons unfaithful Israel to trial, where all creation serves as witnesses. "Where did I fail you?" pleads YHWH, who then recites all the saving deeds in fulfillment of YHWH's promises to Israel. The penitent, though still misguided, defendant seeks to atone for wrongdoing: "What kind of offering will please you: a burnt one, calves, rams, oil, firstborn?" But YHWH requires only an offering of ourselves: to do justly, love mercy, and walk humbly with God.

Anthems
With What Shall I Come Before the Lord, John Ness Beck, (Beckenhorst Press) SATB (M). *What Does the Lord Require,* Erik Routley, *PH90* #405. *Three Things I Require,* Perry and Purifoy (Jenson) SATB, divisi (M).

1 Corinthians 1:18–31 The gospel always seems to turn our world upside down. Here worldly wisdom and strength are characterized as foolish and weak, and the nonsense and weakness of the crucifixion are labeled as wise and strong. The epitome of God's love for us is revealed in the offensiveness of the cross.

Anthem
O for a World, Glaser, arr. Lowell Mason, *PH90* #386.

Matthew 5:1–12 Jesus teaches his disciples the Beatitudes as he begins the Sermon on the Mount.

Anthems
The Beatitudes, Lloyd Pfautsch (Flammer) SATB (MD). *The Beatitudes,* William Reynolds (Broadman) SATB (ME). *Folk Beatitudes,* David Eddelman (Carl Fischer) 2-part (E).

Psalm 15
1. Metrical: *Lord, Who May Dwell Within Your House.* Text: C.M., Christopher L. Webber. Tune: CHESHIRE. *PH90* #164. For text only see *ANMP,* p. 46.
2. Responsorial: *Psalm 15.* Text: Grail. Refrain: Richard Proulx. Gelineau tone. *PS93* #9.
3. Responsorial: *They Who Do Justice Will Live in the Presence of God.* Setting: David Haas. *CS/PFTCY,* vol. 3, p. 56.
See also *WIII* #912 & #929; *PR&T,* pp. 43 & 68.

Anthem
Who Shall Abide, Walter Pelz (Augsburg) SAB guitar, flute.

Organ Music for the Day
1. *Prelude on* RATHBUN (*In the Cross of Christ I Glory, PH90* #84), Seth Bingham (*Twelve Hymn Preludes,* set 2, Gray-Belwin).
2. *Prelude on* RICHMOND (*Blest Are the Uncorrupt in Heart, PH90* #233), Healey Willan (*Ten Hymn Preludes,* vol. 1, p. 6, C. F. Peters Corp. 6011).

Hymns for the Day	HL33	HB55	WB72	PH90
Blest Are the Uncorrupt in Heart	–	–	–	233
Called as Partners in Christ's Service	–	–	–	343
Canto de Esperanza/Song of Hope	–	–	–	432
Fill My Cup	–	–	–	350
O for a World	–	–	–	386
What Does the Lord Require	–	–	–	405

SUNDAY BETWEEN FEBRUARY 4 AND 10 [5] (A)

Isaiah 58:1–9a, (9b–12) Israel has strictly followed the law regarding fasting, but YHWH seems not to take notice. Why? "Because you pursue your own interests," admonishes YHWH. "You call attention to your fasting while continuing to quarrel and fight and oppress others. You think I approve of that? Give aid to the hungry, the homeless, the naked—liberate others, then you will see my favor shine like the dawning of the sun's light."

Anthems

A Beautiful Thing, Jane Marshall (Augsburg) SATB (M). *Where Charity and Love Prevail,* Paul Benoit, *WB72* #641.

1 Corinthians 2:1–12, (13–16) Paul contrasts the wisdom of human speeches and the message of the cross. His own oratorical skills, Paul says, are modest and unpersuasive. But the proclamation of Jesus Christ crucified and the power of the Spirit are what convert hearers to belief, trust, and obedience. If the wisdom of the world had known this, "wise" rulers would not have crucified the Lord.

Anthem

The Prayers I Make, Jane Marshall (Sacred Music Press) 2-part mixed (ME).

Matthew 5:13–20 "You are the salt of the earth." You are a light amid the darkness of the world. Let your light shine before all. How? By good works and deeds of justice so the world will praise the heavenly Father. Jesus has not come to abolish the Law but to fulfill it. Anyone (including scribes and Pharisees) who sets aside or obscures even the least of these commandments will be named by YHWH as "least in the kingdom of heaven."

Anthems

You Are the Salt of the Earth, Avery and Marsh, arr. Wilson (Hope) SATB (E). *Light and Salt,* Erik Routley (G.I.A.) SATB (ME).

Psalm 112:1–9, (10)

1. Metrical: *Hallelujah!* Text: C.M., Christopher L. Webber. *ANMP,* p. 181.
2. Responsorial: *Psalm 112.* Text: Helen L. Wright. Refrain: Presbyterian 6. Tone: Hal H. Hopson. *PS93* #112.

See also *WIII* #877; *GG,* p. 71; *PH87* #112; *PR&T,* pp. 43 & 68.

Anthem

Blessed Are the Ones Who Fear Him, Mendelssohn (*Elijah,* number 9, G. Schirmer) SATB (M).

Organ Music for the Day

1. *Prelude on* DONNE SECOURS (*Hope of the World, PH90* #360), Donald Busarow (*The Concordia Hymn Prelude Series,* vol. 23, p. 20, Concordia 97-5738).
2. *Prelude on* ROCKINGHAM (*When I Survey the Wondrous Cross, PH90* #100), Kenneth Leighton (*Chorale Preludes on English Tunes,* p. 9, Oxford University Press 375135-6).

Hymns for the Day	HL33	HB55	WB72	PH90
Christian Women, Christian Men	–	–	–	348
Lord of Light, Your Name Outshining	–	–	–	425
Once in Royal David's City	454	462	539	49
Today We All Are Called to Be Disciples	–	–	–	434
When I Survey the Wondrous Cross	152	198	635	100, 101
Where Charity and Love Prevail	–	–	641	–

SUNDAY BETWEEN FEBRUARY 11 AND 17
(PROPER 1) [6] (A)

Deuteronomy 30:15–20 YHWH loves the people of Israel and desires well-being for them. The question is, Will Israel love YHWH as a child loves a parent? Every day Israel must decide whether to love YHWH by faithfully obeying the commandments, which leads to prosperity in the good land, or to turn away from YHWH and therefore lose the land and die.

Anthem
I Call Heaven and Earth, R. K. Winslow (Elkan-Vogel) SATB and SAT (M).

1 Corinthians 3:1–9 Jealousy and strife are signs of immature faith or, perhaps, inability or resistance to hearing the gospel: living as people of the flesh. Living as people of the Spirit means all human servants perform God's work together in the vineyard, each according to his or her specific function. God alone gives growth.

Anthem
Help Us to Help Each Other, Lord, S. Drummond Wolff (Concordia) SATB (ME).

Matthew 5:21–37 We must reconcile with our brother or sister before we offer anything to God in public worship. Three signs of fractured human relationships are adultery, divorce, and oath taking. Jesus calls us to trust the promises of God, to become one in love, and to speak the simple truth, as signs of the age to come.

Anthem
Neighbors, Ghana melody, arr. Austin Lovelace (H. W. Gray) SATB (E).

Psalm 119:1–8
1. Metrical: *Blest Are the Uncorrupt in Heart.* Text: C.M., Fred R. Anderson. *SPJP,* p. 67 to the Tune: RICHMOND. *PH90* #233.
2. Responsorial: *Psalm 119:1–8.* Text: Helen L. Wright. Refrain and tone: Presbyterian 5. *PS93* #121.
3. Responsorial: *Happy Are They Who Follow the Law of the Lord.* Text: Grail (see also *GPI,* p. 175 and *GPP,* p. 172). Psalm tone and Gelineau tone *WIII* #880, *GG,* p. 74.
4. Metrical: *How I Love Thy Law, O Lord.* Text: *The Psalter,* 1912, alt. Tune: SPANISH HYMN. *HB55* #253.
See also *ANMP,* p. 194; *PR&T,* pp. 67 & 68.

Anthem
Blest Are the Uncorrupt in Heart, Thomas Haweis, *PH90* #233.

Organ Music for the Day
1. *Chorale Prelude on* JESU, MEINE FREUDE (*Jesu, Priceless Treasure, PH90* #365), Walther (various editions), and Gardner Read (*Meditation on* JESU, MEINE FREUDE, H. W. Gray Co., Inc. 814).
2. *Chorale Prelude on* LOBE DEN HERREN (*Praise Ye the Lord, the Almighty, PH90* #482), Gordon Young (*Five Toccatas,* Harold Flammer, Inc. HF-5009).

Hymns for the Day	HL33	HB55	WB72	PH90
As a Chalice Cast of Gold	–	–	–	336
Help Us Accept Each Other	–	–	–	358
Jesu, Jesu, Fill Us with Your Love	–	–	–	367
Lord, Whose Love Through Humble Service	–	–	–	427
Praise Ye the Lord, the Almighty	6	1	557	482
We Are Your People	–	–	–	436

SUNDAY BETWEEN FEBRUARY 18 AND 24
(PROPER 2) [7] (A)

Leviticus 19:1–2, 9–18 A part of the "Holiness Code" mandates that the people of Israel are not to clean up gleanings in fields and vineyards (leave them for the poor), not to use words to deceive others, not to do injustice against neighbors, and not to hate "brothers" or take revenge against their own people. "I am the Lord your God who makes holy," and you are to reflect in word and deed what has been made holy. Therefore, love your neighbor as your own kin.

Anthem
Blessed the People, Johann C. Geisler (Boosey & Hawkes) SATB (M).

1 Corinthians 3:10–11, 16–23 Christ is the sole foundation of the church. Church leaders are but Christ's servants who are all building upon this unchangeable foundation. The raw material used in constructing this temple is the people of God. This sounds foolish to the world, but it is God's wisdom. So all the church leaders and everything in the church belong to the people who belong to Christ who belongs to God.

Anthems
Temples of God, Ronald A. Nelson (Augsburg) unison (E) suitable for children.
Christ Is Made the Sure Foundation, Henry Purcell *PH90* #416 unison.

Matthew 5:38–48 Mosaic law on retribution restricts excess revenge or compensation. Jesus fulfills and surpasses this law by introducing a new principle: Do not take any action against those who seek to do physical violence to you, insult you, file litigation against you, extract forced labor from you, or make demands for gifts and loans. But love and serve your enemies (*even to the extent of accepting a cross*) and pray for them as a sign of the age to come.

Anthem
Forgive Our Sins as We Forgive, Kentucky Harmony, PH90 #347. *Mercy, Pity, Peace, and Love,* Austin C. Lovelace (Randall Egan) SATB (M).

Psalm 119:33–40
1. Metrical: *Teach Me, O Lord, Your Way of Truth.* Text: Psalm 119. *The Psalter,* 1912. Tune: ST. CRISPIN. *PH87* #276.
2. Responsorial: *Psalm 119:33–40.* Text: Grail. Refrain and tone: Presbyterian 5. *PS93* #122.
See also *ANMP,* pp. 198 & 199; *PR&T,* pp. 47 & 78; *PH87* #119; *HB55* #258.

Anthem
Teach Me, O Lord, B. Rogers-Wienandt (Flammer) SATB (ME).

Organ Music for the Day
1. *Prelude on* NICAEA (*Holy, Holy, Holy!, PH90* #138), Peter Hurford (*Chorale Preludes on English Tunes,* p. 15, Oxford University Press 375135-6).
2. *Prelude on* ST. BRIDE (*Give to the Winds Thy Fears, PH90* #286), Gerhard Krapf (*Music for the Service,* Roger Dean Publishing Co. KK 301).

Hymns for the Day	HL33	HB55	WB72	PH90
Christ Is Made the Sure Foundation	336	433	325	416, 417
Forgive Our Sins as We Forgive	–	–	–	347
God, Whose Giving Knows No Ending	–	–	–	422
How Clear Is Our Vocation, Lord	–	–	–	419
The Church's One Foundation	333	437	582	442
When We Are Living	–	–	–	400

SUNDAY BETWEEN FEBRUARY 25 AND 29*
(PROPER 3) [8] (A)

Isaiah 49:8–16a YHWH speaks to exiled Israel, who laments that YHWH has forgotten Israel. To the contrary, YHWH has brought an end to Israel's suffering—in fact, the restoration is already occurring—and is bringing those who sit in darkness out into the light. It is impossible for YHWH to forget the people of Israel because YHWH's love for them far exceeds that of a mother's love for her nursing child. A picture of the restored Israel is inscribed on YHWH's hands. YHWH keeps YHWH's promises.

Anthem
Sing, O Ye Heavens, Johann Friedrich Peter (H. W. Gray) SSATTB (M).

1 Corinthians 4:1–5 Paul is apparently the target of some hate mail from Corinthian church members who condemn him and his teaching. But all church leaders, writes Paul, are but "servants of Christ and stewards of the mysteries of God." So any judging that takes place is in the hands of Christ. No need then to worry about others judging you. Paul says, "I don't even judge myself, because it is the Lord alone who will judge your faithfulness."

Anthem
The Lord Will Come and Not Be Slow, Richard Peek (H. W. Gray) 2-part mixed (E).

Matthew 6:24–34 A rigorous text that defies circumvention. Why are you so driven to scramble up the social ladder of success; so wretchedly uptight over accumulating cash, cash, and more cash; so obsessed with getting ahead in life? Why? Surely life is worth more than all these ephemeral pleasures combined. Do you think you can ward off death or buy more life? Stop for a moment and behold how creation simply lives by the grace of God. Now try steering your fretful energy into serving God by serving neighbors. Seek first the kingdom of God—feed the hungry, clothe the naked, shelter the homeless—and you may discover that life is richer when it is leaner.

Anthem
Great Are Your Mercies, O My Maker, Chinese folk song, *PH90* #352.

Psalm 131
1. Metrical: *Lord, for Ever at Thy Side. H82* #670.
2. Responsorial: *Psalm 131.* Text: Taizé. Setting: Jacques Berthier. *PS93* #135.
See also *30P&2C; CC* G-2924; *WIII* #955.

Anthem
Psalm 131, Jack Beeson (*Three Settings from the Bay Psalm Book,* Oxford) SATB (E).

Organ Music for the Day
1. WER NUR DEN LIEBEN GOTT (*If Thou but Trust in God, PH90* #382), Walcha (*Choralvorspiele,* vol. 1, p. 44, C. F. Peters Corp. 4850).
2. *Prelude on* ST. PETER (*In Christ There Is No East or West, PH90* #439), Darke (*Three Chorale Preludes,* Novello & Co., Ltd. 1452).

Hymns for the Day	HL33	HB55	WB72	PH90
All Things Bright and Beautiful	–	456	–	267
Give to the Winds Your Fears	294	364	377	286
Great Are Your Mercies, O My Maker	–	–	–	352
Great Is Thy Faithfulness	–	–	–	276
In Christ There Is No East or West	341	479	435	439, 440
Seek Ye First (Matt. 6:33)	–	–	–	333

*Except when this Sunday is The Transfiguration of the Lord.

TRANSFIGURATION OF THE LORD
[SUNDAY PRECEDING LENT] (A)

Exodus 24:12–18 YHWH summons Moses to the top of the mountain at Sinai in order that he may receive the tables of stone YHWH has inscribed. A cloud envelops the mountain for a six-day period of preparation, but on the seventh day YHWH calls Moses to enter the cloud. Fire and light ("the glory of the Lord") suddenly burst through the cloud in full view of the people. Moses remains on the mountain forty days in order to receive all the instructions from YHWH.

Anthems

O Splendor of God's Glory Bright, M. Praetorius, *PH90* #474. *The God of Heaven,* Norman Warren, *PH90* #180.

2 Peter 1:16–21 The writer directly confronts some opponents of the gospel by keeping alive Peter's testimony, which is based not on devised fables but on a historical event of the life of Jesus. Specifically, Peter was an eyewitness of the transfiguration and personally heard the voice confirm Christ's divine sonship. Thus the Old Testament's prophecy of the coming of the Messiah has been certified by God and, therefore, all would do well to pay attention to scripture with the aid of the Spirit.

Anthems

This Is My Beloved Son, Knut Nystedt (Concordia) SAB (E). *This Is My Beloved Son,* Johannes Herbst (Boosey & Hawkes) SATB (M).

Matthew 17:1–9 Before the eyes of the disciples, the ordinary man named Jesus shines with the dazzling brilliance of the light of God. Peter wants to preserve this mountaintop high by stopping the action and living there. But a cloud overshadows them and a hidden voice speaks the same words spoken at the baptism of Jesus: "This is my beloved Son, with whom I am well pleased; listen to him." The glow and the cloud disappear, and the disciples see only the ordinary man named Jesus, who is walking down the mountain toward Jerusalem to die on a cross.

Anthems

Christ Upon the Mountain Peak, Peter Cutts (*Ecumenical Praise,* number 67, Agape) (ME). *Prayer for Transfiguration Day,* John Weaver (Hope) SATB (MD).

Psalm 2

1. Metrical: *Why Are Nations Raging?* Text: 7.7.7.7.D, Fred R. Anderson, alt. Tune: SALZBURG. *PH90* #159.
2. Responsorial: *Psalm 2.* Setting: Hal H. Hopson. *PS93* #2.
3. Responsorial: *Why This Tumult Among Nations?* Text: Grail (see also *GPI,* p. 3 and *GPP,* p. 3). Gelineau tone: *24P&1C,* p. 2.
4. Metrical: *Wherefore Do the Nations Rage?* Text: *The Psalter,* 1912. Tune: MONSEY CHAPEL. *PH87* #2.

See also *ANMP,* p. 41; *PR&T,* pp. 45 & 65.

Anthem

Why Are Nations Raging?, Jacob Hintze, *PH90* #159.

or Psalm 99

1. Metrical: *The Lord Is King: Let People Quake.* Text: L.M., Christopher L. Webber. *ANMP,* p. 165.
2. Responsorial: *Psalm 99.* Text: Helen L. Wright. Setting: Hal H. Hopson. *PS93* #96.
3. Responsorial: *God Is King: The People Tremble.* Text: Grail (see also *GPI,* p. 141). Refrain: A. Gregory Murray. Gelineau tone: *20P&3C,* p. 19.

4. Metrical: *God Is King.* Words: Michael Saward. Music: Michael Baughen, arr. David G. Wilson. *PP* #113.

See also *PH87* #99; *PR&T,* pp. 59 & 73.

Anthems

Entrata, Noel Goemanne (World Library) SATB (M). *The Lord God Reigneth,* Johann Pachelbel (Concordia) SATB continuo (M).

Organ Music for the Day

1. *Prelude on* GENEVA (*Swiftly Pass the Clouds of Glory, PH90* #73), Emma L. Diemer (*With Praise and Love,* vol. 2, p. 27, The Sacred Music Press).

2. The Agincourt Hymn (DEO GRACIAS, *PH90* #75), John Dunstable (*Treasury of Early Organ Music,* p. 6, Mercury Music Corp. A-258), and Paul Manz (*Ten Chorale Improvisations,* vol. 9, p. 22, Concordia 97-5556).

Hymns for the Day	HL33	HB55	WB72	PH90
All Creatures of Our God and King	–	100	282	455
Come, Christians, Join to Sing	191	131	333	150
From All That Dwell Below the Skies	388	33	373	229
Jesus on the Mountain Peak	–	–	–	74
O Splendor of God's Glory Bright	32	46	529	474
O Wondrous Type, O Vision Fair	142	182	531	75
Swiftly Pass the Clouds of Glory	–	–	–	73

Easter Cycle
Season of Lent
ASH WEDNESDAY (ABC)

Joel 2:1–2, 12–17 Blow the trumpet, for the Day of YHWH is coming! YHWH's judgment is near! Turn back to YHWH with all your heart. Fast, weep, mourn. Return to YHWH, who manifests *hesed* ("steadfast love"). Perhaps YHWH will forgive you and bless you. Gather together all the people and turn back to YHWH.

Anthems
O My God, Bestow Thy Tender Mercy, Pergolesi-Hopson (Carl Fischer) 2-part (E). *Ye People, Rend Your Hearts* and *If with All Your Hearts,* Mendelssohn (*Elijah,* G. Schirmer) tenor solo. *A Lenten Proclamation,* James Chepponis (G.I.A.) 3 mixed voices (E). *Judgment,* Alec Wyton (*Two Choral Hymns,* H. W. Gray) SSATB (M).

or **Isaiah 58:1–12** Israel has strictly followed the law regarding fasting, but YHWH seems not to take notice. Why? "Because you pursue your own interests," admonishes YHWH. "You make a show of your fasting, you call attention to it while continuing to quarrel and fight and oppress others. You think I approve of that? Give aid to the hungry, the homeless, the naked—liberate others—and then you will see my favor shine like the dawning of the sun's light."

Anthems
Cry Aloud, Spare Not, David Krane (Hinshaw) SATB (D). *A Lenten Carol,* W. Glen Darst (H. W. Gray) unison (ME).

2 Corinthians 5:20b–6:10 Do you remember what God in Christ has done for you all? Then accept the reconciliation that God offers you in Christ. Let God transform you! Christ shared our human estrangement from God so that we sinners might be joined with Christ and reconciled with God. So work with God today, for the day of salvation is now.

Anthems
Grant Us Thy Peace, Felix Mendelssohn (Boosey & Hawkes) SATB (E). *Lord, for Thy Tender Mercies' Sake,* Richard Farrant (H. W. Gray) SATB (E). *Kind Maker of the World, PH90* #79. *Treasures in Heaven,* Joseph Clokey (Summy-Birchard) SATB, soprano solo (E).

Matthew 6:1–6, 16–21 Three acts of personal piety (charity, private prayer, and fasting) and a note on treasuring God's will—all are signs of the age to come. Do not broadcast your acts of personal piety to the world. God sees what you do and, therefore, will reward you in the future. What you value in life is where you will devote your time, energy, emotional commitment, everything.

Anthems
When Thou Prayest, Carl Mueller (Carl Fischer) SATB (M). *A Beautiful Thing,* Jane Marshall (Augsburg) SATB (ME). *Have Mercy, Lord, on Me,* M. Montoya, *PH90* #395.

Psalm 51:1–17
1. Metrical: *Have Mercy on Us, Living Lord.* Text: C.M., Fred R. Anderson. Tune: PTOMEY. *PH90* #195. For text only see *SPJP,* p. 3.
2. Responsorial: *Psalm 51:1–17.* Text: *Book of Common Prayer.* Setting: David Clark Isele. *PS93* #48.
3. Responsorial: *Psalm 51* (1–12). Text: *Book of Common Prayer.* Setting: Peter R. Hallock. *PS93* #47. (See also *TIP/PSCY* #5.)
4. Responsorial: *The Sacrifice You Accept.* Text: The Grail. Refrain and psalm tone by David Clark Isele. *PH90* #196. (See also *APS,* p. 18.)

See also *ANMP,* p. 101; *HB55* #282; *TIP/PSCY* #5; *WIII* #41 & #787; *PH87* #51; *PR&T,* pp. 19 & 21.

Anthems

Create in Me, O God, Johannes Brahms (G. Schirmer) SATBB (MD). *Wash Me Thoroughly from My Wickedness,* S. S. Wesley (*Church Anthem Book,* Oxford) SATB (ME). *Have Mercy on Us, Living Lord, PH90* #195.

Organ Music for the Day

1. *Chorale Prelude on* ERHALT UNS, HERR (*The Glory of These Forty Days, PH90* #87), Georg Böhm (*Choral Works and Miscellaneous Pieces,* vol. 2, Kalmus 4098).
2. *Chorale Prelude on* HERZLIEBSTER JESU (*Ah, Holy Jesus, PH90* #93), Ernst Pepping (*Kleines Orgelbuch,* B. Schotts Söhne 3735).
3. *Prelude on* AUS DER TIEFE RUFE ICH (*Forty Days and Forty Nights, PH90* #77), Gordon Phillips (*Advent to Whitsuntide,* vol. 3, Hinrichsen Edition, Ltd. 742b).
4. *Prelude on* O QUANTA QUALIA (*God of Compassion, in Mercy Befriend Us, PH90* #261), Clarence Dickinson (*The Modern Anthology,* vol. 2, H. W. Gray Co., Inc. GB 622).

Hymns for the Day	*HL33*	*HB55*	*WB72*	*PH90*
Forty Days and Forty Nights	–	–	–	77
God of Compassion, in Mercy Befriend Us	290	122	392	261
I'm Gonna Live So God Can Use Me	–	–	–	369
Lord, from the Depths to You I Cry	240	277	459	–
Lord, Who Throughout These Forty Days	144	181	470	81
Let All Who Pray the Prayer Christ Taught	–	–	–	349
Kind Maker of the World	–	–	–	79
O for a Closer Walk with God	259	319	–	396, 397
The Glory of These Forty Days	–	–	–	87
Wild and Lone the Prophet's Voice	–	–	–	409
Dear Lord and Father of Mankind	302	416	350	345
Have Mercy, Lord, on Me	–	–	–	395
Just as I Am, Without One Plea	230	271	–	370
O God of Bethel, by Whose Hand	98	342	496	269

FIRST SUNDAY IN LENT (A)

Genesis 2:15–17; 3:1–7 YHWH plants a garden as a good place for the earth creature and gives the earth creature a specific job, freedom, and boundaries in which to live. Enter the serpent with a new agenda. Result: The set boundaries are seen as an option and then violated. Human freedom is perverted and the specific job given by YHWH is neglected. Humans now focus on themselves and therefore see their own nakedness.

Anthem
The Apple Tree, Scottish folk song, arr. K. Lee Scott (Hinshaw) SATB (ME).

Romans 5:12–19 Paul asserts that sin and death became part of our human experience "through one man," yet "all sinned." All humanity reenacts what this "one man" introduced: aspiring to become like God. But, in Christ, God's free gift of grace for all humanity was deliberately introduced. This one righteous act sets free all humanity and gives life to all.

Anthem
Since by Man Came Death, G. F. Handel (*Messiah,* any edition) SATB (M).

Matthew 4:1–11 Jesus has just been called and "ordained" in baptism. Now he is tempted to become three different kinds of messiah: prosperity giver, miracle worker, or political leader. But Jesus repudiates each temptation with a quote from Deuteronomy and says he will let God define his ministry.

Anthem: *The Temptation of Christ,* Lloyd Pfautsch (Lawson-Gould) SATB (D).

Psalm 32
1. Metrical: *How Blest Are Those.* Text: Fred R. Anderson. Tune: ES FLOG EIN KLEINS WALDVÖEGELEIN. *PH90* #184.
2. Responsorial: *Psalm 32.* Text: Grail. Refrain: David Clark Isele. Tone: Tonus peregrinus, arr. Hal H. Hopson. *PS93* #29.
3. Responsorial: *I Turn to You, O Lord, in Time of Trouble.* Text: Grail. (See also *GPI,* p. 40.) *WIII* #881. Also #897 with refrain: *Lord, Forgive the Wrong I Have Done.* (See also *30P&2C,* p. 10.)
4. Metrical: *How Blest Are They Whose Trespass.* Text: The Psalter, 1912, alt. Tune: RUTHERFORD. *PH87* #32; *HB55* #281. (See also *RITL* to the Tune: AU FORT DE MA DÉTRESSE.)

See also *ANMP,* p. 74; *PR&T,* pp. 42 & 75.

Anthem
Psalm 32, Paul Weber (Augsburg) SAB and congregation (ME).

Organ Music for the Day
1. *Out of the Depths* (AUS TIEFER NOT, *PH90* #240), Langlais (*Neuf Pièces,* p. 24, Bornemann SB 5337).
2. *Prelude on* ST. FLAVIAN (*Lord, Who Throughout These Forty Days, PH90* #81), F. Peeters (*Hymn Preludes for the Liturgical Year,* vol. 24, p. 19, C. F. Peters Corp. 6424).

Hymns for the Day	HL33	HB55	WB72	PH90
A Mighty Fortress Is Our God	266	91	274	260
Forty Days and Forty Nights	–	–	–	77
God Marked a Line and Told the Sea	–	–	–	283
I Sing the Mighty Power of God	65	84	628	288
Lord, Who Throughout These Forty Days	144	181	470	81
When We Are Tempted to Deny Your Son	–	–	640	86

SECOND SUNDAY IN LENT (A)

Genesis 12:1–4*a* YHWH chooses a barren, landless, futureless couple and promises descendants, land, and a future in which their name will be magnified. Abram faithfully embraces YHWH's promises and begins his pilgrimage of wandering in the new land.

Anthems
God's Promise, Samuel Adler (Oxford) SSA (M). *God of the Promise,* Richard Hillert (Augsburg) SATB (ME).

Romans 4:1–5, 13–17 For working hard or performing good deeds, people earn wages or rewards and, therefore, can boast of their achievements. For trusting the promises of God, who justifies the impious and the irreligious, people receive God's free gift of grace. Look at Abraham, who was justified not by works but by grace through faith.

Anthem
Faith While Trees Are Still in Blossom, Alec Wyton (*Ecumenical Praise,* number 74, Agape) unison (E).

John 3:1–17 By day, Nicodemus is everything you could want to be; by night, he comes secretly in search of Jesus. By day, Nicodemus controls the affairs of his kingdom; by night, he comes looking for the kingdom of God. Replies Jesus, "Unless one is born of water and the Spirit, he cannot enter the kingdom of God." "How can this be?" asks Nicodemus.

Anthem
God So Loved the World, Jan Bender (Concordia) 2-part (E) and SATB (MD).

Psalm 121
1. Metrical: *I to the Hills Will Lift Mine Eyes. The Psalter,* 1912, alt. *PH90* #234. (See also *RITL* #131, *HB55* #377, and *PH87* #121 to the Tune: GUIDE.)
2. Responsorial: *Psalm 121.* Setting: Hal H. Hopson. *PS93* #125.
3. Responsorial: *I Lift Up My Eyes.* Text: Grail. (See also *GPI,* p. 187.) For additional refrains see *24P&1C,* p. 30. (See *WIII* #951 for additional psalm tone and refrain.)

See also *ANMP,* p. 205; *SPJP,* p. 64; *PH87* #180 & #448; *PR&T,* pp. 57 & 75.

Anthem
I Will Lift Up My Eyes Unto the Hills, Leo Sowerby (Boston Music) SATB alto solo (M).

Organ Music for the Day
1. *If Thou but Trust in God to Guide Thee* (WER NUR DEN LIEBEN GOTT, *PH90* #282), Walcha (*Choralvorspiele,* vol. 1, p. 44, C. F. Peters Corp. 4850), J. S. Bach (*Orgelbüchlein,* various publishers).
2. *Prelude on* LEONI (*The God of Abraham Praise, PH90* #488), Isadore Freed (*Six Liturgical Pieces,* Number 1—"Praise to the Living God," Transcontinental Music Publications T. I. 151).

Hymns for the Day	HL33	HB55	WB72	PH90
If Thou but Trust in God to Guide Thee	105	344	431	282
O Wondrous Sight, O Vision Fair	142	182	531	75
Spirit	–	–	–	319
Strong Son of God, Immortal Love	175	228	578	–
The God of Abraham Praise	8	89	587	488
Where Cross the Crowded Ways of Life	410	507	642	408

THIRD SUNDAY IN LENT (A)

Exodus 17:1–7 The Israelites "contend with" and "test" YHWH as they trek through the desert, for they are about to perish for lack of water. At YHWH's instruction, Moses strikes a rock with his rod, and YHWH miraculously produces living water as a sign of the life that YHWH pours forth upon the people.

Anthem
Springs in the Desert, Kenneth Jennings (H. W. Gray) SATB (M).

Romans 5:1–11 Since we are justified by faith, we are at peace with God. So let's stand up straight and rejoice, for "God has poured out his love into our hearts through the Holy Spirit." While we were sinning against God by resisting and seeking to destroy the Son, God reconciled us to God's self through the death of the Son. At the cross, we are overwhelmed by the incredible depth of God's love for us.

Anthem
God Is a Spirit, Alexander Kopylov (E. C. Schirmer) SATB (E).

John 4:5–42 Jesus sits down by Jacob's well for conversation with a Samaritan (despised) woman (second-class citizen). The metaphor of water permeates their strange dialogue and recalls for hearers the multitude of images of water both in John's Gospel and throughout the Bible.

Anthem
I Heard the Voice of Jesus Say, Tallis' Third Mode, setting by Donald Busarow (Concordia) SATB, flute (M).

Psalm 95
1. Metrical: *Come, Sing with Joy to God.* Text: paraphrased by Arlo D. Duba. Tune: TO GOD WITH GLADNESS. D. C. Isele. *APS,* p. 25; *PH90* #215.
2. Responsorial: *Psalm 95* (1–7). Text: *Book of Common Prayer.* Setting: Jack Noble White. *PS93* #88.
3. Responsorial: *Psalm 95.* Text: *New Church Hymnal.* Setting: William Boyce. *PS93* #89.
4. Responsorial: *Psalm 95.* Setting: Hal H. Hopson. *PS93* #90.
See also *PH90* #214; *HB55* #29; *WIII* #793; *SPJP,* p. 49; *PR&T,* pp. 60 & 81.

Anthem
O Come, Let Us Sing Unto the Lord, Donald Swann (Curwen) 2-part (ME).

Organ Music for the Day
1. *Prelude on* IRISH (*O Come and Sing Unto the Lord*—Psalm 95, *PH90* #214), Henry Coleman (*Twenty-Four Interludes Based on Communion Hymn Tunes,* p. 8, Oxford University Press 375330-8).
2. *Improvisation on* CWM RHONDDA (*Guide Me, O Thou Great Jehovah, PH90* #281), Paul Manz (*Ten Chorale Improvisations,* vol. 5, Concordia 97-5257), and Flor Peeters (*Hymn Preludes for the Liturgical Year,* vol. 20, p. 4, C. F. Peters Corp. 6420).

Hymns for the Day	HL33	HB55	WB72	PH90
Come, Holy Spirit, Our Souls Inspire	–	237	335	125
Guide Me, O Thou Great Jehovah	104	339	409	281
I to the Hills Will Lift My Eyes	–	377	430	234
If Thou but Trust in God to Guide Thee	105	344	431	282
O Come and Sing Unto the Lord	–	29	488	214
Out of Deep, Unordered Water	–	–	–	494

FOURTH SUNDAY IN LENT (A)

1 Samuel 16:1–13 YHWH commands Samuel to offer a sacrifice at Bethlehem as a ruse for anointing the one whom YHWH has chosen as king. At the sacrifice, Samuel surveys seven sons of Jesse who are present, but YHWH selects none of these. The youngest, most inexperienced, least likely son is taking care of the sheep. YHWH says, "Arise, anoint him; for this is he."

Anthem
Lord, When I Came Into This Life, American folk melody, arr. Buchanan, *PH90* #522.

Ephesians 5:8–14 Jesus Christ is the victorious, transforming light in person. Living "in Christ" is living "in the light." So you who are the Lord's people, live as creatures of the light, give witness to the light, and the light will transform all darkness into light.

Anthem
You Were Sometimes Darkness, Mimi Armstrong (G.I.A.) unison (E).

John 9:1–41 The first seven verses recount a sight-giving miracle in which Jesus heals a blind man. Now the real action: neighbors, Pharisees, Jewish leaders interrogate the blind man and his parents on the credentials and techniques of the healer. Ironically, each conversation shows the blind man seeing more clearly— "The man called Jesus," "He is a prophet," "Lord, I believe"—and those who walk by their own light are increasingly blinded. "I am the light of the world," says Jesus; "I give sight to those in darkness."

Anthems
Jesus Said to the Blind Man, M. Vulpius (Concordia) SATB (M). *Open My Eyes That I May See,* C. H. Scott, *PH90* #324.

Psalm 23
1. Metrical: *The Lord's My Shepherd, All My Need.* Text: C.M., Christopher L. Webber. Tune: EVAN. *PH90* #175.
2. Responsorial: *Psalm 23.* Text: Grail. Gelineau tone. *PS93* #18.
3. Responsorial: *Psalm 23.* Text: International Commission on English in the Liturgy. Setting: Howard Hughes. *PS93* #19.
4. Responsorial: *Psalm 23.* Setting: Hal H. Hopson. *PS93* #20.
5. Metrical: *The King of Love My Shepherd Is.* Text: Henry Williams Baker. Tune: ST. COLUMBA. *PH90* #171. (See also *HB55* #106.)

See also *TIP/PSCY* #12; *PH90* #172–175; *PR&T*, pp. 72 & 77.

Anthem
The Lord Is My Shepherd, John Rutter (Oxford) SATB, oboe (MD).

Organ Music for the Day
1. *Prelude on* CRIMOND (*The Lord's My Shepherd, PH90* #170), Gordon Young (*Nine Hymn Preludes for Organ,* Hope Publishing Co. 336).
2. *Prelude on* DOMINUS REGIT ME (*The Lord's My Shepherd, PH90* #174), Christopher Dearnley (*The Cathedral Organist,* vol. 1, J. B. Cramer & Co., Ltd. AP 481) and Robert Elmore (*Three Miniatures for Organ,* Harold Flammer, Inc. HF-5032).

Hymns for the Day	HL33	HB55	WB72	PH90
Christ Is the World's True Light	–	492	326	–
Live Into Hope	–	–	–	332
O God, What You Ordain Is Right	291	366	633	284
O Christ, the Healer	–	–	–	380
Open My Eyes That I May See	–	390	–	324
The True Light That Enlightens Man	–	–	598	–

FIFTH SUNDAY IN LENT (A)

Ezekiel 37:1–14 The vision of the valley of dry bones. Asks YHWH, "Can these bones live?" "Perhaps you know," replies Ezekiel. "Preach to the dry bones," commands YHWH, "that they shall live." So Ezekiel does as commanded. And, astonishingly, the bones come together and breath comes into them, all by the power of the word of God.

Anthems
Breathe on Me, Breath of God, Robert Jackson, *PH90* #316. *Ezekiel Saw the Wheel,* spiritual, arr. Gilbert Martin (Hinshaw) SATB.

Romans 8:6–11 According to Paul, our human situation leads to self-destruction or to striking out against others (including God) who frustrate our desires. The way of our human world leads to sin and death. The way of the Spirit frees us from our world of sin and death and leads us to life—a world where all are servants.

Anthem
The Prayers I Make, Jane Marshall (Sacred Music Press) 2-part mixed (ME).

John 11:1–45 Lazarus dies and Jesus goes to "awake" him. On the way, Jesus encounters Martha and Mary. He arrives at Lazarus's tomb and miraculously restores him to life. "I am the resurrection and the life," says Jesus; "whoever lives and believes in me shall never die."

Anthems
I Am the Resurrection and the Life, Bob Burroughs (Carl Fischer) SSATTB (MD). *I Am the Resurrection and the Life,* Ronald A. Nelson (Augsburg) SATB (M).

Psalm 130
1. Metrical: *Out of the Depths.* Text: Martin Luther. Tune: AUS TIEFER NOT. *PH90* #240.
2. Responsorial: *Psalm 130.* Setting: Hal H. Hopson. *PS93* #134.
3. Metrical: *Lord, from the Depths to Thee I Cried.* Text: The Scottish Psalter, 1650. Tune: SONG 67. *HB55* #277.
See also *CC* G-2308; *TIP/PSCY* #6; *APS*, p. 33; *PR&T*, pp. 49 & 70.

Anthem
Out of the Depths, Alan Hovhaness SATB, soprano solo (MD).

Organ Music for the Day
1. *Partita on* WAS GOD TUT (*O God, What You Ordain Is Right, PH90* #284), Johann Pachelbel (*Selected Organ Works,* vol. 4, Kalmus).
2. *Prelude on* AUS TIEFER NOT (*Out of the Depths*—Psalm 130, *PH90* #240), Samuel Scheidt (*The Church Organist's Golden Treasury,* vol. 1, p. 63, Oliver Ditson Co.), and Max Reger (*Thirty Short Chorale Preludes,* p. 6, C. F. Peters Corp. 3980).

Hymns for the Day	HL33	HB55	WB72	PH90
Breathe on Me, Breath of God	213	235	–	316
Hope of the World	–	291	423	360
O Jesus Christ, May Grateful Hymns . . .	–	–	509	424
Spirit Divine, Attend Our Prayers	212	243	574	325
Spirit of God, Descend Upon My Heart	204	236	575	326
Walk On, O People of God	–	–	–	296
When Jesus Wept	–	–	636	312

PASSION/PALM SUNDAY
[SIXTH SUNDAY IN LENT] (ABC)

Liturgy of the Palms:

Year A	**Matthew 21:1–11**
Year B	**Mark 11:1–11** *or* **John 12:12–16**
Year C	**Luke 19:28–40**

Liturgy of the Passion:

Year A: **Isa. 50:4–9a**	**Phil. 2:5–11**	**Matt. 26:14–27:66** *or* **27:11–54**
Year B: **Isa. 50:4–9a**	**Phil. 2:5–11**	**Mark 14:1–15:47** *or* **15:1–39, (40–47)**
Year C: **Isa. 50:4–9a**	**Phil. 2:5–11**	**Luke 22:14–23:56** *or* **23:1–49**

Isaiah 50:4–9a The third of the four Songs of the Servant of YHWH: Each day YHWH wakens me and opens my ears to the Word, which sustains me. Though I have suffered ridicule, insults, hostility, and physical abuse, I have not turned from my task. I trust YHWH's help; YHWH will vindicate me. So who will declare me guilty?

Anthems
Surely He Hath Borne Our Griefs, Antonio Lotti (E. C. Schirmer) SAB or ATB (M). *He Was Despised,* G. F. Handel (*Messiah,* any edition) alto, solo, or unison (M). *Ah, Holy Jesus,* Crüger, arr. Petrich (Oxford) SATB (MD). *Surely He Hath Borne Our Griefs,* Karl Heinrich Graun (Concordia) SATB (M). *Lord, to Thee We Turn,* Orlando di Lasso (*Second Concord Anthem Book,* E. C. Schirmer) SATB (ME).

Philippians 2:5–11 A primitive christological hymn about the descent and ascent of a divine Savior. By divesting himself of divine glory, he voluntarily assumed the form of a human servant who impoverished himself and "became obedient unto death, even death on a cross." That's why God raised him up and gave him the name above every other name: Lord.

Anthems
All Praise to Thee, M. Lee Suitor (Hope) SAB (ME). *Let This Mind Be in You,* Lee Hoiby (Presser) SAB (MD). *Let This Mind Be in You,* Austin Lovelace (J. Fischer) SATB alto solo (ME).

Matthew 21:1–11 Jesus instructs his disciples to prepare for the entry into Jerusalem. All is done in deliberate fulfillment of Zechariah's prophecy (Zech. 9:9), even to the extent of providing an ass and a colt, so that Jesus may enter as a humble kingly figure. Most of the crowd spread their garments or branches upon the road for this solemn, majestic procession and shout "Hosanna!" Upon entering Jerusalem, the people ask, "Who is this?" And the crowd replies, "This is the prophet Jesus from Nazareth of Galilee."

Anthems
Procession of Palms, Malcolm Williamson (Weinberger [G. Schirmer]) SATB, soprano, alto solos (MD). *Come, Faithful People, Come Away,* Richard Peek (Hope) 1-part (E). *Hosanna,* Christian Gregor, arr. R. Bitgood (H. W. Gray) SATB and children's choir (ME).

Matthew 26:14–27:66 The passion narrative according to Matthew.

Anthems
Canticle of Jean Racine, Gabriel Fauré (Broude) SATB (M). *The Passion According to St. Matthew,* Tomas Victoria, ed. Austin Lovelace (Summy-Birchard) SATB and 3 readers (MD).

or **Matthew 27:11–54** The Roman governor Pilate questions a silent Jesus about his alleged kingship. A frenzied crowd demands that Pilate set free Barabbas and crucify Jesus. Whipped, mocked, and spat upon, Jesus the "King of the Jews" is crucified. "If you are the Son of God," taunt the people, "come down from the cross." The lonely, suffering Jesus cries out only despair—"My God, my God . . ." —and dies. Behold, the Temple curtain is torn in two, the earth shakes, tombs are opened, and soldiers at the cross confess Jesus as the Son of God.

Mark 11:1–11 Jesus instructs two of his disciples to fetch a colt on which no one has sat. If anyone asks why, simply say, "The Lord needs it" (an unacceptable reason to any owner). The two disciples do everything according to Jesus' plan, and all goes well. Jesus then sits upon the colt, and many people spread either their garments or branches on the road and cry out, "Hosanna! Blessed is the one who comes in the name of the Lord" (Ps. 118:26). In this manner, a lowly Jesus silently enters Jerusalem (the place he has thrice predicted where he will suffer and die), goes into the Temple, looks around at everything, and then returns to Bethany with the Twelve.

Anthem

Procession of Palms, Malcolm Williamson (G. Schirmer) SATB (M).

or **John 12:12–16** A great crowd in Jerusalem goes out to acclaim Jesus as messianic king and to pay him homage with palm branches. Jesus finds a young ass and sits upon it in fulfillment of Zechariah 9:9 (*but noticeably omitting all reference to military triumph and humility*). His disciples do not understand all this until he is "glorified."

Anthems

A Sacred Song for Palm Sunday, Richard DeLong (E. C. Schirmer) unison (ME).
Hosannah, Blessed Is He, Knut Nystedt (Augsburg) SAB (ME).

Mark 14:1–15:47 The passion narrative according to Mark.

Anthem

O Come and Mourn with Me, Hal H. Hopson (Agape) 2-part mixed, optional C instrument (ME).

or **Mark 15:1–39, (40–47)** Religious leaders deliver a bound Jesus to the civil authorities—namely, Pilate—for interrogation. "Are you the king of the Jews?" Jesus laconically replies, "You have said so." The mindless crowd, manipulated by the religious leaders, then twice rejects Jesus as king and calls for his death. So the people-pleasing Pilate releases the resistance-movement rebel, Barabbas, and sentences Jesus to be flogged and executed. Soldiers crown Jesus as king, spit on him, mock him, strip him, and crucify him. "My God, my God . . . ," cries Jesus, and then dies, as does the whole world, inaugurating the New Age. Confesses a Roman soldier, "This man was the Son of God!"

Anthem

Behold the Savior of Mankind [Us All], S. Drummond Wolf (Concordia) SATB (ME).

Luke 19:28–40 Jesus instructs two of his disciples to fetch a colt on which no one has ever sat. So they do everything according to Jesus' plan, and all goes well. They then set Jesus upon the colt, and spread their garments in his path as if this were a royal procession. As Jesus draws near to Jerusalem, the whole multitude of disciples praises God for all the mighty works of Jesus they have witnessed. But not everyone is jubilant over this regal parade. Some killjoy Pharisees demand that Jesus curb his noisy disciples. Replies Jesus, "Even if they were silent, the very stones would cry out" (because heaven is about to establish its peace on earth).

Anthem

Hosanna to the Son of David, Ronald A. Nelson (Augsburg) 2-part (E).

Luke 22:14–23:56 The passion narrative according to Luke.

Anthem

A Lamb Goes Uncomplaining Forth, J. S. Bach, arr. Paul Christiansen (AMSI) SATB (ME).

or **Luke 23:1–49** The Sanhedrin brings Jesus before Pilate and accuses him of proclaiming himself a king and of inciting the people to riot. "Are you," inquires Pilate, "the king of the Jews?" "So you say," replies Jesus. Announces Pilate, "I find no crime in this man." But since Jesus is a Galilean, he is taken before Herod, who asks numerous questions to which Jesus gives no answers. So his hearers mock him and send him back to Pilate, who still contends that he and Herod find Jesus not guilty. But the frenzied multitude shouts down Pilate three times, demanding that Jesus be crucified and Barabbas be freed. Then Simon of Cyrene is seized and forced to carry the cross. The innocent yet condemned Jesus laments over the judgment coming to guilty Jerusalem, and calls for repentance. Still, he is crucified between two criminals, while mockers tempt him to save himself and one criminal proclaims that Jesus has done nothing wrong. Since he united himself to us in our guilt and shared our death, surely we can trust his promise that we will be with him "in Paradise."

Anthems

What Wondrous Love Is This, arr. James Melby (Concordia) SATB flute (E). *Cross of Jesus,* John Stainer, arr. Robert Leaf (AMSI) SATB (ME).

Psalm 118:1–2, 19–29 (*Liturgy of the Palms*)

1. Metrical: *This Is the Day the Lord Hath Made* (stanzas 3–5). Text: Isaac Watts. Tune: ARDEN. *RITL* #128. (See also *HB55* #69 to the Tune: ARLINGTON.)
2. Responsorial: *Psalm 118* (19–29). Setting: Hal H. Hopson. *PS93* #118.
3. Responsorial: *Psalm 118* (1, 4–5, 14, 17, 24). Text: Taizé. Setting: Jacques Berthier. *PS93* #120.
4. Responsorial: *Open to Me the Gates of Righteousness.* Text: NRSV. Psalm tone: Laurence Bevenot, 1986. Refrain: A. Gregory Murray, 1963. *PH90* #232.
5. Responsorial: *The Liturgy of the Palms: Processional.* Music: Ancient Gallican Chant. Adapted by Howard E. Galley. *H82* #157.

See also *HB55* #71; *PR&T*, pp. 22 & 23.

Anthems

Psalm 118, Melchior Teschner, arr. Hal H. Hopson (*Eighteen Psalms for the Church Year,* Hope) SATB and congregation (E). *Processional Psalm,* Richard Proulx (G.I.A.) 2 equal voices, 4 handbells (E). *Give Thanks to the Lord,* Richard Felciano (*Songs for Darkness and Light* (E. C. Schirmer) unison (ME).

or Psalm 31:9–16 (*Liturgy of the Passion*)

1. Metrical: *In You, Lord, I Have Put My Trust.* Text: Adam Reissner, trans. Catherine Winkworth. Tune: IN DICH HAB' ICH GEHOFFET. *PH90* #183.
2. Responsorial: *Psalm 31:9–16.* Text: Grail. Refrain and psalm tone by Hal H. Hopson. *PH90* #182.
3. Responsorial: *Psalm 31:1–16.* Text: Grail. Setting: Hal H. Hopson. *PS93* #28.
4. Responsorial: *Lord, God, Be My Refuge and Strength* (all stanzas). Text: Grail (see also *GPI*, p. 37). Refrain, psalm tone, and Gelineau tone: *WIII* #35 (see also *WIII* #814 & #889).

See also *ANMP*, p. 71; *PH87* #31; *PR&T*, pp. 42 & 48.

Anthem

Psalm 31:9–16, Hal H. Hopson, *PH90* #182.

Organ Music for the Day

Liturgy of the Palms:

1. *All Glory, Laud and Honor* (VALET WILL ICH DIR GEBEN, *PH90* #88), J. S. Bach (various editions).
2. *The Palms,* Langlais (*Poèmes Evangéliques,* Philippo).
3. *Prelude on* THE KING'S MAJESTY (*Ride On! Ride On in Majesty!, PH90* #90), Leo Sowerby (H. W. Gray Co., Inc.).

4. *Prelude on* ELLACOMBE (*Hosanna, Loud Hosanna, PH90* #89), Flor Peeters (*Hymn Preludes for the Liturgical Year,* vol. 12, p. 9, C. F. Peters Corp. 6412).

5. *Chorale Prelude on* VALET WILL ICH DIR GEBEN (*All Glory, Laud, and Honor, PH90* #88), Max Reger (*Choralvorspiele,* Op. 67, p. 68, Bote & Bock).

Liturgy of the Passion:

1. *Ah, Holy Jesus* (HERZLIEBSTER JESU, *PH90* #93), Walcha (*Choralvorspiele,* vol. 1, p. 22, C. F. Peters Corp. 4850), Brahms (*Chorale Preludes,* C. F. Peters Corp. and other publishers), and Sigfrid Karg-Elert (*Choral-Improvisations,* vol. 2, p. 20, Edward B. Marks Music Corp.).

2. *Choral Prelude on* HERZLICH TUT MICH VERLANGEN (*O Sacred Head, Now Wounded, PH90* #98), Johann Sebastian Bach (various editions).

Hymns for the Day	*HL33*	*HB55*	*WB72*	*PH90*
Liturgy of the Palms:				
All Glory, Laud, and Honor	146	187	284	88
At the Name of Jesus	–	143	303	148
Hosanna, Loud Hosanna	147	185	424	89
I Greet Thee, Who My Sure Redeemer Art	–	144	625	457
Lift Up Your Heads, Ye Mighty Gates	114	152	454	8
O Jesus Christ, May Grateful Hymns . . .	–	–	509	424
O Day of Radiant Gladness	18	70	–	470
Open Now Thy Gates of Beauty	–	40	544	489
Ride On! Ride On in Majesty!	150	188	563	90, 91
Liturgy of the Passion:				
Ah, Holy Jesus	158	191	280	93
Beneath the Cross of Jesus	162	190	308	92
Creator of the Stars of Night	–	–	348	4
In the Cross of Christ I Glory	154	195	437	84
Take Up Your Cross, the Savior Said	–	293	–	393
Throned Upon the Awful Tree	–	197	605	99
Jesus, Remember Me (Luke 23:42)	–	–	–	599
Make Me a Captive, Lord	247	308	–	378
O Sacred Head, Now Wounded	151	194	524	98
When I Survey the Wondrous Cross	152	198	635	100, 101
When We Are Tempted to Deny Your Son	–	–	640	86

MONDAY OF HOLY WEEK (ABC)

Isaiah 42:1–9 The first of the four Songs of the Servant of YHWH (vs. 1–4) and the response to it (vs. 5–9). YHWH officially presents the chosen servant, upon whom YHWH has put the Spirit, who is to perform the task of bringing forth *mishpat* ("justice") to the nations by his own suffering. YHWH gives the servant as a light to the people who live in darkness. Verses 8–9 affirm that YHWH will give no glory or praise to any idol, and that YHWH declares in advance new things of the future.

Anthems

Behold the Savior of Mankind (Us All), Christopher Tye (*A First Motet Book*, (Concordia) SATB (E). *Jesus, So Lowly*, Harold Friedell (H. W. Gray) SATB (ME). *Behold My Servant*, Jack Boyd (Boston Music) SATB (M). *Hail to the Lord's Anointed*, Malcolm Williamson (*Dove Chorales*, Agape) unison (E).

Hebrews 9:11–15 Christ enters not the earthly Holy of Holies, offering a ritual sacrifice, but he enters once for all the holy dwelling place of God, offering a sacrifice of himself—his own life-giving blood. In his sacrifice, Christ attains what none other ever could—eternal redemption for his people. Christ is truly the high priest of the "good things that have come."

Anthem

The Promise of Eternal Inheritance, Rudolf Moser (Concordia) unison (E).

John 12:1–11 Irrepressible Mary gets carried away at dinner and shocks everyone by pouring thousands of dollars' worth of perfume on Jesus' feet. "An extravagant waste," cries the morally upright Judas; "the money could have been given to the poor." Replies Jesus, "You'll always have the opportunity to serve the poor—so leave her alone, for you'll not always have me. She has saved her perfume for my burial." Mary anoints her only Lord and Savior.

Anthems

A Litany (Drop, Drop, Slow Tears), William Walton (Oxford) SATB (MD). *The Best of Rooms*, Randall Thompson (E. C. Schirmer) SATB (MD). *Master, No Offering Costly or Sweet*, HB55 #299.

Psalm 36:5–11

1. Metrical: *Thy Mercy and Thy Truth, O Lord.* Text: *The Psalter*, 1912. Tune: CADDO. *HB55* #82.
2. Responsorial: *Psalm 36:5–11.* Text: Grail. Refrain: David Clark Isele. Gelineau tone. *PS93* #34.
3. Metrical: *Your Love and Faithfulness, O Lord.* Text: L.M., Christopher L. Webber. *ANMP*, p. 86.
4. Metrical: *My Heart Speaks Out on Those Who Sin.* Text: Bert Witvoet. Tune: PALMARUM. *PH87* #36.
5. Responsorial: Text: optional. Psalm tones and refrains by Hal H. Hopson. *PR&T*, pp. 69 & 77.

Anthems

O How Precious, Raymond Haan (Hinshaw) 2-part (E). *How Precious Is Thy Loving Kindness*, Samuel Adler (Oxford) SATB (MD).

Organ Music for the Day

1. *Prelude on* ROCKINGHAM (*When I Survey the Wondrous Cross, PH90* #100), Kenneth Leighton (*Chorale Preludes on English Tunes*, p. 9, Oxford University Press 375135-6).
2. *Prelude on* HAMBURG (*When I Survey the Wondrous Cross, PH90* #101), Carl McKinley (*Ten Hymn Tune Fantasies*, H. W. Gray).
3. *Prelude on* MARYTON (*O Master, Let Me Walk with Thee, PH90* #357), Flor Peeters (*Hymn Preludes for the Liturgical Year*, vol. 17, p. 22, C. F. Peters Corp. 6417).
4. *Prelude on a Theme by Tallis* (*Thy Mercy and Thy Truth, O Lord*, TALLIS' ORDINAL, *PH90* #186), Richard Peek (Brodt Music Co.), and Healey Willan (*Ten Hymn Preludes*, vol. 2, p. 11, C. F. Peters Corp. 6012).

Hymns for the Day	HL33	HB55	WB72	PH90
All Hail to God's Anointed	111	146	–	205
Blessed Assurance, Jesus Is Mine!	–	139	–	341
Come, Thou Almighty King	52	244	343	139
In the Cross of Christ I Glory	154	195	437	84
Jesus Walked This Lonesome Valley	–	–	–	80, 81
O Master, Let Me Walk with Thee	364	304	520	357
Thy Mercy and Thy Truth, O Lord	–	82	–	186
When I Survey the Wondrous Cross	152	198	635	100, 101

TUESDAY OF HOLY WEEK (ABC)

Isaiah 49:1–7 The second of the four Songs of the Servant of YHWH. YHWH's chosen servant summons the nations to hear YHWH's word. The servant publicly announces his prenatal call and his subsequent despondency about performing the task in vain. But now YHWH has expanded the call to be a light to all the nations (Gentiles), in order that "salvation may reach the ends of the earth."

Anthems
O Send Thy Light, M. A. Balakireff (J. Fischer) SATB (E). *And with His Stripes We Are Healed,* G. F. Handel (*Messiah,* any edition) SATB (M). *Canticle of Trust,* Richard Purvis (Sacred Music) SATB (ME).

1 Corinthians 1:18–31 The gospel always seems to turn our world upside down. Here worldly wisdom and strength are characterized as foolish and weak, and the nonsense and weakness of the crucifixion are labeled as wise and strong. The epitome of God's love for us is revealed in the offensiveness of the cross.

Anthems
Simple Gifts, American folk melody, arr. Heffley (Plymouth) SATB, optional flute, guitar (ME). *The Foolishness Carol,* Austin Lovelace (Somerset) SATB (ME). *Yet a Litle While,* Knut Nystedt (Summy Birchard) SSATB. *Almighty God, the Fountain of All Wisdom,* Ernest Farrar (*Anthems for Choirs,* vol. 1, Oxford) SATB (ME).

John 12:20–36 Some Gentiles seek to see Jesus. "The hour has come . . . ," says Jesus, "for when a single grain of wheat falls into the earth and dies, it produces many grains." Jesus then wrestles with the full import of "the hour" and decides to submit obediently to the Father's will. An affirming voice from heaven accepts the Son's obedience and promises the Son his own glorification. In fact, Jesus' decision to die will open the possibility for others to be liberated from the ruler of this world. Jesus' hour of glory, his death, brings forth life for Jesus and for all those who follow him and serve him.

Anthems
Walk in the Light, Winston Cassler (Augsburg) SATB (E). *Thy Perfect Love,* John Rutter (Oxford) SATB (M). *The Promise Which Was Made,* Edward Bairstow (Novello) SATB (M).

Psalm 71:1–14
1. Metrical: *I Find My Refuge in You, Lord.* Text: C.M., Christopher L. Webber. *ANMP,* p. 119.
2. Responsorial: *Psalm 7* (1–16). Text: Grail. Setting: James E. Barrett. Tone: Harmony, Hal H. Hopson. *PS93* #63.
3. Metrical: *In You, O Lord, I Put My Trust.* Text: Clarence P. Walhout. Tune: JUDSON. *PH87* #71.
4. Responsorial: *I Will Sing of Your Salvation.* Text: Grail (see also *GPI,* p. 97). Refrain, psalm tone, and Gelineau tone: *WIII* #44 & #876.
5. Responsorial: Text: optional. Psalm tones and refrains by Hal H. Hopson. *PR&T,* pp. 45 & 48.

Anthem
In Thee, O Lord, Do I Put My Trust, Jane Marshall (Augsburg) SATB (M).

Organ Music for the Day

1. JESU DULCIS MEMORIA (*Jesus, Thou Joy of Loving Hearts, PH90* #511), Jean Langlais (*Suite Médiévale:* Méditation, p. 9, Salabert).
2. *Prelude on* ANGEL'S STORY (*O Jesus, I Have Promised, PH90* #388), Gerhard Krapf (*O Savior, Precious Savior* in *The Concordia Hymn Prelude Series,* vol. 19, Concordia 97-4710).
3. *Chorale Prelude on* WAS GOTT TUT (*O God, What You Ordain Is Right, PH90* #284), J. S. Bach (*Organ Chorales from the Neumeister Collection,* Bärenreiter 5181), and Max Reger (*Thirty Short Chorale Preludes,* Op. 135a, C. F. Peters Corp. 3980).
4. *Prelude on* DEO GRACIAS (*O Love, How Deep, How Broad, How High, PH90* #83), Flor Peeters (*Hymn Preludes for the Liturgical Year,* vol. 4, C. F. Peters Corp. 6404).

Hymns for the Day	HL33	HB55	WB72	PH90
A Mighty Fortress Is Our God	266	91	274	259, 260
Beneath the Cross of Jesus	162	190	308	92
Christ Is the World's True Light	–	492	326	–
O for a World	–	–	–	386
O Jesus, I Have Promised	268	307	–	388, 389
O Love, How Deep, How Broad, How High	139	–	518	83
O God, What You Ordain Is Right	291	366	633	284

WEDNESDAY OF HOLY WEEK (ABC)

Isaiah 50:4–9a The third of the four Songs of the Servant of YHWH: Each day YHWH wakens me and opens my ears to the word that sustains me. Though I have suffered ridicule, insults, hostility, physical abuse, I have not turned from my task. I trust YHWH's help; YHWH will vindicate me. So who will declare me guilty?

Anthem

He Was Despised, G. F. Handel (*Messiah,* any edition) alto solo or unison (ME).

Hebrews 12:1–3 A lifelong marathon race: that's what you're in for when you join the crowd trying to keep pace with Jesus. So strip off your warm-up suit, throw away your pride, scrap your blueprints for success and any other sins that weigh you down. To endure in this race, you must be lean. And you must be determined and tenacious in keeping your eyes fixed on Jesus. He did not become discouraged or give up because of hostility from sinners or even death on the cross. So persevere in following the pacesetter Jesus. And remember, you're not alone— all the racers from the past are cheering you on.

Anthems

He Endured the Cross, Carl Graun, ed. Robert Wetzler (Augsburg) SATB (M). *He That Shall Endure,* Felix Mendelssohn (*Elijah,* G. Schirmer) SATB (ME). *Fight the Good Fight,* John Gardner (Oxford) SATB (ME).

John 13:21–32 Following the act of foot washing, Jesus announces that one who is present will betray him. Such a disclosure perks up the disciples' conversation and introduces to us the Beloved Disciple. Jesus then dips some bread in the sauce and gives it to Judas, presumably to indicate him as the betrayer. Then, at Jesus' request, Judas leaves "to do what he has to do."

Anthems

Solus ad Victimam (*Alone to Sacrifice Thou Goest*) Kenneth Leighton (Oxford) SATB (MD). *I Caused Thy Grief,* Paul Manz (Augsburg) SATB (M). *Ah, Holy Jesus,* Johann Crüger, arr. William H. Mathis (Oxford) SATB (M).

Psalm 70

1. Metrical: *Be Pleased, O God, to Save My Life.* Text: C.M., Christopher L. Webber. *ANMP,* p. 70.

2. Responsorial: *Psalm 70.* Text: *Book of Common Prayer.* Setting: Peter R. Hallock. *PS93* #62.
3. Metrical: *Come Quickly, Lord, to Rescue Me.* Text: Bert Polman. Tune: DISTRESS. *PH87* #70.
4. Responsorial: *O God, Make Haste to My Rescue.* Text: Grail (see also *GPI,* p. 97). Refrain and Gelineau tone: *30P&2C,* p. 21.

See also *PR&T,* pp. 42 & 49.

Anthems

Haste Thee, O God, Adrian Batten (*Anthems for Choirs,* vol. 1, Oxford) SATB (M).
Thou, Lord, the Refuge of the Meek, Josquin Desprez (J. Fischer) SAB (ME).

Organ Music for the Day

1. DEO GRACIAS or THE AGINCOURT HYMN (*O Love, How Deep, How Broad, How High, PH90* #83), Percy Whitlock (*Six Hymn Preludes,* vol. 1, p. 9, Oxford 375902-0), and Paul Manz (*Ten Hymn Improvisations,* vol. 9, p. 22, Concordia 97-5556).
2. *Chorale Prelude on* HERZLIEBSTER JESU (*Ah, Holy Jesus, PH90* #93), Helmut Walcha (*Choralvorspiele,* vol. 1, p. 22, C. F. Peters Corp. 4850), and Sigfrid Karg-Elert (*Choral-Improvisations,* vol. 2, p. 20, Edward B. Marks Music Corp.).
3. *Hymn Prelude on* MARTYRDOM (*Alas! and Did My Savior Bleed, PH90* #78), Healey Willan (*Ten Hymn Preludes,* vol. 2, p. 33, C. F. Peters Corp. 6012).

Hymns for the Day	HL33	HB55	WB72	PH90
Ah, Holy Jesus	158	191	280	93
Fight the Good Fight	270	359	–	307
For All the Saints	429	425	369	526
Great Is Thy Faithfulness	–	–	–	276
Guide My Feet	–	–	–	354
I Greet Thee, Who My Sure Redeemer Art	–	144	625	457
O Love, How Deep, How Broad	139	–	518	83

MAUNDY THURSDAY (ABC)

Exodus 12:1–4, (5–10), 11–14 The Priestly account of the preparation and celebration of the Passover. Though conducted within each family (or group of families able to consume a whole lamb), this meal is the time at which all Israelites thank God for having redeemed them and made them a people, and they renew their hope in the coming salvation.

Anthems
O Lamb of God Most Holy, PH90 #82. *With a Voice of Singing,* Martin Shaw (Curwen) SATB (ME).

1 Corinthians 11:23–26 The tradition Paul received "from the Lord" he now passes on to others: that the Lord Jesus took bread, gave thanks, broke it, and distributed it, and in the same manner the cup. Christ gave himself away, his own body and blood. So if any eat the bread or drink the cup in a way that contradicts the self-giving body of Christ, the true nature of the church, then those persons eat and drink judgment upon themselves. Wait for one another so you may serve others as the reconciled body of Christ.

Anthem
Bread of the World, Stephen Paulus (Hinshaw) 2-part (E).

John 13:1–17, 31*b***–35** Jesus kneels to scrub dirt from the feet of his disciples. Appalled by such an undignified act, Peter exclaims, "You'll never wash my feet, ever." "Unless you let me wash you," replies Jesus, "then you'll have no share in my life." "In that case, then," says Peter, "wash me all over." "Don't you understand what I have done for you?" asks Jesus. "If I, your Lord and Teacher, have washed your feet, you also ought to wash one another's feet. Serve, forgive, give as I have. Love one another, as I have loved you."

Anthems
Neighbors, Ghana melody, arr. Austin Lovelace (Hope) 2-part mixed (E). *This Is My Commandment,* Thomas Tallis (Oxford) AATB (M). *An Upper Room Did Our Lord Prepare, PH90* #94.

Psalm 116:1–2, 12–19
1. Metrical: *O Thou, My Soul, Return in Peace.* Text: *Murrayfield Psalms* and *The Psalter,* 1912, alt. Tune: MARTYRDOM. *PH90* #228. (See also *RITL* #125.)
2. Responsorial: *Psalm 116.* Text: Helen L. Wright. Refrain: Richard T. Proulx. Tone: Saint Meinrad 1. *PS93* #115.
3. Responsorial: *Psalm 116* (12–19). Text: Helen L. Wright. Setting: Samuel Weber. *PS93* #116.
4. Metrical: *We Love You, Lord, for You Have Heard.* Text: C.M.D., Fred R. Anderson. *SPJP,* p. 61.
5. Responsorial: *How Can I Repay the Lord?* Text: Grail (see also *GPI,* p. 170). Refrain, psalm tone, and Gelineau tone: *WIII* #61, #791, #811, & #863.

See also *PH87* #116; *PR&T,* pp. 24 & 25.

Anthems
This Do in Remembrance of Me, Austin Lovelace (Hope) SATB (E). *What Shall I Render to My God,* Austin Lovelace (Canyon) SATB (E).

Organ Music for the Day
1. *Chorale Prelude on* RENDEZ À DIEU (*Bread of the World, PH90* #502), Helmut Walcha (*Choralvorspiele,* vol. 3, p. 36, C. F. Peters Corp. 5999).
2. SCHÖNSTER HERR JESU, Schroeder (*Sechs Orgelchorale,* B. Schotts Söhne).
3. *Prelude on* ARFON (*Bread of Heaven, PH90* #501), Austin C. Lovelace (*Fourteen Hymn Preludes,* Augsburg 11-6152).
4. *Prelude on Drop, Drop Slow Tears,* Vincent Persichetti (Elkan-Vogel).

Hymns for the Day	HL33	HB55	WB72	PH90
An Upper Room Did Our Lord Prepare	–	–	–	94
Become to Us the Living Bread	–	–	305	500
Bread of the World in Mercy Broken	353	445	–	502
Deck Yourself, My Soul	–	–	351	506
Jesu, Jesu, Fill Us with Your Love	–	–	–	367
O God of Bethel, by Whose Hand	98	342	496	269
O Love, How Deep, How Broad	139	–	518	83
Strong Son of God, Immortal Love	175	228	578	–
There's a Wideness in God's Mercy	93	110	601	298
Where Charity and Love Prevail	–	–	641	–

GOOD FRIDAY (ABC)

Isaiah 52:13–53:12 The fourth of the four Songs of the Servant of YHWH. YHWH promises the coming vindication of YHWH's servant. Thus many are shocked to see an afflicted, disfigured, marred servant. Has God smitten him for past sins? No, the servant has participated in our human brokenness. He has "borne our griefs and carried our sorrows" according to God's will. This humiliated servant is the one whom YHWH will vindicate.

Anthems

Surely He Hath Borne Our Griefs, K. H. Braun (Concordia) SATB (M). *O Vos Omnes* (O Ye People), Pablo Casals (Broude) SATB (D). *Man of Sorrows,* Frank Pooler (Augsburg) SAB (ME). *Isaiah's Song,* Hank Beebe (Carl Fischer) 2-part mixed (E). *Surely He Has Borne Our Griefs,* Carl Heinrich Graun, ed. Walter Collins (Hinshaw) SATB, small orchestra optional (M).

Hebrews 10:16–25 The fulfillment of Jeremiah 31:33–34 abrogates the need for any further sacrifices, since God will no longer remember our sin. Christ's sacrifice truly is once and for all. Now that all guilt is lifted from us, we may freely and confidently respond to God's love offered in Jesus Christ by encouraging one another to trust God's faithful promises. Such trust may lead to a caring, supportive, loving community of faith.

Anthems

With Awe and Confidence, George Brandon (G.I.A.) SATB (ME). *Deep Were His Wounds and Red, PH90* #103.

or **Hebrews 4:14–16; 5:7–9** We have a great high priest to represent us to God, a simple human being named Jesus, who lived in the same kind of power-hungry, achievement-oriented, complacently religious, me-first world. But this Jesus was sinless. He is the perfect one, who is the source of salvation and now reigns with God.

Anthem

I Caused Thy Grief, Paul Manz (Augsburg) SATB (M).

John 18:1–19:42 The passion narrative according to John.

Anthems

And God Looked Down at God That Day, John Stanley (New Music) SATB (E). *O Come and Mourn with Me Awhile,* Hal H. Hopson (Agape) 2 equal voices (E). *O Come and Mourn with Me Awhile,* Dale Wood (Flammer) SAB (ME). *Wondrous Love,* arr. Douglas Wagner (Flammer) SATB (E). *A Lamb Goes Uncomplaining Forth,* J. S. Bach, arr. Paul Christiansen (AMSI) SATB (M). *Thy Love to Me,* Welsh melody, arr. Leland Sateren (AMSI) SATB (E).

Psalm 22

1. Metrical: *Lord, Why Have You Forsaken Me?* Text: L.M., Christopher L. Webber. Tune: SARUM PLAINSONG, MODE IV. *PH90* #168. For text only see *ANMP,* p. 55.
2. Responsorial: *Psalm 22* (1–2, 7–8, 14–22). Setting: Hal H. Hopson. *PS93* #15.
3. Responsorial: *Psalm 22* (1–15). Text: International Commission on English in the Liturgy, *A New Zealand Prayer Book.* Refrain: Jerry R. Brubaker. Tone: Presbyterian 8. *PS93* #16.
4. Responsorial: *My God, My God, Why Have You Forsaken Me?* Text: *Book of Common Prayer.* Music: Peter R. Hallock. *TIP/PSCY* #7.

See also *PH87* #22; *WIII* #31 & #806; *30P&2C,* p. 5; *CC* G-2329; *PR&T,* pp. 26 & 27.

Anthems

My God, My God, Look Upon Me, Maurice Greene (Broude) SSATB tenor solo (M). *All You That Know God's Holy Name,* G. F. Handel, arr. Hal H. Hopson (Coronet) SATB (M). *My God, My God, Why Hast Thou Forsaken Me?* Gerald Near (H. W. Gray) SATB (D).

Organ Music for the Day

1. *O Sacred Head, Now Wounded* (PASSION CHORALE/HERZLICH TUT MICH VERLAN-GEN, *PH90* #98), Johannes Brahms (various editions), Dietrich Buxtehude (*Sämtliche Orgelwerke,* vol. 4, Wilhelm Hansen 3928).
2. *Were You There?* (WERE YOU THERE, *PH90* #102), Dale Wood (*Wood Works,* The Sacred Music Press KK357), and Leo Sowerby (*Ten Preludes,* H. W. Gray Co., Inc. GB 651).
3. *O Sacred Head* (HERZLICH TUT MICH VERLANGEN), J. S. Bach (various editions), Karg-Elert (*Chorale-Improvisations,* Op. 65, Breitkopf), and Langlais (*Neuf Pièces,* Bornemann).

Hymns for the Day	HL33	HB55	WB72	PH90
Ah, Holy Jesus	158	191	280	93
Alone You Journey Forth, O Lord	–	–	294	–
Calvary	–	–	–	96
Deep Were His Wounds, and Red	–	–	–	103
Go to Dark Gethsemane	–	193	–	97
He Never Said a Mumbalin' Word	–	–	–	95
O Sacred Head, Now Wounded	151	194	524	98
Throned Upon the Awful Tree	–	197	605	99
Were You There		201	–	102
O Love, How Deep, How Broad (st. 1–3)	139	–	518	83

72

Season of Easter
EASTER VIGIL (ABC)

1. Genesis 1:1–2:4a All was dark upon the formless, chaotic, unordered waters of creation. God spoke a word, and there was light. When God speaks, action occurs. God spoke again and again and there was firmament-dome, sky, dry land, vegetation, lights (sun, moon, and stars), and living beings—animal life and, finally, human beings—a community of male and female. And God saw that all of creation was very good. Chaos is transformed into cosmos by the majesty and mystery of God, whose will for creation is unity and harmony.

Anthem

In the Beginning of Creation, Daniel Pinkham (E. C. Schirmer) SATB tape (ME).

Psalm 136:1–9, 23–26
1. Metrical: *We Thank You, Lord, for You Are Good.* Text: John G. Dunn. Tune: WAS GOTT TUT. *PH90* #243.
2. Responsorial: *Psalm 136* (1–18, 21–26). Text: Grail. Setting: Joseph Gelineau. *PS93* #139. (See also *24P&1C,* p. 38.)
3. Metrical: *Let Us with a Gladsome Mind.* Text: John Milton. Tune: MONKLAND. *PH90* #244.
4. Responsorial: *Love Is Never Ending.* Text: Based on Psalm 136, Marty Haugen. Tune: MARTY HAUGEN. *CS/PFTCY,* vol. 2, p. 46. (Also found in *GTHR* #58.)

Anthem

Let Us with a Gladsome Mind, Alan Ridout (Stainer and Bell) SATB (ME).

2. Genesis 7:1–5, 11–18; 8:6–18; 9:8–13 Both Yahwist and Priestly sources are interwoven to form an abridged version of the flood narrative. The rebellion against God (sin) by God's creatures leads creation to disorder, disharmony, and disunity. YHWH therefore decides to destroy all except Noah and his family. So the death-dealing power of water is unleashed as YHWH fulfills YHWH's promise. Yet God mysteriously makes a unilateral covenant with Noah and his descendants and all living beings: Never again will I destroy creation by flood. As a sign of God's eternal promise to all creation, God lays down a bow in the sky.

Anthem

If Thou but Suffer God to Guide Thee, Jody Lindh (Concordia) SATB (E).

Psalm 46
1. Metrical: *God, Our Help and Constant Refuge.* Text: 8.7.8.7.3.3.7, Fred R. Anderson. Tune: MICHAEL. *PH90* #192. For text only, see *SPJP,* p. 34.
2. Responsorial: *The Lord of Hosts Is with Us.* Text: NRSV. Psalm tone: Richard Proulx, 1986. Refrain: A. Gregory Murray, 1986. *PH90* #193. Appears with Grail text and Gelineau tone: *WIII* #39.
3. Responsorial: *Psalm 46.* Text: *The United Methodist Liturgical Psalter.* Refrain and Tone: Presbyterian 6. *PS93* #40.
4. Responsorial: *Psalm 46.* Setting: Hal H. Hopson. *PS93* #41.
5. Metrical: *God Is Our Refuge and Our Strength.* Text: *The Psalter,* 1912, alt. 1988. Tune: WINCHESTER OLD. *PH90* #191. (See also *HB55* #38 and *RITL* #102. Melody from *The Scottish Psalter.*)

See also *ANMP,* p. 96; *PH87* #46; *PR&T,* pp. 58 & 76.

Anthem

A Mighty Fortress, Johann Schein (Concordia) 2-part (ME).

3. Genesis 22:1–18 God tests Abraham in order to find out whether Abraham trusts only God's promise. "Give up your only son," summons God—a repugnant, disturbing test—yet Abraham faithfully obeys. Asks Isaac, "Where is the lamb?" "God will provide," replies Abraham, and an angel of the Lord cries out, "Now I know you trust only God's promise because you have not withheld from God that which is most precious to you." Miraculously, God provides a ram for the offering and again blesses Abraham.

Anthem
On God and Not on Human Trust, Johann Pachelbel (Concordia) SATB (M).

Psalm 16
1. Metrical: *When in the Night I Meditate.* Text: *The Psalter,* 1912. Tune: ST. FLAVIAN. *PH90* #165. (See *HB55* #68 to the Tune: MAITLAND.)
2. Responsorial: *Psalm 16.* Text: Grail. Refrain: James E. Barrett. Tone: Gregorian II, alt. Accompaniment: Hal H. Hopson. *PS93* #10.
3. Responsorial: *Keep Me Safe, O God.* Text: Grail (see also *GPI,* p. 15). Refrain, psalm tone, and Gelineau tone: *WIII* #820, #839, #903.
4. Responsorial: *You Are My Inheritance.* Setting by Richard Proulx. *CC* G-2405.
See also *ANMP,* p. 47; *SPJP,* p. 17; *PH87* #16; *PR&T,* pp. 54 & 78.

Anthem
Preserve Me, O Lord, Benedetto Marcello (Concordia) SATB (E).

4. Exodus 14:10–31; 15:20–21 Moses' prebattle, motivational speech to the Israelites: "Fear not, stand firm, keep still, for YHWH will fight for you." YHWH commands Moses to raise his walking stick over the waters so they will divide. An angel of God and the pillar of cloud move to the rear of the Israelites and veil them from the Egyptians. And all comes to fulfillment according to the word of God. YHWH drives back the sea by a strong east wind, throws the Egyptians into panic, causes their wheels to become mired in mud, and tosses them into the sea. Thus YHWH saves Israel from the Egyptians, and Israel believes in YHWH and YHWH's servant Moses. So Moses and the people sing a song to YHWH.

Anthem
Thanks Be to Thee, O Lord, G. F. Handel, arr. Saar (E. C. Schirmer) SATB, alto solo (E).

Exodus 15:1*b*–13, 17–18 (Canticle of Miriam and Moses)
1. Responsorial: *Canticle of Miriam and Moses* (Ex. 15:1–6, 11–13, 17–18). Text: *Book of Common Prayer.* Setting: John Weaver. *PS93* #174.
2. Responsorial: *Exodus Canticle (Song of Miriam and Moses).* Setting: Howard Hughes. *CC* G-3102.

Anthem
The Lord Is My Strength, Howard Hughes (from *Praise God in Song,* GIA).

5. Isaiah 55:1–11 An imperative invitation to the eschatological banquet. Come! Buy! Eat! Free wine and milk. Why futilely try to buy your way into the banquet or purchase unsatisfying pleasures? Heed my word and you shall eat well. Summon your neighbors while YHWH is near. And return to YHWH, our God, who is merciful and quick to forgive, for YHWH's ways are not our ways. When God speaks, action occurs. Does rain fall from the skies and return there before fulfilling its purpose of watering the earth? Neither does God's word. It shall accomplish that which God intends.

Anthem
For as the Rain and Snow Come Down, Hal H. Hopson (Sacred Music Press) SATB (M).

Isaiah 12:2–6 (Song of Thanksgiving)
1. Metrical: *Surely It Is God Who Saves Me.* Text 8.7.8.7.D, Carl P. Daw, Jr. Tune: RAQUEL. *WIII* #584. (See also *PH87* #193 to the Tune: REVIVE US.)
2. Responsorial: *Canticle of Thanksgiving.* Text: *Book of Common Prayer.* Setting: Norman Mealy. *PS93* #175.

3. Responsorial: *Truly, God Is My Salvation.* Refrain, psalm tone, and Gelineau tone: *WIII* #81.

Anthem
The First Song of Isaiah, Jack Noble White (H. W. Gray) SADB (E).

6. Baruch 3:9–15, 32–4:4 Why, O Israel, are you in exile, alienated from God? Because you have forsaken the fountain of wisdom, you are growing old in a foreign land. If you had walked in God's way (Torah), then you would be living forever in peace. Turn away from all seductive ephemeral pleasures, and walk toward God's enduring gift of wisdom's shining light. Happy indeed are those who know what is pleasing to God.

Anthem
Hear Ye, Israel!, Felix Mendelssohn (*Elijah,* G. Schirmer) soprano solo (M).

or **Proverbs 8:22–31** I, Wisdom, was present at the ordering of creation, when YHWH had yet to shape the springs of water, mountains, hills, and fields; when the sky and horizon were positioned; when clouds were placed in the sky above and seas were opened below; when boundaries were set for ocean tides. At that time, I was beside YHWH like an architect and a firstborn child, constantly rejoicing in creation and delighting in the human race.

Anthem
Anthem of Wisdom, Robert Linn (Lawson-Gould) SATB.

Psalm 19
1. Metrical: *The Heavens Above Declare God's Praise.* Text: Christopher L. Webber. Tune: CAITHNESS. *PH90* #166.
2. Responsorial: *Psalm 19* (1–6). Text: Grail. Melody: Monks of Saint Meinrad. Harmony, Samuel Weber. *PS93* #12.
3. Responsorial: *Psalm 19* (7–14). Setting: Hal H. Hopson. *PS93* #13.
4. Metrical: *The Heavens, O Lord, Proclaim Your Power.* Text: C.M. D., Fred R. Anderson. *SPJP,* p. 20.
See also *RITL* #87; *PH87* #19; *30P&2C,* p. 3; *PR&T,* pp. 67 & 68.

Anthem
God's Law Is Perfect and Gives Life, G. F. Handel, *PH90* #167, SATB (E).

7. Ezekiel 36:24–28 Thus says the Lord God: "I will gather together you exiles and bring you home. I will sprinkle you with clean water, forgiving you and cleansing you from all that has defiled you. I will renew you by taking away your stubborn heart and giving you a new heart and a new mind. And I will empower you by putting my spirit among you so that you can walk in my ways. Then you shall live in the land I gave your ancestors; and you shall be my people, and I shall be your God. We shall be inseparable."

Anthem
You Shall Dwell in the Land, John Stainer (Novello) SATB (ME).

Psalm 42
1. Metrical: *As Deer Long for the Streams.* Text: L.M.,Christopher L. Webber. Tune: ROCKINGHAM. *PH90* #189. For text only see *ANMP,* p. 94.
2. Responsorial: *My Soul Is Thirsting for the Lord.* Text: NRSV. Psalm tone: Douglas Mews, 1986. Refrain: J. Gelineau, 1986. *PH90* #190. For Grail text and Gelineau tone see *WIII* #37 (see also *WIII* #825 for alternate refrain and psalm tone).
3. Responsorial: *Psalm 42.* Text: Grail. Refrain: Gelineau. Tone: Frederick A. Gore Ouseley. *PS93* #37.
4. Metrical: *As Pants the Hart for Cooling Streams.* Text: Tate and Brady. Tune: SPOHR. *HB55* #322.
See also *RITL* #101; *PH87* #42; *PR&T,* pp. 45 & 48.

Anthem

Why Afflict Thyself, O My Soul, Heinrich Schütz (Mercury) 2-part, continuo and 2 instruments (ME).

and **Psalm 43**

1. Metrical: *Defend Me, Lord, from Those Who Charge Me.* Text: Marie J. Post. Tune: GENEVAN 43. *PH87* #43.
2. Responsorial: *Psalm 43.* Text: Grail. Refrain: Gelineau. Tone: Frederick A. Gore Ouseley. *PS93* #38.
3. Responsorial: *I Will Go to the Altar of the Lord.* Text: Grail. Refrain, psalm tone, and Gelineau tone: *WIII* #38. (See also *24P&1C,* p. 14.) For text only, see *GPI,* p. 59 and *GGP,* p. 64.
4. Metrical: *Give Judgment, Lord, Defend My Cause.* Text: L.M., Christopher L. Webber. Tune: ROCKINGHAM. *ANMP,* p. 94.

See also *RITL* #101; *PR&T,* pp. 42 & 48.

Anthem

Why Art Thou Cast Down, O My Soul?, Jean Berger (Augsburg) SATB (ME).

8. Ezekiel 37:1–14 The vision of the valley of dry bones, dead dry bones of Israel everywhere. Asks YHWH, "Can these bones live?" "Perhaps you know," replies Ezekiel. "Preach to the dry bones," commands YHWH, "that they shall live." So Ezekiel does as commanded. And astonishingly the bones come together and breath comes into them, all by the power of the word of God.

Anthem

Ezekiel Saw the Wheel, spiritual, arr. Gilbert Martin (Hinshaw) SATB (M).

Psalm 143

1. Metrical: *When Morning Lights the Eastern Skies.* Text: *The Psalter,* 1912. Tune: ST. STEPHEN. *PH90* #250.
2. Responsorial: *Psalm 143* (1–8). Text: Helen L. Wright. Tone and Refrain: Melodies: Columba Kelly. Harmony, Samuel Weber. *PS93* #146.
3. Metrical: *Lord, Hear My Prayer, My Supplication.* Text: James Vanden Bosch, 1981. Tune: GENEVAN 143. *PH87* #143.
4. Metrical: *Lord, Hear Me in Your Faithfulness.* Text: C.M., Christopher L. Webber. *ANMP,* p. 223.
5. Responsorial: Text: optional. Psalm tones and refrains by Hal H. Hopson. *PR&T,* pp. 42 & 49.

Anthem

I Call to the Lord, Felix Mendelssohn, arr. Hal H. Hopson (Broude) SATB (ME).

9. Zephaniah 3:14–20 A psalm of celebration sung by the faithful remnant: Sing, shout, rejoice, and exult, O Israel, because YHWH has taken away, has cast out the menacing threat, and is "in your midst" reigning as King. Fear not! YHWH, your God, will renew you. Promises YHWH, "I will transform the shame of the lame and the outcast into praise, and I will bring you home."

Anthem

Sing, O Daughters of Zion, Jan Bender (Concordia) SAB soprano solo (M).

Psalm 98

1. Metrical: *New Songs of Celebration Render.* Text: Erik Routley. Tune: RENDEZ À DIEU. *PH90* #218. (See also *RITL* #119, *H82* #413, and *PH87* #98 with text by Dewey Westra.)
2. Metrical: *To God Compose a Song of Joy.* Text: Ruth C. Duck. Tune: KEDDY. *PH90* #219.
3. Responsorial: *Psalm 98.* Text: International Commission on English in the Liturgy. Tone: Presbyterian 3. *PS93* #94.

4. Responsorial: *Psalm 98* (1–6). Text: *Book of Common Prayer.* Setting: Peter R. Hallock. *PS93* #95.

See also *WIII* #781; *PH87* #98; *ANMP*, p. 161; *SPJP*, p. 53; *PR&T*, pp. 10 & 13.

Anthem

New Songs of Celebration Render, Genevan Psalter, arr. Carlton R. Young (Agape) 2-part, congregation (E).

10. Romans 6:3–11 Why not continue in sin so God's grace and glory may overflow? Responds Paul, "How can we who died to sin still live in it? When we were baptized into union with Christ, we became one with him in death and were set free from the power of sin, and then we were raised with Christ to new life. So our old being is dead to sin, and we now have a new life in Christ."

Anthem

Let Us Ever Walk with Jesus, Paul Manz (Concordia) unison (E).

Psalm 114

1. Metrical: *When Israel Came, and Judah's House.* Text: L. M., Christopher L. Webber. *ANMP*, p. 183.
2. Responsorial: *Psalm 114.* Text: Helen L. Wright. Refrain: Presbyterian 1. Tone: Lutheran 9. *PS93* #114.
3. Responsorial: *God Has Freed Us and Redeemed Us.* Text: Grail (see also *GPI*, p. 168). Refrain, psalm tone, and Gelineau tone: *WIII* #60.
4. Metrical: *When Israel Fled from Egypt Land.* Text: Henrietta Ten Harmsel. Tune: ANDRE. *PH87* #114.
5. Responsorial: Text optional: Psalm tone and refrain by Hal H. Hopson. *PR&T*, pp. 73 & 76.

Anthem

Psalm 114, Zoltan Kodaly (Boosey & Hawkes) SATB (M).

11. (Year A) Matthew 28:1–10 Two women at Jesus' tomb encounter God's power in the form of an earthquake and an angel. They hurriedly leave the tomb in fear and great joy.

Anthem

The Angel Said to the Women, Harald Rohlig (Concordia) unison or 2-part (E).

11. (Year B) Mark 16:1–8 Three women go to Jesus' tomb to anoint his body. Instead, they find the tomb unsealed and a young man in a white robe sitting on the right side, who says, "Jesus has risen. Go, tell his disciples that he is going before you to Galilee." The women flee from the tomb, for they are afraid.

Anthem

The Morning of the Day of Days, Malcolm Williamson (G. Schirmer) SATB, soprano and tenor solos (M).

11. (Year C) Luke 24:1–12 The message of the two men to the women at the empty tomb, who then relay this good news to the apostles, who disbelieve such idle tales.

Anthem

He Is Risen, Alleluia, Eugene Englert (G.I.A.) 2-part mixed (E).

Organ Music for the Day

1. *Praeludium and Fugue on* CHRIST LAG IN TODESBANDEN (*Christ Jesus Lay in Death's Strong Bands, PH90* #110), Hermann Schroeder (B. Schotts Söhne 2554).
2. *Prelude on* EASTER DAWNING, Argento (AGO 90th Anniversary Anthology).
3. *Chorale Prelude on* CHRIST IST ERSTANDEN (*Christ the Lord Is Risen Again, PH90* #112), Max Reger (*Thirteen Chorale-Preludes,* Hans Sikorski Verlag 116).

Hymns for the Day	HL33	HB55	WB72	PH90
At the Name of Jesus	–	143	–	148
Baptized in Water	–	–	–	492
Cantad al Señor/O Sing to the Lord	–	–	–	472
Come, Ye Faithful (stanza 1)	168	205	344	114, 115
Creating God, Your Fingers Trace	–	–	–	134
Give to the Winds Your Fears	294	364	377	286
God Moves in a Mysterious Way	103	112	391	270
God, Who Stretched the Spangled Heavens	–	–	–	268
Immortal, Invisible, God Only Wise	66	85	433	263
I Sing the Mighty Power of God	65	84	628	288
Let All Things Now Living	–	–	–	554
Like the Murmur of the Dove's Song	–	–	–	314
O God of Bethel, by Whose Hand	98	342	496	269
Of the Father's Love Begotten	–	7	534	309
Out of Deep, Unordered Water	–	–	–	494
O Worship the King, All Glorious Above	2	26	533	476
Sing with Hearts	–	–	–	484
The Day of Resurrection!	166	208	584	118
The Strife Is O'er	164	203	597	119
We Know That Christ Is Raised	–	–	–	495

EASTER DAY (A)

Acts 10:34–43 At Cornelius's house in Caesarea, Peter recounts how his own life has been transformed by the power of the risen Lord, and everyone else (Jews and Gentiles) also can be transformed by that power.

Anthem
Today Is Risen Christ the Lord, Melchior Vulpius (Concordia) SATB, brass (M).

or **Jeremiah 31:1–6** YHWH promises to rebuild and renew an Israel—the object of YHWH's *hesed* ("covenant love").

Anthem
We Will Rejoice, G. F. Handel, arr. Robert S. Hines (Augsburg) SATB (M).

Colossians 3:1–4 In our baptism in Christ, we were given the gift of resurrection with Christ and therefore called to new life through the eyes of resurrection faith.

Anthems
Easter, John Leavitt (Augsburg) SATB with instruments (M). *If Ye Be Risen Again with Christ,* Kenneth Jennings (Concordia) SATB (MD).

or **Acts 10:34–43** See above.

John 20:1–18 Peter and the Beloved Disciple seek the truth about the empty tomb. Mary engages the "gardener" in conversation, who says, "Tell them I am ascending."

Anthems
Easter Fanfare, Paul Fetler (Augsburg) SATB, three trumpets (ME). *I Have Seen the Lord,* Alan Hovhaness (C. F. Peters) SATB, soprano solo, trumpet (MD).

or **Matthew 28:1–10** Two women at Jesus' tomb encounter God's power in the form of an earthquake and an angel. They hurriedly leave the tomb in fear and great joy.

Anthem
The Angel Said to the Women, Harald Rohlig (Concordia) unison or 2-part (E).

Psalm 118:1–2, 14–24
1. Metrical: *God Is My Strength and Song.* Text: S.M., S.M.D., Christopher L. Webber. *ANMP,* pp. 188–90.
2. Responsorial: *The Lord Is My Strength and My Might.* Text: NRSV. Psalm tone: Laurence Bevenot, 1986. Refrain: A. Gregory Murray, 1986. *PH90* #231.
3. Responsorial: *Psalm 118* (14–17, 22–24). Text: *Book of Common Prayer.* Setting: Peter R. Hallock. *PS93* #119. (See also *TIP/PSCY* #8.)
4. Responsorial: *Psalm 118* (1, 4–5, 14, 17, 24). Text: Taizé. Setting: Jacques Berthier. *PS93* #120. (See also *MFTII,* p. 51.)
5. Metrical: *This Is the Day the Lord Hath Made* (verses 3–5). Text: Isaac Watts. Tune: ARDEN. *RITL* #128. (See also *HB55* #69 to the Tune: ARLINGTON.)
6. Responsorial: *Alleluia! Let Us Rejoice!* (guitar) Words and music by David Haas. *CS/PFTCY,* vol. 3, p. 20.

See also *PH87* #118; *PR&T,* pp. 29 & 30.

Anthem
This Is the Day, Richard Proulx (G.I.A.) unison with descant, 11 handbells, triangle, tambourine, organ (E).

Organ Music for the Day
1. CHRIST IST ERSTANDEN (*Christ the Lord Is Risen Again, PH90* #112), J. S. Bach (various editions), and Hermann Schroeder (*Six Organ Chorales,* B. Schotts Söhne 2265).

2. *Resurrection,* King (AGO 90th Anniversary Anthology).
3. *Suite of Easter Hymns,* Emma L. Diemer (The Sacred Music Press KK 322).

Hymns for the Day	HL33	HB55	WB72	PH90
Christ the Lord Is Risen Today!	165	–	330	113
Come, Ye Faithful, Raise the Strain	168	205	344	114, 115
Guide Me, O Thou Great Jehovah	104	339	409	281
Jesus Christ Is Risen Today	163	204	440	123
O Sons and Daughters, Let Us Sing!	167	206	527	116
The Day of Resurrection	166	208	584	118
The Head That Once Was Crowned	195	211	589	149

EASTER EVENING (ABC)

Isaiah 25:6–9 One day the Lord of Hosts will make for all peoples a grand feast. The cloud of sorrow and troubles and death will vanish so that all tears shall succumb to laughter and joy, for YHWH has spoken.

Anthems

Day of Rejoicing, Walter Pelz (Augsburg) SATB trumpet (M). *To Thy Heavenly Banquet,* Alexis Lvov, arr. Westenberg (Walton) SATB (M). *We Have Waited for the Lord,* Richard Wienhorst (Concordia) SATB and handbells (ME).

1 Corinthians 5:6b-8 You are the new people of God by God's gracious act of salvation through the sacrifice of the Son, the true paschal lamb.

Anthems

Christ, Our Passover, Healey Willan (*A First Motet Book,* Concordia) SATB (E). *Christ Our Passover,* Richard Dirkson (H. W. Gray) SATB brass quartet (MD). *Christ Our Passover,* Ronald Arnatt (Augsburg) SATB (MD). *This Is the Feast of Victory,* Daniel Moe (*Ecumenical Praise,* number 13, Hope) unison (E).

Luke 24:13–49 Two of Jesus' followers walking from Jerusalem to Emmaus are joined by the risen Jesus, but they fail to recognize him. Astounded at his unawareness of events in Jerusalem, the two travelers relate their hopes concerning Jesus of Nazareth, who they thought was the one to redeem Israel, and their disillusionment upon his death on the cross. Jesus responds to their despair by interpreting the scriptures to them. Then they go into a home where at the table "Jesus took the bread and blessed, and broke it, and gave it to them. And their eyes were opened and they recognized him." The travelers immediately return to Jerusalem to tell others that "the Lord has risen." Then Jesus suddenly appears to his disciples. They are terrified. He shows them his hands and feet, eats some fish, and opens their minds about how the scriptures have been fulfilled.

Anthems

Stay with Us, Walter Pelz (Concordia) SATB flute (ME). *Breaking of the Bread,* Austin Lovelace (Hope) SATB (E). *This Joyful Eastertide,* Alec Wyton (H. W. Gray) SATB optional brass (ME).

Psalm 114

1. Metrical: *When Israel Came, and Judah's House.* Text: L.M., Christopher L. Webber, *ANMP,* p. 183.
2. Responsorial: *Psalm 114.* Text: Helen L. Wright. Refrain: Presbyterian 1. Tone: Lutheran 9. *PS93* #114.
3. Responsorial: *God Has Freed Us and Redeemed Us.* Text: Grail (see also *GPI,* p. 168). Refrain, psalm tone, and Gelineau tone: *WIII* #60.
4. Metrical: *When Israel Fled from Egypt Land.* Text: Henrietta Ten Harmsel. Tune: ANDRE. *PH87* #114.
5. Responsorial: Text optional: Psalm tone and refrain by Hal H. Hopson. *PR&T,* pp. 73 & 76.

Anthems

Psalm 114, Zoltan Kodaly (Boosey & Hawkes) SATB (MD). *When Israel Came Out of Israel,* S. S. Wesley (Novello) SATB/SATB (M).

Organ Music for the Day

1. O FILII ET FILIAE (*O Sons and Daughters, Let Us Sing!, PH90* #116), Nicolas Lebègue (*Les maîtres français de l'orgue aux XVII et XVIII siècles,* p. 14, Editions Musicales de la Schola Cantorum).
2. *Toccata on* O FILII ET FILIAE, Lynnwood Farnam (Theodore Presser Co. 113-25819).
3. *Prelude on* PUER NOBIS NASCITUR (*That Easter Day with Joy Was Bright, PH90* #121), Alexandre Guilmant (*Organ Music of Alexandre Guilmant,* vol. 2, McAfee Music Corp. DM 241).

Hymns for the Day	HL33	HB55	WB72	PH90
All Glory Be to God on High	–	–	283	133
Be Known to Us in Breaking Bread	356	446	–	505
Come, Risen Lord	–	–	340	503
Earth and All Stars	–	–	354	458
Hear the Good News of Salvation	–	–	–	355
O Sons and Daughters, Let Us Sing!	167	206	527	116, 117
O Love, How Deep, How Broad	139	–	518	83
Praise Ye the Lord, the Almighty	6	1	557	482
The Strife Is O'er, the Battle Done	164	203	597	119

SECOND SUNDAY OF EASTER (A)

Acts 2:14a, 22–32 A portion of Peter's Pentecost speech: God performed signs and wonders through Jesus' life and ministry to certify his divinity. Yet the lawless crucified Jesus (in the name of the law). But God freed him from death and raised him up. David himself said God would not abandon God's faithful servant in death (see Ps. 16:8–11).

Anthem
At God's Right Hand He Doth Stand, J. S. Bach (no. 2, *Christ lag in Todesbanden,* Cantata no. 4, Shawnee Press) SA (ME).

1 Peter 1:3–9 By God's mercy we who are baptized in Christ are born again to a living hope—that God keeps for us—through Christ's resurrection. Though you may suffer some trials now that test your faith, rejoice because God has brought about your rebirth. Let the genuineness of your faith praise and honor Jesus, in whom you believe without even seeing.

Anthem
Thy Name We Bless, O Risen Lord, Melchior Vulpius (Flammer) unison choir and SATB (E).

John 20:19–31 Verses 19–23 are a series of symbolic episodes. The risen Jesus appears to his frightened disciples and says, "Peace." Then he shows them his hands and his side (which fills the disciples with joy) and again says, "Peace." He gives them the Holy Spirit by breathing on them and concludes with an eschatological saying about resisting forgiveness. In verses 24–31, Thomas says he must see with his eyes before he will believe. So again Jesus appears. He tells Thomas to touch his side. Thomas confesses. Blessed are those who believe on the basis of the word alone.

Anthem
We Have Seen the Lord, Robert Wetzler (Augsburg) SATB soprano and bass solos (M). *We Walk by Faith and Not by Sight,* Samuel McFarland. Harmony, Richard Proulx. *PH90* #399.

Psalm 16
1. Metrical: *When in the Night I Meditate.* Text: *The Psalter,* 1912. Tune: ST. FLAVIAN. *PH90* #165. (See *HB55* #68 to the Tune: MAITLAND.)
2. Responsorial: *Psalm 16.* Text: Grail. Refrain: James E. Barrett. Tone: Gregorian II, alt. Accompaniment: Hal H. Hopson. *PS93* #10.
3. Responsorial: *Keep Me Safe, O God.* Text: Grail. (See also *GPI,* p. 15.) Refrain, psalm tone, and Gelineau tone: *WIII* #820, #839, & #903.

See also *CC* G-2405; *ANMP,* p. 47; *PH87* #16; *PR&T,* pp. 54 & 78.

Anthem
Preserve Me, O God, Joseph Goodman (Merrymount) SATB (ME).

Organ Music for the Day
1. VICTORY (*The Strife Is O'er, PH90* #119), C. S. Lang (*Festal Voluntaries—Easter,* p. 10, Novello 1402).
2. *An Easter Suite,* Gordon Young (Hope Publishing Co. 919).

Hymns for the Day	HL33	HB55	WB72	PH90
All Who Love and Serve Your City	–	–	293	413
He Did Not Want to Be Far	–	–	412	–
O Sons and Daughters, Let Us Sing!	167	206	527	116, 117
The Day of Resurrection!	166	208	584	118
Thine Is the Glory	–	209	–	122
We Walk by Faith and Not by Sight	–	–	–	399

THIRD SUNDAY OF EASTER (A)

Acts 2:14a, 36–41 The concluding segment of Peter's Pentecost speech: This Jesus whom you crucified is the one whom God raised from the dead and made Lord. "What shall we do?" cries the guilt-stricken crowd. Repent, and be baptized in the name of Christ for the forgiveness of your sins, and you shall receive the gift of the Holy Spirit.

Anthem
Brethren, We Have Met to Worship, arr. R. Currie (Choristers Guild, Lorenz) 2-part mixed (E).

1 Peter 1:17–23 Conduct yourselves in awe of the holy God, the impartial judge. For you know that Christ's death has ransomed you from your worthless ways, and that his incarnation marked the beginning of the last days according to God's eternal plan now manifested in Christ's resurrection.

Anthem
See That You Love One Another, Joseph Roff (H. W. Gray) SATB soprano solo (M).

Luke 24:13–35 Two of Jesus' followers walk from Jerusalem; they are joined by the risen Jesus, but their eyes prevent them from recognizing him. Since he seems unaware of recent events in Jerusalem, the two relate their hopes concerning Jesus, who they thought was the one to redeem Israel, and their disillusionment upon his death on the cross. Jesus responds to their despair by interpreting the scriptures to them. They go into a home where, at the table, "Jesus took the bread and blessed, and broke it, and gave it to them. And their eyes were opened and they recognized him." The travelers immediately return to Jerusalem to tell others that "the Lord has risen."

Anthem
Stay with Us, Walter Pelz (Concordia) SATB flute (ME).

Psalm 116:1–4, 12–19
1. Metrical: *O Thou, My Soul, Return in Peace.* Text: *Murrayfield Psalms* and *The Psalter,* 1912, alt. Tune: MARTYRDOM. *PH90* #228. (See also *RITL* #125.)
2. Responsorial: *Psalm 116.* Text: Helen L. Wright. Refrain: Richard T. Proulx. Tone: Saint Meinrad 1. *PS93* #115.
3. Responsorial: *Psalm 116* (12–19). Text: Helen L. Wright. Setting: Samuel Weber. *PS93* #116.

See also *SPJP,* p. 61; *WIII* #61, #791, #811, & #863; *PR&T,* pp. 24 & 25.

Anthem
What Shall I Render to My God? Austin Lovelace (Sacred Music Press) 2-part (E).

Organ Music for the Day
Chorale Prelude on LLANFAIR (*Christ the Lord Is Risen Today!,* PH90 #113), Hermann Schroeder (*The Parish Organist,* vol. 8, Concordia 97-1404), and Emma L. Diemer (*Suite of Easter Hymns,* p. 12, The Sacred Music Press KK 322).

Hymns for the Day	HL33	HB55	WB72	PH90
Baptized in the Water	–	–	–	492
Be Known to Us in Breaking Bread	356	446	356	505
Christ the Lord Is Risen Today!	165	–	330	113
Come, Christians, Join to Sing	191	131	333	150
O Sons and Daughters, Let Us Sing!	167	206	527	116, 117
That Easter Day with Joy Was Bright	–	–	581	121

FOURTH SUNDAY OF EASTER (A)

Acts 2:42–47 Luke's well-known idealized picture of the fourfold marks of apostolic church life—devoted study, fellowship, bread-breaking, and praying together—sounds like what we do today. But wait, there's a fifth mark: They sold all their possessions, redistributed their money according to human need, and shared everything in common. Result: The Lord daily added to their community those who were being saved.

Anthem
We Are Your People, Lord, by Your Grace, John W. Wilson, *PH90* #436.

1 Peter 2:19–25 You will be blessed for your innocent suffering on behalf of your faith. After all, the shepherd Christ himself suffered unjustly for you—he bore your sins in his body on the cross and gave his life for all lost sheep, which made possible new life.

Anthem
Greater Love Hath No Man, John Ireland (Galaxy) SATB with soprano, bass solo (M).

John 10:1–10 The first six verses depict Jesus as the single gate to the sheepfold. Through this one gate is the only proper way for the sheep to enter. The last four verses depict Jesus both as the true shepherd whose voice the sheep will obey and as the sole gate leading to salvation for all sheep.

Anthems
I Am the Good Shepherd, Dale Wood (Augsburg) unison (E). *I Am the Good Shepherd,* Thomas Matthews (Presser) 2-part (E).

Psalm 23
1. Metrical: *The Lord's My Shepherd, All My Need.* Text: C.M., Christopher L. Webber. Tune: EVAN. *PH90* #175.
2. Responsorial: *Psalm 23.* Text: Grail. Gelineau tone. *PS93* #18.
3. Responsorial: *Psalm 23.* Text: International Commission on English in the Liturgy. Setting: Howard Hughes. *PS93* #19.
4. Responsorial: *Psalm 23.* Setting: Hal H. Hopson. *PS93* #20.
5. Metrical: *The King of Love My Shepherd Is.* Text: Henry Williams Baker. Tune: ST. COLUMBA. *PH90* #171. (See also *HB55* #106.)
6. Responsorial: *The Lord Is My Shepherd.* Text: *Book of Common Prayer,* 1976. Music: Peter R. Hallock. *TIP/PSCY* #12.

See also *PH90* #172, #173, #174, & #175; *PR&T,* pp. 72 & 77.

Anthem
The Lord Is My Shepherd, John Rutter (Oxford) SATB (MD).
Psalm 23, Michael Hennagin (Walton) SATB (M).

Organ Music for the Day
The King of Love My Shepherd Is (ST. COLUMBA, *PH90* #171), Robin Milford (*Wedding Music,* vol. 2, Concordia 97-1370), and Kenneth Leighton (*Six Fantasies on Hymn Tunes,* Basil Ramsey Publisher of Music).

Hymns for the Day	HL33	HB55	WB72	PH90
God, Be Merciful to Me	–	282	–	–
Lord Christ, When First You Came	–	–	–	7
O for a World	–	–	–	386
Savior, Like a Shepherd Lead Us	458	380	–	387
There's a Wideness in God's Mercy	93	110	601	298
You Servants of God	198	27	645	477

FIFTH SUNDAY OF EASTER (A)

Acts 7:55–60 Obeying Christ, and unconcerned about building his own success-ful ministry, Stephen faithfully preaches the word of God. His listeners respond to the word of God by becoming enraged, shaking their fists and hurling verbal epithets, as well as stones and rocks, after checking their hats and coats with Saul. But Stephen, faithful to the end, dies as a servant of Christ, forgiving his stoners, for they know not what they do.

Anthem
When Stephen Full of Power and Grace, Richard Peek (H. W. Gray) SATB (E).

1 Peter 2:2–10 Once you were nobodies, but God has called you out of darkness into his own marvelous light. Why? To declare, to witness about God's mercy re-vealed in Jesus Christ, the keystone that holds all together yet is a stumbling block for the world.

Anthem
God's Own People, Jane Marshall (H. W. Gray) SATB (ME).

John 14:1–14 Jesus' departure means his return to the Father. "But where are you going?" asks Peter. "To prepare a place for you all," replies Jesus, "where there are enough rooms for everyone. Be not afraid, I'll return to take you all." Thomas quickly speaks out: "But we don't know the way." "I am the way to the Father," says Jesus. "Then show us," Philip pleads. "Whoever has seen me has seen the Fa-ther," says Jesus.

Anthems
The Call, Ralph Vaughan Williams (Galaxy) SATB (MD). *Come My Way, My Truth, My Life,* Philip Dietterich (H. W. Gray) SATB (ME).

Psalm 31:1–5, 15–16
1. Metrical: *In You, Lord, I Have Put My Trust.* Text: Adam Reissner, trans. Cather-ine Winkworth. Tune: IN DICH HAB' ICH GEHOFFET. *PH90* #183.
2. Responsorial: *Psalm 31* (9–16). Text: Grail. Refrain and psalm tone by Hal H. Hopson. *PH90* #182.
3. Responsorial: *Psalm 31* (1–16). Text: Grail. Setting: Hal H. Hopson. *PS93* #28.
See also *WIII* #35; *ANMP,* p. 71; *PH87* #31; *PR&T,* pp. 42 & 48.

Anthem
In Thee, Lord, Have I Put My Trust, Halsey Stevens (C. F. Peters) SATB, some di-visi (M).

Organ Music for the Day
Sing Praise to God, Who Reigns Above (MIT FREUDEN ZART, *PH90* #483), Ernst Pep-ping (*Grosses Orgelbuch,* vol. 3, Schott 3731), and Distler (*Short Chorales,* Op. 8, Bärenreiter).

Hymns for the Day	HL33	HB55	WB72	PH90
Blessing and Honor and Glory and Power	196	137	311	147
Christ Is Made the Sure Foundation	336	433	325	416, 417
He Is the Way	–	–	413	–
Here, O Lord, Your Servants Gather	–	–	417	465
Lead On, O King Eternal	371	332	448	447, 448
Sing Praise to God, Who Reigns Above	–	15	568	483
When Stephen, Full of Power and Grace	–	–	638	–

SIXTH SUNDAY OF EASTER (A)

Acts 17:22–31 Paul preaches the gospel to some Athenians. Appealing first to the common ground of human yearning to worship God, Paul defines who their unknown God is. God is Creator of all, who lives not in any human-made shrines nor needs anything the creatures can make, since God is the giver of all life and breath. The way to know God is through Jesus Christ, who was crucified but raised from death.

Anthem

O Speak to Me of Jesus' Sorrow, Johann G. Gebhard (Carl Fischer) SATB (M).

1 Peter 3:13–22 A rhetorical question begins this text: Would anyone harm a righteous person? No? Well that's precisely why the readers of this letter are suffering. Maybe suffering for your faith is a possibility. So be fearless, be prepared, maintain the right relationship with God, and the world will be put to shame and God will be glorified. For Christ himself suffered—he died for your sins—but he was resurrected and exalted.

Anthem

We Know That Christ Is Raised, C. V. Stanford, *PH90* #495 unison.

John 14:15–21 "Whoever loves me keeps my commandments," says Jesus. How do you do that in a world without Jesus to tell us what to do? Tell his teachings to one another, interpret his teachings for our own age, live out his teachings in relation to one another. Amazingly, that's just what the Holy Spirit prompts in us, and that's why Jesus promised to send us another "companion interpreter."

Anthem

If Ye Love Me, Keep My Commandments, Thomas Tallis (G. Schirmer) SATB (M).

Psalm 66:8–20

1. Metrical: *Be Joyful, All You Lands, in God.* Text: C.M., Christopher L. Webber. *ANMP,* p. 109.
2. Responsorial: *Psalm 66* (1–8). Text: *A New Zealand Prayer Book.* Setting: Richard T. Proulx. *PS93* #57.
3. Responsorial: *Psalm 66:8–20.* Text: *A New Zealand Prayer Book.* Setting: Richard T. Proulx. *PS93* #58.

See also *WIII* #848; *PH87* #66; *HB55* #296; *PR&T,* pp. 66 & 77.

Anthem

The Voice of His Praise, Malcolm Williamson (from *Psalms of the Elements,* Boosey & Hawkes) unison and congregation (E).

Organ Music for the Day

Prelude on HYFRYDOL (*Love Divine, All Loves Excelling, PH90* #376), Gerre Hancock (H. W. Gray Co., Inc. GSTC 1006), Henry Coleman (*A Book of Hymn Tune Voluntaries,* p. 20, Oxford University Press 375115-1), and Gerald Near (*Preludes on Four Hymn Tunes,* p. 9, Augsburg 11-828).

Hymns for the Day	HL33	HB55	WB72	PH90
Christ of the Upward Way	277	295	–	344
Come Down, O Love Divine	–	–	334	313
Holy Spirit, Truth Divine	208	240	422	321
Love Divine, All Loves Excelling	308	399	471	376
Rejoice, the Lord Is King	193	140	562	155

THE ASCENSION OF THE LORD (ABC)

Acts 1:1–11 Jesus charges the apostles to wait in Jerusalem for "the promise of the Father," which is the gift of the Holy Spirit. The apostles ask the risen Jesus if he will now restore the kingdom to Israel. "That's not your worry but God's," replies Jesus. "You'll receive power when the Holy Spirit comes, and then you shall be my witnesses, proclaiming the gospel everywhere." Then Jesus is lifted up and departs on a cloud.

Anthems

The Lord Ascendeth Up on High, Leo Sowerby (Sacred Music) SATB (ME). *Sing We Triumphant Hymns of Praise,* Erik Routley (Hinshaw) SATB, congregation and brass (ME). *O for a Shout of Sacred Joy,* Alice Parker (E. C. Schirmer) SATB snare drum (ME). Hal H. Hopson (Augsburg) 2-part mixed (E). *Christ Is Alive, PH90* #108.

Ephesians 1:15–23 May God give you the Spirit who will make you wise and understanding in the knowledge of Christ. In this way you will know the hope to which Christ has called you (the kind of New Age that is coming), and can recognize God's power among us, especially his power in raising Christ to a position above all earthly powers.

Anthems

Alleluia, Sing to Jesus, Hal H. Hopson (Augsburg) 2-part (E). *Look, Ye Saints, the Sight Is Glorious,* Robert Wetzler (Augsburg) SAB (ME).

Luke 24:44–53 Jesus preaches a kerygmatic sermon on Christ as Lord and the message of repentance and forgiveness. He then constitutes his disciples as the New Israel, promises them the gift of the Spirit, and ascends.

Anthems

The Friends of Christ Together, WB72 #586. *Alleluia! Sing to Jesus, PH90* #144. *O God, the King of Glory,* Henry Purcell (*Anthems for Choirs,* vol. 1, Oxford) SATB (M).

Psalm 47

1. Metrical: *Peoples, Clap Your Hands!* Text: *The Psalter,* 1912. Tune: GENEVAN PSALTER. *PH90* #194. (See also *PH87* #47.)
2. Responsorial: *Psalm 47.* Text: International Commission on English in the Liturgy. Music: Hal H. Hopson. *PS93* #42.
3. Responsorial: *Sing Praise to Our King.* Text: Grail (see also *GPI,* p. 65). Refrain, psalm tone, and Gelineau tone: *WIII* #40. (See also *WIII* #851.)
4. Metrical: *People Gather Round.* Text: Marie J. Post. Tune: PSALM 45. General Psalter. *RITL* #103.

See also *ANMP,* p. 97; *CS/PFTCY,* vol. 1, p. 51; *20P&3C,* p. 14; *PR&T,* pp. 32 & 33.

Anthems

God Has Gone Up, Jack C. Goode (H. W. Gray) SATB (M). *Clap Your Hands,* Carlton Young (Broadman) unison and 2-part (E). *O Clap Your Hands,* John Rutter (Oxford) SATB (MD). *O Clap Your Hands,* Ralph Vaughan Williams (Galaxy) SATB optional brass and percussion (M). *Clap Your Hands,* Michael Jothen (Broude) SATB (ME).

or **Psalm 93** (Years A&B)

1. Metrical: *God, Our Lord, a King Remaining.* Text: John Keble. Tune: BRYN CALFARIA. *PH90* #213. (See also *HB55* #90 and *RITL* #117.)
2. Responsorial: *Psalm 93* (1–2, 5). Text: International Commission on English in the Liturgy, New American Bible. Setting: J. Gerald Phillips. *PS93* #87.
3. Responsorial: *The Lord Is King for Evermore.* Refrain, psalm tone, and Gelineau tone: *WIII* #50 (see also *WIII* #965; for alternate refrain and psalm tone see *24P&1C,* p. 21).

4. Metrical: *The Lord Is King, Enthroned.* Text: *The Psalter,* 1912, alt. Tune: RIALTO. *PH87* #93. See also *The Lord Is King.* Text: Clarence P. Walhout. Tune: GENEVAN 93. *PH87* #172.

See also *ANMP,* p. 152; *SPJP,* p. 48; *PR&T,* pp. 60 & 61.

Anthems

The Lord Reigneth, Paul Manz (Augsburg) SATB (M). *The Lord Is Ruler,* Johann Geisler (Boosey & Hawkes) SSAB (M). *God, Our Lord, a King Remaining,* W. Owen, *PH90* #213.

or **Psalm 110** (Year C)

1. Metrical: *The Lord Unto My Lord Has Said.* Text: *The Psalter,* 1912, alt. Tune: ALL SAINTS NEW. *PH87* #110.
2. Responsorial: *The Lord's Revelation to My Master.* Text: Grail. Refrain, psalm tone, and Gelineau tone: *WIII* #864. (See also *20P&3C,* p. 24.)
3. Responsorial: *The Lord Said to My Lord.* Setting: Betty Pulkingham (with flute) *CTCY,* p. 50.

Anthem

Dixit Dominus, W. A. Mozart (*Solemn Vespers,* K.339, Lawson Gould) English translation, SATB (M).

Organ Music for the Day

1. *Prelude on* DIADEMATA (*Crown Him with Many Crowns, PH90* #151), Flor Peeters (*Thirty Short Preludes on Well-Known Hymns,* p. 7, C. F. Peters Corp. 6195), and Wilbur Held (*Hymn Preludes for the Pentecost Season,* Concordia 97-5517).
2. *The Ascension Suite,* Messiaen (Leduc).
3. *Prelude on* KING'S WESTON (*At the Name of Jesus, PH90* #148), Richard Wienhorst, and Herbert Gotsch (*The Concordia Hymn Prelude Series,* vol. 15, Concordia 97-5706).

Hymns for the Day	HL33	HB55	WB72	PH90
A Hymn of Glory Let Us Sing	–	–	–	141
Alleluia! Sing to Jesus!	–	–	–	144
All Hail the Power of Jesus' Name!	192	132	285	142, 143
Blessing and Honor and Glory and Power	196	137	311	147
Christ, Above All Glory Seated	–	–	324	–
Christ, Whose Glory Fills the Skies	26	47	332	462, 463
Crown Him with Many Crowns	190	213	349	151
Jesus Shall Reign	377	496	443	423
Lord, Enthroned in Heavenly Splendor	–	–	–	154
Open My Eyes That I May See	–	–	–	324
Our King and Our Sovereign, Lord Jesus	–	–	–	157

SEVENTH SUNDAY OF EASTER (A)

Acts 1:6–14 In vss. 6–11, the apostles ask the risen Jesus if he will now restore the kingdom to Israel. "That's not your worry but God's," replies Jesus. "You will receive power when the Holy Spirit comes, and then you shall be my witnesses proclaiming the gospel everywhere." Then Jesus is lifted up and departs on a cloud, while the apostles stand gazing at the sky. "Why are you apostles standing there looking at the sky?" ask two angels. "Jesus will return the same way he departed. So get on with your ministry here and now." In vss. 12–14, the apostles return to Jerusalem and gather in the upper room.

Anthem
You Men of Galilee, Edmund Martens (Concordia) unison, handbells (E).

1 Peter 4:12–14; 5:6–11 Rejoice in your sufferings as a Christian. You shouldn't be surprised at this test of your faith, for suffering belongs to Christ, whose way you are called to follow. So when you suffer for your faith, you know that's a sign of God's blessing. Be alert, be firm in your faith because enemies are seeking to devour you, but after your suffering, God will bring all to perfection.

Anthem
Awake, My Heart, Jane Marshall (H. W. Gray) SATB (ME).

John 17:1–11 Jesus reveals to us not only God but God's will for us. Christ is gone now, but the church is here to show the world what God's will is. No wonder Christ prays for the church. If the church is to show God's will, then the church must be unified and faithful.

Anthems
Celebrate the Good News!, Tom Mitchell (Choristers Guild, Lorenz) 2-part, optional handbells and string bass. *To the Glory of Our King,* Robert Leaf (Choristers Guild, Lorenz) unison (E).

Psalm 68:1–10, 32–35
1. Metrical: *Great God, Arise.* Text: Norman Kansfield. Tune: GENEVAN 68. *RITL* #109.
2. Responsorial: *Psalm 68:1–10, 32–35.* Text: Helen L. Wright. Melody: Columba Kelly. Harmony, Samuel Weber. *PS93* #61.

See also *ANMP,* p. 111; *PR&T,* pp. 59 & 66.

Anthem
Let God Arise, Malcolm Williamson (from *Psalms of the Elements,* Boosey & Hawkes) unison and congregation (E).

Organ Music for the Day
1. *Prelude on* DARWALL'S 148TH (*Rejoice, the Lord Is King, PH90* #155), Percy Whitlock (*Six Hymn Preludes,* Oxford University Press 375902-0).
2. *Prelude on* DEO GRACIAS (*A Hymn of Glory Let Us Sing, PH90* #141), Gordon Young (*Fourteen Pieces for Organ,* The Sacred Music Press KK 111).

Hymns for the Day	HL33	HB55	WB72	PH90
A Hymn of Glory Let Us Sing	–	–	273	141
Alleluia! Sing to Jesus!	–	–	–	144
All Hail the Power of Jesus' Name!	192	132	285	142, 143
Crown Him with Many Crowns	190	213	349	151
Give to the Winds Thy Fears	294	364	377	286
Jesus Shall Reign	377	496	443	423

Pentecost
THE DAY OF PENTECOST (A)

Acts 2:1–21 Wind and tongues of fire—the Holy Spirit—descend and spread among all the believers. Are they drunk? "No," says Peter, "it's only nine in the morning. But while I have your attention, let me tell you about Jesus Christ."

Anthems

Introit for Pentecost, John Weaver (Boosey & Hawkes) SATB (ME). *Whitsunday Canticle,* Erik Routley (*Two for Pentecost,* Hinshaw) SATB (ME).

or **Numbers 11:24–30** Around the tent, Moses gathers seventy elders of the people. YHWH descends in a cloud, speaks to Moses, takes some of the spirit given to Moses and spreads it among the seventy who, except for Eldad and Medad, then prophesy but once.

Anthem

Forth in Thy Name, O Lord, David H. Williams (Shawnee Press) SATB (ME).

1 Corinthians 12:3b–13 The Spirit bestows different gifts to each person, but all are from one and the same Spirit.

Anthem

Therefore, Give Us Love, Daniel Moe (Augsburg) 2-part mixed (E).

or **Acts 2:1–21** See above.

John 20:19–23 A series of symbolic episodes: The risen Jesus appears to his frightened disciples and says, "Peace." Then he shows them his hands and his side (which fills the disciples with joy) and again says, "Peace." He gives them the Holy Spirit by breathing on them, and concludes with an eschatological saying about resisting forgiveness.

Anthem

Peace Be with You, Robert Wetzler (Art Masters) SATB (M).

or **John 7:37–39** Jesus stands up in the Temple court and proclaims that he is the source of living water.

Anthem

O Love Divine, Benedetto Marcello, arr. Douglas Wagner SAB (ME).

Psalm 104:24–34, 35b
1. Metrical: *Bless the Lord with All My Being.* Text: 8.7.8.7.D, Fred R. Anderson. Tune: RUSTINGTON. *PH90* #224. For text only see *SPJP,* p. 56.
2. Responsorial: *Psalm 104* (1–9). Text: Grail. Tone and Refrain: Presbyterian 3. *PS93* #104.
3. Responsorial: *Psalm 104* (24, 27–34). Text: Arlo D. Duba. Setting: Richard T. Proulx. *PS93* #105.
4. Responsorial: *Lord, Send Out Your Spirit.* Setting: Robert Edward Smith. *CC* G-2122.
5. Responsorial: *O Lord, How Manifold Are Your Works!* Text: *Book of Common Prayer.* Music: Peter R. Hallock. *TIP/PSCY* #10.

See also *ANMP,* p. 174; *PH87* #104; *WIII* #855 & #856; *PR&T,* pp. 34 & 35.

Anthem

The Glory of the World, Jack Goode (H. W. Gray) SATB (M).

Organ Music for the Day
1. *Prélude, Adagio et Choral Varié,* VENI CREATOR, Maurice Duruflé (Durand & Cie).
2. *Prelude on* VENI CREATOR SPIRITUS (or KOMM GOTT SCHÖPFER), (*Come, Holy Spirit, Our Souls Inspire, PH90* #125), J. S. Bach (various editions).

Hymns for the Day	HL33	HB55	WB72	PH90
Breathe on Me, Breath of God	213	235	–	316
Come, Holy Spirit, Heavenly Dove	206	239	–	126
Come, Holy Spirit, Our Souls Inspire	–	237	335	125
O Spirit of the Living God	207	242	528	–
Spirit Divine, Attend Our Prayers	212	243	574	325
Spirit of God, Unleashed on Earth	–	–	–	124
The Day of Pentecost Arrived	–	–	583	–
Wind Who Makes All Winds That Blow	–	–	–	131

Ordinary Time
TRINITY SUNDAY
[FIRST SUNDAY AFTER PENTECOST] (A)

Genesis 1:1–2:4a All was dark upon the formless, chaotic, unordered waters of creation. God spoke a word, and there was light. When God speaks, action occurs. God spoke again and again, and there was firmament-dome (or sky), dry land, vegetation, lights (sun, moon, and stars), living beings, animal life and, finally, human beings—a community of male and female. And God saw that all of creation was very good. Chaos is transformed into cosmos by the majesty and mystery of God, whose will for creation is unity and harmony.

Anthem
My Crown of Creation, Charles W. Ore (Morningstar) SATB (ME).

2 Corinthians 13:11–13 A series of pastoral charges to the community of faith, and the well-known and often-used triadic liturgical formula, conclude this letter.

Anthem
Grant Us Thy Peace, Felix Mendelssohn (Boosey & Hawkes) SATB (E).

Matthew 28:16–20 An account of the Great Commission, in which the exalted Jesus appears to his followers on a mountaintop and, in his lordly authority, charges them to "make disciples of *all* nations, baptizing them . . . and teaching them all I have commanded you." The fulfillment of this mission depends not on human authority or ingenuity but on the promised continuing presence of the Lord.

Anthems
Lo, I Am with You, Daniel Moe (Augsburg) SATB (MD). *Go Ye Into All the World,* Robert Wetzler (Augsburg) 2-part mixed (E).

Psalm 8
1. Metrical: *O Lord, Our God, How Excellent.* Text: Fred R. Anderson. Tune: WINCHESTER OLD. *PH90* #162. For text only see *SPJP,* p. 15.
2. Responsorial: *Psalm 8.* Setting: Hal H. Hopson. *PS93* #5.
3. Metrical: *Lord, Our Lord, Thy Glorious Name.* Text: *The Psalter* 1912, alt. Tune: GOTT SEI DANK DURCH ALLE WELT. *PH90* #163. (See also *RITL* #83 to the Tune: SAVANNAH.)
See also *HB55* #95; *WIII* #861; *ANMP,* p. 44; *PR&T,* pp. 37 & 52.

Anthems
How Excellent Is Thy Name, Howard Hanson (C. Fischer) SATB (MD). *How Excellent Is Your Name,* Robert Wetzler ("Blizzard Anthems 2," AMSI) 2-part (E).

Organ Music for the Day
1. *Prelude on* NICAEA (*Holy, Holy, Holy!, PH90* #138), Peter Hurford (*Chorale Preludes on English Tunes,* Oxford University Press 375135–6).
2. *Chorale Prelude on* WIR GLAUBEN ALL' AN EINEN GOTT (*We All Believe in One True God, PH90* #137), J. S. Bach (various editions).

Hymns for the Day	HL33	HB55	WB72	PH90
All Creatures of Our God and King	–	100	282	455
God, Who Stretched the Spangled . . .	–	–	–	268
Holy God, We Praise Your Name	–	–	420	460
Holy, Holy, Holy!	57	245	421	138
I Sing the Mighty Power of God	65	84	628	288
Lord, You Give the Great Commission	–	–	–	429

SUNDAY BETWEEN MAY 29 AND JUNE 4
(PROPER 4) [9] (A) [*USE ONLY IF AFTER TRINITY SUNDAY*]*

Genesis 6:9–22; 7:24; 8:14–19 The rebellion (sin) against God by God's creatures leads creation to disorder, disharmony, and disunity. YHWH, therefore, decides to destroy all except Noah and his family by releasing the death-dealing power of water. Then Noah and his descendants and all living beings leave the ark so they may be fruitful and multiply.

Anthem
If Thou but Suffer God to Guide Thee, Jody Lindh (Concordia) 2-part (E).

Romans 1:16–17; 3:22b–28, (29–31) Sometimes the good news can be bad news. For those living under the illusion that good deeds and obedience to the law can gain and preserve God's acceptance, Paul's words are offensive. He says we all are sinners, but by the free gift of God's grace all gain God's acceptance through Christ Jesus. You can rely only on the mercy and graciousness of God offered to all through Christ. Such news may be frightening, because we can no longer boast about being righteous. God is the righteous one who justifies us through love for us.

Anthem
The Prayers I Make, Jane Marshall (Sacred Music Press) 2-part mixed (E).

Matthew 7:21–29 Evildoers who do mighty works and faith healings in the name of Christ shall not enter the kingdom of heaven because Christ never knew them. Those who hear *and* obey Christ's words are like those who build stone houses on a rock base, and those who do not hear and obey are like those who build mud houses in an arroyo. The crowds were astonished at Jesus' teaching, for he taught with authority.

Anthem
Built on a Rock, S. Drummond Wolff (Concordia) SATB.

Psalm 46
1. Metrical: *God, Our Help and Constant Refuge.* Text: 8.7.8.7.3.3.7, Fred R. Anderson. Tune: MICHAEL. *PH90* #192.
2. Responsorial: The Lord of Hosts Is with Us. Text: NRSV. Psalm tone: Richard Proulx, 1986. *PH90* #193.
See also *PS93* #40 & #41; *PH90* #191; *PH87* #46; *PR&T*, pp. 58 & 76.

Anthem
God Is Our Strength and Refuge, Philip Landgrave (Hope) unison (E).

Organ Music for the Day
1. *Prelude on* WINCHESTER OLD (*God Is Our Refuge and Our Strength*—Psalm 46, *PH90* #191), Flor Peeters (*30 Short Preludes on Well-Known Hymns,* p. 36, C. F. Peters Corp. 6195).
2. *Postlude on* MICHAEL (*God, Our Help and Constant Refuge*—Psalm 46, *PH90* #192), Arthur Wills (Royal School of Church Music 06).

Hymns for the Day	HL33	HB55	WB72	PH90
In Christ There Is No East or West	341	479	435	439, 440
My Hope Is Built on Nothing Less	–	368	–	379
O God, Beneath Your Guiding Hand	462	523	495	–
O God of Bethel, by Whose Hand	98	342	496	269

---

*NOTE: If the Sunday between May 24 and May 28 follows Trinity Sunday, use readings for the Sunday between February 25 and 29 (A) on that day.

SUNDAY BETWEEN JUNE 5 AND JUNE 11
(PROPER 5) [10] (A) [*USE ONLY IF AFTER TRINITY SUNDAY*]

Genesis 12:1–9 YHWH chooses a barren, landless, futureless couple and promises descendants, land, and a future in which their name will be magnified. Abram faithfully embraces YHWH's promises and begins his pilgrimage of wandering in the new land.

Anthem
Prayer, Alice Parker (Lawson-Gould) Double SATB (M).

Romans 4:13–25 For trusting the promises of God, who justifies the impious and the irreligious, people receive God's free gift of grace. Look at Abraham, who was justified not by works but by grace through faith. God's promise to Abraham and all his descendants is guaranteed solely by God's free grace. There is absolutely no way you can earn God's promise, especially by good works or adherence to the law. Abraham trusted God to do what he promised. That's faith.

Anthem
God of the Promise, Richard Hillert (Augsburg) SATB (ME).

Matthew 9:9–13, 18–26 Jesus not only calls a tax collector (i.e., racketeer) to follow him, but sits down to a meal with a host of outcasts and sinners. Why does Jesus eat with such disreputable, immoral people? "Because," replies Jesus, "I have not come to call the respectable, righteous people, but sinners." Imagine that! There's room at Christ's table for all who hear Christ's words and know they can let go of their self-righteousness and enter as forgiven sinners.

Anthems
He Did Not Wait, Ronald Melrose (Carl Fischer) SAB (M). *Immortal Love, Forever Full,* Crawford R. Thoburn (Coronet) SATB (E).

Psalm 33:1–12
1. Metrical: *How Blest the People God the Lord.* Text: C.M., Christopher L. Webber. *ANMP,* p. 79.
2. Responsorial: *Lord, Let Your Mercy Be on Us.* Text: NRSV. Psalm tone: Laurence Bevenot, 1987. Refrain: Richard Proulx, 1987. *PH90* #185.
3. Responsorial: *Psalm 33* (1–22). Text: *The United Methodist Liturgical Psalter.* Refrain and Tone: Presbyterian 2. *PS93* #30.
4. Responsorial: *Psalm 33* (12a, 15–22). Setting: Hal H. Hopson. *PS93* #31.
5. Responsorial: *The Earth Is Full.* Setting by Robert E. Kreutz. *CC* G-2490.
See also *PH87* #33; *PR&T,* pp. 52 & 53.

Anthem
O Fear the Lord, Ye His Saints, Dale Wood (Augsburg) SATB (E).

Organ Music for the Day
Chorale Prelude on WAS GOTT TUT (*O God, What You Ordain Is Right, PH90* #284), settings by Walther, Kellner, and Krebs (*The Church Organist's Golden Treasury,* vol. 3, pp. 119–28, Oliver Ditson Co.).

Hymns for the Day	HL33	HB55	WB72	PH90
Come, Thou Fount of Every Blessing	235	379	341	356
Great God, We Sing That Mighty Hand	470	527	408	265
Jesus Calls Us	223	269	439	–
We Come as Guests Invited	–	–	–	517
Whate'er Our God Ordains Is Right	291	366	633	284

SUNDAY BETWEEN JUNE 12 AND JUNE 18
(PROPER 6) [11] (A) [*USE ONLY IF AFTER TRINITY SUNDAY*]

Genesis 18:1–15, (21:1–7) In the heat of the day, Abraham sits in the shade of his tent. Three strangers approach, so he serves them an on-the-spot banquet. When one of them promises that Sarah will bear a son, she laughs to herself. YHWH, however, knowing of Sarah's skepticism, rebukes her. Sarah denies that she laughed, for she is afraid. But YHWH insists she did laugh and, therefore, reaffirms the promise (cf. 12:1–3) which, despite ongoing obstacles, is fulfilled in the birth of Isaac (21:1–7).

Anthem
God Is Our Life, D. Scarlatti, adapted by H. Lowe (Choristers Guild) unison (E).

Romans 5:1–8 Since we are justified by faith, we are at peace with God. So let's stand up straight and rejoice, for "God has poured out his love into our hearts through the Holy Spirit." While we were sinning against God by resisting and seeking to destroy the Son, God "reconciled us to God's self" through the death of the Son. At the cross, we are overwhelmed by the incredible depth of God's love for us.

Anthem
Lord, Grant Grace, Orlando Gibbons (Concordia) SATB/SATB (M).

Matthew 9:35–10:8, (9–23) Jesus has visited "cities and villages," teaching, preaching, and healing. What Jesus experienced was helpless people, sheep without a shepherd, a bountiful harvest without enough reapers. So Jesus invites his disciples to pray for laborers to bring in the harvest; then he commissions the Twelve with his authority to preach the same message he preaches (cf. Matt. 4:17) to the lost sheep of Israel, and to perform the same signs of the kingdom that he performs.

Anthem
The Lord Gave the Word, G. F. Handel (*Messiah,* any edition) SATB (M).

Psalm 116:1–2, 12–19
1. Metrical: *O Thou, My Soul, Return in Peace.* Text: *Murrayfield Psalms* and *The Psalter,* 1912, alt. Tune: MARTYRDOM. *PH90* #228. (See also *RITL* #125.)
2. Responsorial: *Psalm 116.* Text: Helen L. Wright. Refrain: Richard T. Proulx. Tone: Saint Meinrad 1. *PS93* #115.
See also *PS93* #116; *WIII* #61, #791, #811, & #863; *PR&T*, pp. 24 & 25.

Anthem
What Shall I Render to My God, Austin Lovelace (Canyon) SATB (E).

Organ Music for the Day
Prelude on DUNDEE (*O God of Bethel, by Whose Hand, PH90* #269), settings by C. Hubert H. Parry (*Seven Chorale Preludes,* Novello & Co., Ltd. 1546), and Flor Peeters (*Hymn Preludes for the Liturgical Year,* C. F. Peters Corp. 6412).

Hymns for the Day	HL33	HB55	WB72	PH90
Amazing Grace	–	275	296	280
All Glory Be to God on High	–	–	283	133
Come, Labor On	366	287	–	415
God of Bethel, by Whose Hand	98	342	496	269
O Love, How Deep, How Broad	139	–	518	83
Praise Ye the Lord, the Almighty	6	1	557	482

SUNDAY BETWEEN JUNE 19 AND JUNE 25
(PROPER 7) [12] (A) [*USE ONLY IF AFTER TRINITY SUNDAY*]

Genesis 21:8–21 A story of anguished settlement, and also of God's mercy. Though jealousy and fear seem to motivate Sarah's demand for Hagar and Ishmael's expulsion, God assures Abraham that "as for the son of the slave woman, I will make a nation of him also." In the wilderness, mother and son suffer, death hovers. But, through God's abiding presence, not only are they saved, but Ishmael marries an Egyptian woman. Despite ongoing obstacles, the promises of God (21:13) advance.

Anthem
Like as a Father, Luigi Cherubini, arr. Austin Lovelace (Choristers Guild) 3-part canon for children and adults (E).

Romans 6:1–11 Why not continue in sin so God's grace and glory may overflow? Responds Paul, "How can we who died to sin still live in it? When we were baptized into union with Christ, we became one with him in death and were set free from the power of sin; then we were raised with Christ to new life. So our old being is dead to sin, and we now have a new life in Christ."

Anthem
God's Son Has Made Me Free, Edvard Grieg, arr. by Overby (Augsburg) SATB (MD).

Matthew 10:24–39 Disciples, expect to receive the same response and treatment as your master. There is nothing to fear—the worst they can do is to kill you. So shout what I whisper to you, and boldly face the consequences, knowing you are ultimately under God's care.

Anthem
Thee Will I Love, My Strength, My Tower, Craig Courtney (Beckenhorst) SATB (ME).

Psalm 86:1–10, 16–17
1. Metrical: *To My Humble Supplication.* Text: J. Bryan, c. 1620. Tune: GENEVAN. Harmony, Gustav Holst. *RITL* #111.
2. Responsorial: *Psalm 86.* Text: Grail. Refrain: John Schiavone. Gelineau tone. *PS93* #79.
3. Responsorial: *Lord, You Are Good and Forgiving.* Text: Grail. Psalm tone and Gelineau tone: *WIII* #910.
See also *PH87* #86; *ANMP,* p. 137.

Anthem
Comfort, O Lord, the Soul of Thy Servant, William Crotch (Novello) SATB (ME).

Organ Music for the Day
Prelude on ST. BRIDE (*Give to the Winds Thy Fears, PH90* #286), settings by Healey Willan (*Thirty-Six Short Preludes and Postludes on Well-Known Hymn Tunes,* vol. 2, C. F. Peters Corp. 6162), and Flor Peeters (*Hymn Preludes for the Liturgical Year,* vol. 19, C. F. Peters Corp. 6419).

Hymns for the Day	*HL33*	*HB55*	*WB72*	*PH90*
Baptized in Water	–	–	–	492
Give to the Winds Thy Fears	294	364	377	286
God of Our Life	88	108	395	275
Great Is Thy Faithfulness	–	–	–	276
Take Up Your Cross, the Savior Said	–	293	–	393
There's a Wideness in God's Mercy	93	110	601	298

SUNDAY BETWEEN JUNE 26 AND JULY 2
(PROPER 8) [13] (A)

Genesis 22:1–14 God tests Abraham to find out whether Abraham trusts only God's promise. "Give up your only son," summons God—a repugnant, disturbing test—yet Abraham faithfully obeys. Asks Isaac, "Where is the lamb?" "God will provide," replies Abraham, and an angel of the Lord cries out, "Now I know you trust only God's promise because you have not withheld from God that which is most precious to you." Miraculously, God provides a ram for the offering and again blesses Abraham.

Anthem
On God and Not on Human Trust, Johann Pachelbel (Concordia) SATB (M).

Romans 6:12–23 The seemingly naive, but true, proposition is that humans are slaves of either God or sin. Thus, sin's vast power seeks to enslave human beings and, therefore, competes with the power of God. The bottom-line difference: sin pays the wage of death, while God freely grants eternal life "in Christ Jesus our Lord."

Anthems
Amazing Grace, arr. Richard Proulx (G.I.A) SATB (flute) (ME). *Mercy, Pity, Peace, and Love,* Austin Lovelace (Randall Egan) SATB (M).

Matthew 10:40–42 Whoever hospitably receives Christ's representatives or messengers or disciples, even if only by offering a cup of water, also receives Christ and will therefore be rewarded by God in the age to come.

Anthem
Where Charity and Love Prevail (J. Clifford Evers, para., *WB* #641).

Psalm 13
1. Metrical: *How Long Will You Forget Me, Lord.* Text: C.M., Christopher L. Webber. *ANMP,* p. 45.
2. Responsorial: *Psalm 13.* Setting: Hal H. Hopson. *PS93* #7.
3. Metrical: *How Long Will You Forget Me, Lord.* Text: Psalm 13, vers. Marie J. Post. Tune: THE CHURCH'S DESOLATION. Harmony, Dale Grotenhuis. *PH87* #13.
4. Metrical: *Forgotten for Eternity.* Text: Michael Saward. Music: David G. Wilson. *PP,* p. 69.
See also *PR&T,* pp. 45 & 50; *WIII* #28.

Anthems
How Long Wilt Thou Forget Me, O Lord, Ned Rorem (E. C. Schirmer) SATB (M). *Psalm 13,* Johannes Brahms (G. Schirmer) SSA (M).

Organ Music for the Day
Prelude on RATHBUN (*In the Cross of Christ I Glory, PH90* #84), settings by Seth Bingham (*Twelve Hymn Preludes,* H. W. Gray Co., Inc.), and Flor Peeters (*Thirty Short Preludes on Well-Known Hymns,* C. F. Peters Corp. 6195).

Hymns for the Day	HL33	HB55	WB72	PH90
At the Name of Jesus	–	143	303	148
Christian Women, Christian Men	–	–	–	348
Cuando el Pobre/When a Poor One	–	–	–	407
O God, in a Mysterious Way	103	112	391	270
If Thou but Trust in God to Guide Thee	105	344	431	282
There's a Spirit in the Air	–	–	–	433
Where Cross the Crowded Ways of Life	410	507	642	408

98

SUNDAY BETWEEN JULY 3 AND JULY 9
(PROPER 9) [14] (A)

Genesis 24:34–38, 42–49, 58–67 Abraham's servant tells Laban how Abraham's wealth and YHWH's blessing have been bestowed on Isaac, who needs a wife. The servant then recounts his encounter at the well with Rebekah, and requests her father and brother to deal honorably with Abraham. They defer to Rebekah. She chooses Isaac, who loves her. Despite ongoing obstacles, the promises of God (cf. 12:1–3) advance.

Anthem
God Is Life, Domenico Scarlatti, arr. Helenclair Lowe (Choristers Guild) unison (E).

Romans 7:15–25a Paul's confession about the universal human condition: "Somehow I make a bumbling mess out of all my good intentions and end up doing evil. The power of sin imprisons me. Who shall liberate me from this vicious cycle? Thanks be to God, who does this through Jesus Christ!"

Anthem
Lord, for Thy Tender Mercy's Sake, John Hilton, also attr. to Farrant (Church Music Society) SATB (M).

Matthew 11:16–19, 25–30 The masters of the law seem to be the most confused or obstinate about Jesus' message of grace. Thanks be to God, then, for revealing this message to the unlearned and the foolish. Yet, you are still invited to trade your yoke of law for the yoke of grace, which paradoxically demands more from you, yet will give you rest.

Anthem
The Lord of the Dance, Shaker hymn, arr. John Ferguson (E. C. Schirmer) SATB (ME).

Psalm 45:10–17
1. Metrical: *I Will Praise the King with All My Verses.* Text: Marie J. Post and Bert Polman. Tune: O DASS ICH TAUSENT. *PH87* #45.
2. Responsorial: *Psalm 45.* Text: Grail. Tone: Presbyterian 3. *PS93* #39.

See also *WIII* 1046; *CC* G-2028; *PR&T*, pp. 18 & 44.

Anthem
Let Us Celebrate God's Name, Anton Bruckner, ed. Richard Peek (Augsburg) SATB.

or **Song of Solomon 2:8–13**

Anthems
I Sat Down Under His Shadow (stanzas 3–4), Edward C. Bairstow (Oxford University Press 43.002). *I Am the Rose of Sharon* (stanzas 1–5, 6–7, 10–11), William Billings, ed. Lawrence Bennett (Broude Bros. WW 7). *Arise, My Love, My Fair One,* Gerald Near (Augsburg) SATB (MD).

Organ Music for the Day
1. *Prelude on* ABERYSTWYTH (*Jesus, Lover of My Soul, PH90* #303), settings by Ralph Vaughan Williams (Oxford University Press 375943–8)
2. *Prelude on* O QUANTA QUALIA (*God of Compassion, PH90* #261), F. Peeters (*Hymn Preludes for the Lit. Year,* vol. 21, C. F. Peters Corp. 6421).

Hymns for the Day	HL33	HB55	WB72	PH90
God of Compassion, in Mercy Befriend Us	–	122	392	261
God of the Ages	–	515	394	262
I Danced in the Morning	–	–	426	302
If Thou but Trust in God to Guide Thee	105	344	431	282
Lord Jesus, Think on Me	239	270	–	301
Spirit of God	204	234	575	326

SUNDAY BETWEEN JULY 10 AND JULY 16
(PROPER 10) [15] (A)

Genesis 25:19–34 YHWH blesses barren Rebekah and old Isaac with the gift of twin sons, who struggle with each other in Rebekah's womb (as well as throughout the rest of their lives). Why this conflict? Because YHWH scandalously inverted the conventional order by choosing the elder to serve the younger, the last to become first. Amazingly, YHWH's purposes are fulfilled in the human exchange of the birthright.

Anthems

God Moves in a Mysterious Way, Thomas Harborne (Belwin) SATB (ME). *O God, in a Mysterious Way,* The Scottish Psalter, 1615, arr. Ravenscroft, *PH90* #270.

Romans 8:1–11 According to Paul, our human situation leads to self-destruction or to striking out against others (including God) who frustrate our desires. The way of our human world leads to sin and death. The way of the Spirit frees us from our world of sin and death and leads us to life—a world where all are servants.

Anthem

You Are Not in the Flesh, J. S. Bach (Motet III, *Jesu, Meine Freude,* Peters) SSATB (D).

Matthew 13:1–9, 18–23 A foolish farmer indiscriminately sows seeds along the highway, in thornbushes, on rock piles, all about his fields. Yet, there's going to be a harvest—thirty-, sixty-, a hundredfold. God keeps God's word! So preach the gospel and trust God.

Anthem

The Word of God, Jean Berger (Augsburg) SATB optional instruments (D).

Psalm 119:105–112

1. Responsorial: *Psalm 119* (97–112). Text: Grail. Refrain and Tone: Presbyterian 5. *PS93* #123.
2. Responsorial: *Your Word Is a Lamp for My Steps.* Text: Grail. Gelineau tone *GGP,* p. 175. (See also *GPI,* p. 182.) For refrains see *WIII* #880, #913, and #1023.

Anthem

Thy Word Is a Light, Haydn Morgan (C. Fischer) SSAATTBB (M).

Organ Music for the Day

1. *Chorale Prelude on* JESU, MEINE FREUDE (*Jesus, Priceless Treasure, PH90* #365), J. S. Bach (various editions).
2. *Meditation on* JESU, MEINE FREUDE, Gardner Read (H. W. Gray Co., Inc. 814).

Hymns for the Day	HL33	HB55	WB72	PH90
Deep in the Shadows of the Past	–	–	–	330
I'm Gonna Live So God Can Use Me	–	–	–	369
Immortal, Invisible, God Only Wise	66	85	433	263
O God, What You Ordain Is Right	291	366	633	284
Spirit	–	–	–	319
Walk On, O People of God	–	–	–	296

SUNDAY BETWEEN JULY 17 AND JULY 23
(PROPER 11) [16] (A)

Genesis 28:10–19a See the fugitive Jacob, the slick con man, cowardly fleeing for his life from an enraged Esau bent on revenge. The clever cheat, a common crook, runs until, weary in the dark, he curls up against a stone and sleeps. At daybreak, Jacob awakes and exclaims, "Surely YHWH was in this place." Ostensibly, YHWH gave this dreaming purloiner the same unconditional, guaranteed promise made to Abraham and Isaac. YHWH seems unfair or, worse, immoral. Of all the people in the world to pick, YHWH chooses Jacob, a coward and a crook.

Anthems
Ladder of Mercy, Hal H. Hopson (Sacred Music) 2-part (E). *The Gate of Heaven,* Randall Thompson (E. C. Schirmer) SATB (M).

Romans 8:12–25 An exhortation to live not according to the anxiety and fear of human nature but according to the life-giving Spirit. Though we constantly get tangled in the slavery of our pious self-interest and cravings for acceptance, God's Spirit works among us to bring about a new relationship that enables us to cry out boldly, "Abba!" Our sufferings pale in light of the glory that will be revealed to us. Yet all creation groans for redemption as do we who have the firstfruits of the Spirit. But we have an advantage: The gift of the Spirit supports our confident hope that we shall be saved.

Anthem
Be a New and Different Person, Paul Christiansen (Schmitt) SATB (ME).

Matthew 13:24–30, 36–43 What must be done about the presence of weeds amid growing crops? Usually you yank out the weeds lest they choke the crops, but here you are counseled to wait until harvesttime. Strange. Ah, but then you remember Jesus' words in Matthew 7:1 ("Do not judge . . .").

Anthems
Wild and Lone the Prophet's Voice, Joseph Parry, *PH90* #409. *Then Shall the Righteous Shine Forth,* Felix Mendelssohn (*Elijah,* number 39, G. Schirmer) tenor solo (M).

Psalm 139:1–12, 23–24
1. Metrical: *You Are Before Me, Lord.* Text: Ian Pitt-Watson. Tune: SURSUM CORDA. *PH90* #248.
2. Responsorial: *Psalm 139* (1–5, 7–12, 23–24). Setting: Hal H. Hopson. *PS93* #142.
See also *PH87* # 139 (stanzas 1 & 2); *WIII* #1034; *PR&T,* pp. 34 & 35.

Anthem
Psalm 139, Carlton Young (Hope) SATB oboe (M).

Organ Music for the Day
Prelude on AMAZING GRACE (NEW BRITAIN) (*Amazing Grace, How Sweet the Sound, PH90* #280), Hal H. Hopson (*Five Preludes on Familiar Hymns,* Harold Flammer, Inc. HF 5123), Jean Langlais (*American Folk-Hymn Settings for Organ,* H. T. Fitz-Simons Co., Inc. FO 623).

Hymns for the Day	HL33	HB55	WB72	PH90
Amazing Grace	–	275	296	280
Come, Ye Thankful People, Come	460	525	346	551
Hear the Good News of Salvation	–	–	–	355
Hope of the World	–	291	423	360
Praise, My Soul, the King of Heaven	14	31	551	478
There's a Wideness in God's Mercy	93	110	601	298

SUNDAY BETWEEN JULY 24 AND JULY 30
(PROPER 12) [17] (A)

Genesis 29:15–28 To earn the right to marry Rachel, Jacob labors for Laban seven years. The morning after the wedding, Jacob opens his eyes, and sees—surprise!—Leah. The deceiver Jacob is deceived. He complains about this shell game, so Laban feigns forgetfulness in explaining the fine print. Jacob's additional seven years of labor (totaling fourteen!) so he could wed Rachel would be called "deep love" by some, but in the end, God's will prevails and the divine promise of offspring is advanced (see 28:13–15).

Anthem

Sing God a Simple Song, Leonard Bernstein (*Ecumenical Praise,* number 96, Agape) unison (M).

Romans 8:26–39 We do not know how to pray, yet the Spirit transforms our weak groanings into prayer. The Spirit pleads with God on our behalf so we may share in the glory that God prepares for those who love God. Who can be against us? Nobody, for God spared not God's own Son for us all. Who dares accuse us? Nobody, for God has acquitted us; Christ stands before us. Who can separate us from the love of Christ? Nobody, for God has a hold over us in Christ, and God's hold on us is inexorable.

Anthems

We Do Not Know How to Pray as We Ought, Erik Routley (*Ecumenical Praise,* number 110, Agape) unison (E). *Who Shall Separate Us?,* John Ness Beck (AMSI) SATB (ME). *Who Shall Separate Us?,* Heinrich Schütz (Chantry) SATB (M).

Matthew 13:31–33, 44–52 (a) An unpopular, despised, rejected weed is where foolish birds find refuge and make their home. (b) Without even searching, a man unexpectedly stumbles upon a pot of gold at the beginning of the rainbow. The treasure is simply a free gift he cannot own, but can only receive in joy. A man, on finding a great pearl, discovers its purchase price will cost him everything, including himself. (c) A net, all by itself, gathers fish of every kind—the good, the bad, and the ugly—which are sorted only when the net is full. "Do you understand all this?" asks Jesus. "Yes," respond his disciples. "Good, then you will find your identity in God's will and live according to the treasures of the kingdom."

Anthems

Jesu, Priceless Treasure, J. S. Bach (Augsburg) SATB (E). *Lord, Above All Other Treasures,* J. S. Bach, arr. by Roberta Bitgood (H. W. Gray) unison for sopranos (ME).

Psalm 105:1–11, 45*b*

1. Metrical: *Trumpet the Name! Praise Be Our Lord!* Text: Calvin Seerveld. Tune: GENEVAN 105. *PH87* #105.
2. Responsorial: *Psalm 105* (1–11). Text: Helen L. Wright. Setting: Hal H. Hopson. *PS93* #106.
3. Metrical: *Give Thanks to God, Make Known His Name* (1–8). Text: C.M., Christopher L. Webber. *ANMP,* p. 175.
4. Metrical: *Lift Up Your Hearts.* Text: Jim Seddon. Music: Norman Warren. *PP,* #116.
5. Text optional: Psalm tone and refrain by Hal H. Hopson. *PR&T,* pp. 54 & 56.

Anthem

Sing Ye Praises to Our King, Aaron Copland (Boosey & Hawkes) SATB (M).

or **Psalm 128**

1. Metrical: *How Happy Is Each Child of God.* Text: Dwight M. Mounter, 1986. Tune: WINCHESTER OLD. *PH90* #239.
2. Responsorial: *Psalm 128.* Setting: Hal H. Hopson. *PS93* #133.
3. Responsorial: *O Happy Are Those Who Fear the Lord.* Text: Grail. (See also *GPI,* p. 192.) Refrain, psalm tone, and Gelineau tone: *WIII* #782 & #961. (See also *WIII* #944 and *24P&1C,* p. 35 for additional refrains.)
4. Metrical: *Happy Are They Who Fear the Lord.* Text: C.M., Christopher L. Webber. *ANMP,* p. 211.

See also *PH87* #128; *CC* G-2858; *PR&T,* pp. 52 & 68.

Anthem

Psalm 128, Robert Wetzler (Augsburg) SATB (E).

Organ Music for the Day

1. *Prelude on* LEONI (*The God of Abraham Praise, PH90* #488), Richard Proulx (Augsburg 11–843), and *Toccata on* LEONI, Seth Bingham (H. W. Gray Co., Inc. 858).
2. *Chorale Improvisation on* CWM RHONDDA (*Guide Me, O Thou Great Jehovah, PH90* #281), Paul Manz (*Ten Chorale Improvisations,* Concordia 97–5257).

Hymns for the Day	*HL33*	*HB55*	*WB72*	*PH90*
Guide Me, O Thou Great Jehovah	104	339	409	281
Jesus, Priceless Treasure	–	414	442	365
Jesus, Thy Boundless Love to Me	314	404	–	366
O Jesus, I Have Promised	268	307	–	389
O Love That Wilt Not Let Me Go	307	400	519	384
Rejoice, Ye Pure in Heart!	297	407	561	145
The God of Abraham Praise	8	89	587	488

SUNDAY BETWEEN JULY 31 AND AUGUST 6
(PROPER 13) [18] (A)

Genesis 32:22–31 An all-night wrestling match between the swindler Jacob and a mysterious opponent seems to be a draw until the enigmatic rival cripples Jacob's hip, and requests release because day is breaking. The trickster Jacob, however, seeks a blessing but receives a new name. When he asks the name of the inscrutable stranger, he receives a blessing. "I have seen God face to face," exclaims Jacob, "and yet my life is preserved."

Anthem
Come, O Thou Traveler Unknown, Erik Routley (*Ecumenical Praise*, number 30, Agape) unison (E).

Romans 9:1–5 Paul mourns for his Jewish brothers and sisters who are God's people—recipients of the glory, covenants, law, and promises of God. Before them came the patriarchs, and from them comes Christ, who assures them of salvation. For these people, his own flesh and blood, Paul would surrender his own salvation.

Anthem
Hail to the Lord's Anointed, T. Tertius Noble, *HB55* #146.

Matthew 14:13–21 One of the multitude of remembered meals involving God-with-us. Jesus takes five loaves and two fish and, after giving thanks to God, breaks the bread, and gives all to the disciples to distribute among 5,000-plus people. Miraculously, in the midst of this human meal, God's grace is sufficient to feed all the hungry.

Anthem
Thou Hast Given Us Bread from Heaven, Johann Geisler (H. W. Gray) SATB (M).

Psalm 17:1–7, 15
1. Metrical: *Lord, Listen to My Righteous Plea.* Text: Psalm 15. Tune: BERNARD. *PH87* #17.
2. Responsorial: *Psalm 17* (1–8, 15). Text: *Book of Common Prayer.* Refrain: Hal H. Hopson. Tone: Gregorian VIIIg. *PS93* #11.
3. Responsorial: *Lord, When Your Glory Appears.* Text: Grail. Refrain, psalm tone, and Gelineau tone: *WIII* #960.
4. Responsorial: Text: optional. Psalm tones and refrains by Hal H. Hopson. *PR&T*, pp. 45 & 48.

Anthem
O, Hold Thou Me Up, Benedetto Marcello (Concordia) 2-part (E).

Organ Music for the Day
1. *Let Us Break Bread Together*, Dale Wood (*Preludes and Postludes*, Augsburg 11–9320), and Gordon Young (*Spirituals and Folk Tunes*, Hope Publishing Co. 228).
2. *Prelude on* ST. FLAVIAN (*Be Known to Us in Breaking Bread, PH90* #505), Healey Willan (*Ten Hymn Preludes*, C. F. Peters Corp. 6011).

Hymns for the Day	HL33	HB55	WB72	PH90
Be Known to Us in Breaking Bread	356	446	–	505
Break Thou the Bread of Life	216	250	317	329
Give to the Winds Your Fears	294	364	377	286
Holy God, We Praise Your Name	–	–	420	460
O for a Thousand Tongues	199	141	493	466
Our God, to Whom We Turn	–	128	–	278

SUNDAY BETWEEN AUGUST 7 AND AUGUST 13
(PROPER 14) [19] (A)

Genesis 37:1–4, 12–28 A story of intrafamily jealousy, even hatred, generated by Joseph's tattle-tales, dreams of a world turned upside down, and his father's greater love for him—symbolized by a special robe with long sleeves. The dreamer Joseph is set upon by killers of the dream, his brothers, who rip off Joseph's long robe. Though his life is spared by Reuben's and then Judah's intervention, Joseph is sold to Midianite traders and taken to Egypt. Behind the scenes work the purposes of God through and in spite of Joseph, his brothers, and Egypt.

Anthem
God Moves in a Mysterious Way, arr. Benjamin Britten (*Ecumenical Praise,* number 41, Agape) 2-part (E).

Romans 10:5–15 When your lips confess "Jesus is Lord" because your heart trusts "God raised him from the dead," you acknowledge the nearness of Christ and his salvation offered to all, which Isaiah said will not be transitory. Therefore, the Lord of all bestows such enduring riches on everyone who calls upon the name of the Lord.

Anthem
How Beautiful Are the Feet of Them, G. F. Handel (*Messiah,* any edition) soprano solo (ME).

Matthew 14:22–33 The disciples are in a boat, a strong wind flinging them from wave to wave. Jesus has been off praying, yet here he comes toward the disciples, "walking on the water"—wouldn't you be afraid? "Have no fear," says Jesus, "it is I." "If it is you, Lord," yells Peter, "then bid me to come to you on the water." "Come," says Jesus. So Peter leaves the security of the boat and walks on the water toward Jesus, but suddenly in the face of wind and rain and storm, Peter's faith ebbs and, afraid, he begins to sink. Jesus immediately rescues him, and the disciples confess Jesus as the "Son of God."

Anthem
In the Night, Christ Came Walking, Noble Cain (G. Schirmer) SATB (M).

Psalm 105:1–6, 16–22, 45*b*
1. Metrical: *Trumpet the Name! Praise Be Our Lord!* Text: Calvin Seerveld. Tune: GENEVAN 105. *PH87* #105.
2. Responsorial: *Psalm 105* (1–6, 16–22, 45*b*). Text: Helen L. Wright. Refrain and Tone: Presbyterian 4. *PS93* #107.
3. Text optional: Psalm tone and ref. by Hal H. Hopson. *PR&T,* pp. 54 & 56.

Anthem
O Give Thanks Unto the Lord, Jean Berger (Hinshaw) SATB (M).

Organ Music for the Day
Prelude on ST. BRIDE (*Give to the Winds Thy Fears, PH90* #286), W. T. Best (*English Romantic Classics,* McAfee Music Corp. DM 248), and Gerhard Krapf (*Music for the Service,* Roger Dean Pub. Co. KK 301).

Hymns for the Day	HL33	HB55	WB72	PH90
Deep in the Shadows of the Past	–	–	–	330
Give to the Winds Your Fears	294	364	377	286
Here, O Lord, Your Servants Gather	–	–	417	465
Lord, Speak to Me That I May Speak	399	298	–	426
O Come and Sing Unto the Lord	49	29	488	214
Strong Son of God, Immortal Love	175	228	578	–

SUNDAY BETWEEN AUGUST 14 AND AUGUST 20
(PROPER 15) [20] (A)

Genesis 45:1–15 The simple, self-disclosing words, "I am Joseph," send waves of alarm, shock, dismay through his brothers, because their cunning and deceptive past now jeopardizes their future. But, instead of revenge, Joseph breaks with the past and offers a gift of a new future, because "God sent me to preserve life." God's will for life is at work in spite of all resistant human efforts. Make haste, therefore, in telling the world that God mysteriously works for life in the midst of our leanness.

Anthem
A Song of Praise and Thanksgiving, Allen Pote (Hinshaw) 2-part (E).

Romans 11:13–16, 29–32 Has God rejected the Jews? No! Ironically, the Jews' disobedience (hardness of heart) provides the disobedient Gentiles an opportunity: When the first disciples are rebuffed by their own people, they turn to the Gentiles and preach the good news revealed in Jesus Christ. Doubly ironic it is that the Jews' disobedience (unbelief) is also a necessary stage for their return to faith. For both Jew and Gentile, the journey to God's mercy leads through disobedience. Imagine the joy when all are reconciled—it will be life from the dead!

Anthem
If Thou but Suffer God to Guide Thee, J. S. Bach (C. Fischer) SATB (M).

Matthew 15:(10–20), 21–28 A Canaanite woman cries out to Jesus about her daughter's trouble, saying, "Lord, help me." Despite his disciples' protestations, Jesus responds to this non-Israelite woman's faith and to her wit (about undeserving dogs eating crumbs from the master's table).

Anthems
An Anthem of Faith, Carl F. Mueller (G. Schirmer) SATB (ME). *O Lord, Increase My Faith*, Orlando Gibbons (H. W. Gray) SATB (M).

Psalm 133
1. Metrical: *Behold the Goodness of Our Lord*. Text: Fred R. Anderson. Tune: CRIMOND. *PH90* #241. For text only see *SPJP*, p. 67.
2. Responsorial: *Psalm 133*. Setting: Hal H. Hopson. *PS93* #137.
See also *ANMP*, p. 214; *PH87* #133; *PR&T*, pp. 28 & 82.

Anthem
Together in Unity, Malcolm Williamson (Boosey & Hawkes) unison and congregation (E).

Organ Music for the Day
1. *Prelude on* CRIMOND (*Behold the Goodness of Our Lord*—Psalm 133, *PH90* #241), settings by Gordon Young (*Nine Hymn Preludes for Organ*, Hope Publishing Co. 336), and Alec Rowley (*Choral Preludes Based on Famous Hymn Tunes*, Edwin Ashdown, Ltd.).
2. *Prelude on* AZMON (*O for a Thousand Tongues to Sing*, *PH90* #466), Hal H. Hopson (*Praise to the Lord*, The Sacred Music Press KK 389).

Hymns for the Day	HL33	HB55	WB72	PH90
All People That on Earth Do Dwell	1	24	288	220
God of Compassion, in Mercy Befriend Us	–	122	392	261
I Sing the Mighty Power of God	65	84	628	288
O for a Thousand Tongues	199	141	493	466
O God of Every Nation	–	–	498	289
The King of Love My Shepherd Is	99	106	590	171

SUNDAY BETWEEN AUGUST 21 AND AUGUST 27
(PROPER 16) [21] (A)

Exodus 1:8–2:10 Joseph's generation all died while in Egypt, but the descendants amazingly increased. "Too many and too mighty," complains the new king of Egypt. So the Israelites are enslaved to taskmasters. But the more the Israelites are oppressed, the more they multiply. So Pharaoh commands all male Hebrew babies to be thrown into the Nile. A Hebrew couple give birth to a son who is set adrift among the reeds on the Nile's edge. Ironically, Pharaoh's daughter draws the infant out of the water, approves the infant's mother as nurse, and gives the Hebrew boy an Egyptian name, Moses.

Anthem
The Birth of Moses, Norman Lockwood (Mercury) SSA (flute) (M).

Romans 12:1–8 Present your bodies as a living sacrifice, for that is spiritual worship. Do not conform to the way the (self-fulfillment culture of the) world thinks and values. Be transformed. How do you present your body? Use your gifts according to the grace given you: preach, serve, teach, give away your cash, encourage others, love one another, practice hospitality, share your belongings with others, serve the Lord—that's spiritual worship.

Anthem
To Do God's Will, Jean Berger (Augsburg) SATB (M).

Matthew 16:13–20 Through God's revelation, Peter confesses Jesus as the Christ, though he doesn't understand his own words. Yet upon this follower, a rock of a disciple, Jesus promises to build his church and bestow the kingdom's keys.

Anthem
Built on a Rock, Lindeman-Brandon (Augsburg) SAB (E).

Psalm 124
1. Metrical: *Now Israel May Say.* Text: *The Psalter,* 1912. Tune: OLD 124TH. *PH90* #236.
2. Responsorial: *Psalm 124.* Text: Helen L. Wright. Setting: Peter R. Hallock. *PS93* #128.
3. Responsorial: *If the Lord Had Not Been on Our Side.* Text: Grail. (See also *GPI,* p. 189.) Ref.: G. Murray. Gelineau tone, *30P&2C,* p. 34.
See also *ANMP,* p. 208; *PR&T,* pp. 57 & 59.

Anthems
Now Israel May Say, PH90 #236. *Psalm 124,* Alice Parker (G. Schirmer) SATB (ME).

Organ Music for the Day
1. *Prelude on* OLD 124TH (*Now Israel May Say*—Psalm 124, *PH90* #236), settings by Healey Willan (*Ten Hymn Preludes,* vol. 2, C. F. Peters Corp. 6012), and Flor Peeters (*Thirty Short Preludes on Well-Known Hymns,* C. F. Peters Corp. 6195).
2. *Prelude on* MUNICH (*O Word of God Incarnate, PH90* #327), Emma L. Diemer (*Seven Hymn Preludes,* Harold Flammer, Inc. HF-5008).

Hymns for the Day	HL33	HB55	WB72	PH90
As Those of Old Their Firstfruits Brought	–	–	301	414
O God, in a Mysterious Way	103	112	391	270
Lord, Whose Love Through Humble Service	–	–	–	427
O Word of God Incarnate	215	251	532	327
Take My Life	242	10	–	391
When God Delivered Israel (Ps. 126)	–	–	–	237

SUNDAY BETWEEN AUGUST 28 AND SEPTEMBER 3
(PROPER 17) [22] (A)

Exodus 3:1–15 YHWH freely chooses to be revealed to Moses in a burning bush in the desert. "I will save my people by sending you to lead them out of Egypt." "But," protests Moses, "I am a nobody." So God gives Moses a sign: "When you lead my people out of Egypt, you shall serve God upon this mountain." Still Moses balks: "But whom shall I say sent me?" "Tell them," replies God, "I AM WHO I AM. The God of Abraham and Isaac and Jacob."

Anthem
Cosmic Festival, Richard Felciano (*Ecumenical Praise,* number 49, Agape) unison and electronic tape from E. C. Schirmer (M).

Romans 12:9–21 Paul's catalog of conduct within the Christian community: hate evil, love one another, be constant in prayer, practice hospitality, bless those who persecute you (noted twice so we'll know he means what he says), weep with those who weep, associate with the lowly, overcome evil with good, and more.

Anthems
Neighbors, arr. Austin Lovelace (H. W. Gray) SATB (E). *Jesu, Jesu, Fill Us with Your Love,* Tom Colvin, trans., *PH90* #367.

Matthew 16:21–28 Jesus speaks of his impending death and resurrection. Peter, who seeks a triumphant Messiah, misunderstands, whereupon Jesus rebukes him and teaches about discipleship.

Anthem
Thou Art Jesus, Savior and Lord, Heinrich Schütz (Augsburg) SATB (M).

Psalm 105:1–6, 23–26, 45c
1. Metrical: *Trumpet the Name! Praise Be Our Lord!* Text: Calvin Seerveld. Tune: GENEVAN 105. *PH87* #105.
2. Responsorial: *Psalm 105* (1–11). Text: Helen L. Wright. Setting: Hal H. Hopson. *PS93* #106.
3. Responsorial: *Psalm 105* (1–6, 16–26, 37–45). Text: Helen L. Wright. Refrain and Tone: Presbyterian 4. *PS93* #107.
4. Text optional: Psalm tone and ref. by Hal H. Hopson. *PR&T,* pp. 54 & 56.

Anthem
Seek Ye His Countenance in All Places, Johannes Herbst (Carl Fischer) SATB (M).

Organ Music for the Day
1. *Prelude on* AURELIA (*The Church's One Foundation, PH90* #442), settings by Theodore Beck (*Fourteen Organ Chorale Preludes,* Augsburg 11–6156), and Charles Ore (*Eleven Compositions,* Concordia 97–5702).
2. *Prelude on* WESTMINSTER ABBEY (*Christ Is Made the Sure Foundation, PH90* #416), Henry Purcell (*Purcell Made Practical for the Church Organist,* Lorenz Industries KK 285).

Hymns for the Day	HL33	HB55	WB72	PH90
Christ Is Made the Sure Foundation	336	433	325	416
Guide My Feet	–	–	–	354
Lord, Whose Love Through Humble Service	–	–	–	427
O God, Our Faithful God	–	–	500	277
Take Up Your Cross, the Savior Said	–	293	–	393
The Church's One Foundation	333	437	582	442

SUNDAY BETWEEN SEPTEMBER 4 AND SEPTEMBER 10
(PROPER 18) [23] (A)

Exodus 12:1–14 Instructions on celebrating the paschal sacrifice, which will take on new meaning as the Passover festival—the family meal at which Israel thanks God for redeeming them and making them a people, and at which the people renew their hope in the salvation to come.

Anthem
Christ, Our Passover, Willis Bodine (H. W. Gray) SATB with brass quartet, timpani, and organ (MD).

Romans 13:8–14 The *kairos* ("hour") of the Second Coming of the Lord is dawning. So awake, all believers, and be dressed; "put on Christ" and live as the people of light.

Anthem
O Day Full of Grace, Weyse, David Johnson (Augsburg) SAB (E).

Matthew 18:15–20 Personal offenses must be subject to discipline, for they affect the life of the whole community. First, strive for reconciliation privately; second, seek the counsel of others; third, the church must discipline its members, even if that means excommunication. In all three ways, Christ will be present in the community, for church members who cannot disagree openly with each other cannot love each other.

Anthem
Draw Us in the Spirit's Tether, Harold Friedell (H. W. Gray) SATB (ME).

Psalm 149
1. Metrical: *Give Praise to the Lord.* Text: *The Psalter,* 1912, alt. 1984. Tune: LAUDATE DOMINUM. *PH90* #257.
2. Responsorial: *Psalm 149.* Setting: Hal H. Hopson. *PS93* #156.
3. Metrical: *Sing Praise to the Lord.* Text: *The Psalter,* 1912, alt. Tune: HANOVER. *PH87* #149.
4. Responsorial: *Sing a New Song to the God of Salvation.* Text: Grail. Refrain, psalm tone, and Gelineau tone: *WIII* #80.

See also *ANMP,* p. 76; *APS,* p. 38; *PR&T,* pp. 38 & 39.

Anthem
Praise Ye the Lord, Emma Lou Diemer (Flammer) SATB (ME).

Organ Music for the Day
1. *Prelude on* HYFRYDOL (*Love Divine, All Loves Excelling, PH90* #376), settings by Ralph Vaughan Williams (*Three Preludes Founded on Welsh Hymn Tunes,* Stainer & Bell Ltd.), and Henry Coleman (*A Book of Hymn Tune Voluntaries,* Oxford University Press 375115–1).
2. *Processional of Joy* (based on *Joyful, Joyful, We Adore Thee, PH90* #464), Hal H. Hopson (Carl Fisher, Inc. P 3236).

Hymns for the Day	HL33	HB55	WB72	PH90
Draw Us in the Spirit's Tether	–	–	–	504
Jesus, Thy Boundless Love to Me	314	404	–	366
Joyful, Joyful, We Adore Thee	5	21	446	464
Love Divine, All Loves Excelling	308	399	471	376
O Worship the King	2	26	533	476
We Are One in the Spirit	–	–	–	619

SUNDAY BETWEEN SEPTEMBER 11 AND SEPTEMBER 17
(PROPER 19) [24] (A)

Exodus 14:19–31 Moses' prebattle, motivational speech to the Israelites: "Fear not, stand firm, keep still, for YHWH will fight for you." YHWH commands Moses to raise his walking stick over the waters so they will divide. An angel of God and the pillar of cloud move to the rear of the Israelites and veil them from the Egyptians. And all comes to fulfillment according to the word of God. YHWH drives back the sea by a strong east wind, throws the Egyptians into panic, causes their wheels to become mired in mud, and tosses them into the sea. Thus YHWH saves Israel from the Egyptians, and Israel believes in YHWH and YHWH's servant Moses.

Anthem

Thanks Be to Thee, O Lord, G. F. Handel, arr. Saar (E. C. Schirmer) SATB alto solo (E).

Romans 14:1–12 Often we are fastidious about peripheral concerns such as virtuous diets, principled religious observances, and righteous Christian lifestyle. However, we are to serve not ideologies, rules, laws, or principles, but God revealed in Jesus Christ, who lived and died for us that we might belong to him in life and death.

Anthems

When We Are Living, Spanish melody, *PH90* #400. *We Are the Lord's,* Gerhard Krapf (*Six Scriptural Affirmations,* Sacred Music) 2-part (E).

Matthew 18:21–35 A servant pleads for "a little more time" to repay his multimillion-dollar debt, while absurdly demanding immediate repayment of a twenty-dollar debt from another servant. Would you behave this way if you were really gripped by the stupendous forgiveness of God in Jesus Christ?

Anthems

Be Merciful, Even as Your Father Is Merciful, Gerhard Krapf (Concordia) unison (ME). *Have Mercy on Us, O My Lord,* Aaron Copland (Boosey & Hawkes) SATB (MD).

Psalm 114

1. Metrical: *When Israel Came, and Judah's House.* Text: L.M., Christopher L. Webber. *ANMP,* p. 183.
2. Responsorial: *Psalm 114.* Text: Helen L. Wright. Refrain: Presbyterian 1. Tone: Lutheran 8. *PS93* #114.
3. Responsorial: *God Has Freed Us and Redeemed Us.* Text: Grail. (See also *GPI,* p. 168.) Refrain, psalm tone, and Gelineau tone: *WIII* #60.
4. Metrical: *When Israel Fled from Egypt Land.* Text: Henrietta Ten Harmsel. Tune: ANDRE. *PH87* #114.
5. Responsorial: Text optional: Psalm tone and refrain by Hal H. Hopson. *PR&T,* pp. 73 & 76.

Anthem

When Israel Went Out of Egypt, Hans Leo Hassler (Lawson Gould) SATB (M).

or Exodus 15:1b–11, 20–21

1. Responsorial: *Canticle of Miriam and Moses* (Ex. 15:1–6, 11–13, 17–18). Text: *Book of Common Prayer.* Setting: John Weaver. *PS93* #174.
2. Responsorial: *Exodus Canticle* (*Song of Miriam and Moses*). Setting: Howard Hughes. *CC* G-3102.

Anthem

I Will Sing to the Lord, Alec Wyton (Hinshaw) unison (E).

Organ Music for the Day
Prelude on DETROIT (*Forgive Our Sins as We Forgive, PH90* #347), settings by Gardner Read (*Eight Preludes on Old Southern Hymns,* H. W. Gray Co., Inc. GB 293), and Walter L. Pelz (*The Concordia Hymn Prelude Series,* vol. 22, pp. 40 & 41, Concordia 97–5737).

Hymns for the Day	*HL33*	*HB55*	*WB72*	*PH90*
A Mighty Fortress Is Our God	266	91	274	260
At the Name of Jesus	–	143	303	148
Down to Earth, as a Dove	–	–	–	300
Forgive Our Sins as We Forgive	–	–	–	347
Help Us Accept Each Other	–	–	–	358
O Jesus Christ, May Grateful Hymns	–	–	509	424
When God Delivered Israel (Ps. 126)	–	–	–	237

SUNDAY BETWEEN SEPTEMBER 18 AND SEPTEMBER 24
(PROPER 20) [25] (A)

Exodus 16:2–15 The Israelites find themselves in the desert without food and water. Literally starving to death, they begin complaining; some want to rebel and some want to return to Egypt. Aaron asks, "What do you want?" "We want bread!" shout the people. Aaron shockingly replies, "Good, you will see the glory." YHWH then miraculously rains down *manna* (which means "What is it?") from heaven, which the people are invited to share with one another. The people then turn their backs on Egypt and its power, and face the wilderness and its uncertainty, where they amazingly see the glory.

Anthem
Thou Hast Given Us Bread from Heaven, Johann Geisler (H. W. Gray) SATB (M).

Philippians 1:21–30 An imprisoned Paul writes to the threatened and, therefore, fearful Philippians, "If you die, you will be with Christ. If you live, you can bear witness to Christ. So don't fear death; be obedient to Christ."

Anthem
Art Thou Weary, Art Thou Laden, Philip Gehring (Concordia) unison, antiphonal (E).

Matthew 20:1–16 Some laborers grumble because they toiled all day in the scorching heat for a fair wage, but received the same pay as those who worked only an hour. Apparently God's free grace contravenes our sense of fairness.

Anthem
Sing, My Soul, His Wondrous Love, Ned Rorem (Peters) SATB (M).

Psalm 105:1–6, 37–45
1. Metrical: *Trumpet the Name! Praise Be Our Lord!* Text: Calvin Seerveld. Tune: GENEVAN 105. *PH87* #105.
2. Responsorial: *Psalm 105* (1–6, 16–26, 37–45). Text: Helen L. Wright. Refrain and Tone: Presbyterian 4. *PS93* #107.
3. Metrical: *Lift Up Your Hearts.* Text: Jim Seddon. Music: Norman Warren. *PP* #116.
4. Text optional: Psalm tone and refrain by Hal Hopson. *PR&T,* pp. 54 & 56.

Anthem
O Give Thanks Unto the Lord, Jean Berger (Hinshaw) SATB (M).

Organ Music for the Day
1. *Prelude on* ST. CATHERINE (*Jesus, Thy Boundless Love to Me, PH90* #366), settings by Robert J. Powell (*The God of Abraham Praise,* p. 14, Genevox 4570–84), and Gordon Young (*Nine Hymn Preludes for Organ,* Hope Publishing Co. 336).
2. *Prelude on* CWM RHONDDA (*Guide Me, O Thou Great Jehovah, PH90* #281), Austin C. Lovelace (*Fourteen Hymn Preludes,* Augsburg 11–6152).

Hymns for the Day	HL33	HB55	WB72	PH90
Amazing Grace	–	275	296	280
Glorious Things of Thee Are Spoken	339	434	379	446
Guide Me, O Thou Great Jehovah	104	339	409	281
Hope of the World	–	291	423	360
Jesus, Thy Boundless Love to Me	314	404	–	366
More Love to Thee, O Christ	315	397	–	359

SUNDAY BETWEEN SEPTEMBER 25 AND OCTOBER 1
(PROPER 21) [26] (A)

Exodus 17:1–7 On their journey through the wilderness, the Israelites lack water. Parched tongues waggle, complain, quarrel, find fault, contend against Moses. "What am I to do?" cries Moses. "Surely they'll stone me." Once again, YHWH miraculously provides for the testing, trying, challenging people. From a rock, life-giving water pours forth as a sign of YHWH's glory to the unbelieving, resistant people.

Anthem
By the Springs of Water, Cecil Effinger (Augsburg) SATB.

Philippians 2:1–13 A primitive christological hymn about the descent and ascent of a divine Savior. By divesting himself of divine glory, he voluntarily assumed the form of a human servant who impoverished himself and "became obedient unto death, even death on a cross." That's why God raised him up and gave him the name above every other name: Lord.

Anthems
Let This Mind Be in You, Lee Hoiby (Presser) SATB (MD). *Let This Mind Be in You,* John Yarrington (Chantry) SATB solo (M).

Matthew 21:23–32 A father tells two sons to work in the vineyard. "I won't," says one son, but he does. "I will," says the other son, but he doesn't. Actions do speak louder than words. Do we do God's will? The first action demanded is repentance.

Anthem
The Ten Words, Lloyd Pfautsch (Fortress) SATB (M).

Psalm 78:1–4, 12–16
1. Metrical: *Hear, O My People, What I Say* and *All the Night Through with Glow of Fire.* Text: L.M., Christopher L. Webber. *ANMP,* pp. 125 & 126.
2. Responsorial: *Psalm 78* (1–4, 12–15, 23–25, 29, 37–38). Setting: Hal H. Hopson. *PS93* #67.
3. Responsorial: *The Lord Gave the Bread.* Text: Grail. (See also *GPI,* pp. 109–14.) Refrain, psalm tone, and Gelineau tone: *WIII* #917. (See also *WIII* #1050 with refrain *Do Not Forget the Work of the Lord.*) (See also *GG,* p. 166.)
See also *PH87* #78; *PR&T,* pp. 19 & 21.

Anthem
Let My Complaint Come before Thee, Adrian Batten (*A Sixteenth Century Anthem Book,* Oxford) SATB (ME).

Organ Music for the Day
Prelude on CORONATION (*All Hail the Power of Jesus' Name!, PH90* #142), settings by Jean Langlais (*Modern Organ Music,* vol. 2, p. 16, Oxford University Press 375142–9), and Emma L. Diemer (*With Praise and Love,* vol. 2, p. 19, The Sacred Music Press).

Hymns for the Day	HL33	HB55	WB72	PH90
All Hail the Power of Jesus' Name!	192	132	285	142,143
At the Name of Jesus	–	143	303	148
Christ the Lord Is Risen Today!	165	–	330	113
Creator of the Stars of Night	–	–	348	4
When We Are Tempted to Deny Your Son	–	–	640	86
Wild and Lone the Prophet's Voice	–	–	–	409

SUNDAY BETWEEN OCTOBER 2 AND OCTOBER 8
(PROPER 22) [27] (A)

Exodus 20:1–4, 7–9, 12–20 YHWH spoke to Moses at Mt. Sinai concerning Israel's relationship with YHWH and with neighbors. This Mosaic covenant is one of human obligation, which prohibits Israel from violating the exclusive claims of the divine Lord who liberated them from bondage in Egypt. Conversely, these words distinctively assert the sovereignty of YHWH and the exclusivity of the YHWH-Israel bond. In addition, this covenant protects the fundamental rights of all free Israelite citizens.

Anthem
The Holy Ten Commands, F. J. Haydn (Mercury) canons for 3 equal voices (ME).

Philippians 3:4b–14 Paul has discarded all that was precious to him—achievements, respectability, reputation, moral uprightness, obeying the law—for the sake of something far more valuable: knowledge of Christ Jesus as his Lord, and being in union with him. To know the power of Christ's resurrection, Paul and those "in Christ" must model their life on Christ's sufferings and death. For though Christ Jesus has made Paul and us his own, we still must paradoxically "press on" and "strain forward" to make the prize of the upward call of God our own.

Anthem
A Prayer for Pressing On, Jane Marshall (Agape) SATB.

Matthew 21:33–46 A self-incriminating parable about the human world's rejection of God's invitation to the kingdom. "Therefore, the kingdom will be given to a nation producing the fruits of it." Praise God for this second chance.

Anthem
Lord of the Dance, arr. J. Ferguson (E. C. Schirmer) SATB (ME).

Psalm 19
1. Metrical: *The Heavens Above Declare God's Praise* (1–6). Text: C.M., Christopher L. Webber. Tune: CAITHNESS. *PH90* #166.
2. Responsorial: *Psalm 19* (1–6). Text: Grail. Melody: Monks of Saint Meinrad. Harmony, Samuel Weber. *PS93* #12.
See also *SPJP*, p. 20; *PS93* #13; *PH90* #167; *GPI*, p. 22; *HB55* #257; *WIII* #794, #841, & #873; *PR&T*, pp. 67 & 68.

Anthem
The Law of the Lord, William Mathias (Oxford) SATB (MD).

Organ Music for the Day
1. *Prelude on* FOUNDATION (*How Firm a Foundation, PH90* #361), Jean Langlais (*American Folk-Hymn Settings for Organ*, H. T. FitzSimons Co., Inc. F0623).
2. *Prelude on* SLANE (*Be Thou My Vision, PH90* #339), settings by Hal H. Hopson (*Five Preludes on Familiar Hymns*, Harold Flammer Inc. HF-5123), and Healey Willan (C. F. Peters Corp. 66034).

Hymns for the Day	HL33	HB55	WB72	PH90
Be Thou My Vision	325	303	304	339
Christ Is Made the Sure Foundation	336	433	325	416, 417
God's Law Is Perfect (Ps. 19:7–14)	–	–	–	167
I Danced in the Morning	–	–	426	302
O God, What You Ordain Is Right	291	366	633	284
How Firm a Foundation	283	369	425	361

SUNDAY BETWEEN OCTOBER 9 AND OCTOBER 15
(PROPER 23) [28] (A)

Exodus 32:1–14 Moses has been on the mountain "forty days and forty nights" receiving instructions from YHWH. At the foot of the mountain, a commotion brews among the people. Desiring a sign of the divine presence, the people impatiently, impulsively, truculently demand of Aaron, "Up, make us *elohim* (gods)!" How quickly Israel reneges on its covenant promise. Aaron complies and the "golden calf" is produced, an imitation of what YHWH is about to give them (see Ex. 25:1–9). Says YHWH to Moses, "Let me at these stiff-necked calf worshipers, your people—I'll wipe them out and start over with you." But Moses boldly intercedes for his wayward people. "Why does your anger burn hot against your people? You will be laughed at by the Egyptians if these Israelites fail to survive. You made promises to our ancestors; do you intend to keep your promises?"

Anthem
O for a Closer Walk with God, Arthur Cottman *PH90* #397.

Philippians 4:1–9 Paul exhorts the Philippian community to seek unity, harmony, agreement in the Lord. Above all, he urges them to rejoice. Even in their common suffering, Paul and the Philippians can rejoice because the Lord is at hand and will consummate the work of salvation begun in them.

Anthem
I Will Greatly Rejoice, Donald Rotermund (Concordia) SATB (M).

Matthew 22:1–14 A king invites many guests to a wedding feast, but they all are too busy to come so they offer polite excuses. The king becomes very angry and invites other guests. They all come, good and bad alike, so that the wedding hall is filled. The king enters and shockingly tosses out a guest with soiled clothes. We are appalled! But then again, the least we can do is to attire ourselves appropriately for the messianic banquet. Be transformed!

Anthem
Rejoice in the Lord Always, Daniel Moe (Hope) SATB (M).

Psalm 106:1–6, 19–23
1. Metrical: *O Praise the Lord for He Is Good.* Text: Marie J. Post. Tune: SEDGWICK. *PH87* #106.
2. Responsorial: *Psalm 106* (1–6, 19–23). Text: *A New Zealand Prayer Book.* Setting: Hal H. Hopson. *PS93* #108.
See also *PR&T,* pp. 55 & 59.

Anthem
O Give Thanks Unto the Lord, H. Purcell (E. C. Schirmer) SATB (M).

Organ Music for the Day
1. *Prelude on* MARION (*Rejoice, Ye Pure in Heart!, PH90* #145), Emma L. Diemer (*With Praise and Love,* The Sacred Music Press).
2. *Prelude on* DIVINUM MYSTERIUM (*Of the Father's Love Begotten, PH90* #309), settings by Richard Purvis (*Eleven Pieces for the Church Organist,* MCA Music 00123159), and Gerre Hancock (*Fantasy on* DIVINUM MYSTERIUM, H. W. GRAY CO., INC. GB 627).

Hymns for the Day	HL33	HB55	WB72	PH90
Deck Yourself, My Soul, with Gladness	–	–	351	506
Great Is Thy Faithfulness	–	–	–	276
Guide My Feet	–	–	–	354
Lord, We Have Come at Your Invitation	–	–	–	516
Of the Father's Love Begotten	–	7	534	309
Rejoice, Ye Pure in Heart!	297	407	561	145, 146

SUNDAY BETWEEN OCTOBER 16 AND OCTOBER 22
(PROPER 24) [29] (A)

Exodus 33:12–23 Will YHWH accompany his stiff-necked, sinful, covenant-break-ing people? Thus, Moses prays for the restoration of YHWH's presence denied in Exodus 33:3, 5. He pleads, "Since I have a special relationship with you, show me your character and purposes, and reaffirm that these sinful people are still yours." YHWH consents partially by responding, "My presence will go." So Moses resumes his plea: "If I and your people do not have your presence with us, then do not take us up from here." To this plea, YHWH grants full concession. But maybe this restoration of YHWH's presence will lead to the destruction of Israel, so Moses further pleads for a revelation of YHWH's gracious and merciful nature. Now YHWH takes the initiative in "passing by" Moses and, therefore, revealing an overpowering glimpse of the divine character and purposes.

Anthem
My Presence Shall Go with Thee, Raymond Haan (Sacred Music Press) SATB (ME).

1 Thessalonians 1:1–10 The life and faith of the Thessalonians, despite their suf-fering, is a sign that God has chosen them. They are an example to all believers.

Anthem
Christ Sends the Spirit, Richard Proulx (Augsburg) SAB with flute (ME).

Matthew 22:15–22 The Pharisees deviously seek to trap Jesus by asking him, "Is it right for Jews to pay taxes to the Roman government?" Jesus deftly replies, "Give Caesar his things, and give God the things of God." His response is really a question: What things do not belong to God?

Anthem
Jesus and the Pharisees, M. Franck-Frischmann (Concordia) SATB (M).

Psalm 99
1. Metrical: *The Lord Is King: Let People Quake*. Text: L.M., Christopher L. Web-ber. *ANMP*, p. 165.
2. Responsorial: *Psalm 99*. Text: Helen L. Wright. Setting: Hal H. Hopson. *PS93* #96.
3. Responsorial: *God Is King: The People Tremble*. Text: Grail. (See also *GPI*, p. 141.) Refrain: A. G. Murray. Gelineau tone: *20P&3C*, p. 19.
See also *PP* #113; *PH87* #99; *PR&T*, pp. 59 & 73.

Anthem
Cry Out with Joy, Christopher Walker (Oxford) unison (E).

Organ Music for the Day
Prelude on O GOTT, DU FROMMER GOTT (*O God, Our Faithful God, PH90* #277), set-tings by J. S. Bach (various editions), Johannes Brahms (*Chorale Preludes*, C. F. Pe-ters Corp. and other publishers), and Max Reger (*Thirteen Choral-Preludes*, Hans Sikorski Verlag 116).

Hymns for the Day	HL33	HB55	WB72	PH90
Christ, of All My Hopes the Ground	–	314	–	–
I'm Gonna Live So God Can Use Me	–	–	–	369
Immortal, Invisible, God Only Wise	66	85	433	263
O God of Earth and Space	–	–	–	274
O God, Our Faithful God	–	–	500	277
We Give Thee but Thine Own	394	312	–	428

SUNDAY BETWEEN OCTOBER 23 AND OCTOBER 29
(PROPER 25) [30] (A)

Deuteronomy 34:1–12 Imagine the following: A Hebrew baby is rescued from a watery death by the daughter of Pharaoh, who then gives the Hebrew child an Egyptian name; when the child grows up he impetuously murders a man and flees as a fugitive from justice; while slinking through the wilderness he marries a non-Hebrew woman and, at a mountain, experiences a call from YHWH. Of all people, this man is chosen by God as the prophet without equal. Having served as mediator and intercessor for Israel, Moses now must turn over leadership to Joshua. So Moses views the promised land from afar—because of his wayward people's sin, he must remain outside the land—and is buried in an unknown location in order to prevent any grave cult. He was the first and the greatest of the prophets.

Anthem
God of the Prophets, Paul Bunjes (Concordia) SATB congregation, trumpet (E).

1 Thessalonians 2:1–8 Paul repudiates trumped-up charges by his opponents. "You yourselves know," says Paul, "that in no way did we seek any personal gain. Rather, because of our motherly love for you, God gave us the strength to preach the gospel and devote ourselves to you."

Anthem
Like as a Father, Luigi Cherubini (Summy-Birchard) canon for 3 equal voices (E).

Matthew 22:34–46 The Pharisees try to trap Jesus by asking him a trick question about the "greatest commandment." So Jesus quotes Deuteronomy: "Love God with all your heart, soul, and mind." Then Jesus unexpectedly adds, "Love neighbors as your own kin." You cannot love God without loving your neighbor, or vice versa. Then Jesus questions the Pharisees about the Messiah. Reply the Pharisees, "He is the son of David." "Then how can David call him Lord?" responds Jesus. The Pharisees answer with silence and ask no more questions.

Anthems
Love God with Your Heart, Folk melody (*Three Peace and Brotherhood Canons,* Choristers Guild) 3-part (E). *Thou Shalt Love the Lord Thy God,* Leo Sowerby (H. W. Gray) SATB (M).

Psalm 90:1–6, 13–17
1. Metrical: *Lord, You Have Been Our Dwelling Place.* Text: Fred R. Anderson. Tune: LOBT GOTT IN SEINEM HEILIGTUM. *PH90* #211. (See also *SPJP,* p. 46.)
2. Responsorial: *Psalm 90.* Text: Grail. Refrain: Eugene Englert. Gelineau tone. *PS93* #83.
3. Responsorial: *Psalm 90.* Text: Hal H. Hopson. Refrain and Tone: Hal H. Hopson. Tone B: Based on Eastern Orthodox Tone. *PS93* #84.
4. Metrical: *Our God, Our Help in Ages Past.* Text: Isaac Watts. Tune: ST. ANNE. *PH90* #210. (See also *HB55* #111, *WB72* #549, *PH87* #170, and *H82* #680.)
5. Responsorial: *In Ev'ry Age, O Lord, You Have Been Our Refuge.* Refrain, psalm tone, and Gelineau tone: *WIII* #48 & #933. (See *WIII* #947 & #1048 for additional refrains.)

See also *ANMP,* pp. 142 & 143; *HB55* #88; *PR&T,* pp. 43 & 76.

Anthem
Lord, Thou Hast Been Our Refuge, R. Vaughan Williams (G. Schirmer) SATB/SATB (D).

Organ Music for the Day

1. *Prelude on* DIX (*For the Beauty of the Earth, PH90* #473), settings by Philip Gehring (*Preludes and Postludes,* Augsburg 11–9319), and Flor Peeters (*Hymn Preludes for the Liturgical Year,* vol. 1, C. F. Peters Corp. 6401).
2. *Prelude on* ST. ANNE (*Our God, Our Help in Ages Past*—Psalm 90:1–5, *PH90* #210), C. Hubert H. Parry (*Seven Chorale-Preludes,* Novello & Co., Ltd. 1546).

Hymns for the Day	HL33	HB55	WB72	PH90
Christian Women, Christian Men	–	–	–	348
Christ of the Upward Way	277	295	–	344
For the Beauty of the Earth	71	2	372	473
Great God, We Sing That Mighty Hand	470	527	408	265
Help Us Accept Each Other	–	–	–	358
Jesu, Jesu, Fill Us with Your Love	–	–	–	367
Our God, Our Help (Ps. 90:1–5)	77	111	549	210

118

SUNDAY BETWEEN OCTOBER 30 AND NOVEMBER 5
(PROPER 26) [31] (A)

Joshua 3:7–17 Joshua is instructed by YHWH: "This is the day I will begin to exalt you in the sight of all Israel, so they will know I will be with you as I was with Moses. When you come to the edge of the waters of the Jordan, stand still in the river." Joshua obeys. Thus, when the priests bearing the ark of the covenant step into the Jordan, they stand still, and the rushing, springtime waters stand still, in one heap, permitting the people to cross.

Anthem
If Thou but Suffer God to Guide Thee, Jody Lindh (Concordia) 2-part (E).

1 Thessalonians 2:9–13 Paul obviously is not seeking to be a people-pleasing preacher, because both he and the Thessalonians have suffered as a result of giving witness to God's gospel. For those who welcomed God's word, thanks be to God.

Anthem
Thy Truth Is Great, Ron Nelson (Boosey & Hawkes) SATB (MD).

Matthew 23:1–12 Don't do as the scribes and Pharisees do, for they are poor examples to follow. They are vainly preoccupied with fulfilling the jots and tittles of the law, which has made the law into a burden. Also, do not make claims for yourself. You are all one in Christ. Your greatness is revealed by your service to neighbors.

Anthem
Whoever Would Be Great Among You, Ronald A. Nelson (Augsburg) SAB (E).

Psalm 107:1–7, 33–37
1. Metrical: *Thanks Be to God Our Savior.* Text: David J. Diephouse. Tune: GENEVAN 107. *PH87* #107.
2. Responsorial: *Psalm 107* (35–38, 41–42). Setting: Hal Hopson. *PS93* #110.
3. Metrical: *We Thank You, Lord, for You Are Good.* Text only: Fred R. Anderson. *SPJP,* p. 58.
4. Responsorial: *O Give Thanks to the Lord.* Refrain and Gelineau psalm tone: *20P&3C,* p. 22.
See also *PR&T,* pp. 77 & 81.

Anthem
Thou Visitest the Earth, Maurice Greene (*Church Anthem Book,* Oxford) SATB tenor solo (M); 2-part arr. (*Morning Star Choir Book,* Concordia).

Organ Music for the Day
Prelude on ST. MICHAEL (*O Day of God, Draw Nigh, PH90* #452), settings by Paul Manz (*Ten Chorale Improvisations,* vol. 5, Concordia 97–5257), Robert J. Powell (*Christian Hearts in Love United,* Broadman Press 4570–52), and Flor Peeters (*Hymn Preludes for the Liturgical Year,* vol. 10, C. F. Peters Corp. 6410).

Hymns for the Day	HL33	HB55	WB72	PH90
Cuando el Pobre/When a Poor One	–	–	–	407
Guide Me, O Thou Great Jehovah	104	339	409	281
How Clear Is Our Vocation, Lord	–	–	–	419
Jesus, Thy Boundless Love to Me	314	404	–	366
O Day of God, Draw Nigh	–	–	492	452
You Are Before Me, Lord (Ps. 139)	–	–	–	248

ALL SAINTS' DAY
[November 1 or First Sunday in November] (A)

Revelation 7:9–17 A vision of the glory and joy of the faithful in the New Age. A countless multitude comprised of all peoples, tongues, nations, races, and tribes stands before the throne and before the Lamb. Clothed in white robes (because they have been washed in the blood of the Lamb), and waving palm branches in their hands, the numberless throng and angels sing and shout acclamations. They serve God day and night. They experience the life of salvation where there is no more hunger, no more thirst, no more enervating heat, no more tears, no more pain, for Christ their shepherd guides them to springs of eternal living water.

Anthem

Canticle of the Lamb, Ned Rorem (Boosey & Hawkes) SATB (MD).

1 John 3:1–3 What we shall be ultimately has not been fully revealed. But we do know that when Christ appears at the Parousia, we shall see him as he is and we shall be like him, conformed to him, transformed by him. We may be unfinished people during our journey, but we are God's children. The world may not know who we are because it did not recognize Christ, but we are God's children right now. Look at the love God has already bestowed upon us, that we should be called children of God. And so we are!

Anthem

Until We Rest in Thee, Sue Ellen Page (Choristers Guild) unison SATB (E).

Matthew 5:1–12 Jesus teaches his disciples the Beatitudes as he begins the Sermon on the Mount.

Anthems

The Beatitudes, Lloyd Pfautsch (Flammer) SATB (M). *Folk Beatitudes*, David Eddleman (Carl Fischer) 2-part (E).

Psalm 34:1–10, 22

1. Metrical: *Come, Children, Listen to My Words*. Text: L.M., Christopher L. Webber. *ANMP*, pp. 84 & 85.
2. Responsorial: *Psalm 34* (1–10). Setting: Hal H. Hopson. *PS93* #32.
3. Responsorial: *Psalm 34* (9–22). Text: Helen L. Wright. Refrain: Robert E. Kreutz. Tone: Monks of Saint Meinrad. Harmony, Samuel Weber. *PS93* #33.

See also *WIII* #923, #926, and #954 (note selected verses); *CC* G-2548; *PH87* #34; *PR&T*, pp. 71 & 75.

Anthem

O Taste and See, R. Vaughan Williams (Oxford) SATB (E).

Organ Music for the Day

1. *Prelude on* SINE NOMINE. (*For All the Saints, PH90* #526), settings by Leo Sowerby (*Ten Preludes*, H. W. Gray Co., Inc. GB 651), and Paul Manz (*Ten Short Intonations on Well-Known Hymns*, Augsburg 11–9492).
2. *Prelude on* GELOBT SEI GOTT (*O Lord of Life, Where'er They Be, PH90* #530), Ernst Pepping (*Kleines Orgelbuch*, B. Schotts Söhne 3735).

Hymns for the Day	HL33	HB55	WB72	PH90
For All the Saints	429	425	369	526
Give to the Winds Your Fears	294	364	377	286
I Sing a Song of the Saints of God	–	–	–	364
O Lord of Life, Where'er They Be	–	–	513	530
Our God, Our Help (Ps. 90:1–5)	77	111	549	210

SUNDAY BETWEEN NOVEMBER 6 AND NOVEMBER 12
(PROPER 27) [32] (A)

Joshua 24:1–3a, 14–25 The conclusion of the (Joshua) story of transition from nomadic to settled life in the Promised Land. Since the land offers a multitude of temptations, it is crucial that the tribes remember who they are in the land. At Shechem, Joshua recites their history, and challenges them to declare whom they will serve. "As for me and my household, we will serve the Lord," asserts Joshua. Twice, the people declare the same allegiance. "You are witnesses against yourselves," and thus follows the ceremony of covenant renewal.

Anthem
Choose You This Day, Carl Mueller (Carl Fischer) SATB (ME).

1 Thessalonians 4:13–18 When the Lord comes again, will those believers who have already died still share in the resurrection? Yes! In fact, they shall rise first, and then come with the Parousia to meet the living.

Anthem
If We Believe That Jesus Died, John Goss, ed. Dale Wood (Sacred Music Press) SATB (ME).

Matthew 25:1–13 Ten young women in a bridal party await the coming of the bridegroom. Five of them (the wise ones) take full containers of oil for their lamps so they will be ready at a moment's notice. The other five (the foolish ones) take no oil for their lamps and are unprepared when the delayed bridegroom finally arrives. Be prepared! March with burning torches—keep them blazing. You never know the day or the hour you will be asked to stand loyal and bold for Christ. And when he arrives, surely you don't want to miss the grand messianic feast.

Anthem
Wake, Awake for Night Is Flying, P. Nicolai–Friedrich Zipp (Concordia) SATB and congregation (ME).

Psalm 78:1–7
1. Metrical: *The Mighty Deeds the Lord Has Done.* Text: Calvin Seerveld. Tune: ST. JAMES THE APOSTLE. *PH87* #78.
2. Responsorial: *Psalm 78* (1–4, 12–15, 23–25, 29, 37–38). Setting: Hal H. Hopson. *PS93* #67.
See also *PS93* #68; *WIII* #917; *PR&T*, pp. 19 & 21.

Anthem
O Come, My People, to My Law (*HB55* #255).

Organ Music for the Day
1. *Chorale Prelude on* WACHET AUF (*"Sleepers, Wake!" A Voice Astounds Us, PH90* #17), settings by J. S. Bach (various editions), Hugo Distler (*Orgelpartita on* WACHET AUF, Bärenreiter Verlag 883), and Francis Jackson (*Festal Voluntaries—Advent,* Novello & Co., Ltd. 1400).
2. *Prelude on* LLANGLOFFAN (*Rejoice! Rejoice, Believers, PH90* #15), David Dahl (*The Concordia Hymn Prelude Series,* vol. 30, pp. 42 & 43, Concordia 97–5745).

Hymns for the Day	HL33	HB55	WB72	PH90
God of Our Life	88	108	395	275
I'm Gonna Live So God Can Use Me	–	–	–	369
O Lord of Life, Where'er They Be	–	–	513	530
Rejoice, Rejoice, Believers	115	231	–	15
"Sleepers, Wake!" A Voice Astounds Us	–	–	614	17
Watchman, Tell Us of the Night	109	149	617	20

SUNDAY BETWEEN NOVEMBER 13 AND NOVEMBER 19
(PROPER 28) [33] (A)

Judges 4:1–7 Over and over again, Israel sins, YHWH raises up an oppressor, Israel cries for mercy, and YHWH raises up a deliverer—this time a leader named Deborah. Since YHWH will not allow oppression to endure, Deborah, as YHWH's judge, commands Barak to position himself at Mount Tabor, where YHWH's behind-the-scenes power "throws Sisera and all his army into a panic."

Anthem
Canon of Praise, Natalie Sleeth (Choristers Guild) (E).

1 Thessalonians 5:1–11 You already know the Day of the Lord will arrive like a thief in the night. So be prepared, stay awake, be vigilant. Put on the armor of faith, hope, and love, and look forward to life with Christ.

Anthem
For This Is the Will of God, Frank Pooler (Augsburg) SATB (ME).

Matthew 25:14–30 Three servants are charged with the responsibility of managing a master's property. Two of the servants risk their share of the property by investing it; they double their money. They are good and faithful servants who deserve a reward. The third servant plays it safe by hiding his share and thereby preserving it for the hard master. He is an evil, lazy worker. A simple parable until you remember that God is not a ruthless, hard boss, but God is love. So how do we live in God's free-grace world? Play it safe? Invest ourselves to please a tyrannical master? Neither?

Anthems
Let Us Talents and Tongues Employ, Jamaican folk melody, *PH90* #514. *When I Had Not Yet Learned of Jesus,* Yoosun Lee, *PH90* #410. *We Would Offer Thee This Day,* Jane Marshall (Sacred Music) SATB (M).

Psalm 123
1. Metrical: *To You Have I Lifted Up My Eyes.* Text: *The Psalter,* 1912. Tune: SARAH. *PH87* #123.
2. Responsorial: *Psalm 123.* Text: NRSV. Refrain and Tone: Presbyterian 7. *PS93* #127.
3. Responsorial: *To You Have I Lifted Up My Eyes.* Text: Grail. Refrain, psalm tone, and Gelineau tone: *WIII* #905. (See also *24P&1C,* p. 32.)

Anthem
Thou That Dwellest in the Heavens, Malcolm Williamson (*Psalms of the Elements*) (Boosey & Hawkes) unison and congregation (E).

Organ Music for the Day
Prelude on DUNDEE (*O God, in a Mysterious Way, PH90* #270), settings by John Gardner (*Five Hymn Tune Preludes,* Novello & Co., Ltd. 1475), Godfrey Ridout (*Three Preludes on Scottish Tunes,* Gordon V. Thompson, Ltd.), and W. Lawrence Curry (H. W. Gray Co., Inc. 727).

Hymns for the Day	HL33	HB55	WB72	PH90
Come, Labor On	366	287	–	415
O God, in a Mysterious Way	103	112	391	270
God of Grace and God of Glory	–	358	393	420
O Day of God, Draw Nigh	–	-	492	452
We Are Living, We Are Dwelling	374	356	618	–
As Those of Old Their Firstfruits Brought	–	–	301	414

CHRIST THE KING
[Sunday Between November 20 and November 26] (Proper 29) [34] (A)

Ezekiel 34:11–16, 20–24 Israel's shepherds—political and religious leaders—took care of themselves, and allowed their sheep to be deported to foreign lands. So now YHWH will serve as shepherd of Israel. YHWH will gather his scattered sheep, and return them to their own land, where YHWH will guide, heal, reconcile, feed, rebuke, and punish them with justice. Then YHWH will establish one shepherd as YHWH's servant, a descendant of David, who will faithfully feed and care for YHWH's sheep.

Anthem
Lead Us On, Good Shepherd, Tom Parker (G.I.A.) SATB (E).

Ephesians 1:15–23 May God give you the Spirit who will make you wise and understanding in the knowledge of Christ. In this way you will know the hope to which Christ has called you (the kind of New Age that is coming), and will recognize God's power among us, especially his power in raising Christ to a position above all earthly powers.

Anthems
O How Glorious, Healey Willan (H. W. Gray) SATB (ME).

Matthew 25:31–46 Christ the judge is seated on a throne, separating the wicked from the righteous. All are judged by Christ's call to love endlessly: feed the hungry and the thirsty, welcome strangers, clothe the naked, visit the sick and the imprisoned. The wicked are shocked at their designation, for they did not see the face of Christ in their neighbors, particularly the lowly. Ironically, the righteous are just as surprised, for all they saw was human need, and responded with love.

Anthem
Come, You Have My Father's Blessing, Walter Pelz (Augsburg) SAB (ME).

Psalm 100
1. Metrical: *All People That On Earth Do Dwell.* L.M., Tune: OLD HUNDREDTH. *PH90* #220.
2. Responsorial: *Psalm 100.* Setting: J. Jefferson Cleveland. *PS93* #97.
See also *PS93* #98, #99, #100, #101; *ANMP,* p. 168; *DP/SLR* #95; *WIII* #84; *24P&1C,* p. 24; *PR&T,* pp. 38 & 41.

Anthem
Jubilate Deo, William Walton (Oxford) SATB/SATB (D).

Organ Music for the Day
1. *Prelude on* HYFRYDOL (*Alleluia! Sing to Jesus, PH90* #144), settings by Healey Willan (*Ten Hymn Preludes,* C.F. Peters Corp. 6011), and Gerald Near (*Preludes on Four Hymns,* Augsburg 11–828).
2. *Prelude on* O QUANTA QUALIA (*Blessing and Honor, PH90* #147), R. Hillert (*The Concordia Hymn Prelude Series,* vol. 35, Concordia 97–5750).

Hymns for the Day	HL33	HB55	WB72	PH90
A Hymn of Glory Let Us Sing	–	–	–	141
Christian Women, Christian Men	–	–	–	348
Crown Him with Many Crowns	190	213	349	150
Cuando el Pobre/When a Poor One	–	–	–	407
O Worship the King	2	26	533	476
Our King and Our Sovereign, Lord Jesus	–	–	–	157

Special Days
PRESENTATION OF THE LORD
[FEBRUARY 2] (ABC)

Malachi 3:1–4 Behold, the Day of YHWH is coming and will be heralded by a "messenger" (angel of the Lord? Elijah the prophet? John the Baptist?). This messenger will prepare the way for YHWH's return to the Temple, from where swift judgment on wrongdoers will be executed. The priesthood and Temple will be purified in a refiner's fire so that acceptable offerings may be made to the Lord.

Anthem
Thus Saith the Lord and *But Who May Abide the Day of His Coming*, G. F. Handel (*Messiah*, any edition) bass solo (M).

Hebrews 2:14–18 Jesus shared our flesh and blood, our nature and life, our suffering and temptation, in order to serve as God's high priest and atone for our sins.

Anthem
The Word Became Flesh, George Brandon (E. C. Kirby) unison (E).

Luke 2:22–40 Parents who fulfill the law and prophets, and who break into song and utterances of thanksgiving, frame this narrative of the presentation of Jesus. Simeon the watchman has now seen the Lord's salvation, a light to the nations, and Anna begins telling everyone that the redemption of Jerusalem is at hand.

Anthems
Nunc Dimittis, Darwin Leitz (Chantry) unison (E). *Nunc Dimittis*, Daniel Moe (Agape) unison (E).

Psalm 84
1. Metrical: *How Lovely, Lord.* Text: Arlo D. Duba. Tune: MERLE'S TUNE. *PH90* #207.
2. Responsorial: *Psalm 84.* Text: Helen L. Wright. Setting: Hal H. Hopson. *PS93* #74.
3. Responsorial: *Psalm 84* (1–8). Setting: Hal H. Hopson. *PS93* #75.
4. Responsorial: *Psalm 84.* Text: NRSV. Psalm tone: Chrysogonus Waddell. Refrain: A. Gregory Murray. *PH90* #208.
5. Metrical: *Lord of the Worlds Above.* Text: Isaac Watts. Tune: DARWALL'S 148TH. *HB55* #14; *RITL* #110.

See also *ANMP*, p. 124; *PH87* #84; *PR&T*, pp. 47 & 64.

Anthem
How Lovely, Lord, PH90 #207.

or Psalm 24:7–10
1. Metrical: *Lift Up Your Gates.* Text: Weissel-Winkworth. Tune: TRURO. *PH90* #8. (See also *HB55* #152 and *WB72* #454.)
2. Responsorial: *Psalm 24. PS93* #21.
3. Responsorial: *Lift Up the Gates Eternal.* Text: Jabusch-Duba. Tune: ISRAELI FOLK MELODY. *PH90* #177. (See also *APS*, p. 16.)
4. Responsorial: *Let the Lord Enter.* Text: Grail (see also *GPI*, p. 29). Psalm tone and Gelineau tone: *WIII* #775. (See also *GG* #10 and *24P&1C*, p. 8 for additional refrains.)
5. Responsorial: *Psalm 24.* Text: optional. Psalm tones and refrains by Hal H. Hopson. *PR&T*, pp. 3 & 6.

Anthem
Psalm 24, PH90 #177.

Organ Music for the Day

1. *Chorale Prelude on* LOBE DEN HERREN (*Praise Ye the Lord, the Almighty, PH90* #482), Helmut Walcha (*Choralvorspiele,* vol. 2, C. F. Peters Corp. 4871).
2. *Prelude on* ST. MAGNUS (*The Head That Once Was Crowned, PH90* #149), Healey Willan (*Thirty-Six Short Preludes and Postludes on Well-Known Hymn Tunes,* C. F. Peters Corp. 6161).

Hymns for the Day	*HL33*	*HB55*	*WB72*	*PH90*
Praise Ye the Lord, the Almighty	6	1	557	482
The Head That Once Was Crowned	195	211	589	149
My Faith Looks Up to Thee	285	378	360	383
Song of Simeon	–	–	–	603–605

ANNUNCIATION OF THE LORD
[MARCH 25] (ABC)

Isaiah 7:10–14 Isaiah offers the disbelieving King Ahaz of Judah a sign of God's care, but the king piously refuses to test the Lord for a sign. "Well then," says Isaiah, "the Lord will give you a sign: a young woman shall conceive and bear a son, and shall call his name Immanuel, for God is with God's people."

Anthems

Behold a Virgin Shall Conceive, and *O Thou That Tellest Good Tidings* (air and chorus), G. F. Handel (*Messiah,* any edition) alto, SATB (M).

Hebrews 10:4–10 The preexistent Christ speaks the words of Psalm 40:6–8 in order to define the purpose of his incarnation. No longer will the old Levitical sacrifices be either necessary or efficacious, for the ultimate sacrifice of Christ's body upon the cross will establish the new covenant. The justification for the incarnation is that Christ will take a human body in order to offer this perfect sacrifice in obedience to the will of God.

Anthem

Lo, in the Time Appointed, Healey Willan (Oxford) SATB (M).

Luke 1:26–38 The angel Gabriel announces to a peasant girl that she will be impregnated by the invisible power of God and give birth to a son who "will be called the Son of the Most High; and of his kingdom there will be no end." "Preposterous!" you say. Consider this: From the beginning of time God has been at work in bringing forth Jesus Christ so he could be one with his people. Now, in this final annunciation story in the Bible, God's purpose will be fulfilled. God will act to save God's people. This child is to be born to this woman for the saving of the world. May we join our voices with Mary in saying, "Let it be according to your word; let it happen through our lives."

Anthem

To a Maid Engaged to Joseph, PH90 #19.

Psalm 45

1. Metrical: *I Will Praise the King with All My Verses.* Text: Marie J. Post and Bert Polman. Tune: O DASS ICH TAUSENT. *PH87* #45.
2. Responsorial: *Psalm 45.* Text: Grail. Refrain: Presbyterian 3. Tone: Presbyterian 3 (expanded). *PS93* #39.
3. Responsorial: *Psalm 45* (10–17). *The Queen Stands at Your Right Hand.* Text: Grail (see also *GPI,* p. 62). Refrain, psalm tone, and Gelineau tone: *WIII* #1046. (See also *GG,* p. 165.)
4. Responsorial: *Psalm 45* (10–17). *The Queen Stands at Your Right Hand.* Setting by Howard Hughes. *CC* G-2028.
5. Responsorial: Text: optional. Psalm tones and refrains by Hal H. Hopson. *PR&T,* pp. 18 & 44.

or Psalm 40:5–10

1. Metrical: *I Waited for the Lord My God.* Text: *The Psalter,* 1912. Tune: ABRIDGE. *HB55* #413; *RITL* #100.
2. Responsorial: *Psalm 40* (1–11). Text: Helen L. Wright. Melody: Columba Kelly. Harmony, Samuel Weber. *PS93* #36.
3. Responsorial: *Here Am I, Lord: I Come to Do Your Will.* Text: Grail (see also Grail inclusive *GPI,* p. 54). Psalm tone and Gelineau tone: *WIII* #868. *GG,* p. 107. For other refrains see *WIII* #924. (See also *20P&3C,* p. 8.)

See also *ANMP,* p. 91; *PH87* #40; *PR&T,* pp. 18 & 67.

Anthem

To Do What Pleases You, James Hansen (OCP) SAB congregation (E).

Organ Music for the Day

Prelude on CRUSADERS' HYMN/ST. ELIZABETH (*Fairest Lord Jesus, PH90* #306), F. Melius Christiansen (Augsburg 11–9306), Carl F. Mueller (*Six Preludes Based on Familiar Hymns,* Carl Fischer, Inc. 0 4184).

Hymns for the Day	*HL33*	*HB55*	*WB72*	*PH90*
Come, Thou Fount of Every Blessing	235	379	341	356
Come, Thou Long-Expected Jesus	113	151	342	1, 2
Lo, How a Rose E'er Blooming	–	162	455	48
O Come, O Come, Emmanuel	108	147	489	9
The Angel Gabriel from Heaven Came	–	–	–	16
To a Maid Engaged to Joseph	–	–	–	19

VISITATION OF MARY TO ELIZABETH
[MAY 31] (ABC)

1 Samuel 2:1–10 After years of childlessness, Hannah gives birth to a son named Samuel, whom she now presents at the sanctuary in Shiloh. Here she offers praise to YHWH who can bring a child out of barrenness, abundance out of poverty, princes out of the needy, life out of death, something out of nothing. YHWH is in charge of this world. YHWH's political purposes, economic ways, and social plans will come to fruition.

Anthem
Sing Praise Unto the Name of God, PH90 #226.

Romans 12:9–16b Paul's catalog of conduct within the Christian community: hate evil, love one another, be constant in prayer, practice hospitality, bless those who persecute you (noted twice so we'll know he means what he says), weep with those who weep, associate with the lowly, and more.

Anthem
Let Love Continue, Eugene Butler (Hinshaw) SATB (ME).

Luke 1:39–57 The grand conclusion to the two annunciation stories of John and Jesus. Here Mary's whole being, soul and spirit, offers a canticle of praise to God for "he has done great things for me, and holy is his name."

Anthem
Song of Mary, PH90 #600.

Psalm 113
1. Metrical: *Sing Praise Unto the Name of God.* Text: Fred R. Anderson. Tune: GENEVAN 36. *PH90* #226. For text only see *SPJP*, p. 60.
2. Responsorial: *Psalm 113.* Text: *The United Methodist Liturgical Psalter.* Refrain and Tone: Presbyterian 1. *PS93* #113.
3. Metrical: *Praise the Lord!* Text: Marjorie Jillson. Setting by Heinz Werner Zimmerman. *PH90* #225. (See also *RITL* #123.)
4. Metrical: *Praise God, You Servants of the Lord.* Text: *The Psalter,* 1912. Tune: ANDRE. *HB55* #19. (See also *PH87* #113 to the Tune: FESTUS.)
5. Responsorial: *Praise the Lord Who Lifts Up the Poor.* Text: Grail. Refrain, psalm tone, and Gelineau tone: *WIII* #939. (See also *30P&2C,* pp. 32 & 33 and *GG,* p. 119. For text only see *GPI,* p. 168 and *GGP,* p. 164.)

See also *ANMP,* p. 182; *PR&T,* pp. 69 & 77.

Anthem
Praise the Lord, Ye Servants, Richard Peek (Brodt) unison (E).

Organ Music for the Day
1. *Prelude on* ST. COLUMBA (*The King of Love My Shepherd Is, PH90* #171), Healey Willan (*Ten Hymn Preludes,* C. F. Peters Corp. 6011), and Flor Peeters (*Thirty Short Preludes on Well-Known Hymns,* C. F. Peters Corp. 6195).
2. *Prelude on* MORNING SONG (*Song of Mary, PH90* #600), Theodore Beck (*The Concordia Hymn Prelude Series,* vol. 1, Concordia 97–5536).

Hymns for the Day	HL33	HB55	WB72	PH90
At the Name of Jesus	–	143	303	148
Love Divine, All Loves Excelling	308	399	471	376
O Love, How Deep, How Broad	139	–	518	83
Song of Mary	56	596	–	600
The King of Love My Shepherd Is	99	106	590	171

HOLY CROSS
[SEPTEMBER 14] (ABC)

Numbers 21:4b–9 Impatient Israel wanders in the wilderness murmuring (i.e., complaining) and speaking against God and Moses and the food and water. YHWH has had enough of this murmuring, and so sends judgment in the form of fiery serpents that bite the people so that many die. Result: Israel confesses its sin and prays that the serpents be removed. YHWH instructs Moses to "make an image of a serpent, and set it on a pole; and every one who is bitten, when he sees it, shall live." And it was so. Judgment was and is the means of God's redemption.

Anthem
Bow Down Thine Ear, O Lord, Anton Arensky (*Church Anthem Book,* Oxford) SATB (E).

1 Corinthians 1:18–24 The gospel always seems to turn our world upside down. Here worldly wisdom and strength are characterized as foolish and weak, and the nonsense and weakness of the crucifixion are labeled as wise and strong.

Anthem
Christus Factus Est, Anton Bruckner (Summy-Birchard) SATB (M).

John 3:13–17 The possibility of new life "from above" is available only through Christ, the one who was publicly lifted up on the cross so that all might see and believe, and therefore "have eternal life."

Anthem
God So Loved the World, Jan Bender (*Sing to the Lord a New Song,* Concordia) 2-part (E).

Psalm 98:1–5
1. Metrical: *New Songs of Celebration Render.* Text: Erik Routley. Tune: RENDEZ À DIEU. *PH90* #218. (See also *RITL* #119, *H82* #413, and *PH87* #98 with text by Dewey Westra.)
2. Metrical: *To God Compose a Song of Joy.* Text: Ruth C. Duck. Tune: KEDDY. *PH90* #219.
3. Responsorial: *Psalm 98.* Text: International Commission on English in the Liturgy. Tone: Presbyterian 3. *PS93* #94.
4. Responsorial: *Psalm 98* (1–6). Text: *Book of Common Prayer.* Setting: Peter R. Hallock. *PS93* #95.

See also *WIII* #781; *PH87* #98; *ANMP,* p. 161; *SPJP,* p. 53; *PR&T,* pp. 10 & 13.

Anthem
To God Compose a Song of Joy, PH90 #219.

or Psalm 78:1–2, 34–38
1. Metrical: *Hear, O My People, What I Say* and *All the Night Through with Glow of Fire.* Text: L.M., Christopher L. Webber. *ANMP,* pp. 125 & 126.
2. Responsorial: *Psalm 78* (1–4, 12–15, 23–25, 29, 37–38). Setting: Hal H. Hopson. *PS93* #67.
3. Responsorial: *Psalm 78* (1–7, 34–38a). Text: *The United Methodist Liturgical Psalter,* NRSV. Refrain and Tone: Presbyterian 4. *PS93* #68.
4. Responsorial: *The Lord Gave the Bread.* Text: Grail (see also *GPI,* p. 109–14). Refrain, psalm tone, and Gelineau tone: *WIII* #917 (see also *WIII* #1050 with refrain "Do not forget the work of the Lord"). (See also *GG,* p. 166.)

See also: *PH87* #78; *PR&T,* pp. 19 & 21.

Anthem
Cantate Domino, David McKinley Williams (H. W. Gray) SATB optional brass (MD).

Organ Music for the Day

1. *Prelude on* VICTORY (*The Strife Is O'er, PH90* #119), Wilbur Held (*Six Preludes on Easter Hymns,* Concordia 97–5330).
2. *Prelude on* ROCKINGHAM (*When I Survey the Wondrous Cross, PH90* #100), Richard Purvis (*Impressions,* Fred Bock Music Co. B-G0769).

Hymns for the Day	*HL33*	*HB55*	*WB72*	*PH90*
In the Cross of Christ I Glory	154	195	437	84
The Strife Is O'er	164	203	597	119
Throned Upon the Awful Tree	–	197	605	99
To God Be the Glory	–	–	–	485
When I Survey the Wondrous Cross	152	198	635	100

THANKSGIVING DAY (A)*
[FOURTH THURSDAY IN NOVEMBER IN U.S.A.]

Deuteronomy 8:7–18 Always remember who redeemed you all from bondage, who led you through the perilous wilderness, who brought you water out of solid rock, who fed you in the barren desert, for it is the same one who promises you the land where all your needs will be supplied. You will never go hungry. So don't think you have pulled yourself up by your own bootstraps, but give all the thanks to YHWH, who has done all this for you in the past, and who promises you an abundant future.

Anthem
Sing to the Lord of Harvest, Healey Willan (Concordia) SATB (E).

2 Corinthians 9:6–15 God is the giver of all good gifts. If you are willing to give away your God-given gifts, then God will make sure you always have gifts to give others. After all, God loves cheerful givers who enrich God's creation and who, in turn, are enriched themselves. Truly, the essence of thanksgiving is a life of giving in response to the undeserved grace of God in Christ.

Anthem
O Sing the Glories of Our Lord, H. K. Andrews (Oxford) SATB (E).

Luke 17:11–19 Ten lepers cry out to Jesus for pity. "Go!" commands Jesus (no comfort here). "Show yourselves to the priests." They obey. They do what Jesus tells them to do—that's faith—and they are healed. But one leper, a despised outsider, turns back to give thanks, glorifying God. He obeys and worships. No wonder Jesus says to him, "Your faith has made you whole."

Anthem
Now Thank We All and Praise to the Lord (Quodlibet), Willard Palmer (Alfred) SSATB (ME).

Psalm 65
1. Metrical: *To Bless the Earth, God Sends Us.* Text: *The Psalter,* 1912, alt. Tune: CHRISTUS, DER IST MEIN LEBEN. *PH90* #200.
2. Responsorial: *Psalm 65* (1–8). Text: Grail. Refrain: Hal H. Hopson. Tone: Gregorian VIII. *PS93* #55.
3. Responsorial: *Psalm 65* (9–13). Setting: Hal H. Hopson. *PS93* #56.
See also *PH87* #65; *PH90* #201; *ANMP,* p. 108; *HB55* #99; *RITL* #107; *WIII* #907; *PR&T,* pp. 52 & 53.

Anthem
Thou Visitest the Earth, Maurice Greene (*Church Anthem Book,* Oxford) SATB (E).

Organ Music for the Day
1. *Prelude on* ST. GEORGE'S, WINDSOR (*Come, Ye Thankful People, Come, PH90* #551), Vernon Griffiths (*Festal Voluntaries—Harvest,* Novello & Co., Ltd. 1403).
2. *Prelude on* KREMSER (*We Gather Together, PH90* #559), Gordon Young (*Seven Hymn Voluntaries,* Theodore Presser Co. 413–41118).

Hymns for the Day	HL33	HB55	WB72	PH90
Come, Sing a Song of Harvest	–	–	–	558
Come, Ye Thankful People, Come	460	525	346	551
I Will Give Thanks (Ps. 247)	–	–	–	247
Many and Great, O God, Are Thy Things	–	–	–	271
Now Thank We All Our God	459	9	481	555
We Gather Together	–	18	624	559

---

*NOTE: Readings for Thanksgiving Day are not strictly tied to Year A, B, or C.

Year B

Christmas Cycle
Season of Advent
FIRST SUNDAY OF ADVENT (B)

Isaiah 64:1–9 Be present among us. Make your name known to your adversaries as you did in liberating us from bondage in Egypt. Yes, we have sinned. All of us wandered from your way and are blown about by the wind of our desires. None of us calls upon your name, for your absence has exacerbated our iniquities. But, YHWH, we are the clay and you are our potter. Therefore, mold us!

Anthem
The Prayers I Make, Jane Marshall (Sacred Music Press) 2-part (E).

1 Corinthians 1:3–9 In the opening greeting and thanksgiving, Paul thanks God for his grace given through Christ Jesus. Therefore, we are enriched by spiritual gifts, particularly in all "speech and knowledge." God has given us everything we need and will sustain us to the Day of the Lord, which brings judgment.

Anthem
O Mighty God, Our Lord, Heinrich Schütz (Mercury) 2-part (ME).

Mark 13:24–37 Some people believe they can predict the actual apocalyptic ending of the world. But does anybody know this? Neither angels nor the Son of Man knows. So don't pay any attention to soothsayers. Rather, look alive, keep alert, be responsible all the time, keeping your eye out for the Lord, who is coming from the joyous messianic banquet. This is a word for everybody.

Anthems
Wake, Awake, John Horman (Augsburg) 3-part (E). *Therefore Watch That Ye Be Ready,* Andreas Hammerschmidt (Concordia) SSATB (D).

Psalm 80:1–7, 17–19
1. Metrical: *O Hear Our Cry, O Lord.* Text: Fred R. Anderson. Tune: VINEYARD HAVEN. *PH90* #206 (text only see *SPJP,* p. 43).
2. Responsorial: *Psalm 80* (1–7). Text: Gary Chamberlain. Setting: Hal H. Hopson. *PS93* #70.
3. Responsorial: *Psalm 80.* Text: Grail. Setting: Howard Hughes. Gelineau tone. *PS93* #71.

See also *ANMP,* p. 127; *PH87* #80; *WIII* #767; *30P&2C,* p. 23.

Anthem
Advent Anthem, Richard Proulx (Augsburg) SATB (M).

Organ Music for the Day
1. *Prelude on* VENI EMMANUEL (*O Come, O Come, Emmanuel, PH90* #9), Edward C. Bairstow (*Three Short Preludes,* p. 8, Oxford 375290–5), and Richard Purvis (*An American Organ Mass,* p. 7, Harold Flammer, Inc. HF-5020).
2. *Prelude Improvisation on* ABERYSTWYTH (*Watchman, Tell Us of the Night, PH90* #20), John Huston (H. W. Gray Co., Inc. 866).

Hymns for the Day	HL33	HB55	WB72	PH90
Come, Thou Long-Expected Jesus	113	151	342	1
O Come, O Come, Emmanuel	108	147	489	9
O God of Earth and Altar	419	511	497	291
O God of Every Nation	–	–	498	289
O Lord, How Shall I Meet You?	–	–	–	11
Savior of the Nations, Come	–	–	565	14

134

SECOND SUNDAY OF ADVENT (B)

Isaiah 40:1–11 God announces to a vice-president, "Let Israel know its struggles are ended. Reassure my people." The vice-president shouts to a line manager, "Build the roadway! God is going to Mt. Zion and will pick up God's captive people on the way." The line manager replies, "All grass withers, so what shall I cry to these people? They're in bad shape and won't believe." Answer: Get up on a high place and preach, "Behold, your God comes!"

Anthem
Comfort All Ye My People, Gabriel Fauré (Carl Fischer) SATB (ME).

2 Peter 3:8–15a The human world will end when God says so. Until such time, God is incredibly patient in yearning and hoping that all people will repent before the Day of the Lord arrives. How shall you live now? Expect, anticipate, look forward to the coming of "new heavens and a new earth in which righteousness dwells," and prepare yourselves and the human world to be ready and fit for God's new order.

Anthem
The Lord Will Come and Not Be Slow, Henry Ley (*Oxford Easy Anthem Book,* Oxford) SATB (E).

Mark 1:1–8 In the wilderness, the prophet-like John the Baptizer—dressed like Elijah in 2 Kings 1:8—proclaims the advent of the Lord: "Prepare the way! The mighty one who will baptize you with the Holy Spirit is coming." How shall we prepare? Turn away from your sins of pride, vanity, bigotry. Strip off anything weighing you down. Do as "people from all the country of Judea, and all the people of Jerusalem who were baptized, confessing their sins."

Anthems
Prepare Ye the Way, Allen Pote (Carl Fischer) 2-part (E). *On Jordan's Bank the Baptist's Cry,* Monteverdi, arr. Klammer (G.I.A.) SAB (ME).

Psalm 85:1–2, 8–13
1. Metrical: *Show Us, Lord, Your Steadfast Love.* Text: L.M., Christopher L. Webber. *ANMP,* p. 136.
2. Responsorial: *Psalm 85.* Text: *Book of Common Prayer,* alt. Refrain: Hal H. Hopson. Tone: Lutheran 7. *PS93* #76.
See also *PS93* #77 & #78; *WIII* #770; *PH87* #85; *PR&T,* pp. 1 & 7.

Anthem
That in This Land There May Dwell Glory, Christian Gregor (Boosey & Hawkes) SATB (ME).

Organ Music for the Day
1. *Partita on* PSALM 42 (*Comfort, Comfort You My People, PH90* #3), Georg Böhm (*Sämtliche Orgelwerke,* Breitkopf 8087).
2. *Chorale Improvisation on* HYFRYDOL (*Come, Thou Long-Expected Jesus, PH90* #2), Paul Manz (*Ten Chorale Improvisations,* vol. 1, p. 10, Concordia 97–4554).

Hymns for the Day	HL33	HB55	WB72	PH90
Comfort, Comfort You My People	–	–	347	3
My Lord! What a Morning	–	–	–	449
O Day of God, Draw Nigh	–	–	492	452
On Jordan's Bank the Baptist's Cry	–	–	–	10
Prepare the Way	–	–	–	13
Wild and Lone the Prophet's Voice	–	–	–	409

<h1 style="text-align:center">THIRD SUNDAY OF ADVENT (B)</h1>

Isaiah 61:1–4, 8–11 The prophet announces his calling through God's Spirit. He has been anointed to proclaim the season of YHWH's favor when the afflicted, the disenfranchised, the oppressed, the tormented, the grieving, the imprisoned shall be restored. YHWH: "I despise injustice; so I will restore Israel as a sign of my purposes of salvation." As surely as seeds sprout and grow, the season of YHWH's favor will burgeon and all will praise YHWH.

Anthems

Good Tidings to the Meek, R. Thompson (E. C. Schirmer) SATB (M). *The Spirit of the Lord Is Upon Me,* Edward Elgar (Novello) SATB (M).

1 Thessalonians 5:16–24 Some final admonitions by Paul: Rejoice, pray, give thanks constantly in all that you do. Open yourselves to the work of the Holy Spirit, but always test such actions against God's will as revealed by Christ—if they don't pass the test, then avoid; if they do, then follow. May the God of peace sanctify the whole of your life. And, above all, rejoice always, for God—the faithful one, the one who keeps covenant—will sanctify you so that you are ready for the coming of our Lord Jesus Christ.

Anthem

For This Is the Will of God, Frank Pooler (Augsburg) SATB (ME).

John 1:6–8, 19–28 The rulers send some priests and Levites to interrogate John (the Baptizer) about his identity. Are you the Christ? No! Are you Elijah? No! Are you the prophet? No! (*He isn't anyone important.*) Then why do you baptize? Because among you stands one whom you do not know, but he is the one. And before him, I am nothing.

Anthem

This Is the Record of John, Orlando Gibbons (Lawson-Gould) SAATB tenor solo (MD).

Psalm 126

1. Metrical: *When God Delivered Israel.* Text: Michael A. Saward. Tune: SHEAVES. *PH90* #237. (See also *PP* #134 and *RITL* #133.)
2. Responsorial: *Psalm 126.* Setting: Hal H. Hopson. *PS93* #130.
3. Responsorial: *Psalm 126.* Text: Grail. Setting: J. Gelineau. *PS93* #131.

See also *WIII* #69, #771; *PH87* #126; *ANMP,* p. 209; *PR&T,* pp. 41 & 79.

Anthem

When the Lord Turned Again, Wm. Billings (Concordia) SATB (ME).

or **Luke 1:47–55 (Magnificat)**

See **Fourth Sunday of Advent (B), p. 136.**

Organ Music for the Day

1. *Chorale Improvisation on* PICARDY (*Let All Mortal Flesh Keep Silence, PH90* #5), Paul Manz (*Ten Chorale Improvisations,* vol. 5, p. 30, Concordia 97–5257), and John Joubert (*Easy Modern Organ Music,* vol. 2, p. 5, Oxford 375127–5).
2. *My Soul Exalts the Lord,* J. S. Bach (*Schübler Chorals,* various editions).

Hymns for the Day	HL33	HB55	WB72	PH90
Christian Women, Christian Men	–	–	–	348
Creator of the Stars of Night	–	–	348	4
He Did Not Want to Be Far	–	–	412	–
Lo, How a Rose E'er Blooming	–	162	455	48
Rejoice, Rejoice, Believers	115	231	–	15
The Desert Shall Rejoice	–	–	–	18

FOURTH SUNDAY OF ADVENT (B)

2 Samuel 7:1–11, 16 David aspires to build YHWH a house (temple). Now YHWH replies to David through the mouth of the prophet Nathan: "I took you from the sheep pastures; I chose you as ruler of my people; I have been with you wherever you went; I have made for you a great name; I have given you rest from all your enemies; I will build you a house (dynasty) that will last forever, for my steadfast love will be always with your descendants."

Anthem
Behold the Star of Jacob Rising, Felix Mendelssohn (E. C. Schirmer) SATB (M).

Romans 16:25–27 Glory to the one who can strengthen you in faith according to the good news of Jesus Christ, according to the revelation of the mystery now made known to all, and according to the command of God, who brings about obedience of faith. "To the only wise God be glory for evermore through Jesus Christ!"

Anthems
Blessing, Natalie Sleeth (Choristers Guild) unison and flute (E). *Praise God, O Bless the Lord*, G. F. Handel, arr. H. Hopson (Augsburg).

Luke 1:26–38 The angel Gabriel announces to an ordinary peasant girl that she will be impregnated by the invisible power of God and give birth to a son who "will be called the Son of the Most High; and of his kingdom there will be no end." "Preposterous!" you say. Consider this: From the beginning of time God has been at work in bringing forth Jesus Christ so he could be one with his people. Now, in this final annunciation story in the Bible, God's purpose will be fulfilled. God will act to save the people. This child is to be born to this woman for the saving of the world. We join our voices with Mary in saying, "Let it be according to your word; let it happen through our lives."

Anthems
A Dove Flew Down from Heaven, Hermann Schroeder (Concordia) SATB flute, 2 violins (MD). *And the Angel Came in Unto Mary*, Ian Kellam (Oxford) SATB (M).

Luke 1:47–55 (Magnificat)
1. Metrical: *Song of Mary*. Paraphrase: Miriam Therese Winter. Tune: MORNING SONG. *PH90* #600.
2. Metrical: *Tell Out, My Soul, the Greatness of the Lord*. Tune: WOODLANDS. Text: Timothy Dudley-Smith. *RITL* #182.
3. Responsorial: *Canticle of Mary (Magnificat)* (Luke 1:46–55). Text: Grail. Setting: Joseph Gelineau. *PS93* #161.
4. Responsorial: *Canticle of Mary (Magnificat)* (Luke 1:46–55). Text: English Language Liturgical Consultation, alt. Setting: John Weaver (with additional refrains). *PS93* #162.
5. Responsorial: *Canticle of Mary (Magnificat)* (Luke 1:46–55). Text: *Book of Common Prayer*, alt., English Language Liturgical Consultation. Setting: Tonus peregrinus. Accompaniment: Alec Wyton. Refrain: Bruce Ford. *PS93* #162.

Anthems
O Magnify the Lord with Me, George Lynn (Presser) SATB (M). *Magnificat*, Ralph Vaughan Williams (G. Schirmer) SATB (M). *Song of Mary, PH90* #600.

or Psalm 89:1–4, 19–26
1. Metrical: *My Song Forever Shall Record*. Text: *The Psalter*, 1912. Tune: ST. PETERSBURG. *PH90* #209. (See also *HB55* #516 and *RITL* #113.)
2. Responsorial: *Psalm 89* (1, 3, 19–21, 24). Text: Hal H. Hopson. Setting: Jacques Berthier, arr. Hal H. Hopson. *PS93* #80.
3. Responsorial: *Psalm 89* (1–4, 15–18). Setting: Hal H. Hopson. *PS93* #81.

4. Responsorial: *Psalm 89* (1–4, 15–18). Text: Grail. Refrain and Tone: Presbyterian 6. *PS93* #82.

5. Responsorial: *For Ever I Will Sing*. Setting by Howard Hughes. *CC* G-2027.

See also *ANMP*, p. 139; *PH87* #89; *WIII* #776; *20P&3C*, p. 16; *PR&T*, pp. 5 & 9.

Anthem

I Will Sing of the Mercies, Gerald Near (*Three Introits*, Calvary Press) SATB (M).

Organ Music for the Day

1. *Chorale Prelude on* VALET WILL ICH DIR GEBEN (*O Lord, How Shall I Meet You?*, *PH90* #11), J. S. Bach (various editions), and Paul Manz (*Improvisations for the Christmas Season*, vol. 2, p. 27, Morningstar Music Publishers MSM-10–101).

2. *Chorale Prelude on* ES IST EIN' ROS' (*Lo, How a Rose E'er Blooming, PH90* #48), Johannes Brahms (various editions), and Hermann Schroeder (*Orgelchoräle im Kirchenjahr*, p. 4, B. Schotts Söhne ED 5426).

Hymns for the Day	HL33	HB55	WB72	PH90
Come, Thou Long-Expected Jesus	113	151	342	2
O Come, O Come, Emmanuel	108	147	489	9
"Sleepers, Wake!" A Voice Astounds Us	–	–	614	17
Song of Mary	56	596	–	600
The Angel Gabriel from Heaven Came	–	–	–	16
To a Maid Engaged to Joseph	–	–	–	19
Watchman Tell Us of the Night (antiphonal)	109	149	617	20

138

Season of Christmas
CHRISTMAS EVE/DAY
[DECEMBER 24/25] (ABC)

See Christmas Eve/Day (ABC) in Year A, p. 31.

CHRISTMAS EVE/DAY: ALTERNATIVE LECTIONS 1
[DECEMBER 24/25] (ABC)

See Christmas Eve/Day: Alternative Lections 1 (ABC) in Year A, p. 32.

CHRISTMAS EVE/DAY: ALTERNATIVE LECTIONS 2
[DECEMBER 24/25] (ABC)

See Christmas Eve/Day: Alternative Lections 2 (ABC) in Year A, p. 33.

FIRST SUNDAY AFTER CHRISTMAS DAY (B)

Isaiah 61:10–62:3 Is the land renewed each year so new crops can sprout? Is the Lord God going to restore his people? You know the answer, so rejoice and exult in YHWH. Announce this good news until YHWH's glory and power in saving Jerusalem illuminate all the nations. Israel shall shed its old name and ragged clothes, and be renamed and arrayed in festive clothes and sparkling jewels. YHWH's salvation shall bring complete transformation.

Anthem
I Will Greatly Rejoice, Donald Rotermund (Concordia) SATB (M).

Galatians 4:4–7 When God decided the right time had come, God sent the Son, fully human, to release all those under the law so they might be God's children. Then God sent the Spirit of the Son, who empowered these adopted children to name God as "Abba, Father."

Anthem
Evergreen, Daniel Pinkham (E. C. Schirmer) unison with electronic tape (ME).

Luke 2:22–40 Parents who fulfill the law, and prophets who break into song and utterances of thanksgiving, frame this narrative of the presentation of Jesus. Simeon the watchman has now seen the Lord's salvation, a light to the nations, and Anna begins telling everyone that the redemption of Jerusalem is at hand. Ironically, the birth and the presentation of the child who is "God with us" will eventually demand that child's death as the way to purify and restore life to God's people.

Anthems
Nunc Dimittis, R. Vaughan Williams (G. Schirmer) SATB (ME). *Nunc Dimittis,* John Rutter (Hinshaw) SATB (M).

Psalm 148
1. Metrical: *Let the Whole Creation Cry.* Text: Stopford A. Brooke, 1881. Tune: SALZBURG. Harmony, J. S. Bach. *PH90* #256.

2. Responsorial: *Psalm 148.* Setting: Hal H. Hopson. *PS93* #155.
3. Metrical: *Praise Ye, Praise Ye the Lord.* Text: *The Psalter,* 1912. Tune: AMHERST. *RITL* #141.
4. Responsorial: *Praise the Lord from the Earth* (verses 7–14). Text: *Book of Common Prayer.* Music: Peter R. Hallock. *TIP/PSCY* #9.
See also *PH90* #257; *H82* #432.

Anthems
Lord Who Hast Made Us for Thine Own, Gustav Holst (E. C. Schirmer) SATB (ME).
Praise Hymn, Robert Leaf (AMSI) 2-part or unison (E).

Organ Music for the Day
1. *Prelude on* KINGSFOLD (*O Sing a Song of Bethlehem, PH90* #308), Robert Cundick and John Longhurst (*Twelve Hymn Settings from the Tabernacle,* p. 10, Sonos Music Resources, Inc. SWK058).
2. *Prelude on* PICARDY (*Let All Mortal Flesh Keep Silence, PH90* #5), Henry Coleman (*Twenty-Four Interludes Based on Communion Hymn Tunes,* p. 11, Oxford University Press 375330–8).

Hymns for the Day	HL33	HB55	WB72	PH90
Arise, Your Light Is Come!	–	–	–	411
Hark! The Herald Angels Sing	117	163	411	31
On This Day Earth Shall Ring	–	–	538	46
See Amid the Winter's Snow	–	–	–	50
Song of Simeon	59	597	–	603–605
That Boy-Child of Mary	–	–	–	55
'Twas in the Moon of Wintertime	–	–	–	61

HOLY NAME OF JESUS
[JANUARY 1] (ABC)

See Holy Name of Jesus [January 1] (ABC) in Year A, p. 36.

JANUARY 1
[WHEN OBSERVED AS NEW YEAR'S DAY] (ABC)

See January 1 [When observed as New Year's Day] (ABC) in Year A, p. 38.

SECOND SUNDAY AFTER CHRISTMAS DAY (ABC)

See Second Sunday After Christmas Day (ABC) in Year A, p. 39.

Day of Epiphany
EPIPHANY OF THE LORD
[JANUARY 6] (ABC)

See Epiphany of the Lord (ABC) in Year A, p. 41.

Ordinary Time
BAPTISM OF THE LORD
[SUNDAY BETWEEN JANUARY 7 AND 13] [1] (B)

Genesis 1:1–5 All was dark upon the formless, chaotic, unordered waters of creation. God spoke: "Let there be light." And there was light, for when God speaks, action occurs. Then God separated the light from the darkness and named the light "day." Chaos is transformed into cosmos by God's order and differentiation. "And God saw that the light was good. . . . And there was evening and there was morning, one day."

Anthem
Creation Song, J. Brown (Choristers Guild) unison or 2-part, children.

Acts 19:1–7 In Ephesus, Paul encounters some disciples of John, and asks them if they received the Holy Spirit. "Never heard about, much less received it," they reply; "we were baptized by John." Paul responds, "That's an incomplete baptism of repentance only; even John told you to believe in the one coming after him." So they had themselves baptized in the name of the Lord Jesus, accompanied by Paul's laying his hands on them. Now the Holy Spirit came upon them and they spoke in tongues and prophesied.

Anthem
Come Down, O Love Divine (DOWN AMPNEY), arr. Daniel Gawthrop (H. W. Gray) SATB (ME).

Mark 1:4–11 In the wilderness, the prophet-like John the Baptizer proclaims the advent of the Lord: "Prepare the way! The mighty one who will baptize you with the Holy Spirit is coming." How shall we prepare? Turn away from your sins of pride, vanity, bigotry. Do as "people from all the country of Judea, and all the people of Jerusalem who were baptized, confessing their sins." John then baptizes Jesus of Nazareth. As Jesus emerges from the water, he sees the heavens open and is confirmed by the gift of the Spirit and a voice repeating words reminiscent of a coronation (Ps. 2:7), "You are my beloved Son."

Anthem
Carol of the Baptism, George Brandon (Concordia) SAB (ME).

Psalm 29
1. Metrical: *The God of Glory Thunders.* Text: Michael Perry. Setting: Norman Warren. *PH90* #180 (see also *PP* #82).
2. Responsorial: *Psalm 29.* Setting: Hal H. Hopson. *PS93* #26.
See also *GPI,* p. 35; *CC* G-2421; *ANMP,* p. 66; *PH87* #29; *PR&T,* pp. 17 & 66.

Anthem
Bring to Jehovah, Heinrich Schütz (*Sing Joyfully,* Walton) unison (E).

Organ Music for the Day
1. *Prelude on* CAITHNESS (*Christ, When for Us You Were Baptized, PH90* #70), Healey Willan (*Thirty-Six Short Preludes and Postludes on Well-Known Hymn Tunes,* vol. 1, p. 6, C. F. Peters Corp. 6161).
2. *Prelude on* BUNESSAN (*Morning Has Broken, PH90* #469), Dale Wood (*Wood Works,* p. 20, The Sacred Music Press KK 357).

Hymns for the Day	HL33	HB55	WB72	PH90
Creating God, Your Fingers Trace	–	–	–	134
Down to Earth, as a Dove	–	–	–	300
God, Who Stretched the Spangled Heavens	–	–	–	268
Lord, When You Came to Jordan	–	–	–	71
Of the Father's Love Begotten	–	7	534	309
We Meet You, O Christ	–	–	–	311

SUNDAY BETWEEN JANUARY 14 AND 20 [2] (B)

I Samuel 3:1–10, (11–20) Injustice, infidelity, and corruption permeated temple life at Shiloh. Worse, "the word of YHWH was rare." Yet YHWH persistently calls to the boy Samuel during his sleep so he may deliver the word of YHWH. A suspenseful, dramatic call unfolds four times, reaching its climax when Samuel finally hears YHWH's revelation: Samuel must deliver YHWH's word of judgment upon the whole house of Eli. Amazingly, Eli accepts that word. More amazingly, that word comes true precisely as proclaimed by Samuel, who is then "established as a prophet of YHWH."

Anthem

How Clear Is Our Vocation, Lord, Tune: REPTON, arr. Russell Schultz-Widmar (Augsburg) SATB (ME).

1 Corinthians 6:12–20 For some people, freedom is license to "do your own thing"; so they pursue gluttony or sexual promiscuity, as long as they "don't harm anyone." But such "freedom" is a form of enslavement to—among other things—narcissistic hedonism. That is freedom, writes Paul, but at a staggering cost. We are free from the vicious cycle of endlessly seeking social approval so that we may live in the Spirit, serving the Lord and neighbors. We are free from Platonic dualism of separating body and spirit so that our total self may be joined to Christ and used not for our pleasure but in service to him.

Anthem

Temples of God, R. A. Nelson (Augsburg) 2-part mixed or children (E).

John 1:43–51 Jesus to Philip: "Follow me." Philip to Nathanael: "We have found the one about whom the law and the prophets wrote, Jesus son of Joseph from Nazareth." Nathanael: "Can anything good come out of Nazareth?" Jesus: "I saw you under the fig tree, before Philip called you." Nathanael: "Rabbi, you are the Son of God!" Jesus: "Do you believe because I told you that? All of you [hearers of all times and places] will see heaven opened, and the angels of God ascending and descending upon the Son of Man."

Anthem

He Comes to Us, Jane Marshall (Carl Fischer) SATB (M).

Psalm 139:1–6, 13–18

1. Metrical: *You Are Before Me, Lord.* Text: Ian Pitt-Watson. Tune: SURSUM CORDA. *PH90*#248.
2. Responsorial: *Psalm 139* (1–5, 13–18). Setting: Hal H. Hopson. *PS93* #143.
3. Metrical: *Lord, You Have Searched and Seen Me Through.* Text: L.M., Fred R. Anderson. *SPJP,* p. 70. Tune: MARYTON.

See also *30P&2C,* p. 40; *TIP/MTYL* Cycle (A); *PR&T,* pp. 43 & 48; *WIII* #1034.

Anthem

Lord, Thou Hast Searched Me, Alice Parker (Hinshaw) unison (E).

Organ Music for the Day

1. *Prelude on* SURSUM CORDA (*You Are Before Me, Lord, PH90* #248), Harald Rohlig (*Preludes for the Hymns in Worship Supplement,* vol. 4, p. 24, Concordia 97–5037).
2. *Toccata on* KINGSFOLD (*Today We All Are Called to Be Disciples, PH90* #434), Ralph B. Hastings (H. W. Gray Co., Inc. GSTC 01038).

Hymns for the Day	HL33	HB55	WB72	PH90
God Is Here!	–	–	–	461
Great Is Thy Faithfulness	–	–	–	276
Guide Me, O Thou Great Jehovah	104	339	409	281
If Thou but Trust in God to Guide Thee	–	344	431	282
I'm Gonna Live So God Can Use Me	–	–	–	369
Live Into Hope	–	–	–	332

142

SUNDAY BETWEEN JANUARY 21 AND 27 [3] (B)

Jonah 3:1–5, 10 Corrupt, wicked, and sinful Nineveh deserves nothing less than total destruction—precisely what YHWH intends for this monstrous city. But reluctant and resistant Jonah, YHWH's designated speaker, has to be prodded a second time to proclaim this message of doom. Nevertheless, Jonah obeys, and warns Nineveh that the end is in sight for it. Nineveh, however, believes the word of God and does a 180-degree turnaround from its iniquitous past. When God sees this, God too repents. Immortal, invisible, unchanging God changes God's mind and does not punish Nineveh.

Anthem
Jonah, Dale Wood (Carl Fischer) any combination of voices (E).

1 Corinthians 7:29–31 "The form of this world is passing away." So live "as though you were not" of this world even though you live in this world. Depend not on this world's institutions or values but solely on God, by giving yourself totally to the Lord's service.

Anthem
The Kingdom of God, Austin Lovelace (Hope) SATB (E).

Mark 1:14–20 The *kairos* (time) has been fulfilled because, after John was imprisoned, the intruding sovereignty of God invaded our world in Galilee when Jesus began proclaiming "the gospel of God." Declared Jesus, "The kingdom of God has drawn near; turn around and see and believe the good news." After announcing the kingdom, Jesus calls four everyday people who leave behind everything and immediately follow.

Anthem
Carol of the Baptism, George Brandon (Concordia) SATB (ME).

Psalm 62:5–12
1. Metrical: *My Soul in Silence Waits for God*. Text: *The Psalter*, 1912; alt. Fred R. Anderson. Tune: CHESHIRE. *PH90* #197.
2. Responsorial: *Psalm 62:5–12*. Text: *A New Zealand Prayer Book*. Refrain: Robert Batastini. Tone: source unknown. *PS93* #52.
3. Metrical: *My Soul with Expectation*. Text: The Scottish Psalter 1650. Tune: ST. FLAVIAN. *HB55* #113.
4. Responsorial: *Rest in God Alone*. Text: Grail (see also *GPI*, p. 84). Psalm tone and Gelineau tone: *WIII* #886.
See also *ANMP*, p. 106; *PH87* #67; *PR&T*, pp. 58 & 78.

Anthem
My Soul Truly Waiteth Upon God, John Wood (Novello) SATB (M).

Organ Music for the Day
1. *Prelude on* LANCASHIRE (*Lead On, O King Eternal. PH90* #447), Philip Gehring (*Six Hymn Tune Preludes*, p. 8, Concordia 97–4768).
2. *Prelude on* BOURBON (*Take Up Your Cross, the Savior Said, PH90* #393), Gilbert M. Martin (*Early American Folk Hymns for Organ*, p. 28, Lorenz Industries).

Hymns for the Day	HL33	HB55	WB72	PH90
Be Thou My Vision	325	303	304	339
Christ of the Upward Way	277	295	–	344
Dear Lord and Father of Mankind	302	416	350	345
Immortal, Invisible, God Only Wise	66	85	433	263
Lord, You Have Come to the Lakeshore	–	–	–	377
O God, What You Ordain Is Right	291	366	633	284

SUNDAY BETWEEN JANUARY 28 AND FEBRUARY 3 [4] (B)

Deuteronomy 18:15–20 The Israelites could not bear the fiery presence or voice of YHWH at Horeb. YHWH says to Moses, "Tell them I shall raise up a prophet like you, someone from among your own people, whom everyone shall obey. The prophet I raise up shall speak my words and reveal my will. Anyone who dares to refuse my words, I shall punish. Anyone who dares to speak in my name without authority, or in the name of other gods, shall die."

Anthem
God the Spirit, Guide and Guardian, PH90 #523.

1 Corinthians 8:1–13 It's wonderful that you know "there is no God but one . . . from whom are all things and for whom we exist." You may legitimately be "puffed up" by rightness, but deflate your ego, swollen by correct belief, and subordinate your rightness to concern for others. It is *agape* (love) that "builds up" the community of faith. Flaunting your "knowledge" can become a stumbling block to some and consequently destroy the community.

Anthem
Ubi Caritas, Maurice Durufle (Durand, Presser) SATB (M).

Mark 1:21–28 In a Capernaum synagogue, Jesus teaches not as the scribes but with authority. All are astonished. Suddenly a man with an evil spirit screams, "I know who you are, Jesus of Nazareth. You are the Holy One of God. Have you come to destroy us?" Jesus rebukes him: "Be quiet." The man shudders and the spirit comes out of him. All are astonished, saying, "What is this? He commands evil spirits with authority, and they obey him." News about Jesus spreads quickly throughout Galilee.

Anthems
Good News, Jane Marshall (Carl Fischer) SATB baritone solo (ME). *They Cast Their Nets in Galilee,* Michael McCabe (Carl Fischer) 2-part (E).

Psalm 111
1. Metrical: *Hallelujah! Among the Just.* Text: L.M., Christopher L. Webber. *ANMP,* p. 180.
2. Responsorial: *Psalm 111* (1–4, 9–10). Setting: Hal H. Hopson. *PS93* #111.
3. Responsorial: *I Thank You, Lord, for Your Majesty and Love.* Text: Grail (see also *GPI,* p. 166). Psalm tone and Gelineau tone: *WIII* #58 (see also *20P&3C,* p. 25 for optional refrains).

See also *PH87* #111; *PR&T,* pp. 11 & 13.

Anthem
My Heart Is Full Today, Richard Proulx (Augsburg) 2-part (ME).

Organ Music for the Day
1. *Prelude on* DARWALL'S 148TH (*Rejoice, the Lord Is King, PH90* #155), Percy Whitlock (*Six Hymn Preludes,* p. 1, Oxford University Press 375902–0).
2. *Chorale Prelude on* FOREST GREEN (*Eternal God, Whose Power Upholds, PH90* #412), Richard Purvis (*7 Chorale Preludes,* p. 12, Carl Fischer, Inc. 3450).

Hymns for the Day	HL33	HB55	WB72	PH90
God Has Spoken—by His Prophets	–	–	382	–
Jesus Shall Reign	377	496	443	423
Not for Tongues of Heaven's Angels	–	–	–	531
O Jesus Christ, May Grateful Hymns	–	–	509	424
The God of Abraham Praise	8	89	587	488
Though I May Speak	–	–	–	335

SUNDAY BETWEEN FEBRUARY 4 AND 10 [5] (B)

Isaiah 40:21–31 Exiled Israel perceives itself as abandoned by God. Have you *not* known? . . . *not* heard? . . . *not* understood? Do you ask out of ignorance, poor information, or resistance to hearing? Who is like YHWH as the powerful creator who "sits," "stretches," "spreads," "brings," and "makes"? In all times and places, YHWH ministers to "fainting" (tired) creation. So, wait confidently. God will give life where there was none.

Anthem
They That Wait Upon the Lord, Jean Berger (Augsburg) SATB (M).

1 Corinthians 9:16–23 Why does Paul preach the gospel? Because he is compelled to preach. He has been chosen and divinely commissioned by God. Having no use for personal financial gain from preaching, because it reaps its own rewards of joy, Paul voluntarily submits himself as a slave to all. No special interest groups own him. He is free from all other claims upon his life. True, he is bound to Christ, but he is free to experience the joys and sorrows of others, and to speak their language as he preaches the gospel.

Anthem
Seek to Serve, Lloyd Pfautsch (Agape) 2-part (E).

Mark 1:29–39 Jesus touches Simon's mother-in-law and the fever leaves her. She responds by serving. Jesus then heals many others of various diseases, and expels numerous demons who know who Jesus is, but he does not allow them to reveal the "messianic secret." The next morning Simon and others intrude upon Jesus while he is praying, but Jesus responds to their pleas by announcing he must proclaim the gospel in neighboring towns—that is the purpose of his mission.

Anthem
Immortal Love, Crawford R. Thoburn (Presser) SATB (ME).

Psalm 147:1–11, 20c
1. Metrical: *Now Praise the Lord, All Living Saints.* Text: C.M., Fred R. Anderson. Tune: ST. ANNE. *PH90* #255 (see also *SPJP,* p. 74).
2. Responsorial: *Psalm 147* (1–11). Text: *The United Methodist Liturgical Psalter.* Tone and refrain: Melodies, Columba Kelly. Harmony, Samuel Weber. *PS93* #153.
See also *PS93* #154; *ANMP,* p. 232; *PH87* #147; *PR&T,* pp. 10 & 13.

Anthem
Sing to the Lord with Thanksgiving, George Brandon (Concordia) SATB (ME).

Organ Music for the Day
1. *Chorale Prelude on* MIT FREUDEN ZART (*Sing Praise to God, Who Reigns Above, PH90* #483), Ernst Pepping (*Grosses Orgelbuch,* vol. 3, p. 20, B. Schotts Söhne 3731, and *Böhmisches Orgelbuch,* vol. 2, p. 37, Bärenreiter Verlag 2750).
2. *Partita on* ST. ANNE (*Now Praise the Lord, PH90* #255), Paul Manz (Concordia 97–5307).

Hymns for the Day	HL33	HB55	WB72	PH90
A Mighty Fortress Is Our God	266	91	276	259
At the Name of Jesus	–	143	303	148
God, Whose Giving Knows No Ending	–	–	–	422
I Danced in the Morning	–	–	426	302
Immortal, Invisible, God Only Wise	66	85	433	263
O God, in a Mysterious Way	–	–	–	270

SUNDAY BETWEEN FEBRUARY 11 AND 17
(PROPER 1) [6] (B)

2 Kings 5:1–14 Naaman, a Syrian military commander, suffers from leprosy. Hearing that healing is possible in Israel, he packs his bags and travels to see the king. But the only thing he receives from the king of Israel is the royal runaround—the king is unable to heal Naaman and knows it. But Elisha, the simple man of God, instructs Naaman to wash himself in the Jordan. This makes no sense to Naaman, for he could have done that back home; so he goes away in a rage. At the insistence of his servants, however, Naaman does wash and miraculously is made clean. He almost missed this experience because of his preconceived expectations of God's healing word.

Anthems
Descend, O Spirit, Purging Flame, WB72 #353. *Commit Your Life to the Lord,* Liebhold (Concordia) SATB (M).

1 Corinthians 9:24–27 Paul's recurring image: training for the race, straining toward the goal, and winning the prize. Perhaps a disciplined life of discipleship (prayer, study, and almsgiving?) is what's needed in a "do as you please" culture.

Anthem
Awake, Our Souls, George Brandon (Concordia) 2-part (E).

Mark 1:40–45 A leper, an untouchable outcast, approaches Jesus and says, "If you will, you can make me clean." Jesus' pity or anger (depending on which text you accept) galvanizes him to touch the leper and proclaim him clean. He then charges the leper to fulfill the laws for ritual purification, and to remain silent about Jesus' action and words so that others will not misunderstand who Jesus is. But the man promptly proclaims Jesus' saving words and deeds to everyone he meets. People then come to Jesus from all directions.

Anthem
Two Words of Jesus, L. L. Fleming (Augsburg) SATB (ME).

Psalm 30
1. Metrical: *Come Sing to God, O Living Saints.* Text: C.M.D., Fred R. Anderson. Tune: ELLACOMBE. *PH90* #181.
2. Responsorial: *Psalm 30* (1–2, 4–5, 11–12). Setting: Hal H. Hopson. Tone: William Byrd. *PS93* #27.

See also *WIII* #822; *HB55* #127; *ANMP,* p. 68; *PH87* #30; *PR&T,* pp. 45 & 79.

Anthem
Praise to the Lord, Heinrich Schütz (Belwin-Mills) 2-part (ME).

Organ Music for the Day
1. *Chorale Prelude on* ST. BRIDE (*Give to the Winds Thy Fears, PH90* #286), Alec Rowley (*Chorale Preludes Based on Famous Hymn Tunes,* p. 17, C. F. Peters Corp. 6419), and Healey Willan (*Thirty-Six Short Preludes and Postludes . . .,* vol. 3, p. 22, C. F. Peters Corp. 6163).
2. *Prelude on* AMAZING GRACE/NEW BRITAIN (*Amazing Grace, PH90* #280), Philip Gehring (*Two Folk Hymn Preludes,* Augsburg 11–9507).

Hymns for the Day	HL33	HB55	WB72	PH90
Amazing Grace	–	275	296	280
Fight the Good Fight	270	359	–	307
Give to the Winds Your Fears	294	363	377	286
Guide My Feet	–	–	–	354
Lord Jesus, Think on Me	239	270	–	301
Love Divine, All Loves Excelling	308	399	471	376

146

SUNDAY BETWEEN FEBRUARY 18 AND 24
(PROPER 2) [7] (B)

Isaiah 43:18–25 "Behold, I am doing a new thing," proclaims YHWH. Yes, the exodus from Egypt was formative for Israel's existence, but now YHWH is bringing about a new exodus—"a way in the wilderness and rivers in the desert." Of course, Israel brought this exile on itself. Instead of offering itself to YHWH, it made YHWH into a servant who had to bear the burden of Israel's sins. But because YHWH is the forgiver without equal, Israel's sins will be blotted out by YHWH, who also will bring about a new future for Israel.

Anthem
Springs in the Desert, A. Jennings (H. W. Gray) SATB tenor solo (M).

2 Corinthians 1:18–22 As surely as God is faithful, the word we preach is Jesus Christ, who was constantly faithful in his obedience to the will of God. As God says "Yes" in Christ, we also shout "Amen," for all God's promises find fulfillment in Christ. And it is in Christ that God "establishes us," "commissions us," "puts God's seal upon us," and "gives us God's Spirit."

Anthems
Set Me as a Seal Upon Thine Heart, Wm. Walton (Oxford) SATB (D). *I Thank You, God,* Lloyd Pfautsch (G. Schirmer) SATB (M).

Mark 2:1–12 Four people carry a paralytic to Jesus, who is preaching the word to an overflow crowd at a home. Unable to get near Jesus, the four dig through the roof and lower the paralytic into the home. He comes to be healed, but Jesus unexpectedly forgives his sins. Controversy ensues, for Jesus discerns that the scribes are charging him with blasphemy because they believe only God can forgive sins. So Jesus pronounces healing words, and the paralytic rises and walks as evidence that "the Son of man has authority on earth to forgive sins." It's an illogical deduction, but all are astonished and glorify God because they have never seen anything like this.

Anthem
Jesus Christ Has Come Into Capernaum, Juhani Forsberg (*Ecumenical Praise,* number 14, Agape) (E).

Psalm 41
1. Metrical: *How Blessed Are Those Who Thoughtfully.* Text: Bert Polman, 1985. Tune: GREELEY. *PH87* #41.
2. Responsorial: *Lord, Heal My Soul.* Text: The Grail (see also *GPI,* p. 57). Psalm tone and Gelineau tone: *WIII* #884.

See also *PR&T,* pp. 48 & 70.

Anthem
Be Merciful Unto Me, Stanley Glarum (Augsburg) SSAB or SATB (E).

Organ Music for the Day
1. *Chorale Prelude on* NUN DANKET ALL' UND BRINGET EHR' (*Spirit Divine, Attend Our Prayers, PH90* #325), Helmut Walcha (*Choralvorspiele,* vol. 3, p. 39, C. F. Peters Corp. 5999).
2. *Prelude on* CHARTERHOUSE (*O Jesus Christ, May Grateful Hymns . . ., PH90* #424), Leo Sowerby (*Ten Preludes,* p. 19, H. W. Gray Co., Inc. GB 651).

Hymns for the Day	HL33	HB55	WB72	PH90
God Created Heaven and Earth	–	–	–	290
God of the Ages, Whose Almighty Hand	414	515	386	262
O for a Thousand Tongues	199	141	493	466
O Jesus Christ, May Grateful Hymns	–	–	509	42
O Praise the Gracious Power	–	–	–	471
Where Cross the Crowded Ways	410	507	642	408

SUNDAY BETWEEN FEBRUARY 25 AND 29*
(PROPER 3) [8] (B)

Hosea 2:14–20 YHWH's bride, Israel, has been having an adulterous affair with the Baal gods, and YHWH is fed up with her infidelity. But YHWH strangely promises to start over again with her. YHWH is going to lure Israel back to the wilderness (sometimes you have to go backward in order to go forward), and renew the covenant with her. YHWH intends to reestablish a faithful relationship and thus offers Israel gifts of "righteousness, justice, steadfast love, and mercy." This is an offer Israel cannot refuse, can she?

Anthems
My Song Is Love Unknown, Carl Schalk (Concordia) 2-part (E). *Mercy and Truth Are Met*, Ned Rorem (Boosey & Hawkes) SATB (MD).

2 Corinthians 3:1–6 Paul's credentials for ministry seem suspect: no transcript, no ordination exams, not even a letter of recommendation. But Paul asserts that his ultimate letter of recommendation is the Corinthian church. Its people are the flesh-and-blood testimony, written by the Spirit of the living God, of his authority as an apostle. It is God alone who calls Paul and empowers him to serve.

Anthem
Gracious Spirit, Dwell with Me, HB55 #241.

Mark 2:13–22 Controversy ferments over the propriety of fasting. Righteous people, such as Pharisees or disciples of John the Baptist, are fasting, and Jesus' disciples are not. Why not? "When you're a guest at a wedding feast," says Jesus, "do you fast? As long as you have the bridegroom with you, you cannot fast. Rejoice now, the days for fasting will come when the bridegroom is taken away." New life in Christ cannot be patched onto our old comfortable clothing; neither can it be poured into old predictable molds.

Anthem
Be a New and Different Person, Paul Christiansen (Schmitt, Hall, & McCreary) SATB (ME).

Psalm 103:1–13, 22
1. Metrical: *O My Soul, Bless Your Redeemer*. Text: Para. in the *Book of Psalms*, 1871, alt. Tune: STUTTGART. *PH90* #223.
2. Responsorial: *Psalm 103* (1–4, 6–8, 11–13). Setting: Hal H. Hopson. *PS93* #102.

See also *PS93* #103; *PH90* #222; *HB55* #8; *TIP/PSCY* #14; *ANMP*, p. 169.

Anthem
Bless the Lord, Ippolitov-Ivanov (Boston Music) SATB (M).

Organ Music for the Day
1. *Chorale Prelude on* IN BABILONE (*There's a Wideness in God's Mercy, PH90* #298), Richard Purvis (*Seven Chorale Preludes*, p. 26, Carl Fischer, Inc. 0–3450).
2. *Chorale Prelude on* LOBE DEN HERREN (*Praise Ye the Lord, the Almighty, PH90* #482), Siegfried Reda (*Choral-Spiel-Buch*, p. 14, Bärenreiter Verlag 2064).

Hymns for the Day	HL33	HB55	WB72	PH90
Called as Partners in Christ's Service	–	–	–	343
Deck Yourself, My Soul	–	–	351	506
Great Is Thy Faithfulness	–	–	–	276
How Clear Is Our Vocation, Lord	–	–	–	419
I Come with Joy	–	–	–	507
O God, Our Faithful God	–	–	500	277

---

*Except when this Sunday is The Transfiguration of the Lord.

TRANSFIGURATION OF THE LORD (B)
[Sunday Preceding Lent]

2 Kings 2:1–12 Elijah, on his last journey, tests his disciple Elisha three times concerning his loyalty; each time Elisha vows lifelong commitment. Even the prophets' guilds fail to deter Elisha from following Elijah to the very end. Upon reaching the Jordan River, Elijah parts the waters with his mantle in Moses-like fashion. After crossing to dry ground, Elijah says to Elisha, "What shall I do for you, before I am taken from you?" Elisha asks for a "double share of your *ruach*" (spirit, wind). He asks for the creative power of YHWH, which liberates. Then fire and wind whisk away Elijah while Elisha laments. But then he takes up the mantle of Elijah and parts the Jordan in Moses-like fashion.

Anthem
Prayer for Transfiguration Day, John Weaver (Hope) SATB (MD).

2 Corinthians 4:3–6 It is not ourselves or our denomination that we preach, but Jesus Christ as Lord. We are called to preach, regardless of whether anyone listens, the light of the gospel, the glory of God shining in the face of Jesus Christ, which radiates love, mercy, anger, compassion, pain, forgiveness.

Anthem
The Light of Christ, Marty Haugen (G.I.A.) unison, congregation, optional brass, handbells (E).

Mark 9:2–9 Peter and James and John see Jesus transfigured before them: his garments glisten intensely white. Though they are frightened and confused, Peter briefly perceives the transcendent reality of the blinding light and wants to preserve it right there. But a voice from a cloud utters words that recall Jesus' baptism and anticipate the centurion's proclamation: "This is my beloved Son; listen to him." Jesus then commands the disciples to keep silent about what they have seen, "until the Son of man should have risen from the dead." Then they will understand who Jesus is.

Anthem
Transfiguration, Alec Wyton (Flammer) SATB (M).

Psalm 50:1–6
1. Metrical: *The Lord Has Spoken, God of Gods.* Text: L.M., Christopher L. Webber. *ANMP,* p. 99.
2. Responsorial: *Psalm 50:1–6.* Text: *The Book of Common Prayer,* alt. Setting: Peter R. Hallock. *PS93* #45.
See also *WIII* #892; *PH87* #50; *PR&T,* pp. 45 & 65.

Anthem
Psalm 150, F. Melius Christiansen (Augsburg) SATB (D).

Organ Music for the Day
1. *Fairest Lord Jesus* (CRUSADER'S HYMN/ST. ELIZABETH, *PH90* #306), Philip Moore (*Fantasie-Aria,* Royal School of Church Music 07).
2. *Chorale Improvisation/Prelude* on DEO GRACIAS (*O Wondrous Sight, O Vision Fair, PH90* #75), Paul Manz (*Ten Chorale Improvisations,* vol. 9, p. 22, Concordia 97–5556).

Hymns for the Day	HL33	HB55	WB72	PH90
All Creatures of Our God and King	–	100	282	455
Blessed Assurance, Jesus Is Mine!	–	139	–	341
Come, Christians, Join to Sing	191	131	333	150
From All That Dwell Below the Skies	388	33	373	229
Jesus on the Mountain Peak	–	–	–	74
Swiftly Pass the Clouds of Glory	–	–	–	73

Easter Cycle
Season of Lent
ASH WEDNESDAY (ABC)

See Ash Wednesday (ABC) in Year A, p. 53.

FIRST SUNDAY IN LENT (B)

Genesis 9:8–17 God unilaterally establishes a covenant with Noah and his descendants—in fact, with all creation. Never again shall all flesh, or the earth, be destroyed by floodwaters. Immutable God has changed God's relationship with creation from destructive ire to free grace. As a sign of this covenant, God lays down the bow (a weapon of destruction) in the cloud, which will be a reminder of God's everlasting covenant with creation.

Anthem

Love the Lord, for His Rainbow and His Promise, Walter Horsley (*100% Chance of Rain,* Choristers Guild) 2-part (E).

1 Peter 3:18–22 Christ the righteous suffered and died undeservedly for us the unrighteous (even those who drowned during the "days of Noah"), in order to bring us all to God. The salvific waters of the Flood revealed long ago the faithful love of God now promised to us in the salvific waters of baptism. So the resurrected and exalted Christ, who sits at the right hand of God, rules over all creation and seeks the salvation of all people.

Anthem

We Know That Christ Is Raised, C. V. Stanford (*Ecumenical Praise,* number 111, Agape) unison or SATB (E).

Mark 1:9–15 John baptizes Jesus of Nazareth in the muddy Jordan. As Jesus emerges from the water, he sees the heavens open and is confirmed by the gift of the Spirit and a voice repeating words reminiscent of a coronation (Ps. 2:7), "You are my beloved Son." The New Age has arrived in the person of Jesus Christ. Then the Spirit immediately drives Jesus into the desert where he is tested by Satan and ministered to by angels for forty days. The *kairos* (time) has been fulfilled because, after John is imprisoned, Jesus comes into Galilee proclaiming "the gospel of God."

Anthems

O Love, How Deep, How Broad, How High, Philip Dietterich (Sacred Music Press) 2-part mixed (E). *The Baptism of Christ,* Peter Hallock (G.I.A.) SATB and solo (ME).

Psalm 25:1–10
1. Metrical: *Lord, to You My Soul Is Lifted.* Text: Stanley Wiersma. Tune: GENEVAN 25. PH90 #178 (see also PH87 #25).
2. Responsorial: *Psalm 25.* Text: International Commission on English in the Liturgy. Refrain and Tone: Presbyterian 9. PS93 #23.
3. Responsorial: *To You I Lift Up My Soul.* Text: Grail (see also GPI, p. 30). Refrain, psalm tone, and Gelineau tone: WIII #33 (see also WIII #788 for alternate refrain). See also 20P&3C, p. 6.
4. Metrical: *Show Me Thy Ways, O Lord.* Text: *The Murrayfield Psalms* (1954), adapt. Tune: OLD 25TH. RITL #94.

See also *ANMP,* p. 59; *SPJP,* p. 25; *PR&T,* pp. 46 & 48.

Anthems

To Thee, O Lord, S. Rachmaninoff (Oxford) SATB soprano solo (M). *Show Me Thy Ways,* Walter Pelz (Augsburg) SATB oboe or flute (ME).

Organ Music for the Day

1. *Chorale Prelude on* ERHALT UNS, HERR (*The Glory of These Forty Days, PH90* #87), Johann Pachelbel (*The Church Organist's Golden Treasury,* vol. 1, p. 151, Oliver Ditson Co.), and Dietrich Buxtehude (*Sämtliche Orgelwerke,* vol. 4, pp. 17, 58, Wilhelm Hansen 3928).
2. *Prelude on* ST. FLAVIAN (*Lord, Who Throughout These Forty Days, PH90* #81), C. S. Lang (*Twenty Hymn-Tune Preludes,* vol. 1, p. 14, Oxford University Press 375523-8).

Hymns for the Day	*HL33*	*HB55*	*WB72*	*PH90*
God of Our Life	88	108	395	275
God, Who Stretched the Spangled Heavens	–	–	–	268
Jesus Walked This Lonesome Valley	–	–	–	80
Lord, When You Came to Jordan	–	–	–	71
Lord, Who Throughout These Forty Days	144	181	470	81
Walk On, O People of God	–	–	–	296

SECOND SUNDAY IN LENT (B)

Genesis 17:1–7, 15–16 God's solemn call of Abraham, and the covenant God established with him. God's covenant is everlasting, for it is also established with Abraham's descendants, who will receive the land of Canaan and be God's people. Moreover, God promises a son to aged, barren Sarah.

Anthems

If Thou but Suffer God to Guide Thee, Jody Lindh (Concordia) SATB (ME). *Faith While Trees Are Still in Blossom,* Alec Wyton (*Ecumenical Praise,* number 74, Agape) unison (E).

Romans 4:13–25 God's promise to Abraham and all his descendants is guaranteed solely by God's free grace. There is absolutely no way you can earn God's promise, especially by good works or adherence to the law. Abraham trusted God to do what God promised. That's faith.

Anthems

We Walk by Faith, Hal H. Hopson (Sacred Music Press) SATB (E). *O Lord, Increase My Faith,* Orlando Gibbons (H. W. Gray) SATB (M).

Mark 8:31–38 Jesus' first passion prediction: the Son of Man must suffer, be rejected, be killed, and rise again. Peter remonstrates, saying something like, "We don't want a convicted criminal for our leader. We'll never succeed if you do that." Jesus censures Peter: "You're demonically inspired." Jesus tells the multitude, "If you want to follow me, then deny yourself and take up your cross. You must be willing to lose your life in this world."

Anthem

Lift High the Cross, arr. Donald Busarow (Augsburg) 2-part mixed, trumpet and congregation (E) (also in *PH90* #371).

Psalm 22:23–31

1. Metrical: *My God, O My God!* Text: Calvin Seerveld. Tune: MALDWYN. *PH87* #22 (stanzas 8–10).
2. Responsorial: *Psalm 22:23–31.* Text: *A New Zealand Prayer Book.* Refrain and Tone: Presbyterian 3. *PS93* #17.
3. Responsorial: Text: optional. Psalm tones and refrains by Hal H. Hopson. *PR&T,* pp. 60 & 66.

Anthem

I Will Lift Up Mine Eyes, Lloyd Pfautsch (Hope) SATB (M).

Organ Music for the Day

1. *Prelude on* ROCKINGHAM (*When I Survey the Wondrous Cross, PH90* #100), C. S. Lang (*Twenty Hymn-Tune Preludes,* p. 13, Oxford University Press 375523-8); *Improvisation on* HAMBURG (*PH90* #101), Russell Hancock Miles (*Three Improvisations,* The Arthur P. Schmidt Co.).
2. *My Faith Looks Up to Thee* (OLIVET, *PH90* #383), Hal H. Hopson (*Praise to the Lord,* p. 6, The Sacred Music Press KK 389).

Hymns for the Day	HL33	HB55	WB72	PH90
Christ of the Upward Way	277	295	–	344
God of the Sparrow	–	–	–	272
Guide My Feet	–	–	–	354
O God, in a Mysterious Way	–	–	–	270
Take Up Thy Cross, the Savior Said	–	293	–	393
The God of Abraham Praise	8	89	587	488

152

THIRD SUNDAY IN LENT (B)

Exodus 20:1–17 The words YHWH spoke to Moses at Mt. Sinai concerning Israel's relationship with YHWH and with neighbors, the Mosaic covenant, is one of human obligation that prohibits the Israelites from violating the exclusive claims of the divine Lord who liberated them from bondage in Egypt. Conversely, these words distinctively assert the sovereignty of YHWH and the exclusivity of the YHWH-Israel bond. In addition, this covenant protects the fundamental rights of all free Israelite citizens.

Anthem
Covenant, John Yarrington (Augsburg) 2-part mixed, handbells, congregation optional (E).

1 Corinthians 1:18–25 What the world labels wise and strong, says Paul, is really foolish and weak. And what the world claims is the foolishness of the cross is really the power and wisdom of God. That is one reason we are called to show God's love for the world through such foolish things as loving enemies, handing out food to the hungry, giving away our possessions, or standing with the oppressed.

Anthem
Be Thou My Vision, Alice Parker (Hinshaw) SATB or 2-part (E).

John 2:13–22 When Jesus enters the Temple, he walks into a tumultuous hubbub of financial greed at its worst. The whole enterprise takes place in the court of the Gentiles. Sanctimonious Jewish aristocrats conspired to provide "separate but equal" facilities for Jews and Gentiles, thus giving false legitimacy to prejudice and segregation. Such entrenched evil causes Jesus to drive out everyone and everything, saying, "Destroy this Temple, and in three days I will raise up a new temple-church-people." And he does.

Anthem
God, Bring Thy Sword Over Pulpit and Pew, Ron Nelson (Boosey & Hawkes) SATB (D).

Psalm 19
1. Metrical: *God's Law Is Perfect and Gives Life.* Text: C.M., Christopher L. Webber. Tune: HALIFAX, G. F. Handel. *PH90* #167. Text only *ANMP,* p. 53 (verses 7–14).
2. Responsorial: *Psalm 19* (1–6). Text: Grail. Melody: Monks of Saint Meinrad. Harmony, Samuel Weber. *PS93* #12.
See also *PS93* #13; *HB55* #257 (vs. 7–14); *GPI,* p. 22; *WIII* #794, #841, & #873.

Anthems
God's Law Is Perfect and Gives Life, PH90 #167. *Most Perfect Is the Law of God, HB55* #257.

Organ Music for the Day
1. *Prelude on* DUNDEE (*O God, in a Mysterious Way, PH90* #270), G. Young (*Fourteen Pieces for Organ,* p. 11, The Sacred Music Press KK 1110).
2. *Prelude on* SLANE (*Be Thou My Vision, PH90* #339), Dale Wood (*Wood Works,* p. 17, The Sacred Music Press KK 357).

Hymns for the Day	HL33	HB55	WB72	PH90
Be Thou My Vision	325	303	304	339
Christian Women, Christian Men	–	–	–	348
Make Me a Captive, Lord	247	308	–	378
O for a World	–	–	–	386
O God, What You Ordain Is Right	291	366	633	284
When a Poor One	–	–	–	407

FOURTH SUNDAY IN LENT (B)

Numbers 21:4–9 Impatient Israel wanders in the wilderness murmuring (i.e., complaining) and speaking against God and Moses and the food and water. YHWH has had enough of this murmuring and sends judgment in the form of fiery serpents that bite the people so that many die. Result: Israel confesses its sin and prays that the serpents be removed. YHWH instructs Moses to "make an image of a serpent, and set it on a pole; and everyone who is bitten shall look at it and live." And it was so. Judgment was and is the means of God's redemption.

Anthem
How Goodly Are Thy Tents, F. A. Gore Ouseley (*Anthems for Choirs,* Book 1, Oxford) SATB (ME).

Ephesians 2:1–10 God is love—in fact, so abundantly full of love that God chooses to shower it on us so we will know how extraordinary that love for us is. Though we were spiritually dead, God gave us new life by raising us up with Christ. Our new life is a pure gift of God's grace. We are not self-made people but God's handiwork, created in Christ Jesus for good works.

Anthem
God of Mercy, God of Grace, J. S. Bach, arr. McCurdy (Boosey & Hawkes) SATB (ME).

John 3:14–21 God sent the Son into the world in order that the world might be saved through him. Yet many people reject the light of salvation and choose the darkness of judgment. How odd that we think we can conceal our evil deeds from others and, worse, from ourselves, which results in bringing judgment upon ourselves. Look up and see the crucified Lord—our Savior—and behold the eternal light of life.

Anthem
Wondrous Love, arr. Douglas Wagner (Flammer) SATB (E).

Psalm 107:1–3, 17–22
1. Metrical: *Thanks Be to God Our Savior.* Text: David J. Diephouse. Tune: GENEVAN 107. *PH87* #107 (stanzas 3–4).
2. Responsorial: *O Give Thanks to the Lord.* Refrain and Gelineau psalm tone: *20P&3C,* p. 22 (stanzas 1, 8–10).
3. Metrical: *We Thank You, Lord, for You Are Good.* Text only: Fred R. Anderson. *SPJP,* p. 58.

Anthem
Be Joyful in the Lord, François Couperin, arr. Kenneth Jewel (Concordia) 2-part (E).

Organ Music for the Day
1. *Prelude on* NETTLETON (*Come, Thou Fount of Every Blessing, PH90* #356), Gerre Hancock (*The Bristol Collection,* p. 5, H. Flammer, Inc. HF 5071).
2. *Prelude on* MONKLAND (*Let Us with a Gladsome Mind, PH90* #244), C. S. Lang (*Twenty Hymn-Tune Preludes,* p. 12, Oxford Univ. Press 375523-8).

Hymns for the Day	HL33	HB55	WB72	PH90
Come, Thou Fount of Every Blessing	235	379	341	356
Eternal Light, Shine in My Heart	–	–	–	340
Help Us Accept Each Other	–	–	–	358
Love Divine, All Loves Excelling	308	399	471	376
O God of Earth and Altar	419	511	497	291
To God Be the Glory	–	–	–	485

FIFTH SUNDAY IN LENT (B)

Jeremiah 31:31–34 YHWH is going to make a new covenant with the people. This new covenant will not be like the old Sinai one which the people adulterated, even though YHWH was their faithful husband, but this time YHWH will cut a new covenant into the people's hearts, minds, and wills. They will be YHWH's people; YHWH will be their God. Everyone will know YHWH—no need to teach one another about YHWH—for YHWH will forgive their iniquity and no longer remember their sin.

Anthem

This Is the Covenant, Jean Berger (Augsburg) SATB (M).

Hebrews 5:5–10 Often we forget that Jesus was fully human and, therefore, experienced all that we can ever face—pain, suffering, temptation to sell out God and make a fast buck, fear, loss, every part of the fleshly life we know so well. And in loud cries and tears, Jesus offered his prayers to God, but with a difference. He obeyed God's will and walked faithfully the path chosen for him by God. You can see why Hebrews call Jesus a great high priest, for he is the one who represents the world before God. He is the one whom God appointed to comfort and forgive us, because he is the source of eternal salvation.

Anthem

Christ Was Obedient Unto Death, Manuel de Sumaya (Roger Dean) SATB Latin/English texts (M).

John 12:20–33 Some Greeks (Gentiles) "wish to see Jesus." Answered Jesus, "The hour has come for the Son of man to be glorified"—that is, his crucifixion will reveal the presence and power of God. So if you wish to see Jesus, look at Jesus lifted up on the cross and you will see Jesus for who he is—divine love drawing all to himself. Whoever wants to serve Jesus must be where he is, accept his way, and follow him, even to the cross.

Anthems

Go to Dark Gethsemane, Leland B. Sateren (AMSI) SATB (ME). *Go to Dark Gethsemane,* T. T. Noble (H. W. Gray) SATB (ME).

Psalm 51:1–12
1. Metrical: *Have Mercy on Us, Living Lord.* Text: C.M., Fred R. Anderson. Tune: PTOMEY. *PH90* #195. For text only see *SPJP,* p. 36.
2. Responsorial: *Psalm 51:1–12.* Text: *Book of Common Prayer.* Setting: Peter R. Hallock. *PS93* #47. See also *TIP/PSCY* #5.
3. Responsorial: *Psalm 51* (1–17). Text: *Book of Common Prayer.* Setting: David Clark Isele. *PS93* #48.
4. Responsorial: *The Sacrifice You Accept.* Text: The Grail. Refrain and psalm tone by David Clark Isele. *PH90* #196. See also *APS,* p. 18.
See also *ANMP,* p. 101; *HB55* #282; *TIP/PSCY* #5; *WIII* #41 & #787; *PH87* #51; *PR&T,* pp. 19 & 21.

Anthems

Restore Unto Me, J. Lully, arr. Nelson (Augsburg) 2-part, 2 C instruments (ME). *Have Mercy on Us, Living Lord,* Hal H. Hopson, *PH90* #195.

***or* Psalm 119:9–16**
1. Metrical: *How Shall the Young Direct Their Ways?* Text: The Psalter, 1912. Tune: PRESTON. *HB55* #258.
2. Responsorial: *How Shall a Young Man Cleanse His Way?* Text: *Book of Common Prayer.* Music: Peter R. Hallock. *TIP/PSCY* #4.

Anthem

Blest Are the Uncorrupt in Heart, PH90 #233.

Organ Music for the Day

1. *Prelude on* ST. CHRISTOPHER (*Beneath the Cross of Jesus, PH90* #92), Robert Elmore (*Three Miniatures for Organ*, p. 2, Harold Flammer, Inc. HF-5032).
2. *Prelude on* ST. MAGNUS (*The Head That Once Was Crowned, PH90* #149), Alec
   Rowley (*Chorale Preludes Based on Famous Hymn Tunes*, vol. 2, p. 8, Edwin Ashdown, Ltd.).

Hymns for the Day	*HL33*	*HB55*	*WB72*	*PH90*
Ah, Holy Jesus	158	191	280	93
God, You Spin the Whirling Planets	–	–	–	285
O Jesus, I Have Promised	268	307	–	388, 389
O Love, How Deep, How Broad	139	–	518	83
What Wondrous Love Is This	–	–	–	85
When We Are Tempted to Deny Your Son	–	–	640	86

PASSION/PALM SUNDAY
[SIXTH SUNDAY IN LENT] (ABC)

See Passion/Palm Sunday [Sixth Sunday in Lent] (ABC) in Year A, p. 60.

MONDAY OF HOLY WEEK (ABC)

See Monday of Holy Week (ABC) in Year A, p. 64.

TUESDAY OF HOLY WEEK (ABC)

See Tuesday of Holy Week (ABC) in Year A, p. 65.

WEDNESDAY OF HOLY WEEK (ABC)

See Wednesday of Holy Week (ABC) in Year A, p. 66.

MAUNDY THURSDAY (ABC)

See Maundy Thursday (ABC) in Year A, p. 68.

GOOD FRIDAY (ABC)

See Good Friday (ABC) in Year A, p. 70.

SEASON OF EASTER
EASTER VIGIL (ABC)

See Easter Vigil (ABC) in Year A, p. 72.

EASTER DAY (B)

Acts 10:34–43 At Cornelius's house in Caesarea, Peter recounts how his own life has been transformed by the power of the risen Lord, and everyone else (Jews and Gentiles) also can be transformed by that power.

Anthems
Dear Christians, One and All, Rejoice, Hugo Distler (Concordia) SATB (M). *This Joyful Eastertide,* Alec Wyton (H. W. Gray) SATB optional brass (M).

or **Isaiah 25:6–9** One day the Lord of Hosts will make for all peoples a grand feast. The cloud of sorrow and troubles and death will vanish so that all tears shall succumb to laughter and joy, for YHWH has spoken.

Anthems
This Is the Feast, Daniel Moe (*Ecumenical Praise,* number 13, Agape) unison (E). *The Heavens Rejoice, the Earth Is Filled with Gladness,* J. S. Bach, arr. Harris (Music 70) SSATB (D).

1 Corinthians 15:1–11 This is the good news in which we stand: Christ died for our sins according to the scriptures, was buried, raised on the third day, and appeared to Peter, to the Twelve, and to many faithful witnesses. Finally, he appeared to me, Paul, the least of all apostles.

Anthems
That Easter Day with Joy Was Bright, Robert Leaf (Choristers Guild) children, unison (E). *We Know That Christ Is Raised,* C. V. Stanford, arr. Wolff (Concordia) SATB, congregation (E).

or **Acts 10:34–43** See above.

John 20:1–18 Peter and the Beloved Disciple seek the truth about the empty tomb. Mary engages the "gardener" in conversation, who says, "Tell them I am ascending."

Anthem
I Have Seen the Lord, Alan Hovhaness (C. F. Peters) SATB soprano solo (M).

or **Mark 16:1–8** Three women go to Jesus' tomb to anoint his body. A young man in a white robe says, "Jesus has risen. Go, tell his disciples that he is going before you to Galilee." The women flee from the tomb, for they are afraid.

Anthems
Today Is Risen Christ the Lord, Melchior Vulpius (Concordia) SATB and brass or double choir (M). *Christ the Lord Is Risen Again,* John Rutter (Oxford) SSATB (ME).

Psalm 118:1–2, 14–24
1. Metrical: *God Is My Strength and Song.* Text: S.M., S.M.D., Christopher L. Webber. *ANMP,* pp. 188–90.
2. Responsorial: *The Lord Is My Strength and My Might.* Text: NRSV. Psalm tone: Laurence Bevenot, 1986. Refrain: A. Gregory Murray, 1986. *PH90* #231.
3. Responsorial: *Psalm 118* (14–17, 22–24). Text: *Book of Common Prayer.* Setting: Peter R. Hallock. *PS93* #119. See also *TIP/PSCY* #8.
4. Responsorial: *Psalm 118* (1, 4–5, 14, 17, 24). Text: Taizé. Setting: Jacques Berthier. *PS93* #120. See also *MFTII,* p. 51.
5. Metrical: *This Is the Day the Lord Hath Made* (3–5). Text: Isaac Watts. Tune: ARDEN. *RITL* #128. See also *HB55* #69 to the Tune: ARLINGTON.
6. Responsorial: *Alleluia! Let Us Rejoice!* (guitar) Words and music by David Haas. *CS/PFTCY,* vol. 3, p. 20.

See also *PH87* #118; *PR&T,* pp. 29 & 30.

Anthem
Easter Antiphon, Robert J. Powell (Augsburg) 2-part (E).

Organ Music for the Day
1. *Jesus Christ Is Risen Today* (EASTER HYMN, *PH90* #123), Seth Bingham (*He Is Risen*, H. W. Gray Co., Inc.).
2. *Christ the Lord Is Risen Today!* (LLANFAIR, *PH90* #113), Hermann Schroeder (*The Parish Organist*, vol. 8, p. 12; Concordia 97-1404).

Hymns for the Day	HL33	HB55	WB72	PH90
Christ Is Alive!	–	–	–	108
Christ Is Risen	–	–	–	109
Hear the Good News of Salvation	–	–	–	355
I Danced in the Morning	–	–	426	302
Jesus Christ Is Risen Today	163	204	440	123
This Is the Good News	–	–	263	598

EASTER EVENING (ABC)

See Easter Evening (ABC) in Year A, p. 80.

SECOND SUNDAY OF EASTER (B)

Acts 4:32–35 Since the community of believers in the risen Christ were of one heart and soul, they shared all their possessions in common and gave testimony to the resurrection of the Lord Jesus. As a result of this commitment to economic sharing, not a single needy person lived among them, for distribution of goods was made to each as any had need.

Anthem

A Beautiful Thing, Jane Marshall (Augsburg) SATB (M).

1 John 1:1–2:2 That which was from the beginning, the Word of life, was made manifest, and we have heard, seen, and even touched him with our hands. This is the message we have heard from Christ and proclaim with great joy to you: God is light. How do we know if we are living in the light? When we live in fellowship with one another, we are living in fellowship with God (light). Paradoxically, we all continue to sin (so don't deceive yourselves by saying you have no sin), yet we have an advocate; for when we confess our sins, Christ faithfully forgives us and cleanses us.

Anthem

Walk in the Light, Winston Cassler (Augsburg) SATB (E).

John 20:19–31 Verses 19–23 are a series of symbolic episodes: The risen Jesus appears to his frightened disciples and says, "Peace." Then he shows them his hands and his side (which fills the disciples with joy) and again says, "Peace." He gives them the Holy Spirit by breathing on them and concludes with an eschatological saying about resisting forgiveness. In verses 24–31, Thomas says he must see with his eyes before he will believe. So again Jesus appears. He tells Thomas to touch his side. Thomas confesses. Blessed are those who believe on the basis of the word alone.

Anthems

Peace Be with You, Robert Wetzler (AMSI) SATB (M). *We Have Seen the Lord,* Robert Wetzler (Augsburg) SATB (M).

Psalm 133

1. Metrical: *Behold the Goodness of Our Lord.* Text: Fred R. Anderson. Tune: CRIMOND. *PH90* #241. For text only see *SPJP,* p. 67.
2. Responsorial: *Psalm 133.* Setting: Hal H. Hopson. *PS93* #137.
See also *ANMP,* p. 214; *PH87* #133; *PR&T,* pp. 28 & 82.

Anthems

How Good and Pleasant, K. Kosche (Concordia) unison or SATB (E). *Together in Unity,* Malcolm Williamson (Boosey & Hawkes) unison (E).

Organ Music for the Day

1. *Prelude on* O FILII ET FILIAE (*O Sons and Daughters, PH90* #116), Alexandre Guilmant (*Organ Music for Lent and Easter,* p. 32, Bradley Publications B24M26).
2. *Prelude on* CRIMOND (*Behold the Goodness of Our Lord, PH90* #241), Raymond H. Haan (*A Second Book of Contemplative Hymn Tune Preludes,* p. 12, Harold Flammer, Inc. HF 5127).

Hymns for the Day	HL33	HB55	WB72	PH90
Breathe on Me, Breath of God	213	235	–	316
Christ Is Risen! Shout Hosanna!	–	–	–	104
Good Christians All, Rejoice and Sing!	–	–	407	111
O Sons and Daughters, Let Us Sing!	167	206	527	116, 117
Thine Is the Glory	–	209	–	122
We Walk by Faith and Not by Sight	–	–	–	399

THIRD SUNDAY OF EASTER (B)

Acts 3:12–19 Following the healing of a man lame from birth, Peter preaches to his fellow Israelites, urging them to repent.

Anthem
Turn Ye, Turn Ye, Charles Ives (Mercury) SATB (D).

1 John 3:1–7 What we shall be ultimately has not been fully revealed. But we do know that when Christ appears at the Parousia, we shall see him as he is, and that we shall be conformed to him, transformed by him. We may be unfinished people during our journey, and the world may not know who we are, but we are God's children right now—look at the love God has already bestowed upon us. But know also that there are children of the devil who break the bond of fellowship with Christ and, therefore, with one another. Little children, let them not deceive you, for they break God's law by their sinful acts of unrecognized racism, imperialism, sexism, ageism, consumerism, nationalism, and so on. But all who abide in Christ do not continue in sin, for he came to take away sins and to bind us to himself in fellowship.

Anthem
Until We Rest in Thee, Sue Ellen Page (Choristers Guild) children and SATB (E).

Luke 24:36b–48 The risen Jesus suddenly appears to his disciples. They are terrified. So Jesus shows them his hands and feet, eats some fish, and opens their minds about how the scriptures have been fulfilled.

Anthems
There Came Jesus, Jacob Handl (G.I.A.) SATB (M). *He Is Risen,* Walter Pelz (Augsburg) unison with descant (E).

Psalm 4
1. Responsorial: *Psalm 4.* Text: Refrain, Anthony Teague; stanzas, NRSV. Music: Refrain, Helen Wright. Psalm tone: Saint Meinrad. *PH90* #160. See also *APS,* p. 12 with complete text by Teague.
2. Responsorial: *Psalm 4.* Text: Psalter Task Force, adapted from *Psalms from Taizé.* *PS93* #3.
3. Responsorial: *Have Mercy, Lord, and Hear My Prayer.* Refrain, psalm tone, and Gelineau tone: *WIII* #25 (see also *WIII* #840 for alt. refrain).
4. Metrical: *O God, Defender of My Cause.* Text: S.M., Christopher L. Webber. *ANMP,* p. 42.
See also *PH87* #4; *PR&T,* pp. 69 & 78.

Anthem
Give Ear, O Lord, Heinrich Schütz (Mercury) 2-part (ME).

Organ Music for the Day
1. *Prelude on* VRUECHTEN (*Because You Live, O Christ, PH90* #105), Emma L. Diemer (*Suite of Easter Hymns,* p. 17, The Sacred Music Press KK 322).
2. *Prelude on* TRURO (*Christ Is Alive!, PH90* #108), Gerhard Krapf (*Various Hymn Settings,* p. 7, Edwin F. Kalmus 3603).

Hymns for the Day	HL33	HB55	WB72	PH90
Be Known to Us in Breaking Bread	356	446	–	505
Because You Live, O Christ	–	–	–	105
Christ Is Alive!	–	–	–	108
Lord, I Want to Be a Christian	–	317	–	372
My Song Is Love Unknown	–	–	–	76
The Strife Is O'er, the Battle Done	164	203	597	119

FOURTH SUNDAY OF EASTER (B)

Acts 4:5–12 Peter and John are on trial for healing and preaching. "By what power or name did you do this?" inquire the prosecutors. Filled with the Holy Spirit, Peter seizes the opportunity to bear testimony: "By the name of Jesus, whom you crucified, but whom God raised from the dead. God's power is, iron-ically, revealed in the crucifixion of his suffering servant, Jesus; there is no other. name in whom there is salvation. 'The stone which the builders rejected has be-come the head of the corner' [Ps. 118:22]."

Anthem
Christ Is Made the Sure Foundation, Dale Wood (Sacred Music) SATB (E).

1 John 3:18–24 God commands us: "Believe in the name of Jesus Christ and love one another." That means you ignore the tempting but unreliable tugs of your heart saying "Do this" or "Do that," and you unequivocally reject the pangs of your conscience when it accuses you, for you live confidently in God's presence, which is greater than these. Rather, love in deed and in truth, for "all who obey his commandments abide in him, and he abides in them."

Anthems
Come, My Way, My Truth, John Clements (Oxford) SSATB (ME). *Ubi Caritas* (*Where Charity and Love Abide*), Maurice Durufle (Presser) SATB (ME).

John 10:11–18 "I am the good shepherd," says Jesus, "who chooses to lay down his life for his sheep that they may live—not just the sheep you know or see, but all the sheep in other folds who belong to me. I am the good shepherd who in-timately knows and cares for and loves all his sheep as one flock."

Anthem
I Am the Good Shepherd, Dale Wood (Augsburg) unison (E).

Psalm 23
1. Metrical: *The Lord's My Shepherd, I'll Not Want.* Text: The Scottish Psalter, 1650. Tune: CRIMOND. *PH90* #170; *HB55* #104 (also to the Tunes: EVAN and BEL-MONT).
2. Responsorial: *Psalm 23.* Text: Grail. Gelineau tone. *PS93* #18.
3. Responsorial: *Psalm 23.* Text: International Commission on English in the Liturgy. Setting: Howard Hughes. *PS93* #19.
4. Responsorial: *Psalm 23.* Setting: Hal H. Hopson. *PS93* #20.
See also *PH90* #171; *TIP/PSCY* #12; *PH90* #172–175; *PR&T,* pp. 72 & 77.

Anthem
My Shepherd Will Supply My Need, V. Thomson (H. W. Gray) SATB (E).

Organ Music for the Day
1. *Prelude on* ST. COLUMBA (*The King of Love My Shepherd Is, PH90* #171), Henry Coleman (*Twenty-Four Interludes Based on Communion Hymn Tunes,* p. 15, Ox-ford University Press 375330-8).
2. *Prelude on* RESIGNATION (*My Shepherd Will Supply My Need, PH90* #172), H. Hop-son (*Praise to the Lord,* p. 28, The Sacred Music Press KK 389).

Hymns for the Day	HL33	HB55	WB72	PH90
Ah, Holy Jesus	158	191	280	93
Blest Be the Tie That Binds	343	473	–	438
Christ Is Made the Sure Foundation	336	433	325	416, 417
I Greet Thee, Who My Sure Redeemer Art	–	144	625	457
My Hope Is Built on Nothing Less	–	368	–	379
Take Thou Our Minds, Dear Lord	245	306	579	392

FIFTH SUNDAY OF EASTER (B)

Acts 8:26–40 The familiar story of Philip and the baptism of the Ethiopian finance official. Make no mistake about God's role from beginning to end. An angel of the Lord instigated Philip's journey to the south of Jerusalem. And behold, Philip just happened to see an Ethiopian reading Isaiah 53:7–8 (about the Suffering Servant). Guided by the Spirit, Philip asked, "Do you understand what you're reading?" And at the Ethiopian's invitation, Philip began to proclaim the good news of Jesus, which led to the baptism of the Ethiopian. Truly, God's grace always precedes any human profession of faith.

Anthem
Thanks to God Whose Word Was Written, PH90 #331.

1 John 4:7–21 God is love! Love belongs to God! How do we know that? Because the ultimate revelation of love is God's sending God's only Son into the world. And through Jesus' life and death, God shows us what love is: not our first showing love to God, but Jesus' laying down his life for us as an act of love so we might have new life. Now we know how to love one another.

Anthem
Neighbors, arr. Austin Lovelace (H. W. Gray) SATB (E).

John 15:1–8 Branches that bear no fruit are pruned so they may produce a crop. As Jesus says, you are already pruned clean by the word I have spoken to you, so remain in me, and I in you. Branches that try to produce fruit on their own will wither and be cut off. Apart from me, the true vine, you can do nothing. If you remain in me, and my words remain in you, then you shall bear much fruit, glorify my Father, and prove to be my disciples.

Anthems
I Am the Vine, Allen Pote (Sacred Music) unison or 2-part (E). *The Vine Most Surely I Am,* Heinrich Schütz, ed. Gore (Chantry) SSATTB (MD).

Psalm 22:25–31
1. Metrical: *My God, O My God!* Text: Calvin Seerveld. Tune: MALDWYN. *PH87* #22 (stanzas 8–10).
2. Responsorial: *Psalm 22* (23–31). Text: *A New Zealand Prayer Book.* Refrain and Tone: Presbyterian 3. *PS93* #17.
See also *WIII* #31 (stanzas 12–15); *30P&2C,* p. 5; *PR&T,* pp. 60 & 66.

Anthem
Psalm Tones and Refrains, p. 66, Hal H. Hopson (Hope).

Organ Music for the Day
1. *Carol Prelude on* FOREST GREEN (*Eternal God, Whose Power Upholds, PH90* #412), Gordon Phillips (*Six Carol Preludes,* p. 2, Oxford University Press 375644-7).
2. *Prelude on* BRIDEGROOM (*Like the Murmur of the Dove's Song, PH90* #314), Sue M. Wallace (*Hymn Prisms,* p. 4, Hope Publishing Co. 270).

Hymns for the Day	HL33	HB55	WB72	PH90
Called as Partners in Christ's Service	–	–	–	343
God, Bless Your Church with Strength!	–	–	–	418
Jesu, Jesu, Fill Us with Your Love	–	–	–	367
Like the Murmur of the Dove's Song	–	–	–	314
Near to the Heart of God	–	–	–	527
O Word of God Incarnate	215	251	532	327

SIXTH SUNDAY OF EASTER (B)

Acts 10:44–48 While Peter is preaching in Cornelius' home, the Spirit falls on all the hearers. The Jewish Christians are amazed that the Spirit has been poured out on the Gentiles. But the God revealed in the good news of Jesus Christ is a God who favors no nation, race, class, gender, occupation, or social status, because God intends a Spirit-empowered mission for all people.

Anthem
Spirit, All Holy, Finn Videro (Augsburg) SAT tenor solo (ME).

1 John 5:1–6 If you believe "Jesus is the Christ," you are by definition a child of God and therefore love God, as well as all other children of God. When you love God's children, you love God and obey God's commandments. After all, our belief in Jesus as the Son of God is the conquering power, because the salvific and life-giving water and blood flowed from Jesus Christ.

Anthem
Love God with Your Heart, folk song (*Three Peace and Brotherhood Canons*, Choristers Guild) (E).

John 15:9–17 If you keep Jesus' commandments, you will remain in his love, just as he has kept his Father's commandments and remained in God's love. Jesus' commandment to us and all his friends is to bear fruit that endures, by loving one another as he has loved us.

Anthems
Keep My Commandments, Lloyd Pfautsch (AMSI) SATB (M). *If Ye Love Me, Keep My Commandments*, T. Tallis (G. Schirmer) SATB.

Psalm 98
1. Metrical: *New Songs of Celebration Render.* Text: Erik Routley. Tune: RENDEZ À DIEU. *PH90* #218. See also *RITL* #119, *H82* #413, and *PH87* #98 with text by Dewey Westra.
2. Metrical: *To God Compose a Song of Joy.* Text: Ruth C. Duck. Tune: KEDDY. *PH90* #219.
3. Responsorial: *Psalm 98.* Text: International Commission on English in the Liturgy. Tone: Presbyterian 3. *PS93* #94.
4. Responsorial: *Psalm 98* (1–6). Text: *Book of Common Prayer.* Setting: Peter R. Hallock. *PS93* #95.
See also *WIII* #781; *PH87* #98; *ANMP*, p. 161; *PR&T*, pp. 10 & 13.

Anthem
With Songs of Rejoicing, J. S. Bach, arr. H. Hopson (C. Fischer) 2-part (E)

Organ Music for the Day
1. *Prelude on* HYFRYDOL (*Love Divine, All Loves Excelling, PH90* #376), Henry Coleman (*Twenty-Four Interludes Based on Communion Hymn Tunes*, p. 7, Oxford University Press 375330-8), and F. Peeters (*Little Chorale Suite for Organ*, p. 6, J. B. Cramer & Co., Ltd. APS 493).
2. *Prelude on* ST. PETER (*In Christ There Is No East or West, PH90* #439), Alec Rowley (*Chorale Preludes Based on Famous Hymn Tunes*, vol. 4, p. 16, Edwin Ashdown, Ltd.).

Hymns for the Day	HL33	HB55	WB72	PH90
Called as Partners in Christ's Service	–	–	–	343
Love Divine, All Loves Excelling	308	399	471	376
Not for Tongues of Heaven's Angels	–	–	–	531
Son of God, Eternal Savior	393	–	573	–
Spirit	–	–	–	319
What a Friend We Have in Jesus	257	385	–	403

THE ASCENSION OF THE LORD (ABC)

See The Ascension of the Lord (ABC) in Year A, p. 87.

SEVENTH SUNDAY OF EASTER (B)

Acts 1:15–17, 21–26 Peter announces to a company of about 120 believers that someone must be chosen to replace Judas as fulfillment of Psalm 109:8. Not just anyone can be chosen; only "one of those who accompanied us during all the time the Lord Jesus went in and out among us." So two names are presented and offered to the Lord in prayer, who then chooses Matthias through the casting of lots.

Anthem
Strengthen for Service, Lord, Austin Lovelace (Canyon) unison (E).

1 John 5:9–13 God's testimony is that "God gave us eternal life, and this life is in his Son." Those who belong to the Son have eternal life because the Son belongs to God, who gave eternal life to the Son. Conversely, those who do not belong to the Son do not have eternal life.

Anthem
My Eternal King, Jane Marshall (Carl Fischer) SATB (M).

John 17:6–19 Jesus' prayer for his disciples (in every age): "Holy Father: keep them in the power of your name and your word. While I was with them I kept them safe by the power of your name, and I gave them your word so that none was lost. But now I am coming to you, and they shall be alone, so protect them, especially from the evil [one]. As you sent me into the hostile world that rejected me, so also I have sent them into the same world. So sanctify, consecrate, set them apart with your word and in your name so they may carry out your mission to the world."

Anthem
Lord, You Give the Great Commission, PH90 #429.

Psalm 1
1. Metrical: *The One Is Blest.* Text: *The Psalter,* 1912. Tune: DUNFERMLINE. *PH90* #158.
2. Responsorial: *Psalm 1* (1–4, 6). Setting: Hal H. Hopson. *PS93* #1.
See also *WIII* #24; *TIP/PSCY* #11; *RITL* #81; *ANMP,* p. 40; *PR&T,* pp. 67 & 68.

Anthem
Blessed Is the Man, Corelli, arr. Stone (Boston) SAB (ME).

Organ Music for the Day
1. *Prelude on* DUKE STREET (*Jesus Shall Reign, PH90* #423), Robert J. Powell (*American Organ Music,* vol. 2, p. 47, The Sacred Music Press).
2. *Prelude on* DONNE SECOURS (*Hope of the World, PH90* #360), Donald Busarow (*The Concordia Hymn Prelude Series,* vol. 23, pp. 20 & 23, Concordia 97-5738).

Hymns for the Day	HL33	HB55	WB72	PH90
Come Down, O Love Divine	–	–	334	313
Come, Holy Spirit, Our Souls Inspire	–	237	335	125
God, Bless Your Church with Strength!	–	–	–	418
He Is the Way	–	–	413	–
Hope of the World	–	291	423	–
Jesus Shall Reign	377	496	443	423

THE DAY OF PENTECOST (B)

Acts 2:1–21 Wind and tongues of fire—the Holy Spirit—spread among all the believers. Are they drunk? "No," says Peter, "it's only nine in the morning. But while I have your attention, let me tell you about Jesus Christ."

Anthems
Introit for Pentecost, John Weaver (Boosey & Hawkes) SATB (M). *Whitsunday Canticle,* Erik Routley (*Two for Pentecost,* Hinshaw) SATB (ME).

or **Ezekiel 37:1–14** The vision of the valley of dry bones. "Preach to the dry bones," YHWH tells Ezekiel, "that they shall live." So Ezekiel does as commanded. And astonishingly, the bones come together and breath comes into them, all by the power of the word of God.

Anthem
Holy Spirit, Truth Divine, Jean Pasquet (Elkan-Vogel) 2-part (E).

Romans 8:22–27 All creation groans, as do we who have the firstfruits of the Spirit, for redemption. But we have an advantage: The gift of the Spirit supports our confident hope that we shall be saved. We do not know how to pray, yet the Spirit transforms our weak groanings into prayer. The Spirit pleads with God on our behalf so we may share in the glory that God prepares for those who love God.

Anthem
Come, Spirit Divine, Hugo Distler (Joseph Boonin) SATB (MD).

or **Acts 2:1–21** See above.

John 15:26–27; 16:4b–15 "I," says Jesus, "will send to you from the Father the Paraclete (the Spirit of truth), who will bear witness to me, as also will you. Now I shall go away to the one who sent me in order that the Paraclete may come to you and convince the world of sin and of righteousness and of judgment. When the Spirit of truth comes, that Spirit will guide you into all the truth, and will glorify me."

Anthem
The Spirit of Truth, Knut Nystedt (Concordia) SAB (ME).

Psalm 104:24–34, 35b
1. Metrical: *Bless the Lord with All My Being.* Text: 8.7.8.7.D, Fred R. Anderson. Tune: RUSTINGTON. PH90 #224. For text only see *SPJP,* p. 56.
2. Responsorial: *Psalm 104* (1–9). Text: Grail. Tone and Refrain: Presbyterian 3. PS93 #104.
3. Responsorial: *Psalm 104* (24, 27–34). Text: Arlo D. Duba. Setting: Richard T. Proulx. PS93 #105.
4. Responsorial: *Lord, Send Out Your Spirit.* Setting by Robert Edward Smith. CC G-2122.
5. Responsorial: *Lord, How Manifold Are Your Works!* (25–35). Text: *Book of Common Prayer.* Music: Peter R. Hallock. TIP/PSCY #10.

See also *ANMP,* p. 174; *PH87* #104; *WIII* #855, 856; *PR&T,* pp. 34–35.

Anthem
O Lord, How Manifold Are Thy Works, Martin Shaw (Novello) unison (ME).

Organ Music for the Day
1. *Prelude on* VENI CREATOR SPIRITUS/KOMM GOTT SCHÖPFER (*Come, Holy Spirit, Our Souls Inspire, PH90* #125), Leo Sowerby (*Advent to Whitsuntide,* vol. 4, p. 25, Hinrichsen Edition, Ltd. 743b).
2. *Variations on the Welsh Hymn Tune* ABERYSTWYTH (*Wind Who Makes All Winds That Blow, PH90* #131), Paul L. Thomas (Oxford University Press 385480-5).

166

Hymns for the Day	HL33	HB55	WB72	PH90
Come, Holy Spirit, Heavenly Dove	206	239	–	126
Come, Holy Spirit, Our Souls Inspire	–	237	335	125
Come, Thou Almighty King	52	244	343	139
Holy Ghost, Dispel Our Sadness	–	–	419	317
Holy Spirit, Lord of Love	–	–	–	524
Holy Spirit, Truth Divine	208	240	422	321

Ordinary Time
TRINITY SUNDAY
[FIRST SUNDAY AFTER PENTECOST] (B)

Isaiah 6:1–8 Confronted by the immediate presence of the enthroned God and of seraphim singing "Holy, holy, holy," which rocked the very foundations of the Temple, Isaiah feels his hair stand on end, shirt buttons pop, and shoelaces untie as he is denuded of his pretense of worthiness before the Lord. "Woe is me!" cries out Isaiah. "For I am a man of unclean lips, and I dwell in the midst of a people of unclean lips." Astonishingly, one of the seraphim then touches Isaiah's lips with a burning coal from the altar, saying, "Your guilt is taken away, and your sin forgiven." Upon hearing the voice of the Lord say, "Whom shall I send, and who will go for us?" Isaiah's lips now inexplicably respond, "Here am I! Send me."

Anthem
In the Year That King Uzziah Died, David McKay Williams (H. W. Gray) SATB (D).

Romans 8:12–17 An exhortation to live not according to the anxiety and fear of human nature but according to the life-giving Spirit. Though we constantly get tangled in the slavery of our pious self-interest and cravings for acceptance, God's Spirit works among us to bring about a new relationship that enables us to cry out boldly, "Abba!"

Anthem
Sing and Dance, Children of God, Michael Bedford (Hinshaw) 2-part (E).

John 3:1–17 By day, Nicodemus is everything you could want to be; by night, he comes secretly in search of Jesus. By day, Nicodemus controls the affairs of his kingdom; by night, he comes looking for the kingdom of God. Replies Jesus, "Unless one is born of water and the Spirit, then one cannot enter the kingdom of God." "How can this be?" asked Nicodemus.

Anthems
Truly, Truly I Say to You, Gerhard Krapf (Concordia) unison (E). *God So Loved the World,* Tschesnokoff, ed. Noble Cain (Boosey & Hawkes) SSAATTBB (MD).

Psalm 29
1. Metrical: *The God of Glory Thunders.* Text: Michael Perry. Setting: Norman Warren. *PH90* #180 (see also *PP* #82).
2. Responsorial: *Psalm 29.* Setting: Hal H. Hopson. *PS93* #26.
See also *GPI,* p. 35; *24P&1C,* p. 10 for optional refrains; *CC* G-2421; *ANMP,* p. 66; *SPJP,* p. 29; *PH87* #29; *PR&T,* pp. 17 & 66.

Anthem
Festal Anthem, Robert Leaf (Augsburg) SATB trumpet (M).

Organ Music for the Day
1. *Prelude on* ITALIAN HYMN/MOSCOW/TRINITY (*Come, Thou Almighty King, PH90* #139), Robert Cundick and John Longhurst (*Twelve Hymn Settings from the Tabernacle,* Sonos Music Resources, Inc. SWK058).
2. *Prelude on* ABBOT'S LEIGH (*Come, Great God of All the Ages, PH90* #132), Austin Lovelace (Hope Publishing Co. 274).

Hymns for the Day	HL33	HB55	WB72	PH90
All Creatures of Our God and King	–	100	282	455
Come, Thou Almighty King	52	244	343	139
God Is One, Unique and Holy	–	–	–	135
Holy, Holy, Holy!	57	11	421	138
Of the Father's Love Begotten	–	7	534	309
Spirit Divine, Attend Our Prayers	212	243	574	325

SUNDAY BETWEEN MAY 29 AND JUNE 4
(PROPER 4) [9] (B) [*USE ONLY IF AFTER TRINITY SUNDAY*]*

1 Samuel 3:1–10, (11–20) Injustice, infidelity, and corruption permeated temple life at Shiloh. Worse, "the word of YHWH was rare." Yet YHWH persistently calls to the boy Samuel during his sleep so he may deliver the word of YHWH's judgment upon the whole house of Eli. Amazingly, Eli accepts that word. More amazingly, that word comes true precisely as proclaimed by Samuel, who is then "established as a prophet of YHWH."

Anthem
Here I Am, Lord, PH90 #525.

2 Corinthians 4:5–12 "We don't promote ourselves," says Paul, "we preach Christ as Lord and serve him alone. We are frail human beings, earthenware vessels, in whom God has entrusted the powerful treasure of the gospel. Yes, we are often afflicted, perplexed, and persecuted, but our 'suffering life' reflects Jesus' life. We are not success-devotees but suffering disciples."

Anthem
Good Spirit of God, Jean van de Cauter (*Ecumenical Praise,* number 82, Agape) unison or SATB (E).

Mark 2:23–3:6 Two controversy-pronouncement stories about plucking grain and healing on the Sabbath: Jesus counters Pharisaical accusations with questions about the precedence of human need over legalism, the priority of humans in the order of creation, and the intention of the Sabbath—to save or kill life. Jesus then affirms his authority by pronouncing that "the Son of Man is lord even of the sabbath." Rather than amazement, Jesus' adversaries (religious and political leaders) stare in silence, then conspire to kill him.

Anthem
Can I See Another's Woe, Jane Marshall (Carl Fischer) SATB (ME).

Psalm 139:1–6, 13–18
1. Responsorial: *Psalm 139* (1–5,13–14,16–18). Setting: H. Hopson. *PS93* #143.
2. Metrical: *Lord, You Have Searched and Seen Me Through.* Text: L.M., Fred R. Anderson. *SPJP,* p. 70. Tune: MARYTON.
See also *30P&2C,* p. 40 (st. 1, 2, 6–8); *PH87* #139 (st. 1 & 2); *WIII* #1034.

Anthem
Search Me and Know My Heart, Carlton R. Young (Hope) SATB, solo voice, oboe, narrator, and optional congregation (ME).

Organ Music for the Day
1. *Prelude on* NUN DANKET ALL' UND BRINGET EHR' (*This Is the Day, PH90* #230), Douglas Coates (Bosworth & Co., Ltd. 22077).
2. *Chorale Prelude on* HELFT MIR GOTT'S GÜTE PREISEN (*Help Me Praise God's Goodness,* Johann N. Hanff, *Masterpieces of Organ Music,* number 61, Liturgical Music Press).

Hymns for the Day	HL33	HB55	WB72	PH90
Blest Be the Tie That Binds	343	473	–	438
Great Is Thy Faithfulness	–	–	–	276
If Thou but Trust in God	–	344	431	282
O Master, Let Me Walk with Thee	364	304	520	357
Our Cities Cry to You, O God	–	–	–	437
Today We All Are Called to Be Disciples	–	–	–	434

---

*NOTE: If the Sunday between May 24 and May 28 follows Trinity Sunday, use readings for the Sunday between February 25 and 29 (B) on that day.

SUNDAY BETWEEN JUNE 5 AND JUNE 11
(PROPER 5) [10] (B) [*USE ONLY IF AFTER TRINITY SUNDAY*]

1 Samuel 8:4–11, (12–15), 16–20, (11:14–15) Israel exhorts Samuel to appoint a king, like other nations. Samuel, displeased, prays to YHWH, who says: "They have not rejected you, but me from being king over them. Ever since I brought them out of Egypt, they have forsaken me for other gods. Warn them; show them the practices of kings." So Samuel describes for the people how a king would oppress them. But they refuse to listen; they are determined to get a king, like other nations.

Anthem
God Marked a Line and Told the Sea, PH90 #283.

2 Corinthians 4:13–5:1 "I believed, therefore I spoke," says the Septuagint version of Psalm 115:1. Likewise, we and Paul believe in a resurrection faith; therefore, we all preach the gospel, knowing that God will raise us all and join us to Christ. Though we may occasionally succumb to despair when we realize we are edging closer to our mortal death, still we fix our eyes not on the ephemeral, material securities of this world, but on the eternal, invisible home that God has prepared for us.

Anthem
We Know That Christ Is Raised, C. V. Stanford (Augsburg) SATB (E).

Mark 3:20–35 Neighbors and scribes reject Jesus, saying he is insane and demonic, respectively. He counters with a rhetorical question and three "if . . . then" sayings (all about a divided "house" falling), and a pronouncement about the unforgivable sin of blasphemy against the Holy Spirit, who is at work in Jesus. Then Jesus' family shows its blindness about Jesus' identity, which elicits another question from Jesus and his pronouncement about the doers of God's will being his true family.

Anthem
Lord, for Thy Tender Mercy's Sake, R. Farrant (Novello) SATB (ME).

Psalm 138
1. Metrical: *I Will Give Thanks with My Whole Heart.* Text: L.M., Christopher L. Webber. Tune: HERR JESU CHRIST. *PH90* #247.
2. Responsorial: *Psalm 138.* Text: Arlo D. Duba. Refrain: Arlo D. Duba. Harm., H. Hopson. Instrumentation: Lynelle M. Williams. *PS93* #141.

See also *30P&2C,* p. 39; *WIII* #879; *PR&T,* pp. 57 & 77.

Anthem
With Songs of Rejoicing, J. S. Bach, arr. Hal H. Hopson (Carl Fischer) 2-part mixed (E).

Organ Music for the Day
1. *Prelude on* SEELENBRÄUTIGAM (*Jesus, Lead the Way*), Gerald Near (*Preludes on Four Hymn Tunes,* Augsburg 11-828).
2. *Chorale Prelude on* HERR JESU CHRIST (*I Will Give Thanks*—Psalm 138, *PH90* #247), J. S. Bach and Georg Böhm (*The Church Organist's Golden Treasury,* vol. 2, Oliver Ditson Co.).

Hymns for the Day	HL33	HB55	WB72	PH90
Angels, from the Realms of Glory	124	168	298	22
Come, Thou Almighty King	52	244	343	139
God Is Here!	–	–	–	461
Hope of the World	–	291	423	360
Lift High the Cross	–	–	–	371
We Walk by Faith and Not by Sight	–	–	–	399

SUNDAY BETWEEN JUNE 12 AND JUNE 18
(PROPER 6) [11] (B) [USE ONLY IF AFTER TRINITY SUNDAY]

1 Samuel 15:34–16:13 YHWH commands Samuel to offer a sacrifice at Bethlehem as a ruse. He is to anoint the one whom YHWH has chosen as king. At the sacrifice, Samuel surveys seven sons of Jesse, but YHWH selects none of these. The youngest, most inexperienced, least likely son is taking care of the sheep. And YHWH says, "Arise, anoint him; for this is he."

Anthem
As a Chalice Cast of Gold, PH90 #336.

2 Corinthians 5:6–10, (11–13), 14–17 In our earthly life we live by faith, trusting the invisible rather than the visible, hoping for the unseen rather than the seen, and daring to be courageous in the face of death. For our hope is in Jesus Christ; after all, what more could we ask than a fuller, transformed life at home with the Lord? So we seek to please Christ now and then, for we shall not be judged by human standards but by Christ, the one who died on behalf of us all.

Anthem
We Walk by Faith, Hal H. Hopson (Sacred Music) SATB (ME).

Mark 4:26–34 Two surrealistic parables: Is one about a lazy or pious farmer? No, this is about God's grain growing automatically by stages during the sabbatical year but concluding with a horrid, apocalyptic harvest of the enemies of God (see Joel 3:13). The other is about an unpopular, despised, rejected weed (not a triumphant cedar of Lebanon) in which foolish birds find refuge and make their home.

Anthem
Song of the Mustard Seed, Hal H. Hopson (G.I.A.) unison, children.

Psalm 20
1. Metrical: *In the Day of Need.* Text: Christopher Idle. Tune: SAMSON. *PH90* #169. (See also *PP* #77 and *PH87* #20.)
2. Responsorial: *Psalm 20.* Text: Helen L. Wright. Melody: Columba Kelly. Harmony, Samuel Weber. *PS93* #14.
3. Responsorial: Text: optional. Psalm tones and refrains by Hal H. Hopson. *PR&T*, pp. 2, 15, & 63.

Anthems
We Will Rejoice, William Croft (Broude) ATB solos (M). *In the Day of Need, PH90* #169.

Organ Music for the Day
1. *Prelude on* WINCHESTER OLD (*God Is Our Refuge, PH90* #191), Alfred Whitehead (*A Christmas Pastorale*, H. W. Gray Co., Inc. 645).
2. *Prelude on* FOUNDATION (*How Firm a Foundation, PH90* #361), Wilbur Held (*Seven Settings of American Folk Hymns*, Concordia 97-5829).

Hymns for the Day	HL33	HB55	WB72	PH90
All Hail to God's Anointed	–	–	–	205
Come, Ye Thankful People, Come!	460	525	346	551
God, You Spin the Whirling Planets	–	–	–	285
Walk On, O People of God	–	–	–	296
We Know That Christ Is Raised	–	–	–	495
We Walk by Faith and Not by Sight	–	–	–	399

SUNDAY BETWEEN JUNE 19 AND JUNE 25
(PROPER 7) [12] (B) [*USE ONLY IF AFTER TRINITY SUNDAY*]

1 Samuel 17:(1a, 4–11, 19–23), 32–49 David resolves to take on the Philistine Goliath in a "winner-take-all" battle. Though Saul protests such a mismatch, David is confident (because the God of justice—YHWH—will stand by him). Casting off Saul's armor, David opts for his staff and five smooth stones. When Goliath discerns that ill-equipped David is his foe, he is insulted at being treated with such disdain by the Israelites. Ironically, it is a mismatch: Goliath the mighty Philistine versus David (and YHWH)—no contest!

Anthem

O David Was a Shepherd Lad, Austin Lovelace (H. W. Gray) unison, children.

or **1 Samuel 17:57–18:5, 10–16** David and Jonathan bond themselves together in covenant. Saul retains David in his entourage, and wherever Saul sends him, David's military triumphs continue, also increasing his popularity. An evil spirit invades Saul, who then twice attempts to maim, if not kill, David. Saul is afraid of David. So, to place David in greater danger, Saul makes David a military commander in the field. David, however, is even more successful, endearing himself to all Israel and Judah.

Anthem

If Thou but Suffer God to Guide Thee, Jody Lindh (Concordia) SATB (ME).

2 Corinthians 6:1–13 Work with God *today,* for the day of salvation is *now.* Yes, we "apostles" who work with God have faced obstacles, but we have endured through faithful conduct. Yes, tension exists between the way the world perceives us and who we really are. Nevertheless, we have acted as God's servants in a way that merits commendation, for the way we live, speak, act as a church reflects on the gospel itself. Now, respond to God's magnanimous reconciling act; open wide your hearts.

Anthem

Stand Up and Bless the Lord, arr. William Whitehead (*Simple Solutions for Slim Sundays,* Triune) 2-part (E).

Mark 4:35–41 Jesus and his disciples enjoy an evening boat ride, until a rampaging, howling storm slings their boat from wave to wave. Terrified, helpless disciples scream at the slumbering Jesus, "Teacher, don't you care?" So Jesus puts down the beastly storm by simply saying, "Be quiet!" "Who is this that has such power that the wind and sea obey him?" ask the awestruck disciples. Guess who's really in charge of the world.

Anthem

Grant Us Thy Peace, Felix Mendelssohn (Boosey & Hawkes) SATB (E).

Psalm 9:9–20 (reflecting upon 1 Samuel 17:1a, 4–11, 19–23, 32–49)
1. Responsorial: *Psalm 9:9–20.* Setting: Hal H. Hopson. *PS93* #6.
2. Metrical: *Wholehearted Thanksgiving to You I Will Bring.* Text: *The Book of Psalms for Singing,* 1975. Tune: WALTHER. *PH87* #9.
3. Responsorial: Text: optional. Psalm tones and refrains by Hal H. Hopson. *PR&T,* pp. 59 & 66.

Anthem

They That Know Thy Name, Robert J. Powell (Schmitt, Hall, McCreary) SA(T)B (ME).

or **Psalm 133** (reflecting upon 1 Samuel 17:57–18:5, 10–16)
1. Metrical: *Behold the Goodness of Our Lord.* Text: Fred R. Anderson. Tune: CRIMOND. *PH90* #241. For text only see *SPJP,* p. 67.

2. Responsorial: *Psalm 133.* Setting: Hal H. Hopson. *PS93* #137.
3. Metrical: *When Brethren Live at Peace.* Text: S.M., Christopher L. Webber. *ANMP*, p. 214.
4. Metrical: *Behold, How Good, How Pleasant Is the Union.* Text: Bert Polman. Tune: GENEVAN 133. *PH87* #133.
5. Responsorial: *Together in Unity.* For unison choir, congregation, and organ. Text: Psalm 133. Music: Malcolm Williamson. (Boosey & Hawkes W. 003).
6. Responsorial: Text optional: Psalm tone and refrain by Hal H. Hopson. *PR&T,* pp. 28 & 82.

Anthems
Behold, How Good and Joyful, John Clarke-Whitfeld (Oxford) SATB (ME) bass solo. *A Prayer for Peace,* Michael McCabe (AMSI) SATB, SAB, or 2-part (E).

Organ Music for the Day
1. *Prelude on* ST. BRIDE (*Give to the Winds Your Fears, PH90* #286), Raymond H. Haan (*Contemplative Hymn Tune Preludes,* Harold Flammer, Inc. HF-5103).
2. *Voluntary III in D,* William Croft (*Organ Works,* Oxford University Press).

Hymns for the Day	HL33	HB55	WB72	PH90
Called as Partners in Christ's Service	–	–	–	343
Give to the Winds Your Fears	294	364	377	286
God of the Ages, Whose Almighty Hand	414	515	394	262
Great God, We Sing That Mighty Hand	470	527	408	265
Lonely the Boat	–	–	–	373
O Sing a Song of Bethlehem	138	177	526	308

SUNDAY BETWEEN JUNE 26 AND JULY 2
(PROPER 8) [13] (B)

2 Samuel 1:1, 17–27 "How are the mighty fallen!" David publicly laments the slaying of Saul and Jonathan—"Israel's glory." This song of raw feelings shall "be taught to the people of Judah" so they will know of David's grief as well as the nation's. The shields of Israel's undivided heroes—"who were swifter than eagles, stronger than lions"—lie in disgrace on Gilboa. Weep, women of Israel, for Saul will no longer clothe you. And Jonathan's deep affection will be but a memory. "How are the mighty fallen!"

Anthem
The Lament of David, Daniel Pinkham (E. C. Schirmer) SATB electronic tape (D).

2 Corinthians 8:7–15 Perhaps more than any other word, "giving" best characterizes the lifestyle of Christians. We give to neighbors our faith, speech, knowledge, help, love, and now Paul charges us to give our cash. Our whole life points to the servant Christ who "though he was rich, yet for our sakes he became poor." Christ is the self-giver par excellence.

Anthem
We Would Offer Thee This Day, O God, Jane Marshall (Sacred Music) SATB (M).

Mark 5:21–43 A story within a story about two desperate yet faithful people. Jairus's faith in Jesus restores his daughter to life, and an unknown woman's flow of faith saves her from an incurable illness and makes her whole. No wonder everyone is amazed.

Anthems
O Christ, the Healer, PH90 #380. *Draw Us in the Spirit's Tether,* Harold Friedell (H. W. Gray) SATB.

Psalm 130
1. Metrical: *Out of the Depths.* Text: Martin Luther. Tune: AUS TIEFER NOT. *PH90* #240.
2. Responsorial: *Psalm 130.* Setting: Hal H. Hopson. *PS93* #134.
3. Metrical: *Lord, from the Depths to Thee I Cried.* Text: The Scottish Psalter, 1650. Tune: SONG 67. *HB55* #277.
4. Responsorial: *Out of the Depths* (through-composed). James J. Chepponis. *CC* G-2308.
5. Responsorial: *Out of the Depths.* Text: *Book of Common Prayer.* Music: Peter R. Hallock. *TIP/PSCY* #6.

See also *WIII* #799; *APS,* p. 33; *PR&T,* pp. 49 & 70.

Anthem
From Deepest Woe I Cry to Thee, P. P. Stearns (AMSI) 2-part (ME).

Organ Music for the Day
1. *Prelude on* TRURO (*Lift Up Your Heads, Ye Mighty Gates, PH90* #8), G. Winston Cassler (*Hymn Tune Preludes,* Augsburg 11-9205).
2. *Chorale Prelude on* AUS TIEFER NOT (*Out of the Depths*—Psalm 130, *PH90* #240), Ernst Pepping (*Praeludia Postludia,* B. Schotts Söhne 6041).

Hymns for the Day	HL33	HB55	WB72	PH90
As Deer Long for the Streams	317	322	–	189, 190
God, Whose Giving Knows No Ending	–	–	–	422
I Love the Lord, Who Heard My Cry	–	–	–	362
Lord, Whose Love Through Humble Service	–	–	–	427
O Lord of Life, Where'er They Be	–	–	–	530
We Give Thee but Thine Own	394	312	–	428

SUNDAY BETWEEN JULY 3 AND JULY 9
(PROPER 9) [14] (B)

2 Samuel 5:1–5, 9–10 All the tribes of Israel gather at the sanctuary in Hebron and affirm David as "bone and flesh." Thus, in fulfillment of the promise (1 Sam. 25:30), and in the presence of YHWH, the elders anoint David as king over Israel. David now lives in Jerusalem, renaming it the city of David, and becomes greater and greater because "YHWH was with him."

Anthem
Hallelujah to the God of Israel, F. J. Haydn (J. Fischer) SATB (M).

2 Corinthians 12:2–10 "I've had ecstatic spiritual experiences that rival anyone else's," says Paul, "but what ultimately strengthens me is not such visions and revelations but insults, hardships, persecutions, calamities, and 'thorns in the flesh.'" Despite our list of achievements and presumed self-esteem that create in us a false sense of self-sufficiency, ultimately we are completely dependent upon Christ. Yes, faith in him will generate an assortment of suffering cross-experiences, but paradoxically, when we are weak, then we are strong, for God's grace alone is sufficient to sustain us.

Anthem
Open, Lord, My Inward Ear, Malcolm Williamson (*Ecumenical Praise,* number 31, Agape) unison (E).

Mark 6:1–13 Jesus preaches his homecoming sermon. Many are so astonished at this carpenter's son's teachings that they take offense and reject him. In the midst of such lack of faith, such closed-mindedness to the power of God at work, Jesus "could do no mighty work there." Then, unworthy, incomplete, imperfect disciples are commissioned by Jesus, and given authority. "Do not encumber yourself with material goods," charges Jesus. "Stay where you're welcome and leave where you're rebuffed." So they go obediently, untrained and inexperienced: preaching, exorcizing, anointing, and healing in the name of Jesus.

Anthem
They Saw You as the Local Builder's Son, Verner Ahlberg (*Ecumenical Praise,* number 105, Agape) unison (E).

Psalm 48
1. Metrical: *Great Is the Lord Our God.* Text: The Psalter Hymnal. Tune: DIADEMATA. *PH87* #48.
2. Responsorial: *Psalm 48.* Text: *A New Zealand Prayer Book.* Refrain and Tone: Howard Hughes. *PS93* #43.
See also *PP* #93; *PR&T,* pp. 38 & 65.

Anthem
Great Is the Lord (Grail Gelineau Psalter, G.I.A.) SATB (ME).

Organ Music for the Day
1. *Chorale Prelude on* MIT FREUDEN ZART (*Sing Praise to God, PH90* #483), Max Drischner (*Choralvorspiele für Dorforganisten,* C. L. Schultheiss).
2. *Prelude on* DUNDEE (*O God, in a Mysterious Way, PH90* #270), David N. Johnson (*Deck Thyself, My Soul, with Gladness,* Augsburg 11-9157).

Hymns for the Day	HL33	HB55	WB72	PH90
All Hail to God's Anointed	–	–	–	205
How Firm a Foundation	283	369	425	361
Jesus, Our Divine Companion	–	–	–	305
O Master, Let Me Walk with Thee	364	304	520	357
Take Up Thy Cross, the Savior Said	–	293	–	393
When We Are Living	–	–	–	400

SUNDAY BETWEEN JULY 10 AND JULY 16
(PROPER 10) [15] (B)

2 Samuel 6:1–5, 12b–19 Following victory over the Philistines, David and his "chosen men" jubilantly march back to Jerusalem with the Ark of God leading them. David, however, abandons the Ark at a pagan farmer's home, which is then unexpectedly blessed by the presence of the Lord. So David resumes the "Ark processional" by offering a solemn sacrifice and dancing with all his might before the Lord.

Anthem

Sing and Dance, Children of God, M. Bedford (Hinshaw) 2-part (E).

Ephesians 1:3–14 Thanks to be you, O God, for blessing our union with Christ by bestowing the gift of the Spirit and for choosing us as your servants for the purpose of praising your glorious free grace. May the God of our Lord Jesus Christ continually give us discernment regarding our calling and rich inheritance.

Anthem

Messenger to Ephesus, Eugene Butler (Agape) SATB (M).

Mark 6:14–29 John the Baptist, "a righteous and holy man," is the forerunner of Jesus; the preparer of the way of the Lord; the baptizer of the beloved Son; yet, unjustifiably imprisoned. When bad things happen to good people does it make them better people? Not in John's case, for he suffers violent death at the hands of established power. Better be prepared for the coming trials.

Anthem

O God, Whose Will Is Life and Peace, Thomas Tallis (*Third Mode*) setting, Donald Busarow (Concordia) SATB, optional congregation, flute (ME).

Psalm 24

1. Metrical: *The Earth and All That Dwell Therein.* Text: *The Psalter,* 1912, alt. Tune: CAITHNESS. *PH90* #176.
2. Responsorial: *Psalm 24. (Lift Up the Gates Eternal).* Text: Willard F. Jabusch, Arlo D. Duba. Tune: ISRAELI FOLK MELODY. Arr. John Ferguson. Instrumentation: Kenneth E. Williams, Lynelle M. Williams. *PS93* #21. (See also *PH90* #177 and *APS,* p. 16.)
3. Responsorial: *Psalm 24.* Setting by Arthur Wills in *Popular Psalm Settings,* The Year Book Press, 76-14115.

See also *ANMP,* p. 58; *PH87* #24; *SPJP,* p. 24; *WIII* #775; *PR&T,* pp. 3 & 6.

Anthem

Who Shall Ascend, Hank Beebe (Carl Fischer) 2-part (E).

Organ Music for the Day

1. *Prelude on* LAUDA ANIMA (*Praise, My Soul, the King of Heaven, PH90* #478), Kevin Norris (*Reflections on Six Hymn Tunes,* Art Masters Studios, Inc. OR-5).
2. *Prelude on* AUSTRIA (*Glorious Things of Thee Are Spoken, PH90* #446), John K. Paine (McAfee Music Corp.).

Hymns for the Day	HL33	HB55	WB72	PH90
Here, O Lord, Your Servants Gather	–	–	417	465
I Greet Thee, Who My Sure Redeemer Art	–	144	625	457
Immortal, Invisible, God Only Wise	66	85	433	263
O Lord of Life, Where'er They Be	–	–	–	530
Praise Ye the Lord	–	–	–	258
Ye Watchers and Ye Holy Ones	–	34	–	451

SUNDAY BETWEEN JULY 17 AND JULY 23
(PROPER 11) [16] (B)

2 Samuel 7:1–14a Now that David has established his power, he notices that "God's tent is not as good as my home." Replies Nathan: "Do what's in your heart, for YHWH is with you." But that same night the word of the Lord comes to Nathan: "Do not try to contain and control me in a house (temple), for I have been and will be with you all wherever you are. Go tell David that I chose him, I established him, I will build him an enduring house (family dynasty), and I will keep my steadfast love with him forever."

Anthem
Thou Hast Told Us, Arnold Bax (*Anthems for Choirs,* vol. 4, Oxford) SATB (E).

Ephesians 2:11–22 Remember when we were separated from each other by walls of hostility, accusation, name-calling, hatred? We were strangers to each other. But then Christ's cross rammed our barricades of pride and smashed our fortifications of bitterness and guilt, reconciling us all to him. That's the good news we preach: that we have been re-created as a new people, a new family in union with Christ.

Anthem
One Family, One Faith, Garry Cornell (AMSI) SATB (ME) handbells.

Mark 6:30–34, 53–56 Jesus urges the disciples to rest after their ministry. Yet he feels compassion for the multitude following him because they are like shepherdless sheep, so he teaches them. Crossing over to the region around Gennesaret, Jesus is immediately recognized. Whenever and wherever he is, people constantly bring the sick and the lame and the broken to Jesus, pleading for healing. And they are healed.

Anthem
O Jesus Christ, to You May Hymns Be Rising, Daniel Moe (*Ecumenical Praise,* number 94, Agape) SATB (ME).

Psalm 89:20–37
1. Metrical: *Forever I Will Sing of Your Great Love, O Lord.* Text: Psalm 89. Tune: GENEVAN 89. *PH87* #89 (stanzas 4–5).
2. Responsorial: *Psalm 89:20–37.* Text: Grail. Refrain and Tone: Presbyterian 6. *PS93* #82.
3. Responsorial: *I Have Found David My Servant.* Text: *Book of Common Prayer.* Music: Peter R. Hallock. *TIP/MTYL* Cycle (B).

See also *PR&T,* pp. 56 & 62.

Anthem
My Song Forever Shall Record, PH90 #209.

Organ Music for the Day
1. *Prelude on* WESTMINSTER ABBEY (*Christ Is Made the Sure Foundation, PH90* #416), Clifford Harker (Bosworth & Co., Ltd. 22015).
2. *Festival Postlude on* WESTMINSTER ABBEY (*Christ Is Made the Sure Foundation, PH90* #416), George Towers (J. B. Cramer & Co., Ltd.).

Hymns for the Day	HL33	HB55	WB72	PH90
Blessed Assurance, Jesus Is Mine!	–	–	–	341
Christ Is Made the Sure Foundation	336	433	325	416, 417
Great Is Thy Faithfulness	–	–	–	276
Love Divine, All Loves Excelling	308	399	471	376
O Praise the Gracious Power	–	–	–	471
Savior, Like a Shepherd Lead Us	458	380	–	387

SUNDAY BETWEEN JULY 24 AND JULY 30
(PROPER 12) [17] (B)

2 Samuel 11:1–15 David arises from his afternoon nap and lays his eyes upon a beautiful woman, Bathsheba, bathing in her home. Overcome, he sends his couriers to fetch her. He indulges in sexual intercourse with her, resulting in her pregnancy. David recalls her husband, Uriah, from the battlefield for a brief furlough at home with his wife, but dutiful Uriah keeps watch all night outside the palace. David then plies Uriah with alcohol, but he sleeps in the palace compound. So David plots to send Uriah back to the war, to be killed in a retreat ordered by David via Joab.

Anthem
Have Mercy on Us, Aaron Copland (Boosey & Hawkes) SATB (MD).

Ephesians 3:14–21 Paul falls on his knees and prays that the Spirit will strengthen us, that Christ will make his home among us so we may understand the incredible breadth, length, height, and depth of his love, and that God will fill us with God's nature. To God be the glory!

Anthem
Now Unto Him That Is Able, Jan Bender (Concordia) SATB (M).

John 6:1–21 Near Passover, a multitude follow Jesus "into the hills." "How are we to feed so many?" tests Jesus. Andrew spots a boy with five loaves and two fish. Jesus says, "Tell everyone to sit" (about 5,000 do so). He takes the loaves, gives thanks, and distributes to those seated; so also the fish, as much as they want. The disciples collect twelve basketfuls of leftovers. The people see this "sign" and identify Jesus as "the prophet who is to come." But Jesus' kingdom is not of this world, so he departs. During the night, the disciples try to cross the sea, but the rough winds fling them from wave to wave. They see Jesus "walking on the water." "It is I," says Jesus. "Fear not." Immediately, the boat reaches their destination.

Anthem
Thou Hast Given Us Bread from Heaven, Johann Geisler (H. W. Gray) SATB (M).

Psalm 14
1. Metrical: *The Foolish in Their Hearts Deny.* Text: Marie J. Post. Tune: OLD 107TH. *PH87* #14.
2. Responsorial: *Psalm 14.* Text: Helen L. Wright. Refrain: John Ferguson. Tone: *Lutheran Book of Worship. PS93* #8.
See also *GPI,* p. 14; *PR&T,* pp. 2 & 15.

Anthem
O That Salvation for Israel Would Come, Johann Geisler (Boosey & Hawkes) SS(A)TB (M).

Organ Music for the Day
1. *Prelude on* CWM RHONDDA (*Guide Me, O Thou . . . , PH90* #281), F. Peeters (*Hymn Preludes for the Lit. Year,* vol. 20, C. F. Peters Corp. 6420).
2. *Prelude on* ST. CATHERINE (*Jesus, Thy Boundless . . . , PH90* #366), D. S. Harris (*Ten Hymn Preludes in Trio Style,* H. W. Gray Co., Inc. GB 632).

Hymns for the Day	HL33	HB55	WB72	PH90
Become to Us the Living Bread	–	–	–	500
Guide Me, O Thou Great Jehovah	104	339	409	281
Jesus, Thy Boundless Love to Me	314	404	–	366
Judge Eternal, Throned in Splendor	417	517	447	–
O Love, How Deep, How Broad	139	–	518	83
When We Are Tempted to Deny Your Son	–	–	640	86

178

SUNDAY BETWEEN JULY 31 AND AUGUST 6
(PROPER 13) [18] (B)

2 Samuel 11:26–12:13a YHWH is outraged by David's adultery with Bathsheba and his arranged murder of Uriah, so YHWH sends the prophet Nathan to tell David a story about a rich man commandeering a poor man's precious lamb. Recognizing himself as a sinner, David repents.

Anthem
O God, Be Merciful, Christopher Tye (Oxford) SATB (M).

Ephesians 4:1–16 We have received as a gift from God a way of life in Christ and, therefore, are called to exemplify it: humility, gentleness, patience, and tolerance. Above all, preserve (not presume) the fragile unity the Spirit gives to the community, for there is only one Lord, one faith, and one baptism. "Each of us was given grace according to the measure of Christ's gift." These gifts are "to equip the saints for the work of ministry, for building up the body of Christ." All gifts exist to enhance the larger work of the church, and to maintain the oneness of the body of Christ given to us.

Anthem
Anthem of Unity, John Ness Beck (G. Schirmer) SATB (ME).

John 6:24–35 People searching for Jesus are accused by him of seeking only another free lunch. "Work for imperishable, eternal manna," says Jesus, "which the Son of Man will give you." What kind of works must we do? "Believe in the one whom God has sent," says Jesus. Then show us a sign—like the manna in the wilderness—so we will believe. "That bread," retorts Jesus, "came from heaven." That's the bread we want; give it to us. "Simply open your eyes and see," answers Jesus; "I am the bread of life; whoever comes to me shall not hunger, and whoever believes in me shall never thirst."

Anthem
The Bread of Life, Gerhard Krapf (*Seven Seasonal Sentences,* Sacred Music) SATB (E).

Psalm 51:1–12
1. Metrical: *Have Mercy on Us, Living Lord.* Text: C.M., Fred R. Anderson. Tune: PTOMEY. *PH90* #195. For text only see *SPJP,* p. 36.
2. Responsorial: *Psalm 51:1–12.* Text: *Book of Common Prayer.* Setting: Peter R. Hallock. *PS93* #47. (See also *TIP/PSCY* #5.)
See also *PS93* #48; *PH90* #196; *APS,* p. 18; *ANMP,* p. 101; *HB55* #282; *WIII* #41 & #787; *PH87* #51; *PR&T,* pp. 19 & 21.

Anthem
Wash Me Throughly from My Wickedness, S. S. Wesley (*Church Anthem Book,* Oxford) SATB (ME).

Organ Music for the Day
1. *Prelude on* AURELIA (*The Church's One Foundation, PH90* #442), Charles T. Taylor (*Fifteen Chorale Preludes on Well-Known Hymns,* H. T. FitzSimons Co., Inc.).
2. *Prelude on* BREAD OF LIFE (*Break Thou the . . . , PH90* #329), Seth Bingham (*Twelve Hymn Preludes,* Op. 38, Set 2, H. W. Gray Co., Inc.).

Hymns for the Day	HL33	HB55	WB72	PH90
Bread of Heaven	–	–	313	501
Help Us Accept Each Other	–	–	–	358
Jesus, Thou Joy of Loving Hearts	354	215	–	510, 511
Lord Jesus, Think on Me	239	270	–	301
The Church's One Foundation	333	437	582	442
There's a Wideness in God's Mercy	93	110	601	298

SUNDAY BETWEEN AUGUST 7 AND AUGUST 13
(PROPER 14) [19] (B)

2 Samuel 18:5–9, 15, 31–33 Intrafamily strife over succession to the throne ignites Absalom's revolt against his father, who flees Jerusalem. David, however, orders his officers not to harm Absalom. Though all the people hear David's command, ten armor bearers kill Absalom. A Cushite slave, a commissioned messenger, arrives to recount the Lord's victory over the rebellious forces. "Is Absalom well?" queries David. Knowing that kings usually react to bad news by thrashing the bearer, the Cushite answers circumspectly, "May what happened to him befall all your enemies." David, overcome with grief, reacts in an unkingly way by retiring to the room above the gateway and weeping uncontrollably over the death of his traitorous son: "O my son Absalom. Would I had died instead of you."

Anthem
David's Lamentation, William Billings (Belwin) SATB (M).

Ephesians 4:25–5:2 You are one in the Spirit, so sin not against the Spirit by thriving on slander, bitterness, anger, or divisiveness. Rather, as beloved children of God, imitate God's new life in Christ: speak the truth openly with one another, use words that build up the body, be kind and tenderhearted to each other, and forgive one another, as God in Christ forgave you.

Anthem
Be Ye Kind, One to Another, K. K. Davis (Galaxy) SATB alto.

John 6:35, 41–51 How can this son of Joseph, this man from Nazareth, say he is the bread that came down from heaven? "Do not be so disbelieving, so stubborn, so closed-minded," says Jesus, "for belief is a gift from God. I am the living bread that came down from heaven. My flesh is the sustenance, the very stuff of life that God gives. Whoever believes has eternal life."

Anthem
The Living Bread, Leland Sateren (Augsburg) SATB (E).

Psalm 130
1. Metrical: *Out of the Depths*. Text: Martin Luther. Tune: AUS TIEFER NOT. *PH90* #240.
2. Responsorial: *Psalm 130*. Setting: Hal H. Hopson. *PS93* #134.
See also *HB55* #277; *CC* G-2308; *TIP/PSCY* #6; *WIII* #799; *APS*, p. 33.

Anthem
Psalm 130, Paul Manz (Concordia) SATB (M).

Organ Music for the Day
1. *Prelude on* AUS TIEFER NOT (*Out of the Depths*—Psalm 130, *PH90* #240), J. S. Bach (*Church Organist's Golden Treasury*, vol. 1, Oliver Ditson Co.), and *Sonata III*, Felix Mendelssohn (*Organ Works*, p. 45, G. Schirmer, Inc. 227).
2. *Prelude on* CWM RHONDDA (*Guide Me, O Thou Great Jehovah, PH90* #281), David Cherwien (*Interpretations Based on Hymn-Tunes*, Art Masters Studios, Inc. SP-103).

Hymns for the Day	HL33	HB55	WB72	PH90
Amazing Grace	–	275	296	280
As Deer Long for the Streams	317	322	–	189
Bread of Heaven	–	–	313	501
Help Us Accept Each Other	–	–	–	358
Lord, Make Us Servants of Your Peace	–	–	–	374
O God of Earth and Altar	419	511	497	291

SUNDAY BETWEEN AUGUST 14 AND AUGUST 20
(PROPER 15) [20] (B)

1 Kings 2:10–12; 3:3–14 David dies and is buried, and Solomon accedes to the throne of his father. YHWH appears to Solomon in a dream, asking him what he needs. Solomon, a model of faith, recites YHWH's past *hesed* ("steadfast love") to his father, David, and, therefore, prays for a "listening mind/heart to govern your people." Because he asked not for long life or riches, YHWH was pleased and thus gave Solomon a wise and discerning mind/heart, and also—beyond his request—riches and honor. Obedience to God's ways will also result in lengthened life.

Anthem

Give Thy Servant an Understanding Heart, Virgil T. Ford (Carl Fischer) SATB (ME).

Ephesians 5:15–20 Watch how you walk. You can walk foolishly, hesitatingly, aimlessly, fearfully from birth to death. Or you can walk as God's beloved children in Christ who are at home in God's grace and, therefore, walk wisely, purposefully, joyfully, steadily with each other while singing praise and thanks to God.

Anthem

Be Filled with the Spirit, Ludwig Lenel (Concordia) SATB (ME).

John 6:51–58 For 2,000 years, many an argument has been generated by the nuances between "believing in Jesus" and "eating his flesh and drinking his blood." Advocates of cognitive and experiential "means of grace" have long battled over the "presence of God" and "the way to eternal life." Now hear Jesus' audacity when he proclaims that only those who "have life in," "abide in," "eat and drink," him—the bread of life—have eternal life.

Anthem

Verily, Verily, I Say Unto You, Thomas Tallis (Oxford) SATB (M).

Psalm 111
1. Metrical: *Hallelujah! Among the Just.* Text: L.M., Christopher L. Webber. *ANMP,* p. 180.
2. Responsorial: *Psalm 111* (1–4, 9–10). Setting: Hal H. Hopson. *PS93* #111.
3. Responsorial: *I Thank You, Lord, for Your Majesty and Love.* Text: Grail (see also *GPI,* p. 166). Psalm tone and Gelineau tone: *WIII* #58. (See also *20P&3C,* p. 25 for optional refrains.)
See also *PH87* #111; *PR&T,* pp. 11 & 13.

Anthem

My Heart Is Full Today, R. Proulx (Augsburg) 2-part, 4 handbells (E).

Organ Music for the Day
1. *Prelude on* MORNING SONG (*O Holy City, Seen of John, PH90* #453), Wilbur Held (*Hymn Preludes for the Autumn Festivals,* Concordia 97-5360), David N. Johnson (*Preludes & Postludes,* vol. 2, Augsburg 11-9319).
2. *Voluntary on* SLANE (*Be Thou My Vision, PH90* #339), Gordon Young (*Eight Organ Voluntaries on Familiar Hymn Tunes,* Theodore Presser Co. 413-41034).

Hymns for the Day	HL33	HB55	WB72	PH90
Be Thou My Vision	325	303	304	339
Breathe on Me, Breath of God	213	235	–	316
Eternal Light, Shine in My Heart	–	–	–	340
Holy Spirit, Truth Divine	208	240	422	321
O Word of God Incarnate	215	251	532	327
With Glad, Exuberant Carolings	–	–	–	490

SUNDAY BETWEEN AUGUST 21 AND AUGUST 27
(PROPER 16) [21] (B)

1 Kings 8:(1, 6, 10–11), 22–30, 41–43 Solomon stands before the altar of the newly constructed Temple, raises his outstretched arms, and offers the dedicatory prayer: "YHWH, God of Israel, nothing can compare to you, below. You keep covenant and show *hesed* ("steadfast love") to your people. When a foreigner (who hears about your mighty hand of deliverance of your people from Egypt) offers prayer to you, hear, and answer so that all may know your name and obey you, as do your people Israel."

Anthems
All Wisdom Is from the Lord, William Mathias (Oxford) SATB (D). *O Lord, My God* (*Solomon's Prayer*), S. S. Wesley (Curwen) SAB (ME).

Ephesians 6:10–20 Much to our surprise, we peace-loving Christians discover that trying to keep the faith in our world is a battle against unseen enemies, the "principalities and powers" that live in our mind and our world. With what shall we defend ourselves? Put on the armor of God: truth, righteousness, peace, faith, and salvation. And one offensive weapon is permitted—the Word of God as your sword. Now pray that you may be bold in proclaiming the gospel message.

Anthem
Soldiers of Christ, Robert J. Powell (Carl Fischer) SATB (ME).

John 6:55–69 Many people grumble at Jesus' hard teachings and "eating his flesh and drinking his blood." Some withdraw and some—like Peter—confess Jesus as "the Holy One of God." It truly is the Spirit that gives life.

Anthem
Lord, to Whom Shall We Go?, Wm. Mudde (Augsburg) SATB (ME).

Psalm 84
1. Metrical: *How Lovely, Lord.* Text: Arlo D. Duba. Tune: MERLE'S TUNE. *PH90* #207.
2. Responsorial: *Psalm 84.* Text: Helen L. Wright. Setting: Hal H. Hopson. *PS93* #74.
3. Responsorial: *Psalm 84* (1–8). Setting: Hal H. Hopson. *PS93* #75.
See also *PH90* #208; *HB55* #14; *RITL* #110; *ANMP*, p. 124; *PH87* #84; *PR&T*, pp. 47 & 64.

Anthem
Psalm 84, Richard Proulx (G.I.A.) SATB (ME).

Organ Music for the Day
1. *Prelude on* NATIONAL HYMN (*God of the Nations, Whose Almighty Hand, PH90* #262), Emma L. Diemer (*With Praise and Love,* vol. 2, The Sacred Music Press).
2. *Prelude on* HYFRYDOL (*Love Divine, All Loves Excelling, PH90* #376), David S. Harris (*Ten Hymn Preludes in Trio Style,* H. W. Gray Co., Inc., GB 643).

Hymns for the Day	HL33	HB55	WB72	PH90
A Mighty Fortress Is Our God	266	91	274	259, 260
Bread of Heaven	–	–	313	501
Break Thou the Bread of Life	216	250	317	329
Eternal Light, Shine in My Heart	–	–	–	340
God of Compassion, in Mercy Befriend Us	290	122	392	261
Immortal, Invisible, God Only Wise	66	85	433	263

SUNDAY BETWEEN AUGUST 28 AND SEPTEMBER 3
(PROPER 17) [22] (B)

Song of Solomon 2:8–13 The voice of my beloved! Look, he comes like a leaping strong gazelle or a bounding, agile young stag, and he invites me to come out from behind the lattice, and join him in his life. Winter is past; blossoms appear; the fig ripens. Through the renewing power of love, a new life beckons. Our future life and that of our Lover shall be one.

Anthem
Arise, My Love, My Fair One, Richard DeLong (E. C. Schirmer) SATB (M).

James 1:17–27 Hearing what we want to hear is nothing new—remember Adam and Eve, who heard what they wanted to hear and did what they wanted to do. So we too hear God's word, yet do as we please. We see our broken lives reflected in life's mirror, but deny or ignore or forget what we see and continue on our merry way. Now hear this! Blessed are those who peer into God's liberating word and then act upon it in word and deed.

Anthem
Every Good Gift and Every Perfect Gift, Rudolf Moser (Concordia) SATB (ME).

Mark 7:1–8, 14–15, 21–23 "Why do your disciples eat ritually unclean food?" demand the Pharisees and scribes. Jesus counters by quoting Isaiah 29:1, "You honor me with your words, but your hearts are far from me." Then he pronounces: "You're obsessed with your own laws and have abrogated God's law. Listen, what makes a person unclean is not ingesting unclean things but emitting the evil things in one's heart: theft, envy, slander, pride, and more."

Anthem
Create in Me a Clean Heart, Paul Bouman (Concordia) 2-part (E).

Psalm 45:1–2, 6–9
1. Metrical: *I Will Praise the King with All My Verses.* Text: Marie J. Post and Bert Polman. Tune: O DASS ICH TAUSENT. *PH87* #45.
2. Responsorial: *Psalm 45.* Text: Grail. Refrain: Presbyterian 3. Tone: Presbyterian 3 (expanded). *PS93* #39.
3. Responsorial: Text: optional. Psalm tones and refrains by Hal H. Hopson. *PR&T,* pp. 18 & 44.

Anthem
Grace Is Poured Abroad, Daniel Pinkham (C. F. Peters) SATB (MD).

Organ Music for the Day
1. *Choral Prelude on* DUNDEE. (*I to the Hills Will Lift My Eyes, PH90* #234), W. Lawrence Curry (H. W. Gray Co., Inc. 727).
2. *Choral Prelude on* EIN' FESTE BURG (*A Mighty Fortress Is Our God, PH90* #260), Dietrich Buxtehude (*Sämtliche Orgelwerke,* vol. 4, Wilhelm Hansen 3928).

Hymns for the Day	HL33	HB55	WB72	PH90
As a Chalice Cast of Gold	–	–	–	336
Blessed Assurance, Jesus Is Mine!	–	–	–	341
Forgive Our Sins as We Forgive	–	–	–	347
Joyful, Joyful, We Adore Thee	–	21	446	464
Now Praise the Hidden God of Love	–	–	–	402
We Plow the Fields and Scatter	–	–	–	560

SUNDAY BETWEEN SEPTEMBER 4 AND SEPTEMBER 10
(PROPER 18) [23] (B)

Proverbs 22:1–2, 8–9 If you seek to stockpile riches, ignore the poor, and plant seeds of injustice, disaster will burst up like a death-dealing mushroom cloud. So open your eyes to the rich life in the service of YHWH and experience blessings rather than self-destruction. Share your "bread" with those who have less than you.

Anthem
Seek to Serve, Lloyd Pfautsch (Hope) 2-part (E).

James 2:1–10, (11–13), 14–18 Sisters and brothers in Christ, we are charged to live according to the part of the Holiness Code as revealed in Leviticus 19:18. So we hardly conceive of ourselves as practicing partiality, discrimination, snobbishness, or any other degrading human "relationship," or lack thereof. Yet each of us can easily succumb to the strong temptation to favor the powerful, the rich, the influential and, therefore, immediately create unjust distinctions among social groups. So feed, clothe, and shelter all your neighbors as you care for your own family. In this way you will manifest the conjuncture of faith and actions.

Anthem
Neighbors, Austin Lovelace (H. W. Gray) SATB (E).

Mark 7:24–37 A Syrophoenician woman begs Jesus to cast out a demon from her daughter. To this non-Israelite woman's faith and to her wit (about undeserving dogs eating children's crumbs), Jesus responds. Hearing and speaking are interlinked gifts that depend on each other. Now see a deaf man with a speech impediment. He can neither hear the word of God nor speak it. But Jesus miraculously frees this shackled man to hear and to speak. Now there's just no hiding this good news about Jesus Christ, right? Once again, God astonishingly finds a way to speak to us so we can hear and then speak the word.

Anthem
God Hath Done All Things Well, M. Franck (Concordia) SATB (M).

Psalm 125
1. Metrical: *All Who, with Heart Confiding.* Text: *The Psalter,* 1912, alt. Tune: KNOW-HEAD. *PH87* #125.
2. Responsorial: *Psalm 125.* Text: Hal H. Hopson. Refrain: Hal H. Hopson. Gelineau tone. *PS93* #129.

See also *30P&2C,* p. 35; *PR&T,* pp. 73 & 77.

Anthem
All Who with Heart Confiding, Orlando di Lasso (Elkan-Vogel) SATB (M).

Organ Music for the Day
1. *Prelude on* SLANE (*Be Thou My Vision, PH90* #339), Paul Manz (*Ten Chorale Improvisations,* vol. 9, Concordia 97-5556).
2. *Prelude on* AZMON (*O for a Thousand Tongues to Sing, PH90* #466), Emma L. Diemer (*With Praise and Love,* The Sacred Music Press).

Hymns for the Day	HL33	HB55	WB72	PH90
Christian Women, Christian Men	–	–	–	348
Jesu, Jesu, Fill Us with Your Love	–	–	–	367
O for a Thousand Tongues to Sing	199	141	493	466
Today We All Are Called to Be Disciples	–	–	–	434
We Are Your People	–	–	–	436
When a Poor One	–	–	–	407

184

SUNDAY BETWEEN SEPTEMBER 11 AND SEPTEMBER 17
(PROPER 19) [24] (B)

Proverbs 1:20–33 Wisdom cries out God's word wherever people work or play, calling God's people from their "waywardness" and "complacency." But they refuse to listen to Wisdom's distress signal. Worse, people take pride in their scoffing at and hating knowledge. Yet God yearns for understanding of the ordained orderliness that must be honored, trusted, praised, and heeded.

Anthem
Cause Us, O Lord, Ron Nelson (Boosey & Hawkes) SATB (M).

James 3:1–12 It is imperative that we control our speech, especially teachers who communicate "truth," for the tongue is a powerful and dangerous instrument. A bit guides a horse, a rudder steers a ship, and the tongue keeps the "whole body in check," or "stains the whole body," destroying life. No one can tame the tongue, but a forked tongue brings forth "blessing and cursing," which is like trying to get both fresh and salt water from the same source, or figs from an olive tree. Our speech needs to bless and not curse.

Anthem
Silent Devotion and Response, Ernest Bloch (Broude) SATB (M).

Mark 8:27–38 Peter's confession about Christ is immediately corrected, followed by Jesus' first passion prediction: the Son of man must suffer, be rejected, be killed, and rise again. "Oh no," remonstrates Peter, "we don't want a convicted criminal, a societal failure, for our leader. We'll never succeed if you do that." Surprisingly, Jesus censures Peter with harsh words: "If you want to play human games of power, success, and triumphalism, then you're demonically inspired. If anyone wants to follow me, then deny yourself and take up your cross. You must be willing to lose your life in this world."

Anthem
Thou Art Jesus, Savior and Lord, H. Schütz (Augsburg) SATB (M).

Psalm 19
1. Metrical: *The Heavens Above Declare God's Praise.* Text: Christopher L. Webber. Tune: CAITHNESS. *PH90* #166.
2. Responsorial: *Psalm 19* (1–6). Text: Grail. Melody: Monks of Saint Meinrad. Harmony, Samuel Weber. *PS93* #12.
3. Responsorial: Psalm 19 (7–14). Setting: Hal H. Hopson. *PS93* #13.
See also *SPJP*, p. 20; *RITL* #87; *PH87* #19; *PR&T*, pp. 67 & 68.

Anthem
Lord, You Have the Words, Richard Proulx, 2-part 4 handbells (E).

Organ Music for the Day
1. *Prelude on* CAITHNESS (*The Heavens Above Declare God's Praise*—Psalm 19, *PH90* #166), Edward G. Mead (Willis Music Co. 10909).
2. *Prelude on* ROCKINGHAM (*When I Survey the Wondrous Cross*, *PH90* #100), David S. Harris (*Ten Hymn Preludes in Trio Style*, H. W. Gray Co., Inc. GB 643) or *Prelude on* HAMBURG (*PH90* #101), Paul Bunjes (*The Parish Organist*, Part II, Concordia 97-1151).

Hymns for the Day	HL33	HB55	WB72	PH90
Hear the Good News of Salvation	–	–	–	355
Hope of the World	–	291	423	360
I Want Jesus to Walk with Me	–	–	–	363
Make Me a Captive, Lord	247	308	–	378
O Jesus, I Have Promised	268	307	–	388, 389
Take Up Thy Cross, the Savior Said	–	293	–	393

SUNDAY BETWEEN SEPTEMBER 18 AND SEPTEMBER 24
(PROPER 20) [25] (B)

Proverbs 31:10–31 Portions of an acrostic poem that celebrates everything about a capable woman from A to Z. Her sense of responsibility, generosity, love, and, especially, honoring of YHWH are to be praised.

Anthem
A Woman of Valor, Isadore Freed, SATB (Transcontinental) (M).

James 3:13–4:3, 7–8a Watch people interact with each other and you'll see either earthly wisdom or wisdom "from above." Worldly wisdom prompts jealousy, bitterness, prejudice, covetousness, self-aggrandizement, and every other vile behavior that polarizes people and ignites demonic disorder. The wisdom of God is sown in peace so the harvest yields peaceful, compassionate, and merciful deeds. Be careful if you claim to be wise; your actions will reveal the source of your wisdom.

Anthem
Prayer for Peace, Sam Batt Owen (G.I.A.) SATB (ME).

Mark 9:30–37 Jesus speaks again of impending suffering, death, and resurrection, but his disciples dream of personal grandeur. So Jesus places a child—the lowest-ranking member on society's status list—among the disciples, saying, "True greatness is daring to become 'last of all and the servant of all.'"

Anthems
Let Them Come to Be Blessed, J. Bert Carlson (AMSI) SATB (E). *Whoever Would Be Great Among You,* R. A. Nelson (Augsburg) SAB (E).

Psalm 1
1. Metrical: *The One Is Blest.* Text: *The Psalter,* 1912. Tune: DUNFERMLINE. *PH90* #158.
2. Responsorial: *Psalm 1* (1–4, 6). Setting: Hal H. Hopson. *PS93* #1.
3. Responsorial: *Blessed Are They Who Delight in the Law of the Lord.* Text: Grail (see also *GPI*, p. 1). Refrain, psalm tone, and Gelineau tone: *WIII* #24 (see also *WIII* #882 for alt. refrain).
4. Responsorial: *Happy Are They Whose Delight Is in the Law of the Lord.* Text: *Book of Common Prayer,* 1976. Music: Peter R. Hallock. *TIP/PSCY* #11.
See also *RITL* #81; *ANMP*, p. 40; *PH87* #1; *SPJP*, p. 11; *PR&T*, pp. 67 & 68.

Anthem
Blessed Is the One, Corelli-Stone (Boston) SAB (E).

Organ Music for the Day
1. *Chorale Prelude on* CHRISTUS, DER IST MEIN LEBEN (*God Is Our Strong Salvation, PH90* #179), Ernst Pepping (*Fünfundzwanzig Orgelchoräle,* B. Schotts Söhne 4723), and Johann G. Walther (*The Church Organist's Golden Treasury,* vol. 1, Oliver Ditson Co.).
2. *Prelude on* FOREST GREEN (*Eternal God, Whose Power Upholds, PH90* #412), Wilbur Held (*Six Carol Settings,* Concordia 97-4985).

Hymns for the Day	HL33	HB55	WB72	PH90
Give to Me, Lord, a Thankful Heart	–	–	–	351
Help Us Accept Each Other	–	–	–	358
In Christ There Is No East or West	341	479	435	439, 440
Lord, Make Us Servants of Your Peace	–	–	–	374
O God, We Bear the Imprint of Your Face	–	–	–	385
Though I May Speak	–	–	–	335

SUNDAY BETWEEN SEPTEMBER 25 AND OCTOBER 1
(PROPER 21) [26] (B)

Esther 7:1–6, 9–10; 9:20–22 King Ahasuerus and Haman attend Queen Esther's banquet (trap). The king promises to grant Esther any petition. Her request: "Let my life be given me, and the lives of my people, because we have been sold, and are to be destroyed and killed." King: "Who did this?" Esther: "A foe, an enemy, this wicked Haman." A eunuch points to the gallows that Haman had prepared for Mordecai, and ironically says, "Hang him on that." So they did. This deliverance of the Jews surely was the will of God. So Mordecai sent letters to all the Jews near and far to celebrate annually the feast of Purim.

Anthem
Now Thank We All Our God, J. S. Bach, arr. J. Holler SATB (M).

James 5:13–20 Our speech needs to bless and not curse. If you are suffering, pray to God; cheerful, sing songs of praise to God; sick, call for the elders of the church who will pray to God; if you have committed sin, confess your sins and pray for one another, so you may be healed. "The prayer of the righteous is powerful and effective," for prayer is a gift from God, and it is God who grants the healing. Elijah prayed that it not rain, and it didn't. Then he prayed for rain and it did. Speak the truth to others and rescue others "from death." Our speech needs to bless and not curse.

Anthem
Prayer, Lloyd Pfautsch (Lawson-Gould) 2-part (ME).

Mark 9:38–50 Who is marching with Jesus on the way to the cross? Not necessarily those in the visible pilgrimage, for there may be invisible, yet faithful, followers who are passing a cup of water from one neighbor's hand to the next. It is better to be partial, incomplete people than to cause others to sin and fail to serve God. It is better to go through life broken and humble while serving others than to fulfill our own human potential at others' expense.

Anthem
A Prayer of St. Francis, Richard DeLong (Southern Music) SATB (ME).

Psalm 124
1. Metrical: *Now Israel May Say.* Text: *The Psalter,* 1912. Tune: OLD 124TH. *PH90* #236.
2. Responsorial: *Psalm 124.* Text: Helen L. Wright. Setting: Peter R. Hallock. *PS93* #128.

See also *30P&2C,* p. 34; *ANMP,* p. 208; *PR&T,* pp. 57 & 59.

Anthem
Psalm 124, Alice Parker, arr. Robert Shaw (G. Schirmer) SATB (M).

Organ Music for the Day
1. *Prelude on* ELLACOMBE (*I/We Sing the Mighty Power of God, PH90* #288), Donald Busarow (*The Concordia Hymn Prelude Series,* vol. 7, Concordia 97-5614).
2. *Prelude on* OLD 124TH (*Now Israel May Say*—Ps. 124, *PH90* #236), F. Peeters (*Hymn Preludes for the Lit. Year,* vol. 10, C. F. Peters Corp. 6410).

Hymns for the Day	HL33	HB55	WB72	PH90
As Deer Long for the Streams	317	322	–	189
Come Sing to God	–	–	–	181
O Savior, in This Quiet Place	–	–	–	390
There's a Spirit in the Air	–	–	–	433
We Walk by Faith and Not by Sight	–	–	–	399
Within Your Shelter, Loving God	–	–	–	212

SUNDAY BETWEEN OCTOBER 2 AND OCTOBER 8
(PROPER 22) [27] (B)

Job 1:1; 2:1–10 Everything that Proverbs says to do, Job does: faithful to God—trusting, obeying—and careful not to do anything evil. "There is no one like him on earth." How enduring is such trust? Satan (the tester, the accuser, the prosecuting attorney before God) contends only as long as the sheltered Job experiences a plentiful life. So Job's possessions are destroyed, his family slaughtered, and his skin afflicted. Yet Job does not rebel.

Anthem
The Lament of Job, Dale Jergenson (G. Schirmer) SATB (M).

Hebrews 1:1–4; 2:5–12 How do we hear God's word? Through prophets of old and, ultimately, through a Son whom God appointed as heir of all things and who upholds the world by his word. This Son reflects the nature of God and is superior to angels, for he achieved purification of sin. Yet he also reflects the nature of humankind, for he shared our flesh and blood and tasted suffering and death for us. He is the pioneer of salvation who united himself with all humankind.

Anthem
The Head That Once Was Crowned with Thorns, arr. George Brandon (G.I.A.) SAB or unison (E).

Mark 10:2–16 Adversaries come to test Jesus on the legality of divorce; instead, they learn about marriage. According to the law books—starting with Moses—divorce is lawful. "But," teaches Jesus, "only as a concession to your stubbornness about accepting God's will for creation." God intended male and female to be joined together as one. But marital relationships do rupture in our broken world. May we all receive the kingdom of God as dependent children who rely on direction, love, forgiveness, and care from above.

Anthem
The Kingdom of God, Joseph Roff (H. W. Gray) 2-part (E).

Psalm 26
1. Metrical: *Lord, Speak to Me, for I Am Yours.* Text: Marie J. Post. Tune: PERRY. PH87 #26.
2. Responsorial: *Psalm 26.* Text: Grail. Refrain: David Clark Isele. Gelineau tone. PS93 #24.
3. Responsorial: Text: optional. Psalm tones and refrains by Hal H. Hopson. PR&T, pp. 42 & 48.

Anthem
They That Sow in Tears, Heinrich Schütz (G. Schirmer) SSATB (M).

Organ Music for the Day
1. *Prelude on* DIX *(For the Beauty of the Earth, PH90* #473), William H. Harris *(Festal Voluntaries—Christmas and Epiphany,* Novello & Co., Ltd. 1399).
2. *Chorale Prelude on* LASST UNS ERFREUEN *(From All That Dwell Below the Skies, PH90* #229), Josef F. Doppelbauer *(Sieben Choralvorspiele,* Musikverlag Alfred Coppenrath).

Hymns for the Day	HL33	HB55	WB72	PH90
Great God, We Sing That Mighty Hand	470	527	408	265
Down to Earth, as a Dove	–	–	–	300
Jesus Loves Me!	–	465	–	304
O God, in a Mysterious Way	–	–	–	270
O God, What You Ordain Is Right	291	366	633	284
Walk On, O People of God	–	–	–	296

SUNDAY BETWEEN OCTOBER 9 AND OCTOBER 15
(PROPER 23) [28] (B)

Job 23:1–9, 16–17 Job replies to Eliphaz's assertion that we receive from God precisely what we deserve. "Yes, God is evenhanded, just, and merciful. Therefore, since I am innocent, I need only a hearing before the Almighty to pitch my appeal, and be acquitted. But I cannot locate God's divine court to present my case. If I cannot have my day in court, then it is better to be dead and innocent, than alive and guilty."

Anthem

O That I Knew Where I Might Find Him, W. S. Bennett (*Church Anthem Book,* Oxford) SATB (M).

Hebrews 4:12–16 Be careful of rejecting or disobeying God's word, for it is two-edged and will expose you to the very depths of your soul. We have, however, a great high priest to represent us to God, a simple human being named Jesus, who lived in the same kind of power-hungry, achievement-oriented, complacently religious, me-first world. But this Jesus was sinless: he never turned away from God; though constantly tempted to win the world for himself, he obeyed God's will. So with Christ as our high priest, let us approach God with confidence, that we may receive mercy and grace.

Anthem

God's Word Is Like a Flaming Sword, WB72 #405.

Mark 10:17–31 What's the price of "eternal life"? Total self-giving, even to obeying the will of God as exemplified by the suffering Messiah, Jesus Christ. Impossible for anyone to do that? Right! You cannot save yourself, but with God all things are possible. Respond to Jesus' call to follow him along the way of servanthood; you may discover that eternal life is God's free gift in Christ.

Anthem

Camel in the Eye, Art Allen (*Choir Book for Saints and Sinners,* Agape) (E).

Psalm 22:1–15
1. Metrical: *Lord, Why Have You Forsaken Me?* Text: L.M., Christopher L. Webber. Tune: SARUM PLAINSONG, MODE IV. *PH90* #168. For text only see *ANMP*, p. 55.
2. Responsorial: *Psalm 22:1–15.* Text: International Commission on English in the Liturgy, *A New Zealand Prayer Book.* Refrain: Jerry R. Brubaker. Tone: Presbyterian 8. *PS93* #16.

See also *TIP/PSCY* #7; *WIII* #31; *PH87* #22; *WIII* #31; *CC* G-2329.

Anthem

My God, My God, Look Upon Me, Maurice Greene, ed. Young (Broude) SSATB tenor solo (M).

Organ Music for the Day
1. *Prelude on* ST. ANNE (*Our God, Our Help in Ages Past, PH90* #210), David S. Harris (*Ten Hymn Preludes in Trio Style,* H. W. Gray Co., Inc. GB 632), and Gerhard Krapf (*Various Hymn Settings,* E. F. Kalmus 3603).
2. *Fantasia and Fugue on* ST. ANNE, Richard Peek (Brodt Music Co.).

Hymns for the Day	HL33	HB55	WB72	PH90
Blessing and Honor	196	137	311	147
I'm Gonna Live So God Can Use Me	–	–	–	369
O Hear Our Cry, O Lord	–	–	–	206
O Master, Let Me Walk with Thee	364	304	520	357
Psalm 31:9–16	–	–	–	182
The Head That Once Was Crowned	195	211	589	149

SUNDAY BETWEEN OCTOBER 16 AND OCTOBER 22
(PROPER 24) [29] (B)

Job 38:1–7, (34–41) Job has insisted on a hearing from "on high"; now he gets it, for the one who answers Job is YHWH. "Who is making all that noise? You want a day in court? Then put on your clothes, and let's go." Job wants to question God; instead, God will question Job: "Is God God?" "What constitutes God's Godness?" Answer: God's inscrutability.

Anthem
The Voice of the Whirlwind, Ralph Vaughan Williams (Oxford) SATB (M).

Hebrews 5:1–10 God has chosen someone to represent our world: someone humble enough to deal gently with the ignorant and the wayward; someone who is human—one of us, who is victimized by the world. Yet this person represents the world before God, and offers his whole life to God for us. His name: Jesus, Son of God. Jesus was fully human: in loud cries and tears, Jesus offered his prayers to God, but with a difference. He obeyed God's will. Jesus is the one whom God appointed to comfort and forgive us, because he is the source of eternal salvation.

Anthem
We Know That Christ Is Raised, Charles V. Stanford, arr. Wolff (Concordia) SATB (ME).

Mark 10:35–45 A bald request for power. James and John petition Jesus for seats at the right and left hand of power. Asks Jesus, "Can you drink the cup I must drink, be baptized in the way I am baptized?" "Sure, we can do that!" "Then you will drink the cup and be baptized in the same manner as I, and you will endure rejection and suffering and death on the cross—giving your whole life as a slave of all."

Anthem
Whoever Would Be Great Among You, R. A. Nelson (Augsburg) SAB (E).

Psalm 104:1–9, 24, 35c
1. Metrical: *Bless the Lord with All My Being.* Text: 8.7.8.7.D, Fred R. Anderson. Tune: RUSTINGTON. *PH90* #224. For text only see *SPJP*, p. 56.
2. Responsorial: *Psalm 104* (1–9). Text: Grail. Tone and Refrain: Presbyterian 3. *PS93* #104.
3. Responsorial: *The Earth Is Full of Your Riches, O Lord.* Text: Grail. Ref.: A. G. Murray. Gelineau tone: *WIII* #56 (stanzas 1–5, 11, 17).
See also *CC* G-2122.

Anthem
Bless the Lord, My Soul and Being, PH90 #224.

Organ Music for the Day
1. *Fantasia on* HANOVER (*You Servants of God, Your Master Proclaim, PH90* #477), Kenneth Leighton (Basil Ramsey Publisher of Music).
2. *Prelude on* ST. MAGNUS (*The Head That Once Was Crowned, PH90* #149), Robert J. Powell (*Fifteen Chorale Preludes*, The Sacred Music Press).

Hymns for the Day	HL33	HB55	WB72	PH90
Crown Him with Many Crowns	190	213	349	151
God, Who Stretched the Spangled Heavens	–	–	–	268
Immortal, Invisible, God Only Wise	66	85	433	263
Many and Great, O God, Are Thy Things	–	–	–	271
O Jesus, I Have Promised	268	307	–	388, 389
Take Up Thy Cross, the Savior Said	–	293	–	393

SUNDAY BETWEEN OCTOBER 23 AND OCTOBER 29
(PROPER 25) [30] (B)

Job 42:1–6, 10–17 For chapters on end, Job thought he had wisdom enough to criticize, rebuke, challenge, and, ultimately, condemn God's way of running creation. But the overwhelming effect of the theophanic whirlwind, in which he sees what God is really like, results in an immediate repudiation by Job of his former certainty. In dust and ashes, Job finds his rightful place and accepts his vocation as one of God's creatures.

Anthem
Prayer, Lloyd Pfautsch (Lawson-Gould) 2-part (ME).

Hebrews 7:23–28 There is but one (and only one) permanent, unchanging, perpetual, eternal officeholder as high priest. His work, therefore, continues today and tomorrow and tomorrow as he constantly intercedes, pleads, and mediates for those who draw near to God. Jesus Christ is the holy, blameless, unstained One who offered one complete, finished, final sacrifice of his life, once for all. In Christ, God has appointed one who has been made perfect forever; in this One alone we can trust.

Anthem
Lord Jesus, Think on Me, HB55 #270.

Mark 10:46–52 A blind beggar, who doesn't look, walk, act, talk, much less see the way we do, sits by the roadside and dares to call for mercy from the "Son of David." Many shun or even rebuke him. But Jesus asks him, "What do you want me to do for you?" "Let me receive my sight," pleads Bartimaeus. "Your faith has made you well," says Jesus. Though Jesus' followers remain blind to his mission, this blind beggar sees well enough to respond to Jesus' call and follow him "on the way."

Anthems
I Have Longed for Thy Saving Health, William Byrd (H. W. Gray) SATB (M). *O Christ, the Healer, PH90* #380.

Psalm 34:1–8, (19–22)
1. Responsorial: *Psalm 34* (1–10). Setting: Hal H. Hopson. *PS93* #32.
2. Responsorial: *Psalm 34* (1–8). *Taste and See.* Setting: Thomas F. Savoy. *CC* G-2548.

See also *PH87* #34; *PR&T,* pp. 68 & 69.

Anthem
Taste and See, Alexander Peloquin (G.I.A.) SATB solo (ME).

Organ Music for the Day
1. *Chorale Prelude on* WER NUR DEN LIEBEN GOTT (*If Thou but Trust in God to Guide Thee, PH90* #282), Georg Böhm and Johann Walther (*The Church Organist's Golden Treasury,* vol. 3, Oliver Ditson Co.).
2. *Partita über den Choral,* WER NUR DEN LIEBEN GOTT, Ernst Pepping (B. Schotts Söhne 2246).

Hymns for the Day	HL33	HB55	WB72	PH90
Alleluia! Sing to Jesus!	–	–	–	144
Here I Am, Lord	–	–	–	525
I Love the Lord, Who Heard My Cry	–	–	–	362
If Thou but Trust in God to Guide Thee	–	344	431	282
Lord, When I Came Into This Life	–	–	–	522
O God, What You Ordain Is Right	291	366	633	284

SUNDAY BETWEEN OCTOBER 30 AND NOVEMBER 5
(PROPER 26) [31] (B)

Ruth 1:1–18 An Israelite woman, Naomi, feels that the Lord has turned against her. She endured stark famine in her homeland, and fled as a refugee with her family to a strange land where her husband died and her two sons married foreigners. Now, Naomi's two sons have died, leaving no male heir, making her, their widowed mother, a dependent. Upon hearing that YHWH has visited YHWH's people and given them food, Naomi sets out for home. But one of her foreign-born daughters-in-law, Ruth, unilaterally pledges unexpected fidelity to Naomi and thereby embodies the elusive but attainable *hesed* (covenant love) that YHWH wills for human relationships.

Anthem

Wedding Song (Entreat Me Not to Leave Thee), Flor Peeters (C. F. Peters) SATB soprano solo (M).

Hebrews 9:11–14 Christ does not enter the earthly Holy of Holies offering a ritual sacrifice, but he enters once for all the holy dwelling place of God, offering a sacrifice of himself—his own life-giving blood. In his sacrifice Christ attains what none other ever could—eternal redemption for his people. Christ is truly the high priest of "the good things that have come."

Anthem

The Promise of Eternal Inheritance, Rudolf Moser (Concordia) unison (E).

Mark 12:28–34 Jesus answers a trick question about the "greatest commandment" by quoting Deut. 6:4: "Love God with all your heart, soul, mind, and strength." Jesus then unexpectedly adds Lev. 19:18: "Love your neighbors as your own kin." You cannot love God without loving your neighbor, or vice versa. "Right you are!" affirms a scribe. "Your call to such love far outweighs all else we do." Replies Jesus, "You are not far from the kingdom of God."

Anthem

Hear, O Israel, Ron Nelson (Boosey & Hawkes) SATB (ME).

Psalm 146
1. Metrical: *I'll Praise My Maker While I've Breath.* Text: Isaac Watts, alt. Tune: OLD 113TH. *PH90* #253. (See also *RITL* #140.)
2. Responsorial: *Psalm 146* (5–10). Text: NRSV. Psalm tone: Howard Hughes. Refrain: John Schiavone. *PH90* #254.
3. Responsorial: *Psalm 146.* Text: Grail. Refrain: Richard T. Proulx. Gelineau tone. *PS93* #150.

See also *ANMP*, p. 228; *SPJP*, p. 65; *PH87* #146; *PR&T*, pp. 2, 7, 69, & 75.

Anthem

Psalm 146, Robert J. Powell (G.I.A.) 5 handbells SB (ME).

Organ Music for the Day
1. *Prelude on* LEONI (*The God of Abraham Praise, PH90* #488), C. S. Lang (*Three Chorale Preludes*, Oxford University Press 31.935).
2. *Prelude on* OLD 113TH (*I'll Praise My Maker*—Psalm 146, *PH90* #253), Gerald Near (*Prelude on Four Hymn Tunes*, Augsburg 11-828).

Hymns for the Day	HL33	HB55	WB72	PH90
Alas! and Did My Savior Bleed	249	199	–	78
Jesu, Jesu, Fill Us with Your Love	–	–	–	367
Though I May Speak	–	–	–	335
When a Poor One	–	–	–	407
When I Survey the Wondrous Cross	152	198	635	100, 101
Where Cross the Crowded Ways	410	507	642	408

ALL SAINTS' DAY
[NOVEMBER 1 OR FIRST SUNDAY IN NOVEMBER] (B)

Isaiah 25:6–9 One day the Lord of Hosts will make for all peoples a grand feast. The cloud of sorrow and troubles and death will vanish so that all tears shall succumb to laughter and joy, for YHWH has spoken.

Anthem
Day of Rejoicing, Walter Pelz (Augsburg) SATB trumpet (ME).

Revelation 21:1–6a A vision of a new heaven and a new earth. The new Jerusalem descends from God and joins the transformed earth where chaotic waters, tears, death, mourning, crying have all disappeared. Human beings will see God and live in holy fellowship together. Shouts the great voice from the throne, "I make all things new."

Anthems
And I Saw a New Heaven, Edgar Bainton (Novello) SATB (MD). *I Saw a New Heaven and a New Earth,* A. Eugene Ellsworth (Kjos) SATB 2 trumpets (M).

John 11:32–44 Jesus risks his life in traveling to Bethany to respond to Mary and Martha's call to visit his sick (and now dead) friend Lazarus. Like Lazarus, we cannot raise ourselves out of our own tombs, but when God in Christ sees the death-dealing predicament of our world, he weeps and then calls Lazarus and us out of our tombs, inviting us to share in his victory over death so that we can experience the freedom of new life in Christ.

Anthem
The Raising of Lazarus, Adrian Willaert (Ricordi) SATB (M).

Psalm 24
1. Metrical: *The Earth and All That Dwell Therein.* Text: *The Psalter,* 1912, alt. Tune: CAITHNESS. *PH90* #176.
2. Responsorial: *Psalm 24* (1–6). Setting: Hal H. Hopson. *PS93* #22.
3. Responsorial: *Psalm 24.* Setting by Arthur Wills in *Popular Psalm Settings,* The Year Book Press, 76-14115.
4. Responsorial: *Psalm 24* (*Lift Up the Gates Eternal*). Text: Willard F. Jabusch, Arlo D. Duba. Tune: ISRAELI FOLK MELODY. Arr. John Ferguson. Instrumentation: Kenneth E. Williams, Lynelle M. Williams. *PS93* #21. (See also *PH90* #177 and *APS,* p. 16.)

See also *ANMP,* p. 58; *PH87* #24; *SPJP,* p. 24; *WIII* #775; *PR&T,* pp. 3 & 6.

Anthem
Lift Up Your Heads, Jane Marshall (Hinshaw) unison treble voices, optional handbells (ME).

Organ Music for the Day
1. *Prelude on* SINE NOMINE (*For All the Saints, PH90* #526), Flor Peeters (*Hymn Preludes for the Liturgical Year,* vol. 5, C. F. Peters Corp. 6405), and Charles W. Ore (*Eleven Compositions,* Concordia 97-5385).
2. *Chorale Prelude on* GELOBT SEI GOTT (*O Lord of Life, Where'er They Be, PH90* #530), Joseph Ahrens (*Das Heilige Jahr,* vol. 2, Willy Müller).

Hymns for the Day	HL33	HB55	WB72	PH90
Here, O Our Lord, We See You	–	–	–	520
I Sing a Song of the Saints of God	–	–	–	364
O Holy City, Seen of John	409	508	505	453
O Lord, You Gave Your Servant John	–	–	–	431
Of the Father's Love Begotten	–	7	534	309
We Meet You, O Christ	–	–	–	311

SUNDAY BETWEEN NOVEMBER 6 AND NOVEMBER 12
(PROPER 27) [32] (B)

Ruth 3:1–5; 4:13–17 Naomi instructs Ruth to dress in her "Sabbath best" and go alone at night to the threshing floor near the gate where men celebrate the harvest. YHWH bestows the gift of new life through the union of Ruth and Boaz. Then the women praise YHWH for transforming Naomi's emptiness into fullness through Ruth's faithful *hesed,* and name the newborn Obed, who later became the father of Jesse, who became the father of David.

Anthem

O for a Thousand Tongues, Glaser, arr. Theron Kirk (Oxford) (ME).

Hebrews 9:24–28 Christ, the eternal high priest, solemnly entered the heavenly, invisible, spiritual sanctuary (not the earthbound temple) only one time, and offered his blood, once for all, to put away the sins of many. In Christ, a new age has begun through his act of total self-giving. He will appear again to save those who eagerly await him.

Anthem

All for Love, Robert Young (Carl Fischer) SATB (M).

Mark 12:38–44 Jesus cites the scribes as hypocrites, exposing their greed. Unlike the scribes who calculate their giving according to percentages, a poor widow gives her whole life to God in the form of two small coins. She is the model of genuine piety we are called to emulate.

Anthem

We Would Offer Thee This Day, J. Marshall (Sacred Music) SATB (M).

Psalm 127

1. Metrical: *Unless the Lord the House Shall Build.* Text: *The Psalter,* 1912, alt. Tune: BOURBON. *PH90* #238.
2. Responsorial: *Psalm 127.* Setting: Hal H. Hopson. *PS93* #132.
3. Responsorial: *May the Lord Watch Over This House.* Text: Grail (see also *GPI,* p. 191). Refrain, psalm tone, and Gelineau tone: *WIII* #70. (See also *24P&1C,* p. 34.)

See also *ANMP,* p. 210; *PH87* #127; *PR&T,* pp. 2 & 7.

Anthem

Unless the Lord the House Shall Build, PH90 #238.

Organ Music for the Day

1. *Chorale Prelude on* NUN DANKET ALLE GOTT (*Now Thank We All Our God, PH90* #555), Johann Sebastian Bach (various editions).
2. *Prelude on* HYFRYDOL (*Love Divine, All Loves Excelling, PH90* #376), Gordon Young (*Eight Organ Voluntaries on Familiar Hymn Tunes,* Theodore Presser Co. 413-41034).

Hymns for the Day	HL33	HB55	WB72	PH90
Eternal God, Whose Power Upholds	–	485	357	412
God, Whose Giving Knows No Ending	–	–	–	422
Holy God, We Praise Your Name	–	–	420	460
Lord of Light, Your Name Outshining	–	–	–	425
Love Divine, All Loves Excelling	308	399	471	376
O Love, How Deep, How Broad . . .	139	–	518	83

SUNDAY BETWEEN NOVEMBER 13 AND NOVEMBER 19
(PROPER 28)[33] (B)

1 Samuel 1:4–20 Hannah is perceived by society as an unblessed person, for she is a barren woman and, therefore, unworthy in the sight of God. Hannah may be infertile in her womb, but she is "fertile in spirit"—she petitions God, she hopes, and, ultimately, gives selflessly, forfeiting what she treasures. Miracle of miracles, Hannah, the unworthy one, gives birth to YHWH's servant—priest and prophet— who saves the people of Israel at a decisive moment in their history. God works in mysterious ways, for "unblessed," unworthy Hannah ("grace") becomes the mediator of grace.

Anthem
Thou, O God, Art Praised in Zion, Ian Hare (Oxford) SATB (MD).

Hebrews 10:11–18 Having completed the perfect sacrifice that did away with sin, Christ sat down and rested while awaiting the end when his enemies would serve as his footstool. The fulfillment of Jer. 31:33–34 abrogates the need for any more sacrifices, since God will no longer remember our sin. Now that all guilt is lifted from us, we may freely and confidently respond to God's love offered in Jesus Christ by encouraging one another to trust God's faithful promises. Such trust may lead to a caring, loving community of faith.

Anthem
The New Covenant, David York (Presser) SATB tenor solo (MD).

Mark 13:1–8 The gleaming splendor of the power and majesty of the Temple can captivate us. But the days will come when it shall be razed. When? What will be the signs? Stay away from those who say "I am he! When you hear of wars, earth-quakes, and famines, this is just the beginning, but fear not."

Anthem
O Day of Peace, C. Hubert H. Parry, *PH90* #450.

1 Samuel 2:1–10 (Canticle of Hannah)
1. Metrical: *Song of Hannah.* Text: Emily Brink. Tune: VIOLA. Hughes H. Huffman. *PH87* #158.
2. Responsorial: *1 Samuel 2* (1–4, 7, 8). Text: *A New Zealand Prayer Book.* Setting: John Weaver. *PS93* #172.

Anthem
Praise the Lord, Ye Servants, Richard Peek (H. W. Gray) unison (ME).

Organ Music for the Day
1. *Fantasia on* HELMSLEY (*Jesus Comes with Clouds Descending, PH90* #6), Kenneth Leighton (Basil Ramsey Publisher of Music).
2. *Prelude on* ITALIAN HYMN (*Come, Thou Almighty King, PH90* #139), Healey Willan (*The Parish Organist,* part 8, Concordia 97-1404).

Hymns for the Day	HL33	HB55	WB72	PH90
How Great Thou Art	–	–	–	467
Lead On, O King Eternal	371	332	448	447, 448
Now Praise the Hidden God of Love	–	–	–	402
This Is the Day the Lord Hath Made	23	69	–	230
We Walk by Faith and Not by Sight	–	–	–	399
What Wondrous Love Is This	–	–	–	85

CHRIST THE KING

[SUNDAY BETWEEN NOVEMBER 20 AND NOVEMBER 26] (PROPER 29) [34] (B)

2 Samuel 23:1-7 David—whom YHWH was with—sings his last words as the anointed one: "The Spirit of the Lord speaks his word through my tongue, saying, 'The just ruler beams like the rising sun and makes the grass as richly green as after the early spring rain.' Such is my house (family dynasty), for the Lord has stood by the eternal covenant with me and secured my salvation in God. But the godless people are like wind-blown, prickly tumbleweeds that no one can hold without getting hurt. One must be an iron spear in order to put these thorny enemies to their only use: to burn in the fire."

Anthem

The Last Words of David, R. Thompson (E. C. Schirmer) SATB (MD).

Revelation 1:4b–8 The prophet John sends greetings to the seven churches: "Remember to whom you belong—not to the Caesars of this world, but solely to Christ. Remember by whose grace and peace you live—not by the Caesars' mercy, but only by God's. Yes, the claims about Christ—he reliably testified that God's promises will be fulfilled, he inaugurated a new age, he rules as the King of kings—all seem preposterous, but one day the whole world will recognize that he is the one who loves us, frees us from our sins, and makes us priests. To him be glory and power, forever."

Anthem

Unto Him That Loved Us, Ralph Vaughan Williams (*Morning Star Choir Book,* vol. 1, Concordia) unison (E).

John 18:33–37 Political and religious leaders, obsessed with finding a king who fits their definition, cannot hear the truth to which Jesus bears witness. Everyone who listens to his voice will hear the truth. Those possessed by the frenzy to acquire ephemeral, earthly power will be threatened by the truth to which Jesus bears witness.

Anthem

Arise, the Kingdom Is . . . , G. Martin (Flammer) SATB or 2-part (ME).

Psalm 132:1–12, (13–18)

1. Metrical: *Arise, O Lord.* Text: *The Psalter,* 1912. Tune: FEDERAL STREET. *HB55* #518.
2. Responsorial: *Psalm 132* (1–11). Text: *A New Zealand Prayer Book.* Refrain and Tone: Presbyterian 3. *PS93* #136.

See also *RITL* #135; *PH87* #132; *ANMP,* p. 213; *PR&T,* pp. 62 & 64.

Anthem

I Will Clothe Thy Priests . . . , J. Peter (Boosey & Hawkes) SATB (ME).

Organ Music for the Day

1. *Improvisation on* DIVINUM MYSTERIUM (*Of the Father's Love Begotten, PH90* #309), Halsey Stevens (Peer International Corp.).
2. *Prelude on* BRYN CALFARIA (*God, Our Lord, a King Remaining,* Psalm 93, *PH90* #213), Ralph Vaughan Williams (*Three Preludes Founded on Welsh Hymn Tunes,* Stainer & Bell, Ltd.).

Hymns for the Day	HL33	HB55	WB72	PH90
A Hymn of Glory Let Us Sing	–	–	273	141
Blessing and Honor and Glory and . . .	196	137	311	147
God of Our Life	88	108	395	275
God of the Ages, Whose Almighty Hand	414	515	394	262
Jesus Comes with Clouds Descending	–	–	–	6
Our King and Our Sovereign, Lord Jesus	–	–	–	157

Special Days (B)
PRESENTATION OF THE LORD
[FEBRUARY 2] (ABC)

See Presentation of the Lord [February 2] (ABC) in Year A, p. 123.

ANNUNCIATION OF THE LORD
[MARCH 25] (ABC)

See Annunciation of the Lord [March 25] (ABC) in Year A, p. 125.

VISITATION OF MARY TO ELIZABETH
[MAY 31] (ABC)

See Visitation of Mary to Elizabeth [May 31] (ABC) in Year A, p. 127.

HOLY CROSS
[SEPTEMBER 14] (ABC)

See Holy Cross [September 14] (ABC) in Year A, p. 128.

THANKSGIVING DAY (B)*
[FOURTH THURSDAY IN NOVEMBER IN U.S.A.]

Joel 2:21–27 The quintessential, purest evangelical word everyone wants to hear: "Fear not!" But note that such a word follows verses 1–11, which say, "Fear, fear, fear!" Then, in verse 18, YHWH notices Israel—"These are my very own people"—and has pity on them. Now there is talk of a new creation. Early rain, grain, wine, oil, eat plenty, be satisfied, never again be put to shame, and you will know that I, YHWH, am in the midst of you.

Anthem
Fear Not, O Land, John Goss (G. Schirmer) SATB (M).

1 Timothy 2:1–7 Lift up your hands and hearts and offer intercessions for all people, friends and enemies alike. Pray especially for those with political power, for they are charged with the responsibility of securing and maintaining an orderly life. They need God's word in order to work for God's truth and justice and peace. And above all, remember that there is only one mediator who brings us together and to whom we owe our total allegiance and trust: Christ, who gave himself as a ransom for all.

Anthem
A Song of Praise and Thanksgiving, Allen Pote (Hinshaw) 2-part (E).

Matthew 6:25–33 A rigorous text that defies circumvention. Why are you so driven to scramble up the social ladder of success; so wretchedly uptight over accumulating cash, cash, and more cash; so obsessed with getting ahead in life? Why? Surely life is worth more than all these ephemeral pleasures combined. Do you think you can ward off death or buy more life? Stop for a moment and behold how creation simply lives by the grace of God. Now try steering your fretful energy into serving God by serving neighbors. Seek first the kingdom of God—feed the hungry, clothe the naked, shelter the homeless—and you may discover that life is richer when it is leaner.

Anthem
Sometimes a Light Surprises, Jane Marshall (*Ecumenical Praise,* number 42, Agape) unison (E).

Psalm 126
1. Metrical: *When God Delivered Israel.* Text: Michael A. Saward. Tune: SHEAVES. *PH90* #237. (See also *PP* #134 and *RITL* #133.)
2. Responsorial: *Psalm 126.* Setting: Hal H. Hopson. *PS93* #130.
See also *PS93* #131; *WIII* #69 and #771; *ANMP,* p. 209; *PH87* #126.

Anthem
When the Lord Turned Again, Wm. Billings (Concordia) SATB (ME).

Organ Music for the Day
1. *Prelude on* ST. GEORGE'S, WINDSOR (*Come, Ye Thankful People, Come, PH90* #551), Robert English (Boston Music Co.), Flor Peeters (*Thirty Short Preludes on Well-Known Hymns,* C. F. Peters Corp. 6195).
2. *Prelude on* ROYAL OAK (*All Things Bright and Beautiful, PH90* #267), E. L. Diemer (*Folk Hymn Sketches,* The Sacred Music Press KK 385).

Hymns for the Day	HL33	HB55	WB72	PH90
Come, Sing a Song of Harvest	–	–	–	558
Come, Ye Thankful People, Come	460	525	346	551
I Will Give Thanks with My Heart (Ps. 247)	–	–	–	247
Many and Great, O God, Are Thy Things	–	–	–	271
Now Thank We All Our God	459	9	481	555
We Gather Together	–	18	624	559

*NOTE: Readings for Thanksgiving Day are not strictly tied to Year A, B, or C.

Year C

Christmas Cycle
Season of Advent
FIRST SUNDAY OF ADVENT (C)

Jeremiah 33:14–16 Behold, the days are coming when YHWH will raise up "a righteous Branch" from David's line who will rule with justice and righteousness (cf. Jer. 23:5–6). In the midst of disorder, anguish, desolation, and uncertainty, YHWH proclaims, "I will fulfill my promise to raise up the legitimate successor to the throne, whose name will be 'The Lord is our righteousness.'"

Anthems
O Word That Goest Forth on High, Gerald Near (H. W. Gray) SATB (MD). *A Spotless Rose,* Herbert Howells (Galaxy) SATB (M).

1 Thessalonians 3:9–13 "For your growth in faith and love," writes Paul, "I thank God with great joy. Also, I continually pray that God will soon join us together and that, until such time, God will increase our love for one another, as well as for all God's children. In this way we shall be strengthened for the ultimate test at the Parousia (coming) of our Lord Jesus."

Anthem
E'en So, Lord Jesus, Quickly Come, Paul Manz (Concordia) SATB (M).

Luke 21:25–36 A Chicken Little picture of the end of the world: signs in sun and moon and stars, distress of nations, people fainting, and the Son of man coming. Listen for the word of God in these signs. What's arriving, judgment? No, mercy! So raise your heads, look up and see that your redemption is near. You don't know when, but watch, pray, prepare, live attentively, gladly expecting the coming of the Lord.

Anthem
And There Will Be Signs, Stephen Chatman (*Ecumenical Praise,* number 15, Agape) 2-part (M).

Psalm 25:1–10
1. Metrical: *Lord, to You My Soul Is Lifted.* Text: Stanley Wiersma. Tune: GENEVAN 25. *PH90* #178. (See also *PH87* #25.)
2. Responsorial: *Psalm 25:1–10.* Text: International Commission on English in the Liturgy. Refrain and Tone: Presbyterian 8. *PS93* #23.
See also *WIII* #33; *WIII* #788, for alternate refrain; *20P&3C,* p. 6; *RITL* #94; *ANMP,* p. 59; *SPJP,* p. 25; *PR&T,* pp. 46 & 48.

Anthem
Show Me Thy Ways, Walter Pelz (Augsburg) SATB guitar, oboe (ME).

Organ Music for the Day
1. *Orgelpartita* on NUN KOMM, DER HEIDEN HEILAND (*Savior of the Nations, Come, PH90* #14), Hugo Distler (Bärenreiter Verlag 637).
2. *Fantasy on the Chorale* WACHET AUF (*Sleepers, Wake! A Voice Astounds Us, PH90* #17), Max Reger (Edwin F. Kalmus 4107).

Hymns for the Day	HL33	HB55	WB72	PH90
Come, Thou Long-Expected Jesus	113	151	342	1
Jesus Comes with Clouds Descending	–	–	–	6
My Lord! What a Morning	–	–	–	449
O Come, O Come, Emmanuel	108	147	489	9
"Sleepers, Wake!" A Voice Astounds Us	–	–	614	17
Watchman, Tell Us of the Night	109	149	617	20

SECOND SUNDAY OF ADVENT (C)

Malachi 3:1–4 Behold, the Day of YHWH is coming and will be heralded by a messenger (angel of the Lord? Elijah the prophet? John the Baptist?) who will prepare the way for YHWH's return to the Temple, from where swift judgment on wrongdoers will be executed. The priesthood and Temple will be purified in a refiner's fire so that acceptable offerings may be made to the Lord.

Anthem
Promise, Leland Sateren (*The Redeemer,* Schmitt, Hall, McCreary) SATB (M).

Philippians 1:3–11 Paul expresses his unbounded joy for the ongoing witness of the Philippian community of faith, and thanks God for their partnership with him in the work of the gospel. He prays for their continued growth in *agape* (love), which will lead to discernment of human needs to which they can respond, thereby serving as sign-doers of the day of Christ—through whom God is working—and be filled with "the fruits of righteousness."

Anthem
He Which Hath Begun a Good Work in You, Jan Bender (Concordia) SAB (E).

Luke 3:1–6 The word of God comes to John in the wilderness, who then cries out, "Repent! Turn around! Orient yourself to God's future. Place your hope not in the powers of this world but in the One who will flatten mountains and raise up valleys, straighten the crooked, and smooth the rough-hewn" (in fulfillment of Isa. 40:3–5). John urgently preaches "a baptism of repentance for the forgiveness of sins" because of the imminent arrival of the Messiah, when "all flesh shall see the salvation of God."

Anthem
Advent Message, M. How (Boosey & Hawkes) unison or 2-part (E).

Luke 1:68–79 (Benedictus)
1. Metrical: *Blest Be the God of Israel.* Text: Michael A. Perry, alt. Tune: MERLE'S TUNE. Hal H. Hopson. *PH90* #602. (See also *DP/SLR* #97.)
2. Responsorial: *Song of Zechariah.* Text: English Language Liturgical Consultation. Byzantine Chant. *PS93* #158.
See also *PH90* #601; *PS93* #159 & #160; *20P&3C,* p. 32.

Anthem
Song of Zechariah, PH90 #601.

Organ Music for the Day
1. *Chorale Prelude on* STUTTGART (*Come, Thou Long-Expected Jesus, PH90* #1), Flor Peeters (*Festal Voluntaries: Christmas and Epiphany,* Novello & Co., Ltd. 1399).
2. *Prelude on* HYFRYDOL (*Come, Thou Long-Expected Jesus, PH90* #2), Ralph Vaughan Williams (*A Galaxy of Hymn-Tune Preludes,* Galaxy Music Corp. GMC 2353).

Hymns for the Day	HL33	HB55	WB72	PH90
Let All Mortal Flesh Keep Silence	112	148	449	5
Lift Up Your Heads, O Mighty Gates	114	152	454	8
More Love to Thee, O Christ	315	397	–	359
O Lord, How Shall I Meet You?	–	–	–	11
On Jordan's Bank the Baptist's Cry	–	–	–	10
Prepare the Way	–	–	–	13

THIRD SUNDAY OF ADVENT (C)

Zephaniah 3:14–20 A psalm of celebration sung by the faithful remnant: Sing, shout, rejoice, and exult, O Israel, because YHWH has cast out the menacing threat, and is "in your midst" reigning as King. Fear not! YHWH, your God, will renew you. Promises YHWH, "I will transform the shame of the lame and the outcast into praise, and I will bring you home."

Anthem
Daughter of Zion, Joseph Clokey (Presser) SATB (E).

Philippians 4:4–7 Rejoice and demonstrate to the world gentleness and forbearance, because the Lord is at hand, and the peace of God will guard your hearts and minds from any new threats. So no need to fret over your own well-being: forsake your Sisyphus-like drivenness to secure tomorrow today, and consider practicing the virtues embraced by Paul: truth, honor, justice, purity, agreeableness, excellence, and whatever is praiseworthy.

Anthem
Rejoice in the Lord, anon., arr. J. Rickard (Augsburg) SATB (M).

Luke 3:7–18 See the deluge of people streaming toward John, the voice in the wilderness, standing knee-deep in the muddy Jordan, greeting the baptism seekers with these words: "You snakes! Who told you to flee here so you could smugly receive another ritual cleansing while clutching your social status card? Turn away from yourselves and face God." "How?" ask the people. "Share your food and clothing with less fortunate neighbors, and dispose of your greedy, cheating, and intimidating ways." Hearing such words, the people inquire of John, "Are you the Christ?" "No," replies John, "I baptize only with water, but the One who is to come will baptize with the Holy Spirit and with fire, and will winnow the wheat from the chaff."

Anthem
Thou Shalt Know Him When He Comes, Hal H. Hopson (Flammer) SATB (M).

Isaiah 12:2–6 (Song of Thanksgiving)
1. Metrical: *Surely It Is God Who Saves Me.* Text: 8.7.8.7.D, Carl P. Daw, Jr. Tune: RAQUEL. *WIII* #584. (See also *PH87* #193; Tune: REVIVE US.)
2. Responsorial: *Canticle of Thanksgiving.* Text: *Book of Common Prayer.* Setting: Norman Mealy. *PS93* #175.
See also *WIII* #81.

Anthem
The First Song of Isaiah, Jack Noble White (H. W. Gray) SATB, congregation (ME).

Organ Music for the Day
1. *Prelude on* TRURO (*Lift Up Your Heads, Ye Mighty Gates, PH90* #8), John F. Wilson (*Easy Hymn Settings,* Hope Publishing Co. 286).
2. *Prelude on* WINCHESTER NEW (*On Jordan's Bank the Baptist's Cry, PH90* #10), Finn Videro (*Koralpreludier och Orgelkoraler,* Engstrom & Sodring 342).

Hymns for the Day	HL33	HB55	WB72	PH90
Let All Mortal Flesh Keep Silence	112	148	449	5
Lift Up Your Heads, O Mighty Gates	114	152	454	8
More Love to Thee, O Christ	315	397	–	359
O Lord, How Shall I Meet You?	–	–	–	11
On Jordan's Bank the Baptist's Cry	–	–	–	10
Prepare the Way	–	–	–	13

FOURTH SUNDAY OF ADVENT (C)

Micah 5:2–5a Out of an obscure, insignificant clan shall come a future ruler of Israel with genealogical links to a past shepherd king. At the advent of this new ruler, YHWH promises to start afresh with Israel by returning the remnant home. Then the new shepherd ruler will feed his flock by relying on the strength, majesty, and name of YHWH. Since the greatness of this ruler will be acknowledged by all, YHWH's people shall dwell in safety.

Anthem
He Shall Feed His Flock, G. F. Handel (*Messiah,* any edition) alto solo (E).

Hebrews 10:5–10 The preexistent Christ speaks the words of Psalm 40:6–8 in order to define the purpose of his incarnation. No longer will the old Levitical sacrifices be either necessary or efficacious, for the ultimate sacrifice of Christ's body upon the cross will establish the new covenant. The justification for the incarnation is that Christ will take a human body in order to offer this perfect sacrifice in obedience to the will of God.

Anthem
All Glory Be to God on High, the Only Son from Heaven, Johann Crüger (*Four Christmas Chorales,* Concordia) 2-part, descant (ME).

Luke 1:39–45, (46–55) The conclusion to Luke's two annunciation stories of John and Jesus. A young, single peasant of low estate from Nazareth, a slave of the Lord, is favored by God. Mary's whole being, soul and spirit, offers a canticle of praise to God, for "he has done great things for me, and holy is his name." Mary's words of thanksgiving, recited by her people for centuries (cf. 1 Sam. 2:1–10), testify to her faith in the sovereign God.

Anthem
Mary's Salutation, Johann Eccard (Oxford) SSATB (M).

Luke 1:47–55 (Magnificat)
See Fourth Sunday of Advent (B), p. 136.

or **Psalm 80:1–7**
1. Metrical: *O Hear Our Cry, O Lord.* Text: Fred R. Anderson. Tune: VINEYARD HAVEN. *PH90* #206 (text only see *SPJP,* p. 43).
2. Responsorial: *Psalm 80:1–7.* Text: Gary Chamberlain. Setting: Hal H. Hopson. *PS93* #70.
See also *PS93* #71; *ANMP,* p. 127; *PH87* #80; *WIII* #767; *30P&2C,* p. 23; *PR&T,* pp. 1 & 51.

Anthem
O Hear Our Cry, O Lord, PH90 #206.

Organ Music for the Day
1. *Prelude on* MORNING SONG (*Song of Mary, PH90* #600), Stephen Gabrielsen (*Advent Preludes,* Augsburg 11-5054).
2. *Prelude on* VENI EMMANUEL (*O Come, O Come, Emmanuel, PH90* #9), K. Leighton (*Six Fantasias on Hymn Tunes,* Basil Ramsey).

Hymns for the Day	HL33	HB55	WB72	PH90
Christian Women, Christian Men	–	–	–	348
Lord Christ, When First You Came	–	–	–	7
The Desert Shall Rejoice	–	–	–	18
Rejoice, Rejoice, Believers	115	231	–	15
Rejoice, Ye Pure in Heart!	297	407	561	145, 146
Song of Mary	56	596	–	600

Season of Christmas
CHRISTMAS EVE/DAY
[DECEMBER 24/25] (ABC)

See Christmas Eve/Day (ABC) in Year A, p. 31.

CHRISTMAS EVE/DAY: ALTERNATIVE LECTIONS 1
[DECEMBER 24/25] (ABC)

See Christmas Eve/Day: Alternative Lections 1 (ABC) in Year A, p. 32.

CHRISTMAS EVE/DAY: ALTERNATIVE LECTIONS 2
[DECEMBER 24/25] (ABC)

See Christmas Eve/Day: Alternative Lections 2 (ABC) in Year A, p. 33.

FIRST SUNDAY AFTER CHRISTMAS DAY (C)

1 Samuel 2:18–20, 26 Every year Hannah weaves a little robe for her son Samuel (who faithfully serves YHWH at the sanctuary in Shiloh) and personally delivers it to her son when she and her husband, Elkanah, offer their annual sacrifice. Then Eli, the high priest, blesses Elkanah and Hannah, petitioning YHWH to repay them with seed for children because of the gift of their son Samuel to YHWH's service. And Samuel continues to grow in stature and in favor with YHWH and with humankind.

Anthem
The Hand of God Doth Supply All Our Needs, A. Vivaldi, arr. Vree (*Magnificat,* Presser) SS (M).

Colossians 3:12–17 You are the chosen, holy, beloved people of God. So put on the freely given garments Christ has offered you and model them to the world. Array yourselves with his example of "compassion, kindness, lowliness, meekness, and patience"—clothe yourselves with concern first for others' needs. Be tolerant with one another, forgive one another as Christ has forgiven you, and wrap yourselves with love, which binds you together. Let the peace of Christ and Christ's word govern all you do and say, and remember always to be thankful for what God in Christ has done for you.

Anthem
You Are the People of God, Gerhard Becker (Concordia) unison (E).

Luke 2:41–52 At Passover time, Mary and Joseph take their son Jesus to Jerusalem, where they lose him among the crowd. Their anxious search finds their son in the Temple, listening and asking questions and amazing all with his answers. "Why did you seek all over for me?" queries Jesus. "Didn't you know I must be here, concerned about my Father's things?" Parents simply do not understand such fanciful statements by their children—and Mary and Joseph are no exception. But Jesus went with them and was "obedient to them." And his mother "kept all these things in her heart." And Jesus grew in "wisdom and in stature, and in favor with God and humankind."

Anthem
Son, Why Have You Treated Us So?, Jan Bender (Concordia) SAB (ME).

Psalm 148
1. Metrical: *Let the Whole Creation Cry.* Text: Stopford A. Brooke, 1881. Tune: SALZBURG. Harmony, J. S. Bach. *PH90* #256.
2. Responsorial: *Psalm 148.* Setting: Hal H. Hopson. *PS93* #155.
See also *RITL* #141; *TIP/PSCY* #9; *PH90* #257; *H82* #432.

Anthem
Let the Whole Creation Cry, PH90 #256.

Organ Music for the Day
1. *Prelude on* IRBY (*Once in Royal David's City, PH90* #49), David Cherwien (*Interpretations Based on Hymn-Tunes,* Art Masters Studios, Inc. SP-102).
2. *Prelude on* SALZBURG (*Let the Whole Creation Cry,* Psalm 148, *PH90* #256), Johann Pachelbel (*Musikalische Sterbensgedanken,* C. F. Peters Corp. 8616).

Hymns for the Day	*HL33*	*HB55*	*WB72*	*PH90*
Christ, You Are the Fullness	–	–	–	346
Down to Earth, as a Dove	–	–	–	300
Infant Holy, Infant Lowly	–	–	–	37
In the Bleak Midwinter	–	–	–	36
Once in Royal David's City	454	462	539	49
See Amid the Winter's Snow	–	–	–	51

HOLY NAME OF JESUS
[JANUARY 1] (ABC)

See Holy Name of Jesus [January 1] (ABC) in Year A, p. 36.

JANUARY 1
[WHEN OBSERVED AS NEW YEAR'S DAY] (ABC)

See January 1 [When observed as New Year's Day] (ABC) in Year A, p. 38.

SECOND SUNDAY AFTER CHRISTMAS DAY (ABC)

See Second Sunday After Christmas Day (ABC) in Year A, p. 39.

Day of Epiphany
EPIPHANY OF THE LORD
[JANUARY 6] (ABC)

See Epiphany of the Lord (ABC) in Year A, p. 41.

Ordinary Time
BAPTISM OF THE LORD
[SUNDAY BETWEEN JANUARY 7 AND 13] [1] (C)

Isaiah 43:1–7 Fear not! Exile is no longer a place of fear, because the power of God is at work. From east and west, YHWH will gather into the land of Zion all those scattered in exile. "When you pass through the waters, the rivers, the fire, the flames, I will be with you. Because you are precious in my sight, I am bringing you home."

Anthem
How Firm a Foundation, Dorothy Ohl (Plymouth) SATB (ME).

Acts 8:14–17 The gospel is preached in Samaria; the people receive the word of God and are baptized in the name of the Lord Jesus. When the apostles at Jerusalem hear about this, they send Peter and John to pray for the believers to receive the divine gift of the Holy Spirit. They lay their hands upon the people, who receive the divine gift of the Spirit and can now discern the difference between truth and illusion.

Anthem
O Lord, Give Thy Holy Spirit, Thomas Tallis (*Second Concord Anthem Book*) (E. C. Schirmer) SATB (M).

Luke 3:15–17, 21–22 Upon hearing jolting words from John, the people inquire, "Are you the Christ?" "No," replies John, "I baptize only with water, but the One who is to come will baptize with the Holy Spirit and with fire and will winnow the wheat from the chaff." After all are baptized, including Jesus, who is now praying, the heavens open, the Holy Spirit descends like a dove upon Jesus, and a voice proclaims, "You are my beloved Son, with you I am well pleased."

Anthem
The Baptism of Our Lord, Charles Callahan (Morningstar) unison, descant (E).

Psalm 29
1. Metrical: *The God of Heaven Thunders.* Text: Michael Perry. Setting: Norman Warren. *PH90* #180. (See also *PP* #82.)
2. Responsorial: *Psalm 29.* Setting: Hal H. Hopson. *PS93* #26.
See also *GPI,* p. 35; *24P&1C,* p. 10 for optional refrains; *CC* G-2421; *ANMP,* p. 66; *SPJP,* p. 29; *PH87* #29; *PR&T,* pp. 17 & 66.

Anthem
The God of Heaven, PH90 #180.

Organ Music for the Day
1. *Prelude on* CAITHNESS (*Christ, When for Us You Were Baptized, PH90* #70), Flor Peeters (*Hymn Preludes for the Liturgical Year,* C. F. Peters Corp. 6418).
2. *Prelude on* DOWN AMPNEY (*Come Down, O Love Divine, PH90* #313), Henry G. Ley (Oxford University Press 375534-3).

Hymns for the Day	HL33	HB55	WB72	PH90
Christ, When for Us You Were Baptized	–	–	–	70
How Firm a Foundation	283	369	425	361
Jesus, Our Divine Companion	–	–	–	305
Lord, When You Came to Jordan	–	–	–	71
Of the Father's Love Begotten	–	7	534	309
When Jesus Came to Jordan	–	–	–	72

SUNDAY BETWEEN JANUARY 14 AND 20 [2] (C)

Isaiah 62:1–5 A promise by the prophetic community to intercede without ceasing for Jerusalem—forsaken and desolate—until she is saved and newly named by YHWH. Then her light (glory) shall dawn like the morning brightness, a burning torch, a gleaming jewel, and her children shall farm once again the land promised to the faithful.

Anthem
King of Glory, King of Peace, H. Friedell (H. W. Gray) SATB (M).

1 Corinthians 12:1–11 Though every congregation is a fragile group, one spiritual gift bonds all together: profession of Jesus as Lord. In addition, there are varieties of gifts, services, and working, but it is the same Spirit, Lord, and God operating in all. So Paul's partial list of spiritual gifts to each person—knowledge, faith, healing, miracle-working, prophecy, preaching, speaking or interpreting in tongues—are all from one and the same Spirit and, therefore, must serve the common good.

Anthem
Draw Us in the Spirit's Tether, Harold Friedell (H. W. Gray) SATB (ME).

John 2:1–11 A grand wedding feast is about to come to an embarrassing end because the supply of wine is dwindling. What an opportune hour for Jesus miraculously to change some water into premium wine. What a marvelous story pointing to the new way of Christ's mercy toward us. Water transformed into new wine, guilt into free grace, accusation and retaliation into justification, judgment into forgiveness—all this happened when the time came for Jesus' "hour" on Calvary. Surely God works in mysterious ways.

Anthem
Lord, Who at Cana's Wedding Feast, Dietrich Buxtehude (*Wedding Blessings*, Concordia) unison, 2 violins or C instruments (E).

Psalm 36:5–10
1. Metrical: *Thy Mercy and Thy Truth, O Lord*. Text: *The Psalter*, 1912. Tune: CADDO. *HB55* #82.
2. Responsorial: *Psalm 36* (5–11). Text: Grail. Refrain: David Clark Isele. Gelineau tone. *PS93* #34.

See also *ANMP*, p. 86; *PH87* #36; *PR&T*, pp. 69 & 77.

Anthem
O How Precious, Raymond Haan (Hinshaw) 2-part (E).

Organ Music for the Day
1. *Prelude on* TALLIS' ORDINAL (*Thy Mercy and Thy Truth, O Lord*—Psalm 36, *PH90* #186), Raymond H. Haan (*A Second Book of Contemplative Hymn Tune Preludes*, Harold Flammer, Inc. HF 5127).
2. *Chorale Prelude on* VENI CREATOR SPIRITUS/KOMM, GOTT SCHÖPFER (*Come, Holy Spirit, Our Souls Inspire, PH90* #125), John Cook (*Festal Voluntaries—Ascension, Whitsun and Trinity*, Novello & Co., Ltd. 1401).

Hymns for the Day	HL33	HB55	WB72	PH90
Come, Holy Spirit, Our Souls Inspire	–	–	–	125
Down to Earth, as a Dove	–	–	–	300
God of Compassion	290	122	392	261
I'm Gonna Live So God Can Use Me	–	–	–	369
O Lord, Make Haste to Hear My Cry	–	392	–	249
O Sing a Song of Bethlehem	138	177	526	308

SUNDAY BETWEEN JANUARY 21 AND 27 [3] (C)

Nehemiah 8:1–3, 5–6, 8–10 All the people gather as one when Ezra the scribe brings forth the book of the law of Moses, which YHWH gave to Israel. Ezra reads from it. All ears listen. All eyes watch. Everybody stands. All hands are lifted, and all mouths respond, "Amen." All heads are bowed, and all worship YHWH. Levites explain the law so that all minds understand. And all eyes shed tears when they discern YHWH's incredible care for all humanity. So all the people celebrate YHWH's saving presence among them.

Anthem
Praise the Lord, Heinz Werner Zimmerman (*Five Hymns,* Concordia) SATB (ME).

1 Corinthians 12:12–31a Conventional wisdom believes in the precedence of the individual who decides to associate with others and, thereby, form a group to which each member may contribute prized talents according to the reigning hierarchy. The biblical vision, however, believes in the precedence of the body (of Christ) in which baptized members (a foot, hand, ear, eye) may discern their God-given, essential gifts for contributing to the care of the body.

Anthem
The Church of Christ Is One, Stanley Tagg (*Westminster Praise,* Hinshaw) unison (E).

Luke 4:14–21 Jesus returns home to open his public ministry in Galilee by reading Isaiah 61:1–2 and a modified 58:6. These words not only begin but foreshadow Jesus' entire ministry, for he is the one anointed by the Spirit at his baptism "to preach good news to the poor and to proclaim release to the captives."

Anthem
Good News, Jane Marshall (C. Fischer) SATB (ME).

Psalm 19
1. Metrical: *The Heavens Above Declare God's Praise.* Text: Christopher L. Webber. Tune: CAITHNESS. *PH90* #166.
2. Responsorial: *Psalm 19* (1–6). Text: Grail. Melody: Monks of Saint Meinrad. Harmony, Samuel Weber. *PS93* #12.
3. Responsorial: *Psalm 19* (7–14). Setting: Hal H. Hopson. *PS93* #13.

See also *SPJP,* p. 20; *RITL* #87; *PH87* #19; *30P&2C,* p. 3; *PR&T,* pp. 67 & 68.

Anthem
Silent Devotion and Response, Ernest Bloch (Broude) SATB (M).

Organ Music for the Day
1. *Prelude on* TRURO (*Live Into Hope, PH90* #332), Claudia Drews (*The Concordia Hymn Preludes Series,* vol. 39, Concordia 97-5857).
2. *Prelude on* WESTMINSTER ABBEY (*Christ Is Made the Sure Foundation, PH90* #416), Christopher Steel (*Six from the Sixties,* Novello & Co., Ltd.).

Hymns for the Day	HL33	HB55	WB72	PH90
Arise, Your Light Is Come	–	–	–	411
Called as Partners in Christ's Service	–	–	–	343
Live Into Hope	–	–	–	332
Our God, to Whom We Turn	–	128	–	278
We All Are One in Mission	–	–	–	435
When in Our Music God Is Glorified	–	–	–	264

210

SUNDAY BETWEEN JANUARY 28 AND FEBRUARY 3 [4] (C)

Jeremiah 1:4–10 Jeremiah's vision, in which YHWH anoints him to be a "prophet to the nations." "But I do not know how to speak," laments Jeremiah. "Fear not," answers YHWH, "I am with you. What I command, you shall speak." YHWH then touches Jeremiah's mouth, saying, "I have put my words into your mouth so that you shall speak the double-edged word of judgment and salvation that uproots and smashes, and builds and plants."

Anthem
O Thou Whose Power, Gilbert Martin (H. W. Gray) SATB (M).

1 Corinthians 13:1–13 What is love? Love is action, not a feeling. Love is self-giving, even unto death, in the manner of Christ's self-giving. Love maintains all faithfulness, all hope, all steadfastness. Love is eternal because it is the purpose and nature of God. Today we see that dimly, but someday we shall see clearly and understand fully.

Anthems
The Gift of Love, Hal H. Hopson (Hope) 2-part (E). *Though I May Speak, PH90* #335.

Luke 4:21–30 Everyone is aglow the day the hometown boy, Joseph's son, returns to preach his inaugural sermon. All speak well of him and marvel at his words, until he speaks about the favoring of outsiders—Gentiles by name. Then the crowd's admiration turns to rejection, and they seek to execute vigilante justice on the brow of a hill outside the city. Yet Jesus passes through the midst of this frenzied crowd and goes away.

Anthem
Insult and Reproach, G. Battistini (*Sing Joyfully,* vol. 4, Walton) SATB (M).

Psalm 71:1–6
1. Metrical: *I Find My Refuge in You, Lord.* Text: C.M., Christopher L. Webber. *ANMP,* p. 119.
2. Responsorial: *Psalm 71:1–6.* Text: Grail. Setting: James E. Barrett. Tone: Harmony, Hal H. Hopson. *PS93* #63.
3. Metrical: *In You, O Lord, I Put My Trust.* Text: Clarence P. Walhout. Tune: JUDSON. *PH87* #71.
See also *GPI,* p. 97; *WIII* #44 & #876; *PR&T,* pp. 45 & 48.

Anthem
In Thee, O Lord, Joseph Haydn (Sam Fox) SATB (M).

Organ Music for the Day
1. *Prelude on* BEECHER (*Called as Partners in Christ's Service, PH90* #343), Don Hustad (*Hymns for the Organ,* Hope Publishing Co. 311).
2. *Chorale Prelude on* DAS NEUGEBORNE KINDELEIN (*Great God, Your Love Has Called Us Here, PH90* #353), Harald Rohlig (*Victim Divine, Your Grace We Claim,* in *The Concordia Hymn Prelude Series,* vol. 17, Concordia 97-5708).

Hymns for the Day	HL33	HB55	WB72	PH90
Great God, Your Love Has Called Us Here	–	–	–	353
How Clear Is Our Vocation, Lord	–	–	–	419
Jesus, Our Divine Companion	–	–	–	305
Lord, Speak to Me, That I May Speak	399	298	–	426
Not for Tongues of Heaven's Angels	–	–	–	531
Though I May Speak	–	–	–	335

SUNDAY BETWEEN FEBRUARY 4 AND 10 [5] (C)

Isaiah 6:1–8, (9–13) Confronted by the immediate presence of the enthroned God, and by seraphim singing "Holy, holy, holy," which rocked the very foundations of the Temple, Isaiah feels denuded of his pretense of worthiness before the Lord. "Woe is me!" cries out Isaiah. "For I am a person of unclean lips and I dwell in the midst of a people of unclean lips." One of the seraphim touches Isaiah's lips with a burning coal from the altar, saying, "Your guilt is taken away, and your sin forgiven." Upon hearing the voice of the Lord say, "Whom shall I send, and who will go for us?" Isaiah's lips now inexplicably respond, "Here am I! Send me."

Anthem
In the Year That King Uzziah Died, David McKay Williams (H. W. Gray) SATB (MD).

1 Corinthians 15:1–11 This is the good news in which we stand: Christ died for our sins according to the scriptures, was buried, raised on the third day, and appeared to Peter, to the Twelve, and to many faithful witnesses. Finally, he appeared to me, Paul, the least of all apostles.

Anthem
We Know That Christ Is Raised, C. V. Stanford (Augsburg) SATB (E).

Luke 5:1–11 A crowd presses upon Jesus, who gets into a boat and teaches from it. He then tells Simon to catch fish on a day when all-night labor had yielded empty nets. Peter obeys Jesus' word and, behold, hauls in such a great catch that the boat begins to sink. So Peter falls down at Jesus' feet, confessing, "I am a sinner, Lord." "Fear not," replies Jesus. "From now on you will be catching people alive." Then Simon and his partners leave their successful catch of fish behind and follow Jesus.

Anthem
How Lovely Are the Messengers, Felix Mendelssohn (G. Schirmer) SATB (M).

Psalm 138
1. Metrical: *I Will Give Thanks with My Whole Heart*. Text: L.M., Christopher L. Webber. Tune: HERR JESU CHRIST. *PH90* #247.
2. Responsorial: *Psalm 138*. Text and Refrain: Arlo D. Duba. Harmony, Hal H. Hopson. Instrumentation: Lynelle M. Williams. *PS93* #141.

See also *30P&2C*, p. 39; *WIII* #879; *PR&T*, pp. 57 & 77.

Anthem
With Songs of Rejoicing, J. S. Bach, arr. Hal H. Hopson (C. Fischer) 2-part mixed (E).

Organ Music for the Day
1. *Chorale Prelude on* HERR JESU CHRIST (*I Will Give Thanks with My Whole Heart*— Psalm 138, *PH90* #247), Georg P. Telemann (*Twelve Easy Choral Preludes*, Edwin F. Kalmus 4005).
2. *Prelude on* NICAEA (*Holy, Holy, Holy!*, *PH90* #138), Calvin Hampton (*The Church Organist's Library*, McAfee Music Corp. DM 239).

Hymns for the Day	HL33	HB55	WB72	PH90
Hear the Good News of Salvation	–	–	–	355
Here I Am, Lord	–	–	–	525
Holy God, We Praise Your Name	–	–	420	460
Holy, Holy, Holy!	–	–	–	138
Lord, You Have Come to the Lakeshore	–	–	–	377
This Is the Good News	–	–	263	598

SUNDAY BETWEEN FEBRUARY 11 AND 17
(PROPER 1) [6] (C)

Jeremiah 17:5–10 In whom do you trust? Trust any human being or human-created social structure or institution (even a church denomination), and you are guaranteed to end up a lonely shrub in the desert—isolated, parched, anxious, helpless, wilting, dying a slow death—in a word, cursed. Trust in the Lord, and you are certain to be rooted by the living waters—drinking as needed in times of anguish, pain, distress, and, therefore, always bearing fruit—in a word, blessed. YHWH knows whom you trust, because your actions reveal in whom your heart trusts and, therefore, you live accordingly.

Anthem
Blessed the People, J. Geisler (Boosey & Hawkes) SATB (ME).

1 Corinthians 15:12–20 Writes Paul, "If there is no resurrection, then Christ was not raised, you're locked into your sins forever, and your faith is futile. But," continues Paul, "Christ has been raised from the dead." An irrational and unconvincing deduction. Yet it worked, because churches open to the power of the Spirit experience the presence of the risen Christ in their life together.

Anthem
Christ Is Risen, Pablo Sosa, *PH90* #109.

Luke 6:17–26 Jesus' opening words in his Sermon on the Plain describe the life of a healed community. "Blessings to you who are poor, hungry, weeping, and despised. Woe to you who are rich, full, laughing, and respected." Jesus has a way of turning our values upside down, doesn't he? He also makes us squirm.

Anthem
The Beatitudes, Lawson Lunde (Broude) SATB (M).

Psalm 1
1. Metrical: *The One Is Blest.* Text: *The Psalter,* 1912. Tune: DUNFERMLINE. *PH90* #158.
2. Responsorial: *Psalm 1* (1–4, 6). Setting: Hal H. Hopson. *PS93* #1.
See also *GPI,* p. 1; *WIII* #24; *WIII* #882 for alt. refrain; *TIP/PSCY* #11; *RITL* #81; *ANMP,* p. 40; *PH87* #1; *SPJP,* p. 11; *PR&T,* pp. 67 & 68.

Anthem
The One Is Blest, PH90 #158.

Organ Music for the Day
1. *Prelude on* DONNE SECOURS (*Hope of the World, PH90* #360), Victor Freudenberg (*Ten Chorale Preludes and Settings for Organ,* Victor Freudenberg, 532 Pinar Drive, Orlando, FL 32825).
2. *Prelude on* ST. BRIDE (*Give to the Winds Thy Fears, PH90* #286), Albert Beck (*Seventy-Six Offertories on Hymns & Chorales,* Concordia 97-5207).

Hymns for the Day	HL33	HB55	WB72	PH90
Christ Is Risen	–	–	–	109
Hope of the World	–	291	423	360
If Thou but Trust in God to Guide Thee	–	344	431	282
O for a World	–	–	–	386
Our God, to Whom We Turn	–	128	–	278
There's a Spirit in the Air	–	–	–	433
We Are Your People	–	–	–	436

SUNDAY BETWEEN FEBRUARY 18 AND 24
(Proper 2) [7] (C)

Genesis 45:3–11, 15 The simple, self-disclosing words, "I am Joseph," send waves of alarm, shock, and dismay through his brothers, because their cunning and deceptive past now jeopardizes their future. But instead of revenge, Joseph breaks with the past and offers a gift of a new future. Why? Because "God sent me to preserve life." God's will for life is at work in spite of all resistant human efforts. Make haste, therefore, in telling the world that God mysteriously works for life in the midst of our leanness.

Anthem

In Adam We Have All Been One (*Westminster Praise,* Hinshaw) SATB (E).

1 Corinthians 15:35–38, 42–50 Paul undermines our obsession with preserving our earthly body, as well as our Greek notions of immortality. Our physical body that has been sown will die and be raised as a spiritual body. Death will end our earthly life, but we shall experience the new creation of resurrected life. We shall be changed people.

Anthem

Praise to the Holiest, arr. Erik Routley (*Westminster Praise,* Hinshaw) SATB (E).

Luke 6:27–38 More injunctions from Jesus' Sermon on the Plain that invert our conventional wisdom: "Do not take any retaliatory action against those who do physical violence to you, extract forced labor from you, or make demands for gifts and loans. But love and serve your enemies, and pray for them as a sign of the age to come."

Anthem

On Love of One's Enemies, Virgil Ford (Broadman) SATB (E).

Psalm 37:1–11, 39–40
1. Metrical: *Fret Not for Those Who Do Wrong Things.* Text: C.M., Christopher L. Webber. Tune: CULROSS. *PH90* #188. Text only, Christopher L. Webber. *ANMP,* p. 87.
2. Responsorial: *Psalm 37* (1–11). Setting: Hal H. Hopson. *PS93* #35.
3. Metrical: *Give to the Winds Thy Fears.* Text: Paul Gerhard, trans. John Wesley. Tune: ST. BRIDE. *PH90* #286; *HB55* #364.
See also *PH87* #37; *PR&T,* pp. 57 & 68.

Anthem

O Rest in the Lord, Felix Mendelssohn (*Elijah,* any edition) unison or solo (E).

Organ Music for the Day
1. *Prelude on* LLANGLOFFAN (*O God of Every Nation, PH90* #289), David Dahl (*The Concordia Hymn Prelude Series,* vol. 30, Concordia 97-5745).
2. *Prelude on* DICKINSON COLLEGE (*Lord, Make Us Servants, PH90* #374), Peter Hurford (*The Bristol Collection,* Harold Flammer, Inc. HF-5082).

Hymns for the Day	HL33	HB55	WB72	PH90
Celebrate with Joy and Singing	–	–	–	107
God Moves in a Mysterious Way	103	112	391	270
Lord, Make Us Servants of Your Peace	–	–	–	374
O Day of Peace	–	–	–	450
Take My Life	242	310	–	391
When Will People Cease Their Fighting?	–	–	–	401

SUNDAY BETWEEN FEBRUARY 25 AND 29*
(PROPER 3) [8] (C)

Isaiah 55:10–13 God's intentions for human history may be delayed, but they are not nullified. God's full promises still stand, for the word of God abides forever, and surrounds God's people (cf. Isa. 40:6–8 and 55:11). Sooner or later, God's rule will be visible among all. This means that instead of "thorns and thistles" (cf. Gen. 3:18), "the fall" shall end and "the homecoming" shall begin a new, everlasting creation in which relationships among all exiles are fully restored. You can count on God's promises.

Anthem
For as the Rain and Snow Come Down, Hal H. Hopson (Sacred Music) SATB (M).

1 Corinthians 15:51–58 A mystery: all of us may not die before the eschaton, but all of us shall be changed. At the last trumpet, all shall put on the imperishable, immortal heavenly garment, and thus death itself shall lose its sting, die, and be swallowed up in victory through our Lord Jesus Christ. Thanks be to God! Therefore, confident of this ultimate victory, let us now "be steadfast, immovable, always abounding in the work of the Lord."

Anthem
O Death, Where Is Thy Sting? (*Messiah,* any edition) alto, tenor duet, and SATB (MD).

Luke 6:39–49 We are all so blind, which is why we lead each other into ditches. Worse, we trust our own obstructed sight, condemning ourselves to the pit—after all, "thorns and thistles" do not produce "figs and grapes." So those who hear and obey Christ's words are like those who build stone houses on a rock base, and those who do not hear and obey are like those who build mud houses in an arroyo.

Anthem
A Test of Goodness, Virgil Ford (Broadman) SATB (ME).

Psalm 92:1–4, 12–15
1. Metrical: *To Thank the Lord Our God.* Text: The Scottish Psalter, 1650, var. Tune: SALVATION. Attr. to R. Boyd in *Kentucky Harmony. RITL* #116.
2. Responsorial: *Psalm 92* (1–2, 5, 12–13). Text: Taizé. Setting: Jacques Berthier. Refrain: Harmony by Psalter Task Force. *PS93* #86.

See also *WIII* #888; *PR&T,* pp. 40 & 78.

Anthem
The Just Man Shall Flourish, Richard Proulx (Augsburg) unison, flute, oboe (E).

Organ Music for the Day
1. *Prelude on* VICTORY (*The Strife Is O'er, PH90* #119), David N. Johnson (*Music for Worship—Easy Trios,* Augsburg 11-9291).
2. *Prelude on* BOURBON (*Take Up Your Cross, the Savior Said, PH90* #393), Charles W. Ore (*Eleven Compositions,* Concordia 97-5702).

Hymns for the Day	HL33	HB55	WB72	PH90
Christ the Lord Is Risen Today!	165	–	330	113
God of Our Life	88	108	395	275
Great Is Thy Faithfulness	–	–	–	276
My Hope Is Built on Nothing Less	–	368	–	379
O Holy City, Seen of John	409	508	505	453
The Strife Is O'er	–	–	597	119

*Except when this Sunday is The Transfiguration of the Lord.

TRANSFIGURATION OF THE LORD

[Sunday Preceding Lent] (C)

Exodus 34:29–35 Moses makes his final descent from Mt. Sinai, this time with a shining face. Immediately, the Israelites and their leaders see the glory of God shining in the uncovered face of Moses, "and they were afraid to come near him." But, since Moses was human, they could behold him and receive the commandments that YHWH had given Moses. Whenever Moses spoke with YHWH or mediated YHWH's guidance to the people, Moses' radiant face was unveiled. And when he wasn't performing his mediatorial task, his face was veiled.

Anthem
The Face of Moses Shone, Charles T. Lee (H. W. Gray) SATB (ME).

2 Corinthians 3:12–4:2 When we turn to Christ, we behold the unveiled glory of God in Christ and are, surprisingly, transformed into Christ's likeness. Lest we think our turning to Christ is solely by our choice, remember that it is the Holy Spirit who frees us to turn and to follow Christ.

Anthem
Faces Like Mirrors, Austin Lovelace SATB (M).

Luke 9:28–36, (37–43) Eight days after speaking to his disciples about "taking up the cross," Jesus ascends a mountain with Peter, James, and John. As Jesus is praying, the appearance of his face becomes different, his clothing becomes dazzling white, and Moses and Elijah talk with him about his exodus from Jerusalem. Peter and the others "saw his glory" and want to set up the festival tents right there. But a cloud overshadows them, and a voice proclaims words that recall Jesus' baptism—"This is my Son, my chosen [or Beloved]"—and then adds this charge: "Listen to him!" The disciples open their eyes and see only Jesus, so they keep silent about what they have heard.

Anthem
Christ Upon the Mountain Peak, Peter Cutts (*Ecumenical Praise,* number 67, Agape) unison (E).

Psalm 99
1. Metrical: *The Lord Is King: Let People Quake.* Text: L.M., Christopher L. Webber. *ANMP,* p. 165.
2. Responsorial:*Psalm 99.* Text: Helen Wright. Setting: Hal Hopson. *PS93* #96. See also *GPI,* p. 141; *20P&3C,* p. 19; *PP* #113; *PH87* #99; *PR&T,* pp. 59, 73.

Anthem
The Lord God Reigneth, Johann Pachelbel (Concordia) SATB (M).

Organ Music for the Day
1. *Prelude on* KING'S WESTON (*At the Name of Jesus, PH90* #148), P. Stearns (*Twelve Hymn Preludes for General Use,* H. Flammer, Inc. HF-5145).
2. *Prelude on* DEO GRACIAS (*O Wondrous Sight, O Vision Fair, PH90* #75), Richard Hillert (*The Concordia Hymn Prelude Series,* vol. 5, Concordia 97-5611).

Hymns for the Day	HL33	HB55	WB72	PH90
Holy Spirit, Truth Divine	208	240	422	321
O Splendor of God's Glory Bright	32	46	529	474
O Wondrous Type, O Vision Fair	142	182	531	75
Spirit of the Living God	–	–	–	322
Swiftly Pass the Clouds	–	–	–	73
Take Up Thy Cross, the Savior Said	–	293	–	393

Easter Cycle
Season of Lent
ASH WEDNESDAY (ABC)

See Ash Wednesday (ABC) in Year A, p. 53.

FIRST SUNDAY IN LENT (C)

Deuteronomy 26:1–11 Instructions on offering firstfruits of the land to the Lord so you will not succumb to the temptation to believe you achieved the harvest which the Lord has given you. First, recite the ancient creedal story of YHWH's actions for the people—hearing their distress, delivering them from affliction, and guiding them to the Promised Land. Then offer the firstfruits of your God-given gifts to the Lord. Why all this ritual? So you will remember how YHWH took care of your refugee ancestors, rejoice in such unmerited love, and therefore care for the outsiders who live among you.

Anthem
Thanks to God the Lord, Heinrich Schütz (Concordia) SATB (E).

Romans 10:8b–13 When your lips confess "Jesus is Lord" because your heart trusts "God raised him from the dead," you acknowledge the nearness of Christ and his salvation offered to all, which Isaiah said will not be transitory. The Lord of all bestows such enduring riches upon all who call upon the Lord's name.

Anthem
Lenten Litany, M. How (Boosey & Hawkes) unison, baritone solo (E).

Luke 4:1–13 Jesus has just been "ordained" in baptism and is full of the Holy Spirit, who leads him into the wilderness for forty days, where he is tempted by the devil to become three different kinds of Messiah: prosperity giver, political leader, or miracle worker. Jesus, however, repudiates each temptation with a quote from Deuteronomy, indicating he will let God define his ministry. The devil then departs until an opportune time.

Anthem
O Love, How Deep, How Broad, How High, Philip Dietterich (Sacred Music) 2-part (E).

Psalm 91:1–2, 9–16
1. Metrical: *Within Your Shelter, Loving God.* Text: John G. Dunn. Tune: ABBEY. C.M., *PH90* #212.
2. Responsorial: *Psalm 91* (1–6, 9–16). Text: Helen L. Wright. Refrain and Tone: Presbyterian 6. *PS93* #85.
See also *RITL* #115; *ANMP,* p. 148; *SPJP,* p. 47; *PR&T,* pp. 57 & 75.

Anthem
Happy Are You, Jane Marshall (Augsburg) SATB baritone solo (ME).

Organ Music for the Day
1. *Prelude on* ST. FLAVIAN (*Lord, Who Throughout These Forty Days, PH90* #81), Charles T. Taylor (Harold Flammer, Inc. 4286).
2. *Prelude on* DEO GRACIAS (*O Love, How Deep, How Broad, How High, PH90* #83), Frank Ferko (*Hymn Preludes,* Augsburg 11-6800).

Hymns for the Day	HL33	HB55	WB72	PH90
As a Chalice Cast of Gold	–	–	–	336
As Those of Old Their Firstfruits Brought	–	–	–	414
Lord, Who Throughout These Forty Days	144	181	470	81
O Jesus, I Have Promised	268	307	–	388, 389
O Love That Wilt Not Let Me Go	307	400	519	384
When We Are Tempted to Deny Your Son	–	–	640	86

SECOND SUNDAY IN LENT (C)

Genesis 15:1–12, 17–18 YHWH promises through Abram to be our shield, and that our gifts shall be great. But, like Abram, we protest: "We live in the 'real world' where human ambition breeds carelessness, and unfulfilled divine promises are trusted less than a falling star." YHWH's response: the same promise is pledged and a sign—the countless fixed stars—given. Miraculously, Abram surrenders his craving for control and "believes YHWH." YHWH then seals the covenant with Abram.

Anthem
God Shall Do My Advising, Dietrich Buxtehude (Concordia) SATB (ME).

Philippians 3:17–4:1 Paul's exhortation to imitate him in pressing on toward the goal of true righteousness that God has already given in Christ. Abandon earthly pleasure-seeking, which makes you "enemies of the cross of Christ," and follow the example of the citizens of heaven, whose lowly bodies will be transformed to be like Christ's glorious body.

Anthem
Open Thou Mine Eyes, John Rutter (Hinshaw) SATB soprano solo (M).

Luke 13:31–35 Jesus so passionately yearns to shield God's people under his protective wings that neither warnings nor threats could possibly deter his urgent passion-journey to Jerusalem. In his three-day ministry he laments "Jerusalem's" continual resistance to God's unremitting grace.

Anthem
Jerusalem, Thou That Killest the Prophets, Christoph Bernard (Concordia) SSB 2 violins (M).

Psalm 27
1. Metrical: *God Is My Strong Salvation.* Text: James Montgomery. Tune: CHRISTUS, DER IST MEIN LEBEN. *PH90* #179. (See also *HB55* #347, *RITL* #95, and *WB72* #388 to the Tune: WEDLOCK.)
2. Responsorial: *Psalm 27* (1–6). Text: Taizé, alt. Helen L. Wright. Refrain: Jacques Berthier. Tone: Hal H. Hopson. *PS93* #25.
See also *CC* G-2762; *PH87* #27; *ANMP,* p. 63; *SPJP,* p. 26; *WIII* #792 & #852; *PR&T,* pp. 16 & 57.

Anthem
God Is My Strong Salvation, Melchior Vulpius, *PH90* #179.

Organ Music for the Day
1. *Prelude on* LEONI (*The God of Abraham Praise, PH90* #488), Flor Peeters (*Hymn Preludes for the Liturgical Year,* vol. 6, C. F. Peters Corp. 6406).
2. *Chorale Prelude on* WER NUR DEN LIEBEN GOTT (*If Thou but Trust in God to Guide Thee, PH90* #282), J. S. Bach (various editions).

Hymns for the Day	HL33	HB55	WB72	PH90
Fight the Good Fight	270	359	–	307
Forgive Our Sins as We Forgive	–	–	–	347
If Thou but Trust in God to Guide Thee	–	344	431	282
O Jesus Christ, May Grateful Hymns . . .	–	–	509	424
The God of Abraham Praise	8	89	587	488
Walk On, O People of God	–	–	–	296

THIRD SUNDAY IN LENT (C)

Isaiah 55:1–9 An imperative invitation to the eschatological banquet. Come! Buy! Eat! Free wine and milk. Why futilely try to buy your way into the banquet or purchase unsatisfying pleasures? Heed my word and you shall eat well. Summon your neighbors while YHWH is near. And return to the Lord, our God, who is merciful and quick to forgive, for YHWH's ways are not our ways.

Anthem
The Second Song of Isaiah, Erik Routley (Hinshaw) SATB unison, congregation (E).

1 Corinthians 10:1–13 Paul recalls the exodus-wilderness events. Those who were under the protection of the cloud, led through the sea, given manna to eat and water to drink, presumed they could live as they pleased. But God was not pleased with them, so they were destroyed. But know also that God faithfully struggles with us against the seductive forces—idolatry, immorality, testing God, grumbling—that threaten to drive a wedge between us and God.

Anthem
Lead Me, Lord, in Thy Righteousness, S. S. Wesley (Oxford) SATB (E).

Luke 13:1–9 Were the Galileans destroyed during the sacrificial worship in the Temple because they were worse sinners than all other Galileans? Were the eighteen Jerusalemites killed in the catastrophic collapse of the Siloam tower because they were worse offenders than all other Jerusalemites? Do bad things happen only to bad people? No! But we all are ultimately judged by our fruits. Meanwhile, all barren fig trees will be given a little more time to bear fruit. Only by God's sheer grace and good patience are we given time to repent (*but not forever*).

Anthem
We Are a Garden, Alice Parker (E. C. Schirmer) SATB harp, triangle (MD).

Psalm 63:1–8
1. Metrical: *O Lord, You Are My God.* Text: John G. Dunn. Tune: ALBERTA. *PH90* #199.
2. Responsorial: *Psalm 63:1–8.* Text: Arlo D. Duba. Refrain: Presbyterian 8. Tone: Thomas Tallis. *PS93* #53.

See also *PH90* #198; *ANMP,* p. 107; *PS93* #54; *GPI,* p. 85; *PR&T,* pp. 48 & 75.

Anthem
O God, You Are My God, PH90 #199.

Organ Music for the Day
1. *Prelude on* AMAZING GRACE/NEW BRITAIN (*Amazing Grace, PH90* #280), Gordon Young (*Spirituals and Folk Tunes,* Hope 228).
2. *Prelude on* IN BABILONE (*There's a Wideness in God's Mercy, PH90* #298), Gordon Young (*Collage for Organ,* Harold Flammer, Inc. HF-5011).

Hymns for the Day	HL33	HB55	WB72	PH90
God of Compassion, in Mercy Befriend Us	290	122	392	261
O Come Unto the Lord	–	–	–	381
O for a Closer Walk with God	259	319	–	396, 397
O My Soul, Bless Your Redeemer	–	–	523	223
Out of Deep, Unordered Water	–	–	–	494
Stand Up and Bless the Lord	–	–	–	491

FOURTH SUNDAY IN LENT (C)

Joshua 5:9–12 YHWH has liberated the people of Israel from the disgrace of slavery in Egypt and brought them to Gilgal, where they solemnly celebrate the first Passover in the Promised Land. Down drops the curtain on forty years of wilderness wanderings and sustenance by miraculous manna from the heavens, and up rises the curtain on YHWH's nourishment of Israel by the produce and fruit of the land.

Anthem
O Taste and See, R. V. Williams (Oxford) SATB soprano solo (E).

2 Corinthians 5:16–21 God has entrusted us with the ministry of reconciliation and appointed us as ambassadors for Christ. Our message? God tracked down and made up with our rebellious, guilty, frightened world. Instead of tallying up all our sins, God incarnate, Jesus Christ, strode into our world and loved us and forgave us, transforming our world into a new creation.

Anthem
Reconciliation, L. Pfautsch (Hope) SATB trumpet (M).

Luke 15:1–3, 11b–32 The younger of two sons requests his share of property from his father, who foolishly gives him his inheritance. The younger son then squanders everything, tumbling to the depths of pig herder. Realizing there is bread back home, he seeks to earn his food by working as his father's hired servant. But the father has compassion, embraces and kisses him, and throws an extravagant homecoming party, completely restoring him. The hardworking elder son becomes angry and, though his father pleads with him, keeps his distance from the party. Declares the father, "Child, everything of mine is yours." No repentance, no conversion, but lots of unconditional love.

Anthem
And the Father Will Dance Over You in Joy, Mark Hayes (Hinshaw) SATB (ME).

Psalm 32
1. Metrical: *How Blest Are Those.* Text: Fred R. Anderson. Tune: ES FLOG EIN KLEINS WALDVÖGELEIN. *PH90* #184.
2. Responsorial: *Psalm 32.* Text: Grail. Refrain: David Clark Isele. Tone: Tonus peregrinus, arr. Hal H. Hopson. *PS93* #29.
See also *WIII* #881; *PH87* #32; *HB55* #281; *ANMP,* p. 74; *PR&T,* pp. 42 & 75.

Anthem
How Blest Are Those, PH90 #184.

Organ Music for the Day
1. *Chorale Prelude on* ES FLOG EIN KLEINS WALDVÖGELEIN (*How Blest Are Those*— Psalm 32, *PH90* #184), John Diercks (*The Parish Organist,* Concordia 97-4759).
2. *Prelude on* IN BABILONE (*There's a Wideness in God's Mercy, PH90* #298), Paul Manz (*Ten Chorale Improvisations,* Concordia 97-5342).

Hymns for the Day	HL33	HB55	WB72	PH90
Give Praise to the Lord	–	–	–	257
God, You Spin the Whirling Planets	–	–	–	285
Great Is Thy Faithfulness	–	–	–	276
There's a Wideness in God's Mercy	93	110	601	298
What Wondrous Love Is This	–	–	–	85
Your Faithfulness, O Lord, Is Sure	–	–	–	251

FIFTH SUNDAY IN LENT (C)

Isaiah 43:16–21 "Behold, I am doing a new thing," proclaims YHWH. Yes, the exodus from Egypt was dramatic and formative for Israel's existence, but now YHWH is bringing about a new exodus by making a straight road in the wilderness, and creating thirst-quenching rivers in the desert so that YHWH's chosen people may sing their praise to the Lord.

Anthem
By the Springs of Water, Cecil Effinger (Augsburg) SATB (M).

Philippians 3:4b–14 Paul has discarded all that was precious to him—achievements, respectability, reputation, moral uprightness, obeying the law—for the sake of something far more valuable: knowledge of Christ Jesus as his Lord and being in union with him. To know the power of Christ's resurrection, Paul and those "in Christ" must model their life on Christ's sufferings and death. For though Christ Jesus has made Paul and us his own, we still must paradoxically "press on" and "strain forward" to make the prize of the upward call of God our own.

Anthem
A Reflection of Christ, David Schwoebel (Hinshaw) SAB (ME).

John 12:1–8 Irrepressible Mary gets carried away at dinner, and shocks everyone by pouring thousands of dollars' worth of perfume on Jesus' feet. "An extravagant waste," cries the morally upright Judas; "the money could have been given to the poor." Replies Jesus, "You'll always have the opportunity to serve the poor; so leave her alone, for you'll not always have me. She has saved her perfume for my burial." Mary anoints her only Lord and Savior.

Anthem
O Jesus, My Lord, Karoly Kope (Hinshaw) SAB (ME).

Psalm 126
1. Metrical: *When God Delivered Israel.* Text: Michael A. Saward. Tune: SHEAVES. *PH90* #237 (see also *PP* #134 and *RITL* #133).
2. Responsorial: *Psalm 126.* Setting: Hal H. Hopson. *PS93* #130.
See also *PS93* #131; *WIII* #69, #771; *ANMP,* p. 209; *PR&T,* pp. 41 & 79.

Anthem
Home from Our Exile, Bernard Huijbers (Oregon Catholic Press) SATB (E).

Organ Music for the Day
1. *Prelude on* MONKLAND (*Let Us with a Gladsome Mind, PH90* #244), Heathcote Statham (*Festal Voluntaries—Harvest,* Novello & Co., Ltd. 1403).
2. *Chorale Prelude on* JESU MEINE FREUDE (*Jesu, Priceless Treasure, PH90* #365), Johann G. Walther (*The Church Organist's Golden Treasury,* vol. 2, Oliver Ditson Co.).

Hymns for the Day	HL33	HB55	WB72	PH90
Be Thou My Vision	325	303	304	339
Guide Me, O Thou Great Jehovah	104	339	409	281
Guide My Feet	–	–	–	354
Jesus, Priceless Treasure	–	414	442	365
Jesus, the Very Thought of Thee	309	401	–	310
O God, What You Ordain Is Right	291	366	633	284

PASSION/PALM SUNDAY
[Sixth Sunday in Lent] (ABC)

See Passion/Palm Sunday [Sixth Sunday in Lent] (ABC) in Year A, p. 60.

MONDAY OF HOLY WEEK (ABC)

See Monday of Holy Week (ABC) in Year A, p. 64.

TUESDAY OF HOLY WEEK (ABC)

See Tuesday of Holy Week (ABC) in Year A, p. 65.

WEDNESDAY OF HOLY WEEK (ABC)

See Wednesday of Holy Week (ABC) in Year A, p. 66.

MAUNDY THURSDAY (ABC)

See Maundy Thursday (ABC) in Year A, p. 68.

GOOD FRIDAY (ABC)

See Good Friday (ABC) in Year A, p. 70.

Season of Easter
EASTER VIGIL (ABC)

See Easter Vigil (ABC) in Year A, p. 72.

EASTER DAY (C)

Acts 10:34–43 At Cornelius's house in Caesarea, Peter recounts how his own life has been transformed by the power of the risen Lord, and everyone else (Jews and Gentiles) also can be transformed by that power.

Anthem
Good Christian Friends, Rejoice and Sing!, Melchior Vulpius, arr. Bisbee (Augsburg) SA, SAB, or SATB instruments (M).

or **Isaiah 65:17–25** Behold, YHWH creates new heavens and a new earth where all may truly rejoice.

Anthem
Thou, O God, Art Praised in Zion, Ian Hare (Oxford) SATB (M).

1 Corinthians 15:19–26 Christ has been raised from death; all who belong to him will rise also.

Anthem
Since by Man Came Death, G. F. Handel (*Messiah*, any edition) SATB (M).

or **Acts 10:34–43** See above.

John 20:1–18 Peter and the Beloved Disciple seek the truth about the empty tomb. Mary engages the "gardener" in conversation, who says, "Tell them I am ascending."

Anthem
Magdalen, Cease from Sobs and Sighs, Peter Hurford (Oxford) SATB (ME).

or **Luke 24:1–12** The message of the two men to the women at the empty tomb, who then relay this good news to the apostles, who disbelieve such idle tales.

Anthem
Early Easter Morning, Richard H. Smith (AMSI) SATB (M) no accompaniment.

Psalm 118:1–2, 14–24
1. Metrical: *God Is My Strength and Song.* Text: S.M., S.M.D., Christopher L. Webber. *ANMP*, pp. 188–90.
2. Responsorial: *The Lord Is My Strength and My Might.* Text: NRSV. Psalm tone: Laurence Bevenot, 1986. Refrain: A. Gregory Murray, 1986. *PH90* #231.
3. Responsorial: *Psalm 118* (14–17, 22–24). Text: *Book of Common Prayer.* Setting: Peter R. Hallock. *PS93* #119. (See also *TIP/PSCY* #8.)
4. Responsorial: *Psalm 118* (1, 4–5, 14, 17, 24). Text: Taizé. Setting: Jacques Berthier. *PS93* #120. (See also *MFTII*, p. 51.)
5. Metrical: *This Is the Day the Lord Hath Made* (verses 3–5). Text: Isaac Watts. Tune: ARDEN. *RITL* #128. (See also *HB55* #69 to the Tune: ARLINGTON.)
6. Responsorial: *Alleluia! Let Us Rejoice!* (guitar) Words and music by David Haas. *CS/PFTCY*, vol. 3, p. 20.
See also *PH87* #118; *PR&T*, pp. 29 & 30.

Anthem
This Is the Day the Lord Hath Made, Gerald Near (Augsburg) SAB (M).

Organ Music for the Day
1. *Prelude on* EASTER HYMN (*Jesus Christ Is Risen Today!*, *PH90* #123), William H. Harris (*Festal Voluntaries—Easter*, Novello & Co., Ltd. 1402).
2. *Sonata für Orgel* (*Christ the Lord Is Risen Again*, *PH90* #112), Ernst Pepping (Bärenreiter Verlag 2644).

Hymns for the Day	HL33	HB55	WB72	PH90
Because You Live, O Christ	–	–	–	105
Celebrate with Joy and Singing	–	–	–	107

Christ Jesus Lay in Death's Strong Bands	–	–	327	110
Come, Ye Faithful, Raise the Strain	168	205	344	114, 115
Jesus Christ Is Risen Today!	163	204	440	123
Thine Is the Glory	–	209	–	122

EASTER EVENING (ABC)

See Easter Evening (ABC) in Year A, p. 80.

SECOND SUNDAY OF EASTER (C)

Acts 5:27–32 The apostles' response to the Sanhedrin's prohibition of teaching "in the name of Jesus": We must obey God rather than human authority in giving witness to God's raising of Jesus from death.

Anthem
Easter Carol, Malcolm Williamson (Joseph Weinberger) SATB (M).

Revelation 1:4–8 The prophet John sends greetings to the seven churches: Remember to whom you belong—not to the Caesars of this world but solely to Christ. Remember by whose grace and peace you live—not by the Caesars' mercy but only by God's. Yes, the claims about Christ—he reliably testified that God's promises will be fulfilled, he inaugurated a new age, he rules as the King of kings—all seem preposterous, but one day the whole world will recognize that he is the one who loves us, frees us from our sins, and makes us priests. "To him be glory and power, forever."

Anthem
Unto Him That Loved Us, Ralph Vaughan Williams (*Morningstar Choir Book 1,* Concordia) unison (E).

John 20:19–31 Verses 19–23 are a series of symbolic episodes: The risen Jesus appears to his frightened disciples and says, "Peace." Then he shows them his hands and his side (which fills the disciples with joy) and again says, "Peace." He gives them the Holy Spirit by breathing on them and concludes with an eschatological saying about resisting forgiveness. In verses 24–31, Thomas says he must see with his eyes before he will believe. So again Jesus appears. He tells Thomas to touch his side. Thomas confesses. Blessed are those who believe on the basis of the word alone.

Anthems
Because You Have Seen Me, Thomas, Luca Marenzio (Concordia) SATB (M). *Peace Be with You,* Robert Wetzler (AMSI) SATB (ME). *We Have Seen the Lord,* Robert Wetzler (Augsburg) SATB (M).

Psalm 118:14–29
1. Metrical: *God Is My Strength and Song.* Text: S.M., S.M.D., Christopher L. Webber. *ANMP,* pp. 188–90.
2. Responsorial: *The Lord Is My Strength and My Might.* Text: NRSV. Psalm tone: Laurence Bevenot, 1986. Refrain: A. Gregory Murray, 1986. *PH90* #231.
3. Responsorial: *Psalm 118* (14–17, 22–24). Text: *Book of Common Prayer.* Setting: Peter R. Hallock. *PS93* #119. (See also *TIP/PSCY* #8.)
4. Responsorial: *Psalm 118* (1, 4–5, 14, 17, 24). Text: Taizé. Setting: Jacques Berthier. *PS93* #120. (See also *MFTII,* p. 51.)
5. Metrical: *This Is the Day the Lord Hath Made* (stanzas 3–5). Text: Isaac Watts. Tune: ARDEN. *RITL* #128. (See also *HB55* #69 to the Tune: ARLINGTON.)
6. Responsorial: *Alleluia! Let Us Rejoice!* (guitar) Words and music by David Haas. *CS/PFTCY,* vol. 3, p. 20.

See also *PH87* #118; *PR&T,* pp. 29 & 30.

Anthem
This Is the Day the Lord Hath Made, PH90 #230.

or Psalm 150
1. Metrical: *Praise the Lord, God's Glories Show.* Text: Henry Francis Lyte, alt. Tune: LLANFAIR. *PH90* #481. (See also *HB55* #4, *WB72* #552, and *RITL* #142.)
2. Responsorial: *Psalm 150.* Setting: Hal H. Hopson. *PS93* #157.
3. Responsorial: *Let Everything That Lives Give Praise to the Lord.* Text: Grail (see also *GPI,* p. 216). Refrain, psalm tone, and Gelineau tone: *WIII* #81. (See also *30P&2C,* p. 44.)

4. Responsorial: *Praise Ye the Lord.* Words and music by J. Jefferson Cleveland, 1981. *PH90* #258.

See also *ANMP,* p. 236; *SPJP,* p. 77; *PR&T,* pp. 39 & 80.

Anthem

Praise the Lord with Joyful Cry, Lawrence Bartlett (*Westminster Praise,* Hinshaw) unison (E).

Organ Music for the Day

1. *Prelude on* O FILII ET FILIAE (*O Sons and Daughters, Let Us Sing!, PH90* #116), Leo Sowerby (*Advent to Whitsuntide,* Hinrichsen Edition, Ltd. 743b).
2. *Prelude on* AZMON (*O for a Thousand Tongues to Sing, PH90* #466), Paul Manz (*Ten Chorale Improvisations,* Concordia 97-5556).

Hymns for the Day	HL33	HB55	WB72	PH90
Breathe on Me, Breath of God	213	235	–	316
How Clear Is Our Vocation, Lord	–	–	–	419
Jesus Comes with Clouds Descending	–	–	–	6
Lord, Speak to Me, That I May Speak	399	298	–	426
We Walk by Faith and Not by Sight	–	–	–	399
When We Are Living	–	–	–	400

THIRD SUNDAY OF EASTER (C)

Acts 9:1–6, (7–20) When Saul of Tarsus travels to Damascus, he bears the reputation of a feared, zealous persecutor of those who acknowledge Jesus as the Way. But when Saul departs from Damascus, he is an ardent advocate for the risen Christ. "On the way," Saul was blinded by the light, fell to the roadside, heard and obeyed a voice, experienced the touch of Ananias's hands, regained his sight, and was baptized. The tormentor of Christ has been transformed into a Spirit-filled propagator, who publicly proclaims Jesus as the Son of God, and who will suffer for the sake of the name of the Way.

Anthem

Saul, Egil Hovland (Walton Music) SATB and narrator (D).

Revelation 5:11–14 The prophet John weeps because there is no one worthy to open the seven-sealed scroll containing the proclamation of God's plan. But then he sees a lamb, a leader of the flock, apparently slain yet living. A slaughtered lamb who suffered for our sake, and rose for our sake, is worthy to open the scroll. No wonder the living creatures, elders, angels, numbering in the myriads, burst forth in song.

Anthem

Worthy Is the Lamb, G. F. Handel (*Messiah,* any edition) SATB (M).

John 21:1–19 A fish tale (vs. 1–8) about seven disciples who fish all night and catch nothing. At dawn, a stranger standing on the beach tells them to cast their net on the other side of the boat. They obey. Presto! Their net bulges with fish. Peter exclaims, "It is the Lord!" A eucharistic story (vs. 9–14) about the risen Christ taking bread and fish and giving it to the disciples, while gathered around a charcoal fire—the place of the denial of Jesus by Peter becomes the place at which Jesus forgives and feeds his disciples (cf. 18:18). A commissioning (vs. 15–19) in which Jesus asks Peter three times if he loves him. Following each of three affirmations by Peter, Jesus commissions him to feed his sheep.

Anthem

Feed My Lambs, Natalie Sleeth (Carl Fischer) unison, 2 flutes (E).

Psalm 30

1. Metrical: *Come Sing to God, O Living Saints.* Text: C.M.D., Fred R. Anderson. Tune: ELLACOMBE. *PH90* #18.
2. Responsorial: *Psalm 30* (1–2, 4–5, 11–12). Setting: Hal H. Hopson. Tone: William Byrd. *PS93* #27.

See also *WIII* #822; *ANMP,* p. 68; *PH87* #30; *PR&T,* pp. 45 & 79.

Anthem

Praise Ye, Heinrich Schütz (Belwin) 2-part (ME).

Organ Music for the Day

1. *Prelude on* O QUANTA QUALIA (*Blessing and Honor, PH90* #147), Emma L. Diemer (*Folk Hymn Sketches,* The Sacred Music Press KK 385).
2. *Choralpartita* on LOBE DEN HERREN (*Praise Ye the Lord, the Almighty, PH90* #482), Joseph Ahrens (B. Schotts Söhne 3813).

Hymns for the Day	HL33	HB55	WB72	PH90
Blessing and Honor and Glory and Power	196	137	311	147
God Bless Your Church with Strength!	–	–	–	418
O God, What You Ordain Is Right	291	366	633	284
Take My Life	242	310	–	391
The Church of Christ in Every Age	–	–	–	421
This Is the Feast of Victory	–	–	–	594

FOURTH SUNDAY OF EASTER (C)

Acts 9:36–43 The "widows"—today's "shopping bag ladies"—struggle to survive. These vulnerable, bottom-rung people are the ones to whom Tabitha (Dorcas, the Gazelle), a disciple of Christ, ministers. But she becomes ill and dies, as does her life-giving work. Do you believe in the power of God to bring new life to all persons, even to the helpless, the hopeless, the dying, and the dead? In God's new age, the "widows" will not be left to perish, for they will be restored by a bold word and an act of solidarity. God has promised to stand beside those who have neither power nor hope. "People of God, arise!"

Anthem
God Is Living, God Is Here, J. S. Bach (Oxford) SATB (ME).

Revelation 7:9–17 A vision of the glory and joy of the faithful in the New Age. A countless multitude composed of all peoples, tongues, nations, races, and tribes stands before the throne and the Lamb. Clothed in white robes (because they have been washed in the blood of the Lamb) and waving palm branches in their hands, the numberless throng, with angels, sing and shout acclamations. They serve God day and night. They experience the life of salvation where there is no more hunger, thirst, enervating heat, tears, or pain, for Christ their shepherd guides them to springs of eternal living water.

Anthem
Amen, Praise Ye the Lord, C. Hasse (Carl Fischer) SATB bass solo (E).

John 10:22–30 The Jews (the opposition) want a clear answer from Jesus to their question: "Are you the Christ?" Jesus seems to respond opaquely. "I told you. The works I do in my Father's name bear witness to me. My sheep hear me and follow me, and I give them eternal life." What Jesus really does is ask a plain counter-question: "Do you belong to my flock?"

Anthem
My Shepherd Will Supply My Need, Marie Pooler (Augsburg) unison or 2-part (E).

Psalm 23
1. Metrical: *The Lord's My Shepherd.* Text: The Scottish Psalter. Tune: CRIMOND. *PH90* #170; *HB55* #104. (Also Tunes: EVAN and BELMONT.)
2. Responsorial: *Psalm 23.* Text: Grail. Gelineau tone. *PS93* #18. See also *PS93* #19 & #20; *PH90* #171–#175; *PR&T*, pp. 72 & 77.

Anthem
The Lord Is My Shepherd, John Rutter (Oxford) SATB oboe (M).

Organ Music for the Day
1. *Prelude on* HANOVER (*Ye Servants of God, PH90* #477), C. Hubert H. Parry (*Seven Chorale Preludes,* Novello & Co., Ltd. 1547).
2. *Prelude on* ST. COLUMBA (*The King of Love My Shepherd Is, PH90* #171), Charles V. Stanford (*Six Short Preludes and Postludes for Organ,* Galaxy Music Corp. 3.0160).

Hymns for the Day	HL33	HB55	WB72	PH90
Blessed Assurance, Jesus Is Mine!	–	–	–	341
Cantad al Señor/O Sing to the Lord	–	–	–	472
Celebrate with Joy and Singing	–	–	–	107
Crown Him with Many Crowns	190	213	349	151
Down to Earth, as a Dove	–	–	–	300
Ye Servants of God, Your Master Proclaim	198	27	645	477

228

FIFTH SUNDAY OF EASTER (C)

Acts 11:1–18 "Peter," query some righteous believers in Judea, "what's this we hear about nonkosher people accepting the Word of God?" "God challenged me in a vision," recounts Peter. "I was called to a Gentile home in Caesarea, where I preached, and the same Spirit that came upon us at Pentecost was experienced by those at Caesarea. So said I, 'Who am I to obstruct the work of God?'" Silence then prevails among the pious criticizers, followed by praise to God for giving to "unacceptable people" the eternal gift.

Anthem

Let All the World in Every Corner Sing, Ralph Vaughan Williams, arr. Dale Wood (Sacred Music) SATB optional handbells, brass, and trumpet (ME).

Revelation 21:1–6 A vision of a new heaven and a new earth. The new Jerusalem descends from God and joins the transformed earth, where chaotic waters, tears, mourning, crying, death have all disappeared. Human beings will see God and live in holy fellowship together. Shouts the great voice from the throne, "I make all things new."

Anthem

And I Saw a New Heaven, Edgar Bainton (Novello) SATB (MD).

John 13:31–35 Christ gives God glory by living a life of simple, obedient love: seeking out the lost, the hurt, the suffering, the oppressed, the outcast. He lives a life of poverty and concern for others that ultimately earns him death on the cross. When he is lifted up on the cross to die for us, he gives God glory. He gives himself away in love for us, and commands us to love one another.

Anthem

I Give You a New Commandment, John Shepherd, ed. Watkins Shaw (Oxford) ATBB or TTBB (M).

Psalm 148

1. Metrical: *Let the Whole Creation Cry.* Text: Stopford A. Brooke, 1881. Tune: SALZBURG. Harmony, J. S. Bach. *PH90* #256.
2. Responsorial: *Psalm 148.* Setting: Hal H. Hopson. *PS93* #155.

See also *RITL* #141; *TIP/PSCY* #9; *PH90* #257; *H82* #432.

Anthem

Let the Whole Creation Cry, PH90 #256.

Organ Music for the Day

1. *Chorale Prelude on* UNSER HERRSCHER (*Open Now Thy Gates of Beauty, PH90* #489), Helmut Walcha (*Choralvorspiele,* C. F. Peters Corp. 4850).
2. *Prelude on* DIVINUM MYSTERIUM (*Of the Father's Love Begotten, PH90* #309), John Cook (*Festal Voluntaries—Christmas and Epiphany,* Novello & Co., Ltd. 1399).

Hymns for the Day	HL33	HB55	WB72	PH90
Great God, Your Love Has Called Us Here	–	–	–	353
Here, O Our Lord, We See You	352	442	418	520
Lord, Whose Love Through Humble Service	–	–	–	427
O God, What You Ordain Is Right	291	366	633	284
O Lord, You Gave Your Servant John	–	–	–	431
Spirit of the Living God	–	–	–	322

SIXTH SUNDAY OF EASTER (C)

Acts 16:9–15 A vision, a voice, a man of Macedonia, and mystery interrupted Paul's life in Asia. Therefore, he obediently set sail for Europe, "convinced that God had called us to proclaim the good news to them." Outreach is due to God's intervention. On the Sabbath day, Paul went to "a place of prayer by the river," where the Lord opened the heart of Lydia to listen eagerly to what Paul said. Result: Lydia embraces the gospel and her whole household is baptized. Conversion is due to God's initiative. Lydia believes, therefore she acts: Lydia extends hospitality to Paul and his friends.

Anthem

We Know That Christ Is Raised, Charles V. Stanford (Augsburg) SATB (E).

Revelation 21:10, 22–22:5 John gets a glimpse of the Holy City Jerusalem coming down out of heaven from God. He sees no temple, no natural light (sun), and no closed gates. Rather, the only necessary temple is the one of the Lord God Almighty and the Lamb; the glory of God and the lamp of the Lamb provide sufficient light; and the open-gated city admits friends and foes around the world who are now reconciled. Nothing unclean or profane enters, but only those whose names are inscribed in the Lamb's book of life.

Anthem

The Song of the Tree of Life, Ralph Vaughan Williams (Oxford) unison or 2-part (ME).

John 14:23–29 Says Jesus, "If you love me, then do (keep) my words (which are God's will)." When Jesus departs, God sends the Paraclete (companion interpreter) to teach us and remind us of the same words Jesus spoke.

Anthem

Peace I Leave with You, Knut Nystedt (Augsburg) SSATB (M).

or **John 5:1–9** On the sabbath, Jesus went up to Jerusalem. At a pool by the Sheep Gate lay many invalids—blind, lame, and paralyzed. A man who had been ill for thirty-eight years was asked by Jesus if he wanted to be made well. "Sir, I have no one to put me into the pool when the water is stirred up." Said Jesus, "Stand up, take up your mat, and walk." By the sheer, unmerited grace of God, the man was made well, took up his mat, and began to walk.

Anthem

O Christ, the Healer, PH90 #380.

Psalm 67

1. Metrical: *God of Mercy, God of Grace*. Text: H. F. Lyte, alt. Tune: IMPACT. *PH90* #203. (See also *RITL* #108 to the Tune: HEATHLANDS or *H82* #538 to the Tune: LUCERNA LAUDONIAE.)
2. Responsorial: *Psalm 67*. Text: NRSV. Psalm tone: Laurence Bevenot. Refrain: Marie Kremer. PH90 #202.
3. Responsorial: *Psalm 67*. Setting: Hal H. Hopson. Tone: Gregorian VIf. *PS93* #59 and #60 (with tone based on Eastern Orthodox tone).
4. Responsorial: *May God Be Merciful to Us*. Text: *Book of Common Prayer*. Music: Peter R. Hallock. *TIP/PSCY* #13.
5. Responsorial: *Psalm 67*. Setting by Arthur Wills in *Popular Psalm Settings*, The Year Book Press, 76-14115.

See also *ANMP*, p. 110; *PH87* #67; *SPJP*, p. 39; *WIII* #783; *PR&T*, pp. 80 & 83.

Anthem

Psalm 67, John D. Horman (Choristers Guild) unison and SATB optional handbells, flute, and congregation (E).

Organ Music for the Day
1. *Prelude on* MORNING SONG (*O Holy City, Seen of John, PH90* #453), Richard Warner (*New Every Morning,* The Sacred Music Press).
2. *Prelude on* DOWN AMPNEY (*Come Down, O Love Divine, PH90* #313), John Gardner (*Five Hymn Tune Preludes,* Novello & Co., Ltd. 1475).

Hymns for the Day	*HL33*	*HB55*	*WB72*	*PH90*
Blessed Jesus, at Your Word	–	–	309	454
Come Down, O Love Divine	–	–	334	313
Eternal God, Whose Power Upholds	–	485	357	412
O Holy City, Seen of John	409	508	505	453
O Worship the King, All Glorious Above	2	26	533	476
Yee Jun Ae Joo Nim Eul Nae Ka Mol La/				
When I Had Not Yet Learned of Jesus	–	–	–	410

THE ASCENSION OF THE LORD (ABC)

See The Ascension of the Lord (ABC) in Year A, p. 87.

SEVENTH SUNDAY OF EASTER (C)

Acts 16:16–34 In the Roman city of Philippi, Paul and Silas are stripped, whipped, and imprisoned on trumped-up charges because when they restored a soothsayer to health, they deprived some local owners of further exploitative economic gain. But an earthquake (divine intervention?) turns the city upside down, allowing the jailer and his household to hear the gospel and to be baptized. The story of defeat transformed into victory continues.

Anthem
Christ Sends the Spirit, Richard Proulx (Augsburg) SAB flute, optional congregation (ME).

Revelation 22:12–14, 16–17, 20–21 "Behold, I am coming soon. I am the Alpha and the Omega. Blessed are those who wash their robes in preparation for entry into the city, and for partaking of the tree of life." The Spirit and the Bride say, "Come." And those who are thirsty for the water of life may say, "Come." Amen. Come, Lord Jesus!

Anthem
E'en So, Lord Jesus, Quickly Come, Paul Manz (Concordia) SATB (MD).

John 17:20–26 In the upper room, Jesus concludes his great prayer by praying for us and all others in all times and places who believe in him, so that we may all be one in the same way the Father and Son are one. Such union with Christ and with each other will manifest to the world the mission and work of Christ that the Father sent him to do.

Anthem
Draw Us in the Spirit's Tether, Harold Friedell, *PH90* #504 or (H. W. Gray) SATB (ME).

Psalm 97
1. Responsorial: *A Light Will Shine on This Day.* Text: Grail (see also *GPI,* p. 139). Psalm tone and Gelineau tone: *WIII* #780.
2. Responsorial: *Psalm 97.* Setting: Hal H. Hopson. *PS93* #93.
See also *ANMP,* p. 159; *SPJP,* p. 51; *PH87* #97; *PR&T,* pp. 11 & 13.

Anthem
The Lord Is King O'er Land and Sea, Heinrich Schütz (*Four Psalms,* Mercury) SATB (E).

Organ Music for the Day
1. *Prelude on* DARWALL'S 148TH (*Rejoice, the Lord Is King, PH90* #155), Harold Darke (*Three Chorale Preludes,* Novello & Co., Ltd. 1452).
2. *Chorale Prelude on* WIE SCHÖN LEUCHTET (*O Morning Star, PH90* #69), J. P. Kirnberger (*Die Orgel,* Fr. Kistner & C.F.W. Siegel & Co. 30338).

Hymns for the Day	HL33	HB55	WB72	PH90
Earth's Scattered Isles and Contoured Hills	–	–	–	152
Of the Father's Love Begotten	–	7	534	309
O Morning Star, How Fair and Bright	321	415	521	69
O Praise the Gracious Power	–	–	–	471
Rejoice, the Lord Is King	193	140	562	155
We All Are One in Mission	–	–	–	435

Pentecost

THE DAY OF PENTECOST (C)

Acts 2:1–21 Wind and tongues of fire—the Holy Spirit—spread among all the believers. Are they drunk? "No," says Peter, "it's only nine in the morning. But while I have your attention, let me tell you about Jesus Christ."

Anthems

Whitsunday Canticle, Erik Routley (*Two for Pentecost,* Hinshaw) SATB (ME). *The Day of Pentecost,* John A. Nickson (Kjos) SATB narrator (M).

or **Genesis 11:1–9** The inflammable combination of the fear of loss of control *and* pretentious "possibility thinking" ignites a drivenness to make a name and a place for ourselves, in the name of religion. Such foolish, self-reliant crusades always end in babbling chaos.

Anthem

On Pentecost They Gathered, PH90 #128.

Romans 8:14–17 An exhortation to live not according to the anxiety and fear of human nature but in harmony with the life-giving Spirit. Though we constantly get tangled in the slavery of our pious self-interest and cravings for acceptance, God's Spirit works among us to create a new relationship that enables us to cry out boldly, "Abba!"

Anthems

As Many as Are Led by the Spirit, David McKay Williams (H. W. Gray) SATB (M). *Therefore, Give Us Love,* Daniel Moe (Augsburg) 2-part mixed (E).

or **Acts 2:1–21** See above.

John 14:8–17, (25–27) All of Jesus' life was a revelation of God—his words and deeds were ultimately God's. So whoever believes in and loves God and Jesus will speak and do the words and deeds of Jesus. How? God sends the Paraclete (companion interpreter) to teach and remind us of Jesus' words and deeds so we can speak them and live them.

Anthems

If Ye Love Me, Thomas Tallis (Boosey & Hawkes) SATB (ME). *Peace I Leave with You,* Walter Pelz (Augsburg) SATB (M).

Psalm 104:24–34, 35b

1. Metrical: *Bless the Lord with All My Being.* Text: 8.7.8.7.D, Fred R. Anderson. Tune: RUSTINGTON. *PH90* #224. For text only see *SPJP,* p. 56.
2. Responsorial: *Psalm 104* (1–9). Text: Grail. Tone and Refrain: Presbyterian 3. *PS93* #104.
3. Responsorial: *Psalm 104* (24, 27–34). Text: Arlo D. Duba. Setting: Richard T. Proulx. *PS93* #105.
4. Responsorial: *Lord, Send Out Your Spirit.* Setting by Robert Edward Smith. *CC* G-2122.
5. Responsorial: *Lord, How Manifold Are Your Works!* (25–35). Text: *Book of Common Prayer.* Music: Peter R. Hallock. *TIP/PSCY* #10.

See also *ANMP,* p. 174; *PH87* #104; *PR&T,* pp. 34 & 35.

Anthem

O Lord, How Manifold Are Thy Works, Martin Shaw (Novello) unison (ME).

Organ Music for the Day

1. *Prelude on* VENI CREATOR SPIRITUS/KOMM GOTT SCHÖPFER (*Come, Holy Spirit, Our Souls Inspire, PH90* #125), Nicolas de Grigny (*Organ Book,* Edwin F. Kalmus 4147).

2. *Chorale Prelude on* NUN DANKET ALL' UND BRINGET EHR' (*Spirit Divine, Attend Our Prayers, PH90* #325), Wilbur Held (*Hymn Preludes for the Pentecost Season*, Concordia 97–5517).

Hymns for the Day	HL33	HB55	WB72	PH90
Blessed Jesus, at Your Word	–	–	309	454
Come Down, O Love Divine	–	–	334	313
Come, O Spirit	–	–	–	127
Come, O Spirit, Dwell Among Us	–	–	–	129
Hail Thee, Festival Day!	–	–	–	120
Like the Murmur of the Dove's Song	–	–	–	314

Ordinary Time
TRINITY SUNDAY
[FIRST SUNDAY AFTER PENTECOST] (C)

Proverbs 8:1–4, 22–31 I, Wisdom, was present at the ordering of creation, when YHWH had yet to shape the springs of water, mountains, hills, and fields; when the sky and horizon were positioned; when clouds were placed in the sky above, seas were opened below, and boundaries were set for ocean tides. At that time, I was beside YHWH like an architect and a firstborn child, constantly rejoicing in creation and delighting in the human race.

Anthems
All Wisdom Is from the Lord, William Mathias (Oxford) SATB (M). *My Crown of Creation,* Charles W. Ore (Morningstar) SATB (ME).

Romans 5:1–5 Whether we know it or not, our social world unceasingly tempts us to seek acceptance by being someone, owning something, or living somewhere. Futilely striving to prove our worth, we are hemmed in, restricted, hampered, overburdened, and, eventually, entrapped by "one thing more to achieve." To survive, we submit to a crinkled-up squatting position. Good news! We can stand up straight and rejoice, because we are justified by faith and have peace with God through Jesus Christ. God, who came to us in Jesus Christ, totally accepts us—even our hate and our guilt.

Anthems
Holy Spirit, Lord of Light, Henry Kihlken (AMSI) SATB (ME). *Lord, Grant Grace,* Orlando Gibbons (Concordia) SATB/SATB (M).

John 16:12–15 "When the Spirit of truth comes, he will guide you into all the truth. . . . He will glorify me," says Jesus in his farewell discourse. The same word and work of God will continue to be disclosed by the Spirit of truth, who will instruct you on a way of life that conforms to Jesus Christ.

Anthems
Creating God, Your Fingers Trace, Walter Pelz (Agape) SATB, flute, optional congregation (E). *Hymn to the Trinity,* Paul Lindsley Thomas (Unicorn Music) SATB, optional brass (M).

Psalm 8
1. Metrical: *O Lord, Our God, How Excellent.* Text: Fred R. Anderson. Tune: WINCHESTER OLD. *PH90* #162. For text only see *SPJP*, p. 15.
2. Responsorial: *Psalm 8.* Setting: Hal H. Hopson. *PS93* #5.
See also *PH90* #163; *HB55* #95; *WIII* #861; *ANMP*, p. 44; *PR&T*, pp. 37 & 52.

Anthem
How Excellent Thy Name, Howard Hanson (Carl Fischer) SATB (MD).

Organ Music for the Day
1. *Chorale Prelude on* ALLEIN GOTT IN DER HÖH' (*All Glory Be to God on High, PH90* #133), Johann S. Bach, Georg Böhm, and Johann G. Walther (*The Church Organist's Golden Treasury,* Oliver Ditson Co.).
2. *Prelude on* NICAEA (*Holy, Holy, Holy!, PH90* #138), Healey Willan (*Thirty-Six Short Preludes and Postludes,* C. F. Peters Corp. 6161).

Hymns for the Day	HL33	HB55	WB72	PH90
Ancient of Days	58	46	297	–
Come, Holy Spirit, Heavenly Dove	–	–	–	126
Holy Ghost, Dispel Our Sadness	–	–	–	317
Holy, Holy, Holy!	57	11	421	138
Stand Up and Bless the Lord	–	–	–	491
O Word of God Incarnate	215	251	532	327

SUNDAY BETWEEN MAY 29 AND JUNE 4
(PROPER 4) [9] (C) [*USE ONLY IF AFTER TRINITY SUNDAY*]*

1 Kings 18:20–21, (22–29), 30–39 Drought has bred famine. Starvation stalks people and animals. Who can overcome this death-dealing drought, King Ahab's Baal *or* Elijah's YHWH? The impediment to choosing: our "limp" (serving two masters). Baal responds to the challenge with "no voice, and no answer," exposing himself as a fraudulent "no-god." The promise-keeping YHWH, however, surprises: stones, wood, a drenched burnt offering, Elijah's prayer—the fire of the Lord descends. The people confess, "YHWH reigns!"

Anthem
Elijah!, Dale Wood (Choristers Guild) unison or SATB (ME).

Galatians 1:1–12 A letter from Paul to the churches of Galatia: Grace and peace to you. So much for greetings, on to the harangue proper. "I am shocked that you Galatians are so quickly deserting Christ (who called you by sheer grace) and turning your allegiance to the false teachings of seductive agitators. Let an anathema come upon any who pervert the gospel of Christ."

Anthem
Close in My Breast, Thy Perfect Love, David Lord (*Anthems for Choirs*, vol. 2, Oxford) 2-part (ME).

Luke 7:1–10 Town leaders pressure Jesus to heal a deserving centurion's slave. But the centurion says to Jesus, "Lord, I am not worthy; I am a sinner. But say the word, and my servant will be healed, for I understand the power of real authority." Jesus marvels that "not even in Israel, God's chosen people, have I found such faith."

Anthem
O Lord, I Am Not Worthy, Melchior Franck (Concordia) SATB (ME).

Psalm 96
1. *Metrical*: *O Sing a New Song to the Lord*. Text: Charles H. Gabriel, alt. Tune: GONFALON ROYAL. *PH90* #216.
2. *Responsorial*: *Psalm 96*. Text: *A New Zealand Prayer Book*. Refrain: Clifford W. Howell. Tone: Gregorian V. Harmony, Robert J. Batastini. *PS93* #91.
See also *ANMP*, p. 158; *PH87* #96; *PH90* #217; *PR&T*, pp. 10 & 13.

Anthem
Sing a New Song, Heinrich Schütz, arr. Carolyn Jennings (Belwin) SATB flute, string bass (ME).

Organ Music for the Day
1. *Chorale Prelude on* LASST UNS ERFREUEN (*From All That Dwell Below . . .*, Psalm 117, *PH90* #229), H. Schroeder (B. Schotts Söhne ED 5426).
2. *Chorale Prelude on* OLD HUNDREDTH (*All People That on . . .*, *PH90* #220), P. Hurford (*Ceremonial Music for Organ*, Oxford 375120–8).

Hymns for the Day	HL33	HB55	WB72	PH90
Dear Lord and Father of Mankind	302	416	350	345
How Firm a Foundation	283	369	425	361
Live Into Hope	–	–	–	332
O God of Earth and Altar	419	511	497	291
The God of Heaven	–	–	–	180
When We Are Tempted to Deny Your Son	–	–	640	86

*NOTE: If the Sunday between May 24 and May 28 follows Trinity Sunday, use readings for the Sunday between February 25 and 29 (C) on that day.

SUNDAY BETWEEN JUNE 5 AND JUNE 11
(PROPER 5) [10] (C) [*USE ONLY IF AFTER TRINITY SUNDAY*]

1 Kings 17:8–16, (17–24) In a time of dried-up brooks and faith, and withering trust in the Lord, YHWH sends Elijah to a poor, foreign widow for food. She has only enough flour and oil for a last meal before she and her son starve. "Fear not!" counters Elijah. Miraculously, the widow trusts this word, and risks all she has. But when her son falls deathly ill she accuses Elijah, who then cries out to YHWH. In the face of death, life comes by God's word through ordinary human beings. Result: The widow confesses Elijah's authority—"Now I know the word of YHWH in your mouth is truth."

Anthem
Praise the Lord, Ye Servants, Richard Peek (Belwin-Mills) unison (E).

Galatians 1:11–24 Opponents of Paul have questioned his dubious credentials, for everyone knows Paul's reputation as a persecutor of Christians. Paul's rebuttal: "I was a faithful, law-abiding Jew who zealously obeyed the traditions of my people. But when the risen Christ revealed himself to me through his grace, then by his authority I pursued a different path, preaching to Gentiles the faith that I once tried to destroy. And now others glorify God because of me."

Anthem
Listen, Crystal LaPoint Kowalski (Hinshaw) 2-part mixed (E).

Luke 7:11–17 Jesus sees a funeral procession in Nain—a widow burying her only son, her only source of support. He empathizes with her *but* says, "Do not weep." He then jolts everyone by breaking the law when he touches the bier, and commands the young man to arise. Jesus restores the relationship between mother and son; he heals separation caused even by death.

Anthem
O for a Thousand Tongues, Carl G. Gläser, arr. Theron Kirk (Oxford) SATB (E).

Psalm 146
1. Metrical: *I'll Praise My Maker While I've Breath.* Text: Isaac Watts, alt. Tune: OLD 113TH. *PH90* #253. (See also *RITL* #140.)
2. Responsorial: *Psalm 146* (5–10). Text: NRSV. Psalm tone: Howard Hughes. Refrain: John Schiavone. *PH90* #254.

See also *PS93* #150–152; *ANMP,* p. 228; *SPJP,* p. 65; *PH87* #146.

Anthem
Praise the Lord, John Rutter (Oxford) SATB optional brass (M).

Organ Music for the Day
1. *Chorale Prelude on* O MENSCH, BEWEIN' DEIN' SÜNDE GROSS (*I'll Praise My Maker,* Psalm 146, OLD 113TH, *PH90* #253), Johann Sebastian Bach (various editions), and Gilbert Martin (OLD 113TH, *Pipe Dusters,* Lorenz Industries KK 383).
2. *Prelude on* DARWALL'S 148TH (*Rejoice, the Lord Is King, PH90* #155), John Gardner (*Five Hymn Tune Preludes,* Novello & Co., Ltd. 1475).

Hymns for the Day	HL33	HB55	WB72	PH90
Down to Earth, as a Dove	–	–	–	300
Great God, Your Love Has Called Us . . .	–	–	–	353
Great God, We Sing That Mighty Hand	470	527	408	265
O for a Thousand Tongues to Sing	199	141	493	466
Praise the Lord, God's Glories Show	12	4	552	481
Your Faithfulness, O Lord, Is Sure	–	–	–	251

SUNDAY BETWEEN JUNE 12 AND JUNE 18
(PROPER 6) [11] (C) [*USE ONLY IF AFTER TRINITY SUNDAY*]

1 Kings 21:1–10,(11–14),15–21a In expropriating Naboth's vineyard, King Ahab and Queen Jezebel did everything right and nothing wrong, according to the law. But they did everything wrong and nothing right, according to God's ethics; they are guilty of insidious murder and acquisitive land-grabbing, announces YHWH's speaker, Elijah. Now Ahab will have to live with the consequences of his killing and seizing—his dynasty will end.

Anthem
Wash Me Thoroughly . . ., G. F. Handel (Hinshaw) 2-part (E).

Galatians 2:15–21 "Peter," says Paul, "you and I are Jews by birth, so we learned to keep the obligations of the law. Yet we know a person receives God's favorable judgment not by human achievements but by faith in Jesus Christ. So why should Gentiles, who were never under the law, be compelled to obey it? Because the law is from God? Don't you remember that Christ, who died to the law, redeemed us from its curse? Why then try to rebuild it? We have been put to death with Christ on his cross and now live in Christ."

Anthem
My Faith Looks Up to Thee, Lowell Mason, arr. Erik Routley (Agape) SATB (E).

Luke 7:36–8:3 Simon the Pharisee invites Jesus to an elegant dinner party at which a "woman of the streets" washes Jesus' feet with her tears, wipes them with her hair, kisses them, and pours costly perfume on them. Simon is appalled that Jesus allows such a sinner to touch him. So Jesus tells a story about a creditor who forgave two bankrupt debtors. Which debtor will love him more? Replies Simon, "The one who was forgiven more." Right! Have we and Simon forgotten how much we've been forgiven?

Anthem
A Litany, William Walton (Oxford) SATB (M).

Psalm 5:1–8
1. Metrical: *As Morning Dawns, Lord, Hear Our Cry.* Text: L.M., Fred R. Anderson. Tune: WAREHAM. *PH90* #161. For text only see *SPJP,* p. 14.
2. Responsorial: *Psalm 5:1–8.* Setting: Hal H. Hopson. *PS93* #4.
See also *20P&3C,* p. 2; *PH87* #5; *PR&T,* pp. 43 & 65.

Anthems
Hear My Words, Stephen Paulus (Hinshaw) 2-part mixed (E). *Lead Me, Lord,* S. S. Wesley (Oxford) SATB alto solo (E).

Organ Music for the Day
1. *Prelude on* WAREHAM (*As Morning Dawns,* Psalm 5, *PH90* #161),C. S. Lang, Richard Hillert (*The Concordia Hymn Prelude Series,* vol. 41, Concordia 97–5859).
2. *Prelude on* IN BABILONE (*There's a Wideness . . .,* *PH90* #298), D. S. Harris (*Ten Hymn Preludes in Trio Style,* H. W. Gray Co., Inc. GB 632).

Hymns for the Day	HL33	HB55	WB72	PH90
Alleluia, Alleluia! Give Thanks	–	–	–	106
Forgive Our Sins as We Forgive	–	–	–	347
I Greet Thee, Who My Sure Redeemer Art	–	144	625	457
O Praise the Gracious Power	–	–	–	471
What Wondrous Love Is This	–	–	–	85
When We Are Tempted to Deny Your Son	–	–	640	86

SUNDAY BETWEEN JUNE 19 AND JUNE 25
(PROPER 7) [12] (C) [*USE ONLY IF AFTER TRINITY SUNDAY*]

1 Kings 19:1–4, (5–7), 8–15a By relying on YHWH's power, Elijah triumphs over the Baal priests. Queen Jezebel, however, seeks revenge against Elijah, who flees into the wilderness. "Take my life, Lord," Elijah laments, "victory has turned into defeat, life into death." Instead, an angel cares for Elijah until he is restored and able to walk forty days into the Sinai where he hides in a cave. Asks YHWH, "What are you doing here?" "I'm the only faithful one left," responds Elijah self-righteously. So YHWH commands him to stand upon the mount, and then sends a wind, earthquake, and fire, followed by a majestic "still small voice." YHWH again asks, "What are you doing here?" Elijah complains, "It's me against the world." YHWH: "Go, return."

Anthem

Open, Lord, My Inward Ear, Malcolm Williamson (*Ecumenical Praise,* number 31, Hope) unison (E).

Galatians 3:23–29 Paul tells the Galatians: Law was an intermediate guardian for us minors while God's purposes were coming to maturity. But now that the full revelation has taken place in the coming of Christ, you all are freed from such a custodian, for in Christ you all are heirs, through faith. As you were baptized into union with Christ, you became new people, clothed in Christ's way of living. Regardless of human categories of cultural or religious heritage, socioeconomic class, or gender, "You are all one in Christ," which qualifies you as Abraham's descendants.

Anthem

Because You Are God's Chosen Ones, G. Alan Smith (Hope) (E).

Luke 8:26–39 The Gerasenes hear that Jesus healed a demon-possessed person (a wild man "out of his mind"). The demon(s), however, recognize the power of God in Jesus, Son of the Most High, and shrink back, begging not to be returned to the abyss. So Jesus dismisses these destructive powers into a herd of swine who run headlong into the lake and drown. The curious Gerasenes now see a man restored to his "right mind," "sitting at the feet of Jesus," asking to be a disciple. Jesus, however, commands the man to return home, to show and tell the story of God's unmerited, healing love to the "mentally healthy" Gerasenes, who are so petrified of losing their old selves that they demand that Jesus leave town.

Anthem

The Kingdom of God, Austin Lovelace (Hope) SATB (E).

Psalm 42
1. Metrical: *As Deer Long for the Streams.* Text: L.M.,Christopher L. Webber. Tune: ROCKINGHAM. *PH90* #189. For text only see *ANMP,* p. 94.
2. Responsorial: *My Soul Is Thirsting for the Lord.* Text: NRSV. Psalm tone: Douglas Mews, 1986. Refrain: J. Gelineau, 1986. *PH90* #190. For Grail text and Gelineau tone: *WIII* #37. (See also *WIII* #825 for alternate refrain and psalm tone.)
3. Responsorial: *Psalm 42.* Text: Grail. Refrain: Gelineau. Tone: Frederick A. Gore Ouseley. *PS93* #37.
See also *HB55* #322; *ANMP,* p. 94; *RITL* #101; *PR&T,* pp. 45 & 48.

and **Psalm 43**
1. Metrical: *Defend Me, Lord, from Those Who Charge Me.* Text: Marie J. Post. Tune: GENEVAN 43. *PH87* #43.
2. Responsorial: *Psalm 43.* Text: Grail. Refrain: Gelineau. Tone: Frederick A. Gore Ouseley. *PS93* #38.

3. Responsorial: *I Will Go to the Altar of the Lord.* Text: Grail. Refrain, psalm tone, and Gelineau tone: *WIII* #38. (See also *24P&1C*, p. 14.) For text only see *GPI*, p. 59 and *GGP*, p. 64.

See also *ANMP*, p. 94; *RITL* # 101; *PR&T*, pp. 42 & 48.

Anthem

Psalm 43, Felix Mendelssohn, ed. Lloyd Pfautsch (Hope) SSAATTBB (M).

Organ Music for the Day

1. *Prelude on* ROCKINGHAM (*As Deer Long for the Streams*, Psalm 42, *PH90* #189), Norman Gilbert (*Festal Voluntaries—Lent, Passiontide, and Palm Sunday*, Novello & Co., Ltd. 1404).
2. *Prelude on* BUNESSAN (*Baptized in Water, PH90* #492), Paul Manz (*Ten Chorale Improvisations*, Concordia 97–5556).

Hymns for the Day	HL33	HB55	WB72	PH90
Baptized in Water	–	–	–	492
Christ, You Are the Fullness	–	–	–	346
Dear Lord and Father of Mankind	302	416	350	345
God of Compassion, in Mercy Befriend Us	290	122	392	261
In Christ There Is No East or West	341	479	435	439, 440
To God Be the Glory	–	–	–	485

SUNDAY BETWEEN JUNE 26 AND JULY 2
(PROPER 8) [13] (C)

2 Kings 2:1–2, 6–14 On his last journey, Elijah tests Elisha three times concerning his loyalty; each time Elisha vows lifelong commitment. Even the prophets' guilds fail to deter Elisha from following Elijah to the very end. Upon reaching the Jordan, Elijah parts the waters with his mantle in Moses-like fashion. After crossing, Elijah says to Elisha, "What shall I do for you, before I am taken from you?" Elisha asks for a "double share of your *ruach* (spirit, wind)." He asks for the creative power of YHWH, which liberates. Then fire and wind whisk away Elijah while Elisha laments. But then he takes up the mantle of Elijah, and parts the Jordan in Moses-like fashion.

Anthem
Rekindle the Spirit, Gerhard Krapf (*Six Scriptural Affirmations,* Sacred Music) 2-part mixed (E).

Galatians 5:1, 13–25 Paul tells the Galatians: Christ freed you from the slavery of law in order to set you free to be "servants of one another," to love your neighbor as yourself. If you abuse your freedom by producing works of the flesh, then you destroy others as well as yourself and shall not inherit the kingdom of God. But those who belong to Christ Jesus have crucified the flesh and, therefore, can freely produce fruits of the Spirit.

Anthem
The Fruit of the Spirit Is Love, J. Christian Geisler (Boosey & Hawkes) SATB flute (M).

Luke 9:51–62 As the days draw near when Jesus is "to be received up," he sets his face firmly toward Jerusalem. Because of his commitment, however, some Samaritans will not receive him. His disciples want to punish them, but Jesus rebukes his disciples. They meet some people who want to follow Jesus wherever he is going. "Follow me," invites Jesus, "proclaim the kingdom of God in which we are going to live." Many, however, are tempted to cling to family, job, socioeconomic responsibilities—more rewarding possibilities?

Anthem
The King's Highway, David McKay Williams (H. W. Gray) SATB (M).

Psalm 77:1–2, 11–20
1. Metrical: *I Cried Out to God to Help Me.* Text: Helen Otte. Tune: GENEVAN 77. *PH87* #77 (stanzas 3–4).
2. Responsorial: *Psalm 77:1–2, 11–20.* Text: *A New Zealand Prayer Book.* Setting: Howard Hughes. *PS93* #66.

See also *GGP,* p. 108 (stanzas 5*b*–9); *PR&T,* pp. 36 & 60.

Anthem
I Cry Aloud to God, Lois Land (Plymouth) SATB alto solo (ME).

Organ Music for the Day
1. *Prelude on* MARYTON (*O Master, Let Me Walk with Thee, PH90* #357), Gilbert M. Martin (Lorenz Industries KK 420).
2. *Prelude on* ST. BRIDE (*Make Me a Captive, Lord, PH90* #378), Theodore Beck (*The Parish Organist,* vol. 12, Concordia 97–4759).

Hymns for the Day	HL33	HB55	WB72	PH90
Christ of the Upward Way	277	295	–	344
Eternal God, Whose Power Upholds	–	485	357	412
God the Spirit, Guide and Guardian	–	–	–	588
Make Me a Captive, Lord	247	308	–	378
O Master, Let Me Walk with Thee	364	304	520	357
Today We All Are Called to Be Disciples	–	–	–	434

SUNDAY BETWEEN JULY 3 AND JULY 9
(PROPER 9) [14] (C)

2 Kings 5:1–14 Naaman, a Syrian military commander, suffers from leprosy. Hearing that healing is possible in Israel, he packs his bags and travels to see the king. But the only thing he receives from the king of Israel is the royal runaround—the king is unable to heal Naaman and knows it. But Elisha, the simple man of God, instructs Naaman to wash himself in the Jordan. This makes no sense to Naaman, for he could have done that back home; so he goes away in a rage. At the insistence of his servants, however, Naaman does wash and miraculously is made clean. He almost missed this experience because of his preconceived expectations of God's healing word.

Anthem
I Have Longed for Thy Saving Health, O Lord, William Byrd (H. W. Gray) SATB (ME).

Galatians 6:(1–6), 7–16 Paul's final words to the Galatians: "Don't kid yourselves; God is not mocked. You are accountable for what you do and say. What you sow, you shall reap. Remember, the only thing you may glory in is the cross—the sign of the powers of the old order who humiliated and seemingly defeated our Lord Jesus Christ. Yet by the cross Christ transforms those who constitute God's people into a new creation of mercy and peace."

Anthem
Lift High the Cross, Donald Busarow (Augsburg) SATB (ME).

Luke 10:1–11, 16–20 Jesus appoints seventy others to go out into the world and harvest a ripe crop before it spoils in the field. He sends them ahead of himself, as lambs in the midst of wolves, to announce that "the kingdom of God has come near to you." In the face of adversity, the Seventy discover the incredible power of their Lord's words, but their real joy is in learning that God embraces them forever.

Anthem
Thy Truth Is Great, Ron Nelson (Boosey & Hawkes) SATB (M).

Psalm 30
1. Metrical: *Come Sing to God, O Living Saints.* Text: C.M.D., Fred R. Anderson. Tune: ELLACOMBE. *PH90* #181.
2. Responsorial: *Psalm 30* (1–2, 4–5, 11–12). Setting: Hal H. Hopson. Tone: William Byrd. *PS93* #27.
3. Responsorial: *I Will Praise You, Lord.* Text: Grail (see also *GPI,* p. 36). Refrain, psalm tone, and Gelineau tone: *WIII* #822.
See also *HB55* #127; *RITL* #96 to the Tune: MEIRIONYDD; *ANMP,* p. 68.

Anthem
Praise Ye the Lord, H. Schütz (Belwin Mills) 2-part mixed (ME).

Organ Music for the Day
1. *Prelude on* RATHBUN (*In the Cross of Christ I Glory, PH90* #84), Gordon Young (*Hymn Preludes for the Church Service,* H. Flammer, Inc. HF-5005).
2. *Prelude on* ELLACOMBE (*Come Sing to God, PH90* #181), Hans A. Metzger (*The Parish Organist,* vol. 7, Concordia 97–1403).

Hymns for the Day	HL33	HB55	WB72	PH90
Beneath the Cross of Jesus	162	190	308	92
In the Cross of Christ I Glory	154	195	437	84
Lord, You Give the Great Commission	–	–	–	429
Lord, Make Us Servants of Your Peace	–	–	–	374
Our God, to Whom We Turn	–	128	–	278
When I Survey the Wondrous Cross	152	198	635	100, 101

SUNDAY BETWEEN JULY 10 AND JULY 16
(PROPER 10) [15] (C)

Amos 7:7–17 A vision of destruction in which a plumb line is YHWH's gauge, by which Israel's foundation of justice and faithfulness are measured and found to be out-of-kilter. The inevitable consequences of their sinfulness: the people will be destroyed. When Amos's preaching reaches the ears of the political-religious establishment, the results are predictable. The in-house priest, Amaziah, obtains royal sanction for his marching order to Amos: "Love it, or leave it." Amos, however, answers Amaziah's threat with a further promise of YHWH's judgment.

Anthem
God, Bring Thy Sword, Ron Nelson (Boosey & Hawkes) SATB (D).

Colossians 1:1–14 Intercessory prayers are offered for the community of faith to be filled with the gifts of the knowledge of God's will, the wisdom and understanding wrought by the Spirit, and strength, power, endurance, and patience so the people will conduct themselves in a manner pleasing to God. The community is then exhorted to offer joyful thanks to God for having made them fit to be transferred from the realm of darkness to "the saints in light" (or the kingdom of light made known in Jesus Christ). God authorizes them—and us—to participate in the deliverance and redemption in Christ; therefore, praise God with thanksgiving.

Anthem
God Is Life, Domenico Scarlatti, adapted by Helenclair Lowe (Choristers Guild) unison (E).

Luke 10:25–37 A lawyer tests Jesus' teaching ability, but ends up reciting the commandment to love God *and* neighbor. Whereupon, Jesus tells a story about a traveler victimized by some robbers. Well-intentioned, concerned people are unable to help the injured pilgrim because they must fulfill their responsibilities. But an irreligious, despicable, villainous Samaritan sees the needy, broken person and shows neighborly compassion and mercy. Scandalous! God sends grace to us in neighbors whom we reject.

Anthem
Prayer for Partnership, Tom Mitchell (Choristers Guild) SAB or SATB (E).

Psalm 82
1. Metrical: *There Where the Judges Gather.* Text: Henry Zylstra. Tune: MEIRIONYDD. *PH87* #82.
2. Responsorial: *Psalm 82.* Text: *Book of Common Prayer.* Refrain: Howard Hughes. Tone: Gregorian IVa. Harmony, Kenneth E. Williams. *PS93* #73.
3. Responsorial: *God Stands in the Divine Assembly.* Text: Grail. Gelineau tone: *GGP,* p. 118. For text only see *GPI,* p. 119.
4. Responsorial: Text: optional. Psalm tones and refrains by Hal H. Hopson. *PR&T,* pp. 1 & 15.

Anthem
The Lord Will Come and Not Be Slow, arr. Henry G. Ley (*The Oxford Easy Anthem Book,* number 18, Oxford) SATB (ME).

Organ Music for the Day
1. *Chorale Prelude on* JESU DULCIS MEMORIA (*Jesus, Thou Joy of Loving Hearts, PH90* #511), Flor Peeters (*Ten Chorale Preludes on Gregorian Hymns,* C. F. Peters Corp. 6090), and Jean Langlais (*Méditation, Suite Médiévale,* Francis Salabert Editions).
2. *Prelude on* AZMON (*O for a Thousand Tongues to Sing, PH90* #466), Austin C. Lovelace (*Eight Hymn Preludes,* Augsburg 11–9144).

Hymns for the Day	HL33	HB55	WB72	PH90
Christian Women, Christian Men	–	–	–	348
Lord God of Hosts, Whose Purpose	368	288	460	–
O for a Thousand Tongues to Sing	199	141	493	466
O Jesus Christ, May Grateful Hymns	–	–	509	424
We Are Your People	–	–	–	436
We Meet You, O Christ	–	–	–	311

SUNDAY BETWEEN JULY 17 AND JULY 23
(PROPER 11) [16] (C)

Amos 8:1–12 A vision of a basket of *qayits* ("summer fruit," e.g., apples and pears) that ripen at the *qets* ("end") of the summer, the end of Israel's summertime of security—the result of faithlessness and disobedience. God will not forgive Israel's hypocrisy of religiously attending services while scheming profits, treating the poor as commodities, and peddling trash to the impoverished. Amos sorrowfully warns of the terrible things that will happen: quaking land, an eclipsed sun, mourning for an only son, and a famine of hearing the words of the Lord. It is the *qets* ("end") of the family tree.

Anthem
Have Mercy on Us, Aaron Copland (Boosey & Hawkes) SATB (M).

Colossians 1:15–28 Paul tells the Colossians: You unlikely people (remember, you were once estranged from and actively hostile toward God) are part of what God has done in Christ: reconciled you through his death so that you are now radically new, provided you continue in steadfast faith and do not shift from the hope of the gospel to every other creature under the sun. Now I rejoice in my sufferings for the sake of the body of Christ. Commissioned by the hand of God, I became a minister to make the word of God fully known, for what was mysterious is now made clear in Jesus Christ.

Anthem
Christ, You Are the Fullness, PH90 #346.

Luke 10:38–42 On the way to Jerusalem, Jesus is offered hospitality by Martha. While she busily prepares food for the guest, her sister, Mary, sits at the Lord's feet, listening attentively to his teaching. Martha complains, "Lord, don't you care that Mary neglects her duty while I alone serve? Tell her to help me." But he, surprisingly, replies, "Martha, you're so preoccupied with arranging, cleaning, cooking, preparing, and producing things for this world that you're not ready to receive the grace-filled hospitality of the kingdom."

Anthem
The Best of Rooms, Randall Thompson (E. C. Schirmer) SATB (MD).

Psalm 52
1. Metrical: *Mighty Mortal, Boasting Evil*. Text: Psalm 52, vers. Helen Ott. Tune: MADILL. *PH87* #52.
2. Responsorial: *Psalm 52*. Text: *A New Zealand Prayer Book*. Refrain and Tone: Presbyterian 8. *PS93* #50.
See also *GGP*, p. 74; for text only see *GPI*, p. 72.

Anthem
Forever I Will Praise Thee, J. L. Freydt (Boosey & Hawkes) SATB (ME).

Organ Music for the Day
1. *Prelude on* DONNE SECOURS (*Hope of the World*, PH90 #360), Hans A. Metzger (*Preludes for the Hymns in Worship Supplement*, vol. 3, Concordia 97–50360).
2. *Chorale Prelude on* ST. THOMAS (*I Love Thy Kingdom, Lord*, PH90 #441), C. Hubert H. Parry (*Seven Chorale Preludes*, Novello & Co., Ltd. 1547).

Hymns for the Day	HL33	HB55	WB72	PH90
Be Thou My Vision	325	303	304	339
Call Jehovah Your Salvation	292	123	322	–
Hope of the World	–	–	423	360
If Thou but Trust in God to Guide Thee	105	344	431	282
I Greet Thee, Who My Sure Redeemer Art	–	144	625	457
Lord, When I Came Into This Life	–	–	–	522

SUNDAY BETWEEN JULY 24 AND JULY 30
(PROPER 12) [17] (C)

Hosea 1:2–10 The Lord speaks to Hosea: "Take a whore for your wife, and have children of whoredom, for the land commits great whoredom by forsaking the Lord." Obeying the Lord's repulsive command, Hosea marries a promiscuous woman. She bears three children, each of whom is given an ominous name that announces doom for the nation's future. *Yet* a brighter day will reverse what these children's names declare, for these sinful people are children of the living God.

Anthem
Hosea, Robert J. Powell (Carl Fischer) SATB (ME).

Colossians 2:6–15, (16–19) Paul tells the Colossians: You began in Christ; therefore, root yourself, stand fast, live in union with Christ and no other, abounding in thanksgiving. Resist religious sampling, for it can erode faith in Jesus Christ; cults play on your primal fears and guilts and desires for influence and wealth and, thus, promise self-fulfillment. But Christ disarmed such principalities and powers and delivered you from evil and self-preoccupation. It is with Christ that you were buried and raised, through faith in the working of God. Therefore, with Christ find the fullness of life.

Anthem
New Life, Hal H. Hopson (Sacred Music) SATB (ME).

Luke 11:1–13 Jesus teaches his disciples a simple prayer—five petitions for the reign of God's kingdom. Friends and family may need to be importuned to respond to our needs, but God is always waiting to hear our prayers, serve us, and give us the gift of the Holy Spirit. Simply ask, seek, and knock.

Anthems
The Essence of Prayer, Nylea Butler Moore (G.I.A.) SATB (M). *The Lord's Prayer*, Flor Peeters (Peters Edition) SA or SATB (M).

Psalm 85
1. Metrical: *Show Us, Lord, Your Steadfast Love*. Text: L.M., Christopher L. Webber. *ANMP*, p. 136.
2. Responsorial: *Psalm 85*. Text: *Book of Common Prayer*, alt. Refrain: Hal H. Hopson. Tone: Lutheran 7. *PS93* #76.
3. Responsorial: *Psalm 85*. Setting: Hal H. Hopson. *PS93* #77.
4. Responsorial: *Psalm 85*. Text: Grail. Setting: Jacques Berthier. *PS93* #78.
See also *WIII* #770; *PH87* #85; *PR&T*, pp. 1 & 7.

Anthem
A Psalm of Peace, Jane Marshall (Hinshaw) SATB (ME).

Organ Music for the Day
1. *Chorale Prelude on* CHRISTUS, DER IST MEIN LEBEN (*God Is Our Strong Salvation*, *PH90* #179), Max Reger (*Choralvorspiele*, Op. 67, Bote & Bock).
2. *Prelude on* KING'S WESTON (*At the Name of Jesus*, *PH90* #148), David Cherwien (Art Masters Studios, Inc. SP-103).

Hymns for the Day	HL33	HB55	WB72	PH90
At the Name of Jesus	–	143	303	148
Christ Is Made the Sure Foundation	336	433	325	416, 417
Let All Who Pray the Prayer Christ Taught	–	–	–	349
Now Thank We All Our God	459	9	481	555
Our Father, Which Art in Heaven	–	–	547	589
Our Father, Lord of Heaven and Earth	–	–	–	590

SUNDAY BETWEEN JULY 31 AND AUGUST 6
(PROPER 13) [18] (C)

Hosea 11:1–11 I loved you as a child, but the more I called you near me, the more you withdrew from me. I taught you how to walk, cradled you in my arms, healed you when you were sick, bent down and fed you. Bah! Return to the land of destruction, where the sword will rage against you. Because you are determined to turn away from me, you will bear your earned yoke which no one shall remove. But how can I give up on you? My heart recoils. I will not execute my fierce anger or destroy you, for I am God, the Holy One present among you. I will return you to your homes.

Anthem
Like as a Father, Luigi Cherubini, arr. Austin Lovelace (Choristers Guild) 3-part canon for children and adult choir (E).

Colossians 3:1–11 You have been baptized and, therefore, raised by Christ to new life. So put to death the practices of your old past way, which has died. Set your mind and heart on things above—on Christ alone, following in his way. Because you're raised to new life in Christ, get rid of all these evil practices in which you once walked. Seek your obedience "in Christ" who set you free from all these binding laws and earthly things so that you may be free for love of God and neighbors in the way of Jesus Christ.

Anthem
Baptized in Water, PH90 #492.

Luke 12:13–21 Someone says to Jesus, "Teacher, I want my share of property, to which I am entitled. Tell my brother to give it to me." Replies Jesus, "Beware of and guard against all covetousness." A rich man sought to guarantee tomorrow today by building storehouses to hoard his goods. He wanted to ensure a secure future for himself but forgot that the future—life and death—is in God's hands. So be "rich toward God": Give away your "self" to neighbors rather than foolishly trying to secure your "self" for yourself.

Anthems
Fear Not, Little Flock, Ralph Johnson (Augsburg) SATB (ME). *God, Whose Giving Knows No Ending*, from *Sacred Harp*, 1844 (setting: Hillert) (Agape) SATB congregation, oboe, optional strings (E).

Psalm 107:1–9, 43
1. Metrical: *Thanks Be to God Our Savior*. Text: David J. Diephouse. Tune: GENEVAN 107. *PH87* #107.
2. Responsorial: *Psalm 107* (1–9). Setting: Hal H. Hopson. *PS93* #109.
See also *SPJP*, p. 58; *20P&3C*, p. 22; *PR&T*, pp. 77 & 81.

Anthem
Let the Redeemed of the Lord Say So!, Eugene Butler (Hinshaw) (MD).

Organ Music for the Day
1. *Prelude on* HANOVER (*Ye Servants of God, PH90* #477), Flor Peeters (*Hymn Preludes for the Liturgical Year*, C. F. Peters Corp. 6406).
2. *Prelude on* DUKE STREET (*Fight the Good Fight, PH90* #307), Edward G. Mead (H. W. Gray Co., Inc. 682).

Hymns for the Day	HL33	HB55	WB72	PH90
Christ, You Are the Fullness	–	–	–	346
Fight the Good Fight	270	359	–	307
God of the Prophets!	481	520	398	–
O for a World	–	–	–	386
Strong Son of God, Immortal Love	175	228	578	–
Ye Servants of God, Your Master Proclaim	198	27	645	477

SUNDAY BETWEEN AUGUST 7 AND AUGUST 13
(PROPER 14) [19] (C)

Isaiah 1:1, 10–20 Hear the word of the Lord: I've had enough of your false offerings; they do not please me. Who asked you to bring me such puny offerings when you worship me? Don't bring them anymore—they are an abomination. My soul hates, despises them. When you spread forth your hands, I will close my eyes. Though you utter prayers, I will stop up my ears. Your hands are full of blood. Wash them; make yourselves clean. Do good, seek justice, release the oppressed, protect the orphan, plead for the widow. Come, says the Lord, let's settle this: though your sins are like scarlet, they shall be like snow. Be willing and obedient, and you shall eat the good of the land. Refuse, and you shall be devoured by the sword.

Anthem
O God of Every Nation, Calvin Hampton (*Westminster Praise*, Hinshaw) unison.

Hebrews 11:1–3, 8–16 Faith is belief in God's promises, the only thing upon which to rest one's faith. For example, by faith, Abraham obeyed the call to enter a strange land. By faith, he looked forward to the city of permanent foundations designed and built by God. By faith, barren Sarah received power to conceive. Thus from one aged couple came descendants as plentiful as the "stars in heaven" or "grains of sand." They died before receiving the things God had promised, but they saw them from afar and acknowledged themselves as strangers and sojourners on earth. By faith, Abraham offered to God that which was most precious to him, believing in God's promises.

Anthem
O Lord, Increase My Faith, Orlando Gibbons(H. W. Gray) SATB (M).

Luke 12:32–40 "Fear not, little flock": To give you the kingdom pleases God. Likewise, your almsgiving to neighbors in need pleases God. Keep your lamps burning; wait patiently for the arrival of the bridegroom at an unexpected hour. You may be surprised to discover that he will serve you at table.

Anthem
Treasures in Heaven, J. Clokey (Summy-Birchard) SATB sop. solo (E).

Psalm 50:1–8, 22–23
1. Metrical: *The Lord Has Spoken, God of Gods* (1–6). Text: L.M., Christopher L. Webber. *ANMP*, p. 99.
2. Responsorial: *Psalm 50* (1–6). Text: *The Book of Common Prayer*, alt. Setting: Peter R. Hallock. *PS93* #45.
See also *PS93* #46; *WIII* #892; *PH87* #50; *PR&T*, pp. 45 & 65 (1–6).

Anthem
The Lord Th' Almighty Monarch Spoke, F. J. Haydn (Broude) SATB (M).

Organ Music for the Day
1. *Prelude on* LEONI (*The God of Abraham Praise*, PH90 #488), I. Freed (*Six Liturgical Pieces*, no. 1, Transcontinental Music Pub. T. I. 151).
2. *Prelude on* OLIVET (*My Faith Looks Up to Thee*, PH90 #383), Gordon Young (*Seven Hymn Voluntaries*, Theodore Presser Co. 413–41118).

Hymns for the Day	HL33	HB55	WB72	PH90
Faith of Our Fathers!	267	348	361	–
God, Who Stretched the Spangled Heavens	–	–	—	268
Guide Me, O Thou Great Jehovah	104	339	409	281
How Clear Is Our Vocation, Lord	–	–	–	419
How Firm a Foundation	283	369	425	361
The God of Abraham Praise	8	89	587	488

SUNDAY BETWEEN AUGUST 14 AND AUGUST 20
(PROPER 15) [20] (C)

Isaiah 5:1–7 Isaiah sings of how his beloved friend dug, planted, watered, pruned, and protected a vineyard, expecting *'anabim* ("succulent fruit"), but the vineyard produced *be'ushim* ("rotten stinkers"). The friend anguished. Because of his love for the vineyard, the vintager painfully asks *why* it yielded worthless grapes. The vineyard owner renders the judgment to the listeners: God's protective hedge and wall will be removed, and life-sustaining water withheld from this good-for-nothing vineyard, allowing briars and thorns to strangle it. God looked to the people for *mishpat* ("justice"), but found *mispah* ("bloodshed"); listened for *sedaqah* ("righteousness"), but heard *se'aqah* ("a cry"). How long will God abandon this vineyard that God loves? Until . . .

Anthem
Judge Eternal, Throned in Splendor, WB72 #447.

Hebrews 11:29–12:2 A lifelong marathon race—crossing the Red Sea, circling the walls of Jericho, and more. To endure, you must scrap any sins that weigh you down, and keep your eyes fixed on Jesus. He did not become discouraged or give up because of hostility from sinners or even death on the cross. So persevere in following the pacesetter Jesus. And remember, you're not alone—all the racers from the past are cheering you on: Rahab, Gideon, Barak, Samson, Jephthah, Samuel, David, the prophets, and many others who witnessed and suffered for the faith.

Anthem
Awake, Our Souls!, George Brandon (Concordia) 2-part mixed (E).

Luke 12:49–56 Do you think Christ came to give peace on earth, harmony, tranquillity, serenity? No wonder we're shocked to hear him say he "came to cast fire upon the earth." His baptism demands unflinching allegiance and, therefore, may divide families and separate friends. We can forecast what clouds and winds will bring us, but we're unable to foretell that the fiery Spirit of Christ will sear our self-love and ignite our love for neighbors.

Anthem
How Clear Is Our Vocation, Lord, PH90 #419.

Psalm 80:1–2, 8–19
1. Metrical: *O Hear Our Cry, O Lord.* Text: Fred R. Anderson. Tune: VINEYARD HAVEN. *PH90* #206 (text only see *SPJP,* p. 43).
2. Responsorial: *Psalm 80* (1–7). Text: Gary Chamberlain. Setting: Hal H. Hopson. *PS93* #70.
See also *PS93* #71; *ANMP,* p. 127; *CS/PFTCY,* vol. 2, p. 25; *PH87* #80.

Anthem
O Hear Our Cry, O Lord (Vineyard Haven) *PH90* #206.

Organ Music for the Day
1. *Organ Fantasy on the Hymn Tune* SINE NOMINE (*For All the Saints, PH90* #526), Howard R. Thatcher (Carl Fischer Inc. P3135).
2. *Prelude on* REPTON (*How Clear Is Our Vocation, PH90* #419), C. Callahan (*Six Meditations on English Hymn Tunes,* Organ Lit. Foundation).

Hymns for the Day	HL33	HB55	WB72	PH90
Christ, When for Us You Were Baptized	–	–	–	70
For All the Saints	429	425	369	526
Guide My Feet	–	–	–	354
I Sing a Song of the Saints of God	–	–	–	364
Judge Eternal, Throned in Splendor	417	517	447	–
O Love That Wilt Not Let Me Go	307	400	519	384

SUNDAY BETWEEN AUGUST 21 AND AUGUST 27
(PROPER 16) [21] (C)

Jeremiah 1:4–10 Jeremiah has a vision in which YHWH anoints him to be a "prophet to the nations." "But I do not know how to speak," laments Jeremiah. "Fear not," answers YHWH, "I am with you. What I command, you shall speak." YHWH then touches Jeremiah's mouth, saying, "I have put my words into your mouth so that you shall speak the double-edged word of judgment *and* salvation that uproots and smashes, *and* builds and plants."

Anthem
Lord, When I Came Into This Life, PH90 #522.

Hebrews 12:18–29 Remember Sinai when the first covenant was given: fire, darkness, gloom, whirlwind, trumpet sound, and a voice with frightening words. No wonder Moses "trembled with fear." But you have come to Mt. Zion, the city of the living God, where angels and others who lived in faith now gather together in praise and joy. All meet God, who is judge of all, and also Jesus, mediator of the new covenant, whose blood cries out in mercy and forgiveness. Caution: Do not refuse this joy-filled, merciful gift. Listen to this heaven-and-earth-shaking voice, and pay heed to what you hear, for the Israelites did not listen and were refused entry into the Promised Land.

Anthem
Author of Faith, Whose Spirit Breathes the Active Flame, Kathryn Stephenson (Hinshaw) SATB (ME).

Luke 13:10–17 Jesus teaches in a synagogue on the Sabbath. Present is a daughter of Abraham, for eighteen years crippled, bent over, unable to stand up straight. "Woman," says Jesus, "you are set free from your ailment." At Jesus' touch, she "stands tall," giving all credit to God. But the synagogue leader recites the law (Deut. 5:13, and Ex. 20:9–10)—"You cured on the wrong day." The Lord answers, "You hypocrites! So that your livestock may drink, you untie them on the Sabbath, right? Isn't the Sabbath best honored by doing God's work of salvation in releasing this woman from bondage?"

Anthem
He Did Not Wait, Ronald Melrose (Carl Fischer) SAB (M).

Psalm 71:1–6
1. Metrical: *I Find My Refuge in You, Lord*. Text: C.M., Christopher L. Webber. *ANMP*, p. 119.
2. Responsorial: *Psalm 71:1–6*. Text: Grail. Setting: James E. Barrett. Tone: Harmony, Hal H. Hopson. *PS93* #63.
See also *PH87* #71; *WIII* #44 & #876; *PR&T*, pp. 45 & 48.

Anthem
In Thee, O Lord, Do I Take Refuge, J. Marshall (Augsburg) SATB (ME).

Organ Music for the Day
1. *Chorale Prelude on* UNSER HERRSCHER (*Open Now Thy Gates, PH90* #489), Max Drischner (*Choralvorspiele für Orgel*, Carl L. Schultheiss).
2. *Chorale Prelude on* ERHALT UNS, HERR (*O Christ, the Healer, PH90* #380), Helmut Walcha (*Choralvorspiele*, vol. 1, C. F. Peters Corp. 4850).

Hymns for the Day	HL33	HB55	WB72	PH90
Jesus, Thou Joy of Loving Hearts	354	215	–	511
O Christ, the Healer	–	–	–	380
O God of Every Nation	–	–	498	289
Open Now the Gates of Beauty	–	40	544	489
O Savior, in This Quiet Place	–	–	–	390
We Walk by Faith and Not by Sight	–	–	–	399

SUNDAY BETWEEN AUGUST 28 AND SEPTEMBER 3
(PROPER 17) [22] (C)

Jeremiah 2:4–13 Why would Israel chase after worthless things, becoming worthless? Israel exchanged a faithful God for no-gods. From west to east, you won't see such God-swapping. Even the heavens are appalled. Israel deserted the life-giving waters of God, and built cracked cisterns in the desert. Such behavior results when you cease to recite God's past faithfulness and future promises so you know how to live in the present. It's called an identity crisis, triggered by a leadership team of priests, judges, rulers, and prophets who ignore the credo and, therefore, pollute the land.

Anthem
Help Us, O Lord, Aaron Copland (Boosey & Hawkes) SATB (M).

Hebrews 13:1–8, 15–16 "Let brotherly love continue": Open your home to strangers (you might be entertaining angels), care for the imprisoned and ill-treated, honor marriage, resist love of money—be content with what you have. Not exactly conventional or popular ways to love one another, but no wonder the writer quotes Psalm 118:6, because God is your support and will take care of you. Remember and imitate the fidelity of your leaders, those who spoke the word of God to the community. And, most important, imitate Jesus Christ, the one who is always the same—yesterday, today, and forever.

Anthem
I Saw a Stranger Yestreen, L. Stanley Glarum (G. Schirmer) 2-part mixed (E).

Luke 14:1, 7–14 When you are invited to a marriage feast, resist taking the exalted seat of honor, for you will be covered with shame when a more eminent one arrives and sits in your chair. Rather, sit at a humble place so you may be invited to a seat of honor. Moreover, don't invite friends to your dinner parties; they will simply invite you to theirs. Rather, "invite the poor and the maimed" and you will discover that Christ is present with you too.

Anthem
Whoever Would Be First Among You, R. A. Nelson (Augsburg) 3-part (E).

Psalm 81:1, 10–16
1. Metrical: *Sing a Psalm of Joy.* Text: Marie J. Post. Tune: GENEVAN 81. *PH87* #81 (selected stanzas).
2. Responsorial: *Psalm 81.* Text: Grail. Refrain and Tone: Presbyterian 2. *PS93* #72 (verses 1*a,* 5*b*–8).
See also *30P&2C,* p. 24 (selected stanzas); *PR&T,* pp. 55 & 59.

Anthem
Hold Not Thy Tongue, O God, Anthony Hedges (Novello) SATB (M).

Organ Music for the Day
1. *Chorale Prelude on* WAS GOTT TUT (*O God, What You Ordain Is Right, PH90* #284), Friedrich Wilhelm Marpurg (*Twenty-One Chorale Preludes,* Augsburg 11–9506).
2. *Prelude on* MORNING SONG (*O Holy City, Seen of John, PH90* #453), David Schack (*Preludes on Ten Hymn Tunes,* Augsburg 11–9363).

Hymns for the Day	HL33	HB55	WB72	PH90
Blest Are the Uncorrupt in Heart	–	226	–	233
Called as Partners in Christ's Service	–	–	–	343
Help Us Accept Each Other	–	–	–	358
Where Charity and Love Prevail	–	–	–	641
Where Cross the Crowded Ways of Life	410	507	642	408
Called as Partners in Christ's Service	–	–	–	343

SUNDAY BETWEEN SEPTEMBER 4 AND SEPTEMBER 10
(PROPER 18) [23] (C)

Jeremiah 18:1–11 At YHWH's command, Jeremiah visits a potter's house where he sees some clay resisting being molded into the intended shape by the deft hands of the potter. So the potter patiently reworks the stubborn clay into another shape "as it seemed good to the potter to do so." Then Jeremiah hears the words of YHWH, "I too judge and forgive, pluck up and plant, destroy and build according to the quality of the clay in my hands. Behold, I am shaping evil against you; so repent, turn around, and return from your evil ways."

Anthem
The Prayers I Make, Jane Marshall (Sacred Music) 2-part mixed (E).

Philemon 1–21 Paul appeals to Philemon to accept back a runaway slave, Onesimus, who met Paul in prison and became a Christian. (Punishment for runaway slaves in 1st century Colossae was not much different from 19th-century America.) To ask Philemon to treat a fugitive slave "no longer as a slave, but as a beloved brother" is indeed bold. "Receive him as you would me." Paul trusts God to set free from sin Philemon and all of us captives.

Anthem
Help Us to Help Each Other, S. D. Wolff (Concordia) SATB (E).

Luke 14:25–33 "To be my disciples," declares Jesus, "you must love everyone and everything less than me. You must be willing to bear your own cross and come after me: dedicating yourself to going where I go, associating with outcasts, reaching out your hands to the dependent or helpless, renouncing all that you treasure (including family loyalties). Count the cost of discipleship before committing yourself; otherwise you will fall short and be mocked by others." Isn't that how you would construct towers, wage war, or sue for peace? Tally the cost before committing yourself; otherwise it would be foolish to begin, for others would laugh at your unfinished, bankrupt venture.

Anthem
Take Up Thy Cross, Carlton R. Young (Hope) SATB (E).

Psalm 139:1–6, 13–18
1. Responsorial: *Psalm 139* (1–5, 13–14, 16–18). Setting: Hal H. Hopson. *PS93* #143.
2. Metrical: *Lord, You Have Searched and Seen Me Through.* Text: L.M., Fred R. Anderson. *SPJP,* p. 70. Tune: MARYTON.
See also *30P&2C,* p.40 (st. 1, 2, 6–8); *PH87* #139 (st. 1 & 2); *WIII* #1034.

Anthem
Psalm 139, Carlton R. Young (Hope) SATB solo voice, oboe, congregation with speaking parts (ME).

Organ Music for the Day
1. *Meditation on* ST. ANNE (*Our God, Our Help in Ages Past, PH90* #210), Gordon Young (Shawnee Press, Inc. HF-18).
2. *Prelude on* SLANE (*Be Thou My Vision, PH90* #339), Austin C. Lovelace (*Fourteen Hymn Preludes,* Augsburg 11–6152).

Hymns for the Day	HL33	HB55	WB72	PH90
God of Compassion, in Mercy Befriend Us	290	122	392	261
How Clear Is Our Vocation, Lord	–	–	–	419
Make Me a Captive, Lord	247	308	–	378
Our God, Our Help in Ages Past	77	111	549	210
Take Up Thy Cross, the Savior Said	–	293	–	393
Today We All Are Called to Be Disciples	–	–	–	434

SUNDAY BETWEEN SEPTEMBER 11 AND SEPTEMBER 17
(PROPER 19) [24] (C)

Jeremiah 4:11–12, 22–28 A wake-up call to arouse apathetic Judah, who may look stupid and foolish, but is resourceful and adroit in doing evil. YHWH looked and looked on the earth and the mountains, and saw the disorder of waste and void overcoming the order of creation. Heaven and earth mourn. The searing wind of YHWH is bringing judgment of a D-day-sized army against Judah, who now can only drone funeral songs. *Yet* a full end will not be made by YHWH, whose final word is redemption.

Anthem
Have Mercy on Us, Aaron Copland (Boosey & Hawkes) SATB (MD).

1 Timothy 1:12–17 Thanks to Christ Jesus, who has appointed me to serve him and given me strength for his work. I formerly spoke evil of him and persecuted his people. I didn't know who I was, or what I was doing. Fortunately, Christ came to save sinners, and I am the foremost. So the Lord worked through a wretch like me as an example; he poured out his abundant grace on me and gave me faith and love in him. Now, as an apostle, I spread his good news everywhere. To the eternal King—glory and honor forever!

Anthem
Prayer to Jesus, George Oldroyd (Oxford) SATB (M).

Luke 15:1–10 Is anyone fool-headed enough to risk the safety of ninety-nine sheep in order to look for a single lost sheep? Yet, this shepherd forsakes the greatest good for the most sheep, and seeks a lost sheep "until he finds it," at which time he rejoices with friends and neighbors. Likewise, it's incredible that a woman would turn a home inside out "until she finds" one lost coin, and then throw a party with friends and neighbors to celebrate its recovery. It's amazing how much joy there is in heaven over the finding of a single lost sinner.

Anthem
Amazing Grace, arr. Richard Proulx (G.I.A.) SATB, flute (E).

Psalm 14
1. Metrical: *The Foolish in Their Hearts Deny*. Text: Marie J. Post. Tune: OLD 107TH. *PH87* #14.
2. Responsorial: *Psalm 14*. Text: Helen L. Wright. Refrain: John Ferguson. Tone: Lutheran *Book of Worship*. *PS93* #8.
See also *GPI*, p. 14; *PR&T*, pp. 2 & 15.

Anthem
O That Salvation for Israel Would Come, Johann C. Geisler (Boosey & Hawkes) SS(A)TB (ME).

Organ Music for the Day
1. *Chorale Prelude on* ST. DENIO (*Immortal, Invisible, God Only Wise, PH90* #263), Robert J. Powell (*Chorale Preludes on Hymn Tunes*, Harold Flammer Inc. 4430).
2. *Prelude on* DUNDEE (*O God, in a Mysterious Way, PH90* #270), Henby G. Ley (*An Album of Memorial and Funeral Music*, Oxford 375105–4).

Hymns for the Day	HL33	HB55	WB72	PH90
Amazing Grace	–	275	296	280
God Moves in a Mysterious Way	103	112	391	270
Great Is Thy Faithfulness	–	–	–	276
Immortal, Invisible, God Only Wise	66	85	433	263
Jesus, Thy Boundless Love to Me	314	404	–	366
There's a Wideness in God's Mercy	93	110	601	298

SUNDAY BETWEEN SEPTEMBER 18 AND SEPTEMBER 24
(PROPER 20) [25] (C)

Jeremiah 8:18–9:1 YHWH is "sick to death," grieving over a faithless people. Worse, their indifference intensifies the pain. They question God's job performance, the lack of God's presence among them. "Why," asks YHWH, "do you provoke me by focusing your life on false gods?" The people also question God's job performance regarding tardiness, and prod God to get back on schedule. Over such sin-sick people, YHWH anguishes. Their infirmity is beyond all known cures, and seems too great for a healing balm in Gilead.

Anthem
There Is a Balm in Gilead, PH90 #394.

1 Timothy 2:1–7 Lift up your hands and hearts, and offer intercessions for all people—friends and enemies alike. Pray especially for those with political power, for they are charged with the responsibility of maintaining an orderly life. They need God's word in order to work for God's truth and justice and peace. Above all, only one mediator brings us together, to whom we owe our total allegiance and trust: Christ, who gave himself as a ransom for all.

Anthem
Prayer, Lloyd Pfautsch (Lawson-Gould) 2-part mixed (ME), text by Dag Hammarskjöld.

Luke 16:1–13 A strange story: Jesus praises a crooked steward who cheated his employer and gouged his customers. Only when his boss barked the word "audit" did this slimy steward realize the day of reckoning was at hand for his dishonest dealings. Only then did he seek to save his own neck by serving others and by righting wrongs he had done, which ironically resulted in his doing justly. Thank God we don't need to be threatened to do God's will, because we know about free grace handed out by Christ on the cross. No need to delay another moment in giving away ourselves to neighbors, right?

Anthem
We Seek Your Presence, Jane Marshall (Sacred Music) SATB (E).

Psalm 79:1–9
1. Metrical: *In Your Heritage the Nations.* Text: *The Psalter,* 1912. Tune: O MEIN JESU. Harmony, Paul Bunjes. *PH87 #79.*
2. Responsorial: *Psalm 79:1–9.* Text: Grail. Refrain: Howard Hughes. Gelineau tone. *PS93 #69.*
See also *GGP,* p. 114. For text only see *GPI,* p. 115.

Anthem
Pointed psalm with congregational response, Hal H. Hopson (*Psalm Refrains and Tones for the Common Lectionary,* Hope).

Organ Music for the Day
1. *Chorale Prelude on* NUN DANKET ALLE GOTT (*Now Thank We All Our God, PH90* #555), Johann C. Oley (*Ausgewählte Choralbearbeitungen für Orgel,* Noetzel Edition N 3627).
2. *Chorale Prelude on* HANOVER (*Ye Servants of God, PH90 #477*), A. Rowley (*Chorale Preludes Based on Famous Hymn Tunes,* E. Ashdown, Ltd.).

Hymns for the Day	HL33	HB55	WB72	PH90
At the Name of Jesus	–	143	303	148
God of Our Life	88	108	395	275
Now Thank We All Our God	459	9	481	555
O Love That Wilt Not Let Me Go	307	400	519	384
O God of Earth and Altar	–	–	497	291
Ye Servants of God, Your Master Proclaim	198	27	645	477

SUNDAY BETWEEN SEPTEMBER 25 AND OCTOBER 1
(PROPER 21) [26] (C)

Jeremiah 32:1–3a, 6–15 The end has begun: Babylon is now besieging Jerusalem; Jeremiah is under arrest. Yet another word to Jeremiah from YHWH: "Buy the field at Anathoth from your cousin Hanamel." Proper procedures are complied with: cash, deed, signing, sealing, witnesses, and safekeeping. At the brink of exile, Jeremiah secures legal title to land? If the world were coming to an end, how much real estate would you purchase? Jeremiah, however, trusts in YHWH's promised future. Today: exile. Tomorrow: "houses, fields, and vineyards shall again be bought in this land."

Anthem

Prayer for Blessing, David Schwoebel (Hinshaw) SATB (ME).

1 Timothy 6:6–19 Resist the temptation to desire riches, for love of money will lure you into ruin and destruction. Remember, you entered the world with nothing and you will depart with nothing. Recall your baptism, for, as a new creature "in Christ," God called you to pursue the rich life of "righteousness, godliness, faith, love, steadfastness, and gentleness." Run, run, run on this path of life until the day when our Lord Jesus Christ appears.

Anthem

Fight the Good Fight, John Gardner (Oxford) SATB (M).

Luke 16:19–31 Jesus retells an old familiar Egyptian folktale about a rich man and a poor man. But Jesus' version isn't very funny: we are shocked, outraged, offended to discover that the ostensibly cursed, poor Lazarus rests in the bosom of Abraham, and the seemingly blessed, righteous rich man sizzles in a frying pan of a place, seeking cool relief from Lazarus and pleading for someone to get the word to his brothers that God's judgments reverse everything. But Lazarus isn't running any more errands for the rich man. We already have all we need in the Law and the Prophets and in Jesus Christ. Listen to God's word and turn around (repent) now.

Anthem

Father Abraham, Have Mercy on Me, Gerhard Krapf (Concordia) unison (ME).

Psalm 91:1–6, 14–16
1. Metrical: *Within Your Shelter, Loving God.* Text: C.M., John G. Dunn. Tune: ABBEY. *PH90* #212.
2. Responsorial: *Psalm 92* (1–6, 9–16). Text: Helen L. Wright. Refrain and Tone: Presbyterian 6. *PS93* #85.
See also *RITL* #115; *WIII* #49; *ANMP,* p. 148; *SPJP,* p. 47; *24P&1C,* p. 18.

Anthem

Within Your Shelter, Loving God, PH90 #212.

Organ Music for the Day
1. *Chorale Prelude on* DIX (*For the Beauty of the Earth, PH90* #473), Charles T. Taylor (Harold Flammer, Inc. 4286).
2. *Chorale Prelude on* DUKE STREET (*Fight the Good Fight, PH90* #307), Robert J. Powell (*Fifteen Chorale Preludes,* The Sacred Music Press).

Hymns for the Day	HL33	HB55	WB72	PH90
Fight the Good Fight	270	359	–	307
He Is King of Kings	–	–	–	153
I Sing the Mighty Power of God	65	84	628	288
Now Thank We All Our God	459	9	481	555
O Word of God Incarnate	215	251	532	327
Spirit	–	–	–	319

SUNDAY BETWEEN OCTOBER 2 AND OCTOBER 8
(PROPER 22) [27] (C)

Lamentations 1:1–6 In exile, Israel agonizes; all seems lost. For many, liberation no longer is important; only survival counts, and it often feels like a slow despairing death. Too much suffering for too many years has smothered the fires of hope. In words that etch the pain and hopelessness of their forsakenness, Israel hears the echo of what they feel: "How lonely sits the city that was once full of people! . . . she has no one to comfort her."

Anthem
The Lamentations of Jeremiah, Thomas Tallis (Oxford) SATTB (M).

2 Timothy 1:1–14 You have been called to be speakers of the gospel, and in our world that's not what people want to hear. So you will have to accept your share of suffering. God saved you, chose you, and will give you strength to spread the good news that the love of God was revealed to us in Jesus Christ. But the only way you are going to do that without being afraid or ashamed is by trusting in God. For the sake of this gospel, I suffer, but I am not ashamed because I know whom I've trusted. Keep on telling the gospel, no matter what the cost, because God wants everyone to hear it and be liberated. That's why God came to us in Jesus Christ: to set us all free.

Anthem
Kindle the Gift of God, Gerre Hancock (H. W. Gray) SATB (M).

Luke 17:5–10 Do you invite your letter carrier in for gourmet luncheons, prepare six-course dinners for your trash collector, or serve elegant hors d'oeuvres to your street sweeper? After all, who's serving whom? We expect such workers to serve us and, thereby, earn their pay. Likewise, we expect God to do God's job: take care of us, protect us from any harm, listen to our prayer requests, forgive us for the wrongs we have committed. Stop! Who's serving whom? We are God's servants in the world. So "when you have done all that is commanded you, say, 'We are unworthy servants; we have done only what was our [joyful] duty.' "

Anthem
O Lord, Increase My Faith, Orlando Gibbons (H. W. Gray) SATB (M).

Lamentations 3:19–26 ("The Steadfast Love of the Lord")
1. Responsorial: *Canticle from Lamentations.* Text: NRSV, *A New Zealand Prayer Book.* Setting: John Weaver.
2. Responsorial: *Canticle from Lamentations. PS93* #179.
3. Metrical: *Great Is Thy Faithfulness.* Tune: FAITHFULNESS. Text: William Marion Runyan. *PH90* #276. (See also *PH87* #556.)
4. Metrical: *New Every Morning Is the Love.* Tune: KEDRON. Text: John Keble. *H82* #10.

Anthem
Great Is Thy Faithfulness, PH90 #276.

or Psalm 137
1. Metrical: *By the Babylonian Rivers.* Text: Ewald Bash. Tune: KAS DZIEDAJA. *PH90* #246. (See also *RITL* #137.)
2. Metrical: *By the Waters of Babylon.* Jewish melody (canon). *PH90* #245.
3. Responsorial: *Psalm 137.* Setting: Hal H. Hopson. *PS93* #140.
4. Responsorial: *Let My Tongue Be Silenced.* Text: Grail (see also *GPI,* p. 200). Refrain, psalm tone, and Gelineau tone: *WIII* #797. (See also *30P&2C,* p. 38.)
See also *PH87* #137; *CS/PFTCY,* vol. 3, p. 16; *PR&T,* pp. 2 & 49.

Anthem
By the Babylonian Rivers, PH90 #246.

Organ Music for the Day
1. *Prelude on* ST. DENIO (*Immortal, Invisible, God Only Wise, PH90* #263), Emma L. Diemer (*With Praise and Love,* The Sacred Music Press).
2. *Chorale Prelude on* HANOVER (*Ye Servants of God, Your Master Proclaim, PH90* #477), Gordon Young (*Chorale Preludes on Seven Hymn Tunes,* Harold Flammer, Inc. HF-5002).

Hymns for the Day	*HL33*	*HB55*	*WB72*	*PH90*
Called as Partners in Christ's Service	–	–	–	343
Christian Women, Christian Men	–	–	–	348
Faith of Our Fathers	267	348	361	–
Lord, Whose Love Through Humble Service	–	–	–	427
We All Are One in Mission	–	–	–	435
Ye Servants of God, Your Master Proclaim	198	27	645	477
Kum ba Yah	–	–	–	338

SUNDAY BETWEEN OCTOBER 9 AND OCTOBER 15
(PROPER 23) [28] (C)

Jeremiah 29:1, 4–7 The opening words of a pastoral letter sent to the exiles in Babylon: Get used to it; build a life in exile. Adjust: build, plant, marry. Create a communal infrastructure in exile. Your task: seek the *shalom* (welfare) of the city. Insist on a "welfare system" in Babylon. The mission is not to overthrow a hostile regime, but to hold the regime to its own best promises. The empire can practice *shalom*. The exiled church can influence the empire. Close your ears to liars who say we're going back to normalcy. Dismiss such illusions of escape. Instead, make do, witness in your situation.

Anthem
Father, Help Your People (*Westminster Praise,* number 49, Hinshaw).

2 Timothy 2:8–15 Remember Christ, risen from the dead, as preached in the gospel for which I am suffering. Indeed, I am even chained like a criminal. But God's word is never shackled, so I endure everything for the sake of God's chosen people in order that they too may obtain salvation through Jesus Christ. "If we have died with him, we shall also live with him; if we endure, we shall also reign with him." Remind your people of this so they do not quibble with each other over trivialities—bureaucratic structures, management techniques, budgeting procedures. All this squabbling will only ruin the hearers of the gospel.

Anthem
A Prayer for Pressing On, Jane Marshall (Agape) SATB (ME).

Luke 17:11–19 Ten lepers cry out to Jesus for pity. "Go!" commands Jesus (*no comfort here*). "Show yourselves to the priests." They obey. They do what Jesus tells them to do—that's faith—and they are healed. But one leper, a despised outsider, turns back to give thanks, glorifying God. He obeys *and* worships. No wonder Jesus says to him, "Your faith has made you whole."

Anthem
The Kingdom of God, Austin Lovelace (Hope) SATB or 2-part (E).

Psalm 66:1–12
1. Metrical: *Be Joyful, All You Lands, in God.* Text: C.M., Christopher L. Webber. *ANMP,* p. 109.
2. Responsorial: *Psalm 66* (1–8). Text: *A New Zealand Prayer Book.* Setting: Richard T. Proulx. *PS93* #57.
See also *PS93* #58; *WIII* #848; *PH87* #66; *HB55* #296; *PR&T,* pp. 66 & 77.

Anthem
Jubilate Deo, Laszlo Halmos, ed. Erik Routley (Hinshaw) SATB (ME).

Organ Music for the Day
1. *Improvisation on* ST. CATHERINE (*Jesus, Thy Boundless Love to Me, PH90* #366), Camil Van Hulse (*Eleven Improvisations on Hymn Tunes,* H. T. FitzSimons Co., Inc.).
2. *Prelude on* MARYTON (*O Master, Let Me Walk . . . , PH90* #357), Wilbur Held (*The Concordia Hymn Prelude Series,* vol. 31, Concordia 97–5746).

Hymns for the Day	HL33	HB55	WB72	PH90
All Who Love and Serve Your City	–	–	293	413
I Will Give Thanks with My Whole Heart	–	–	–	247
Let All Things Now Living	–	–	–	554
Lord, from the Depths to You I Cry	240	277	459	–
O for a Thousand Tongues to Sing	199	141	493	466
O God, Our Faithful God	–	–	500	277
What Wondrous Love Is This	–	–	–	85

SUNDAY BETWEEN OCTOBER 16 AND OCTOBER 22
(PROPER 24) [29] (C)

Jeremiah 31:27–34 YHWH is going to make a new covenant with the people. This new covenant will not be like the old Sinai one which the people adulterated, even though YHWH was their faithful husband; this time YHWH will cut the new covenant into people's hearts, minds, and will. They will be YHWH's people, YHWH will be their God. Everyone will know YHWH—no need to teach one another about YHWH—for YHWH will forgive their iniquity and no longer remember their sin.

Anthem
This Is the Covenant, Jean Berger (Augsburg) SATB (M).

2 Timothy 3:14–4:5 Remember what you learned as a child, for all scripture is useful for teaching the truth and giving instructions for right living. Now, in the presence of God and of Christ Jesus, I charge you to preach the Word (regardless of the time). Many will not listen to sound teaching but will prefer to follow their own desires and therefore gather at the feet of teachers who tell them what their egos are itching to hear. Stand firm, endure suffering, and preach the gospel as a servant of God.

Anthem
Be Strong in the Lord, Thomas Matthews (FitzSimons) SATB (M).

Luke 18:1–8 A parable about an "unrighteous" judge and a relentless widow who keeps pleading with this judge to "vindicate me against my adversary." But the judge keeps refusing. So the woman keeps on hounding him. Finally the judge caves in to her bothersome importuning and grants her what she needs. Whew! Isn't it great that the God revealed in Jesus Christ isn't a God you have to "bug" all the time? We can depend on God; can God depend on our persistence in faith? "When the Son of man comes, will he find faith [not religion, but faith] on earth?"

Anthem
We Do Not Know How to Pray, Erik Routley (*Ecumenical Praise,* number 110, Agape) unison (E).

Psalm 119:97–104
1. Metrical: *How I Love Thy Law, O Lord.* Text: *The Psalter,* 1912, alt. Tune: SPANISH HYMN. *HB55* #253.
2. Responsorial: *Psalm 119* (97–112). Text: Grail. Refrain and tone: Presbyterian 5. *PS93* #123.

See also *GGP,* p. 175 (stanzas 13 & 14). For text only see *GPI,* p. 181.

Anthem
Lord, What Love Have I, William Croft (*Anthems for Choirs,* vol. 2, Oxford) (ME).

Organ Music for the Day
1. *Prelude on* MUNICH (*O Word of God Incarnate, PH90* #327), Carl McKinley (*The Lutheran Organist,* H. W. Gray Co., Inc.).
2. *Prelude on* IN BABILONE (*There's a Wideness in . . . , PH90* #298), Flor Peeters (*Hymn Preludes for the Liturgical Year,* C. F. Peters Corp. 6403).

Hymns for the Day	HL33	HB55	WB72	PH90
God of Our Life	88	108	395	275
Lord God of Hosts, Whose Purpose	368	288	460	–
Lord of All Good	–	–	–	375
O Day of God, Draw Nigh	–	–	492	452
Our God, to Whom We Turn	–	128	–	278
O Word of God Incarnate	215	251	532	327

SUNDAY BETWEEN OCTOBER 23 AND OCTOBER 29
(PROPER 25) [30] (C)

Joel 2:23–32 Lots of talk about new creation: "early rain, plentiful grain, wine, oil; eat in plenty, be satisfied, never again be put to shame, and you will know that I, YHWH, am in the midst of you." Afterward, YHWH's spirit/wind will make everybody open to this new creation. Everybody's going to dream and have visions and hope and turn loose of the way things are now organized, because God is establishing a whole new creation.

Anthem
God Is One, Unique and Holy, Peter Cutts (Agape) SATB (ME).

2 Timothy 4:6–8, 16–18 Paul writes: The time is near for me to offer my life as a witness to the gospel. I rejoice that "I have fought the good fight and finished the race." Now the crown of righteousness awaits me and all who have loved Christ's coming on that Day. At my first trial, all deserted me; may God forgive them. But the Lord stood by me, giving me strength to proclaim the word fully that all might hear it. So I was rescued from "the lion's mouth" of death. I am confident the Lord will save me from all evil and deliver me safely into the heavenly kingdom. To God be the glory, forever.

Anthem
I Have Fought the Good Fight, T. Gieschen (Augsburg) SATB (ME).

Luke 18:9–14 A Pharisee offers a typical prayer of thanksgiving that he has been blessed and is not like those who are beyond redemption but is able to do what the law requires—fast twice weekly and tithe his income. He is the ideal model of a pious Jew and therefore must be righteous. A tax collector who knows his outsider's place in the Temple—for he is a sinner—offers a plea acknowledging what everyone knows is true: "I'm no good." But Jesus announces, "I, not the Temple, will determine who is holy. This publican 'beyond redemption' is justified." Free grace boggles our minds every time.

Anthem
The Pharisee and the Publican, Heinrich Schütz (G. Schirmer) SATB tenor and bass solos (M).

Psalm 65
1. Metrical: *To Bless the Earth, God Sends Us.* Text: *The Psalter,* 1912, alt. Tune: CHRISTUS, DER IST MEIN LEBEN. *PH90* #200.
2. Responsorial: *Psalm 65* (1–8). Text: Grail. Refrain: Hal H. Hopson. Tone: Gregorian VIII. *PS93* #55.
See also *PS93* #56; *PH87* #65; *PH90* #201; *ANMP,* p. 108; *HB55* #99.

Anthem
Thou Visitest the Earth, Maurice Greene, ed. Watkins Shaw (Novello) SATB soprano or tenor solo (M).

Organ Music for the Day
1. *Prelude on* CWM RHONDDA (*Guide Me, O Thou . . .,* PH90 #281), R. H. Haan (*Welsh Hymn Tune Preludes,* The Sacred Music Press KK426).
2. *Prelude on* O QUANTA QUALIA (*God of Compassion, in Mercy Befriend Us, PH90* #261), Philip Cranmer (*For Manuals Only,* Oxford 375131–3).

Hymns for the Day	HL33	HB55	WB72	PH90
Fight the Good Fight	270	359	–	307
Guide Me, O Thou Great Jehovah	104	339	409	281
Have Mercy, Lord, on Me	–	–	–	395
O God of Bethel, by Whose Hand	98	342	496	269
O Savior, in This Quiet Place	–	–	–	390
Thine Is the Glory	–	209	–	122

SUNDAY BETWEEN OCTOBER 30 AND NOVEMBER 5
(PROPER 26) [31] (C)

Habakkuk 1:1–4; 2:1–4 We live in an unjust world where the odds seem to favor wickedness, violence, and terrorism. Why doesn't God do something? Habakkuk laments, "How long, O Lord, must I see indiscriminate evil sweep across the earth, without distinction between the righteous and the wicked? How could chaotic forces arrayed against your purposes be an instrument of your judgment?" He climbs his watchtower to look for God's answer, given in plain but cryptic terms: "Behold, the vision tarries," says YHWH; "it may seem slow, but you must wait." In the meantime, when faith is put to the test, the just shall live by faith, confident that God is in control.

Anthem
Write Your Blessed Name, D. Grotenhuis (Sacred Music) SATB (E).

2 Thessalonians 1:1–4, 11–12 A paradox: The Thessalonian church grows in faithfulness at the very moment of its affliction. The comforting word to oppressed, harassed, aggrieved, suffering people is like cool water that strengthens them to carry on the task: "May God complete your work of faith." But a reassuring word to an unafflicted, comfortable church provides what? Threatening judgment? No wonder we struggle with this kind of text.

Anthem
Put Thou Thy Trust in God, Philip Tomblings (Oxford) SATB (ME).

Luke 19:1–10 Jesus approaches Jericho, so the chief tax collector, Zacchaeus—a traitorous crook who has sold out to Rome and constantly cheats his neighbors—perches in a tree to see Jesus. Shockingly, Jesus invites himself into Zacchaeus's home. The crowd is outraged that Jesus has entered a sinner's home. But Zacchaeus—miraculously set free—gives half his goods to the poor and restores past fraudulent deals fourfold. On that day, salvation comes to his house, for he is a son of Abraham ("a keeper of the law").

Anthem
The Best of Rooms, R. Thompson (E. C. Schirmer) SATB (MD).

Psalm 119:137–144
1. Metrical: *The Will of God to Mark My Way.* Text: Timothy Dudley Smith. Music: N. Warren. *PP* #128.
2. Responsorial: *Psalm 119* (129–44). Text: Grail. Refrain and Tone: Presbyterian 5. *PS93* #124.
See also *GPI,* p. 175; *PR&T,* pp. 67 & 68.

Anthem
Righteous, O Lord, Art Thou, Antonio Vivaldi, arr. Ehret (Elkan-Vogel) SATB soprano solo (ME).

Organ Music for the Day
1. *Trio on* CHRISTE SANCTORUM (*Father, We Praise Thee, PH90* #459), David N. Johnson (*Music for Worship: Easy Trios,* Augsburg 11–9291).
2. *Chorale Prelude on* CHRISTUS, DER IST MEIN LEBEN (*God Is My Strong Salvation, PH90* #179), Johann C. Kittel (*Album of Choral Preludes from Olden and Modern Times,* Edwin F. Kalmus 4102).

Hymns for the Day	HL33	HB55	WB72	PH90
From All That Dwell Below the Skies	388	33	373	229
God Is My Strong Salvation	92	347	388	179
How Firm a Foundation	283	369	425	361
O Hear Our Cry, O Lord	–	–	–	206
O Love That Wilt Not Let Me Go	307	400	519	384
Take My Life	242	310	–	391

ALL SAINTS' DAY
[NOVEMBER 1 OR FIRST SUNDAY IN NOVEMBER] (C)

Daniel 7:1–3, 15–18 Daniel experiences a night vision in which the four winds of heaven churn up the great sea, allowing four successive great beasts to emerge. Perplexed by this dream, Daniel seeks an angelic interpreter, who explains that the four great beasts are kings/kingdoms that arise out of the earth but shall be replaced by "the saints of the Most High," who shall receive and possess the kingdom forever.

Anthem
I Heard a Voice from Heaven, John Goss (*Second Concord Anthem Book,* E. C. Schirmer) SATB (ME).

Ephesians 1:11–23 May God give you the Spirit, who will make you wise and understanding in the knowledge of Christ. In this way you will know the hope to which Christ has called you (the kind of New Age that is coming) and recognize God's power among us, especially God's power in raising Christ to a position above all earthly powers.

Anthem
Be Thou My Vision, Alice Parker (Hinshaw) SATB (E).

Luke 6:20–31 Jesus' opening injunctions of his Sermon on the Plain describe the life of a healed community. "Blessings to you who are poor, hungry, weeping, and despised. Woe to you who are rich, full, laughing, and respected. Do not take any retaliatory action against those who do physical violence to you, extract forced labor from you, or make demands for gifts and loans. But as a sign of the age to come, love and serve your enemies, and pray for them." Jesus has a way of turning our values upside down, doesn't he? He also makes us squirm.

Anthems
On Love of One's Enemies, Virgil Ford (Broadman) SATB (ME). *The Beatitudes,* Lloyd Pfautsch (Flammer) SATB (MD).

Psalm 149
1. Metrical: *Give Praise to the Lord.* Text: *The Psalter,* 1912, alt. 1984. Tune: LAUDATE DOMINUM. *PH90* #257.
2. Responsorial: *Psalm 149.* Setting: Hal H. Hopson. *PS93* #156.
3. Metrical: *Sing Praise to the Lord.* Text: *The Psalter,* 1912, alt. Tune: HANOVER. *PH87* #149.

See also *WIII* #80; *ANMP,* p. 76; *APS,* p. 38; *PR&T,* pp. 38 & 39.

Anthem
Give Praise to the Lord, PH90 #257.

Organ Music for the Day
1. *Chorale Prelude on* GELOBT SEI GOTT (*O Lord of Life, PH90* #530), Helmut Walcha (*Choralvorspiele,* vol. 3, C. F. Peters Corp. 5999).
2. *Fantasy on* SINE NOMINE (*For All the Saints, PH90* #526), Jan Bender (Augsburg 11–9108).

Hymns for the Day	HL33	HB55	WB72	PH90
For All the Saints	429	425	369	526
Give Thanks for Life	–	–	–	528
I Sing a Song of the Saints of God	–	–	–	364
Lord of the Living	–	–	–	529
O Lord of Life, Where'er They Be	–	–	–	530
Our God, Our Help in Ages Past	77	111	549	210
The Strife Is O'er	–	–	597	119

SUNDAY BETWEEN NOVEMBER 6 AND NOVEMBER 12
(PROPER 27) [32] (C)

Haggai 1:15*b*–2:9 YHWH speaks to us through Haggai's voice: "Remember how splendid our Temple looked in the good old days? Today it seems in sad shape, nearly in ruins. Don't despair. Get on with the rebuilding. Do the work for which you've been called, for I am with you. When you came out of Egypt, I promised I would stay with you, and I am still with you, so fear not. Sometime soon I will shake heaven and earth, land and sea, and all nations, and bring their treasures here to the new Temple, which will be far more splendid than the old one, for I will give my people shalom."

Anthem

Thus Saith the Lord and *But Who May Abide the Day of His Coming*, G. F. Handel (*Messiah*, any edition) bass solo (M).

2 Thessalonians 2:1–5, 13–17 We thank you, God, for your prior grace in choosing your servants to be saved by the power of the Spirit, for calling them through the gospel we preached to them. May they stand firm and hold on to "the traditions" we taught. May you, and our Lord Jesus, encourage and strengthen them so their work for you may be increased.

Anthem

God Gave Us Music, Dale Wood (Sacred Music) SATB, SAB optional handbells (3), brass quartet, congregation (see *PH90* #328).

Luke 20:27–38 Some Sadducees try to discredit Jesus and expose resurrection as an absurdity. So they ask a soap opera of trick questions about to whom we will be married when resurrected (*our myopic questions too?*). "For heaven's sake," Jesus declares, "resurrection is a whole new order where there is a unity among all who serve each other's needs! You can't project the patterns of this present order on the next. Resurrected life has abolished death and, therefore, marriage as the means to propagate life or assure legal succession becomes irrelevant." Thank God, because the present order is not so hot. But it is troubling how we cling to the present order.

Anthems

I'll Praise My Maker, Lloyd Pfautsch (Abingdon) SATB (ME). *I'll Praise My Maker While I've Breath*, *PH90* #253.

Psalm 145:1–5, 17–21
1. Metrical: *Your Faithfulness, O Lord, Is Sure*. Text: Joy F. Patterson, par. Tune: WINCHESTER NEW. Harmony, William Henry Monk, 1847 alt. *PH90* #251.
2. Responsorial: *Psalm 145* (1–5, 8–9). Setting: Hal H. Hopson. *PS93* #147.
3. Responsorial: *Psalm 145* (13*b*–16, 18, 21). Setting: Hal H. Hopson. *PS93* #148.
4. Scottish Chant: *Psalm 145*. Text: Hal H. Hopson. *PS93* #149.
5. Responsorial: *Psalm 145*. Setting by Howard Hughes (verses 10–12). *CC* G-2617.
See also *WIII* #76; *30P&2C*, pp. 42 & 43; *PR&T*, pp. 57 & 76.

Anthem

O Lord, You Are My God and King, *PH90* #252.

or **Psalm 98**
1. Metrical: *New Songs of Celebration Render*. Text: Erik Routley. Tune: RENDEZ À DIEU. *PH90* #218. (See also *RITL* #119, *H82* #413, and *PH87* #98 text by Dewey Westra.)
2. Metrical: *To God Compose a Song of Joy*. Text: Ruth C. Duck. Tune: KEDDY. *PH90* #219.
3. Responsorial: *Psalm 98*. Text: International Commission on English in the Liturgy. Tone: Presbyterian 3. *PS93* #94.

4. Responsorial: *Psalm 98* (1–6). Text: *Book of Common Prayer*. Setting: Peter R. Hallock. *PS93* #95.

See also *WIII* #781; *PH87* #98; *ANMP*, p. 161; *SPJP*, p. 53; *PR&T*, pp. 10 & 13.

Anthem

New Songs of Celebration Render, The Genevan Psalter, arr. Carlton R. Young (Agape) 2-part mixed, brass, congregation.

Organ Music for the Day

1. *Partita on* MIT FREUDEN ZART (*Sing Praise to God, Who Reigns Above, PH90* #483), Gerhard Krapf (Concordia 97–4689).

2. *Chorale Prelude on* RENDEZ À DIEU (*New Songs of Celebration Render, PH90* #218), Robert J. Powell (*Eleven Chorale Preludes on Hymn Tunes*, Harold Flammer Inc. 4430).

Hymns for the Day	HL33	HB55	WB72	PH90
Alleluia, Alleluia! Give Thanks	–	–	–	106
Blessing and Honor and Glory and Power	196	137	311	147
God of Our Life	88	108	395	275
Help Us Accept Each Other	–	–	–	358
O Holy City, Seen of John	409	508	505	453
Sing Praise to God, Who Reigns Above	–	15	568	483

SUNDAY BETWEEN NOVEMBER 13 AND NOVEMBER 19
(PROPER 28) [33] (C)

Isaiah 65:17–25 A vision of a new earth and new heavens calls for joy, because a self-serving creation is transformed into a world of servants. Union between God and humanity is consummated. All conflict, hostility, and death disappear. And everyone freely lives out God's purposes for creation.

Anthem

O God of Light, Gary Cornell (*Celebrations Unlimited*) SATB, congregation (E).

2 Thessalonians 3:6–13 Some people have quit witnessing to the gospel, for they are preoccupied with waiting for the Lord's future coming. They no longer work in the vineyard but are indolent sloths obsessed with heavenly matters. Stay away from idle folk who disobey the word. They will hold you back, because they have ceased carrying out Christ's present work. You know how to imitate us; we toiled night and day so as not to be a burden to you, but an example for you to follow. Persist in doing well.

Anthems

The True Glory, Peter Aston (Hinshaw) SATB (M). *God, Whose Giving Knows No Ending,* arr. Richard Hillert (Agape) SATB, congregation (E).

Luke 21:5–19 "All that glistens is not gold." It is hard for some people to hear that, especially when the Temple's majesty mesmerizes them. But the days will come when it shall be razed. When? Signs? Stay away from the misguided who predict "the time is at hand." Focus on the time now when creatures and creation futilely seek to control their destiny and turn their rage and frustration upon you. A time to despair? No! A great time to preach the gospel revealed by Christ, who gives words and wisdom to speak so that not one hair of the heads of the faithful can be separated from God.

Anthem

By Gracious Powers, J. Gelineau, arr. Erik Routley (Hinshaw) SATB (M).

Isaiah 12 (Song of Thanksgiving)
1. Metrical: *Surely It Is God Who Saves Me.* Text 8.7.8.7.D, Carl P. Daw, Jr. Tune: RAQUEL. *WIII* #584. (Aslo *PH87* #193 to Tune: REVIVE US.)
2. Responsorial: *Truly, God Is My Salvation.* Refrain, psalm tone, and Gelineau tone: *WIII* #81.
See also *PS93* #175.

Anthem

The First Song of Isaiah, Jack Noble White (H. W. Gray) SATB, optional guitar, handbells, percussion, congregation (ME).

Organ Music for the Day
1. *Prelude on* DONNE SECOURS (*Hope of the World, PH90* #360), Victor Freudenberg (*Ten Chorale Preludes and Settings for Organ,* Victor Freudenberg, 532 Pinar Drive, Orlando, FL 32825).
2. *Prelude on* KINGSFOLD (*Today We All Are Called . . . , PH90* #434), D. Johns (*The Concordia Hymn Prelude Series,* vol. 29, Concordia 97–5744).

Hymns for the Day	HL33	HB55	WB72	PH90
Canto de Esperanza/Song of Hope	–	–	–	432
Christ, Whose Glory Fills the Skies	26	47	332	462, 463
Great Day!	–	–	–	445
Hope of the World	–	291	423	360
Take Up Thy Cross, the Savior Said	–	293	–	393
Today We All Are Called to Be Disciples	–	–	–	434

CHRIST THE KING
[SUNDAY BETWEEN NOVEMBER 20 AND NOVEMBER 26] (PROPER 29) [34] (C)

Jeremiah 23:1–6 Shepherds (rulers) who neglect their flocks and allow them to scatter over the land will be dealt with harshly by YHWH. You can count on it! In fact, YHWH promises to replace such unjust leaders with shepherds who truly care for YHWH's people. Behold, the days are coming when YHWH will raise up "a righteous Branch" from David's line, who will rule with justice and righteousness.

Anthem

Behold, a Branch Is Growing, E. Aufdemberge (Concordia) SAB (ME).

Colossians 1:11–20 One sentence in the Greek text encompasses intercessions for the Colossian church, a thanksgiving, and two strophes of a christological hymn. Praise God for transferring Christ's followers from the realm of darkness to "the saints in light" and thus authorizing them to participate in the deliverance and redemption in Christ, the firstborn of creation and firstborn from the dead, who was the agent by whom creation originated and, therefore, could accomplish the redemption of that creation.

Anthem

Sing, My Soul, His Wondrous Love, Ned Rorem (C. F. Peters) SATB (M).

Luke 23:33–43 At the cross: *before* the people gawk, *before* the rulers scoff, *before* the soldiers mock, *before* a criminal taunts, *before* people tempt Jesus to save himself, he says, "Father, forgive them . . ." For Christ, forgiveness precedes sin. Unconditional, freely offered mercy—that's good news! The question, therefore, is not where we go when we die, but *with whom* will we be? Jesus to the dying criminal: Today you will be *with me* in Paradise. As Christ has been *with us,* so we will be *with Christ* in the love of God.

Anthems

Christ Is the King, Richard Peek (Brodt Music) SATB (ME). *O Christ, Our King,* Robert Wetzler (Augsburg) SATB (ME).

Luke 1:68–79 (Benedictus)
1. Metrical: *Blest Be the God of Israel.* Text: Michael A. Perry, alt. Tune: MERLE'S TUNE. Hal H. Hopson. *PH90* #602. (See also *DP/SLR* #97.)
2. Responsorial: *Song of Zechariah.* Text: English Language Liturgical Consultation. Byzantine Chant. *PS93* #158.
See also *PH90* #601; *PS93* #159 & #160; *20P&3C,* p. 32.

Anthem

Song of Zechariah, PH90 #601.

Organ Music for the Day
1. *Prelude on* DARWALL'S 148TH (*Rejoice, the Lord Is King, PH90* #155), Healey Willan (*Thirty-Six Short Preludes and Postludes on Well-Known Hymn Tunes,* C. F. Peters Corp. 6161).
2. *Prelude on* DIADEMATA (*Crown Him with Many Crowns, PH90* #151), Gordon Young (*Gordon Young's Preludes,* Hope 303).

Hymns for the Day	HL33	HB55	WB72	PH90
Because You Live, O Christ	–	–	–	105
Crown Him with Many Crowns	190	213	349	151
Lift Up Your Heads, O Mighty Gates	114	152	454	8
O Come and Sing Unto the Lord	49	29	488	214
O for a Thousand Tongues to Sing	199	141	493	466
O Worship the King, All Glorious Above	2	26	533	476

Special Days (C)
PRESENTATION OF THE LORD
[FEBRUARY 2] (ABC)

See Presentation of the Lord [February 2] (ABC) in Year A, p. 123.

ANNUNCIATION OF THE LORD
[MARCH 25] (ABC)

See Annunciation of the Lord [March 25] (ABC) in Year A, p. 125.

VISITATION OF MARY TO ELIZABETH
[MAY 31] (ABC)

See Visitation of Mary to Elizabeth [May 31] (ABC) in Year A, p. 127.

HOLY CROSS
[SEPTEMBER 14] (ABC)

See Holy Cross [September 14] (ABC) in Year A, p. 128.

THANKSGIVING DAY (C)*
[FOURTH THURSDAY IN NOVEMBER IN U.S.A.]

Deuteronomy 26:1–11 Instructions on offering firstfruits of the land to the Lord so you will not succumb to the temptation to believe you achieved the harvest that the Lord has given you. First, recite the ancient creedal story of YHWH's actions for the people—hearing their distress, delivering them from affliction, and guiding them to the Promised Land. Then offer the firstfruits of your God-given gifts to the Lord. Why all this ritual? So you can always remember how YHWH took care of your refugee ancestors, rejoice in such unmerited love, and care for the outsiders who live among you.

Anthem
Come, Sing a Song of Harvest, Melchior Vulpius, *PH90* #558.

Philippians 4:4–9 Rejoice and demonstrate to the world gentleness and forbearance, because the Lord is at hand, and the peace of God will guard your hearts and minds from any new threats. No need to fret over your own well-being: forsake your Sisyphus-like drivenness to secure tomorrow today, and consider practicing the virtues embraced by Paul: truth, honor, justice, purity, agreeableness, excellence, and whatever is praiseworthy.

Anthem
Rejoice in the Lord Always, Henry Purcell (Concordia) SATB (MD).

John 6:25–35 People searching for Jesus are accused by him of seeking only another ephemeral nutritional boost. "Work for imperishable, eternal manna," says Jesus, "which the Son of Man will give you." What kind of works must we do? Jesus: "Believe in the one whom God has sent." Then show us a sign like the manna in the wilderness—so we will believe. "That bread," retorts Jesus, "came from heaven." That's the bread we want; give it to us. "Open your eyes and see," answers Jesus; "I am the bread of life . . ."

Anthem
Thou Hast Given Us Bread from Heaven, Johann Geisler (H. W. Gray) SATB (M).

Psalm 100
1. Metrical: *All People That on Earth Do Dwell.* L.M., Tune: OLD HUNDREDTH. *PH90* #220.
2. Responsorial: *Psalm 100.* Setting: J. Jefferson Cleveland. *PS93* #97.
See also *PS93* #98–#101; *ANMP,* p. 168; *DP/SLR* #95; *WIII* #844.

Anthem
Jubilate Deo, Benjamin Britten (Oxford) SATB (M).

Organ Music for the Day
1. *Prelude on* KREMSER (*We Gather Together, PH90* #559), Wilbur Held (*Hymn Preludes for the Autumn Festivals,* Concordia 97–5360).
2. *Chorale Prelude on* NUN DANKET ALLE GOTT (*Now Thank We All Our God, PH90* #555), Max Drischner (*Choralvorspiele für Orgel,* Carl L. Schultheiss).

Hymns for the Day	HL33	HB55	WB72	PH90
All People That on Earth Do Dwell	1	24	288	220, 221
I Will Give Thanks with My Whole Heart	–	–	–	247
Let All Things Now Living	–	–	–	554
Let Us with a Gladsome Mind	64	28	453	244
Now Thank We All Our God	459	9	481	555
Rejoice, Ye Pure in Heart!	297	407	561	145, 146

*NOTE: Readings for Thanksgiving Day are not strictly tied to Year A, B, or C.

BIBLIOGRAPHY ON LECTIONARIES

....

Achtemeier, Elizabeth. "Aids and Resources for the Interpretation of Lectionary Texts." *Interpretation: A Journal of Bible and Theology* 31, no. 2 (April 1977): 154–64.

Allen, Horace T., Jr. "Introduction." In *Common Lectionary: The Lectionary Proposed by the Consultation on Common Texts*, pp. 7–27. New York: Church Hymnal Corporation, 1983.

————. "Emerging Ecumenical Issues in Worship." *Word and World* 9, no. 1 (winter 1989): 16–22.

————. "The Ecumenical Import of Lectionary Reform." In *Shaping English Liturgy: Studies in Honor of Archbishop Denis Hurley*, edited by Peter C. Finn and James M. Schellman, pp. 361–84. Washington, D.C.: Pastoral Press, 1990.

————. "Common Lectionary: Origins, Assumptions, and Issues." *Studia Liturgica* 21, no. 1 (1991): 14–30.

————. "Understanding the Lectionary." In *A Handbook for the Lectionary*, pp. 11–44. Philadelphia: Geneva Press, 1980.

————. "Using the Consensus Lectionary: A Response." In *Social Themes of the Christian Year: A Commentary on the Lectionary*, edited by Dieter T. Hessel, pp. 264–68. Philadelphia: Geneva Press, 1983.

Anglican Church of Canada. *The Lectionary*. Toronto: Anglican Book Centre, 1980.

Babin, David E. *Week In—Week Out: A New Look at Liturgical Preaching*. New York: Seabury Press, 1976.

Bailey, Lloyd R. "The Lectionary in Critical Perspective." *Interpretation: A Journal of Bible and Theology* 31, no. 2 (April 1977): 139–53.

————. "Lectionary Preaching." *Duke Divinity School Review* (winter 1976): 25–35.

Bass, George M. *The Renewal of Liturgical Preaching*. Minneapolis: Augsburg Publishing House, 1967.

Boehringer, Hans. "The Common Lectionary." *Word and World* 10, no. 1 (winter 1990): 27–32.

The Book of Common Prayer and Administration of the Sacraments and Other Rites and Ceremonies of the Church. New York: Church Hymnal Corporation and Seabury Press, 1979.

Bower, Peter C. "Introduction." In *Handbook for the Common Lectionary*, pp. 15–40. Philadelphia: Geneva Press, 1987.

Bradshaw, Paul. "The Use of the Bible in the Liturgy." *Studia Liturgica* 22 (1992): 35–52.

Briner, Lewis A. "Bibliography on the Lectionary and the Church Year." *Reformed Liturgy & Music* 9, no. 4 (fall 1975): 19–25.

————. "A Look at New Proposals for the Lectionary." *Worship* 3, no. 2, pp. 83–87; reprinted in *Reformed Liturgy & Music* 17, no. 3 (summer 1983): 126–29.

―――. "Preaching the Lectionary." *Reformed Liturgy & Music* 13, no. 2 (spring 1979): 5–12.

―――. "Using the Lectionary." *Reformed Liturgy & Music* 9, no. 4 (fall 1975): 13–17.

Buchler, Adolf. "The Reading of the Law and Prophets in a Triennial Cycle." *Jewish Quarterly Review* 5 (1893): 420–68; 6 (1894): 1–73.

Carl, William J., III. "Planning Your Preaching: A Look at the Lectionary." *Journal for Preachers* 4, no. 3 (Easter 1981): 13–17.

Carrington, Philip. *The Primitive Christian Calendar: A Study in the Making of the Marcan Gospel.* Vol. 1, *Introduction and Text.* New York: Cambridge University Press, 1952.

The Church of South India. "The 'Christian Year' Lectionary and Collects." In *The Book of Common Worship,* pp. 23–68. Madras: Oxford University Press, 1963.

Clarke, W. K. Lowther, and Charles Harris. "The Lectionary." In *Liturgy and Worship,* pp. 296–301. New York: Macmillan Co., 1946.

Commission on Worship of the Consultation on Church Union. *A Lectionary.* Princeton, N.J.: Consultation on Church Union, 1974.

Common Lectionary: The Lectionary Proposed by the Consultation on Common Texts. New York: Church Hymnal Corporation, 1983.

Crockett, Larrimore. "Luke 4:16–30 and the Jewish Lectionary Cycle: A Word of Caution." *Journal of Jewish Studies* 17 (1966): 13–45.

Davies, J. G., ed. *The New Westminster Dictionary of Liturgy and Worship.* Philadelphia: Westminster Press, 1979.

Davies, William David. "Reflections on Archbishop Carrington's *The Primitive Christian Calendar.*" In *The Background of the New Testament and Its Eschatology: In Honour of C. H. Dodd,* edited by W. D. Davies and D. Daube, pp. 124–52. New York: Cambridge University Press, 1954. Reprinted in W. D. Davies, *Christian Origins and Judaism* (Philadelphia: Westminster Press, 1962), pp. 67–96.

Dudley, Martin. "The Lectionary." In *Towards Liturgy 2000: Preparing for the Revision of the Alternative Service Book,* edited by Michael Perham, pp. 35–42. London: S.P.C.K./Alcuin Club, 1989.

Finch, Rowland G. *The Synagogue Lectionary and the New Testament: A Study of the Three-Year Cycle of Readings from the Law and the Prophets as a Contribution to New Testament Chronology.* London: S.P.C.K., 1939.

Fuller, Reginald H. *What Is Liturgical Preaching?* London: SCM Press, 1957.

González, Justo, and Catherine González. *Liberation Preaching.* Nashville: Abingdon Press, 1980.

Goulder, M. D. *Midrash and Lection in Matthew.* London: S.P.C.K., 1974.

Gray, Donald, ed. *The Word in Season: Essays by Members of the Joint Liturgical Group on the Use of the Bible in Liturgy.* Norwich, England: Canterbury Press, 1988.

―――. "Towards an Ecumenical Eucharistic Lectionary." *Liturgy* 12, no. 4 (1988): 149–54.

―――. "The Contribution of the Joint Liturgical Group to the Search for an Ecumenical Lectionary." *Studia Liturgica* 21, no. 1 (1991): 31–36.

Grisbrooke, W. Jardine. "A Contemporary Liturgical Problem: The Divine Office and Public Worship," *Studia Liturgica* 9, no. 3 (1973): 81–106.

Guilding, Aileen. *The Fourth Gospel and Jewish Worship: A Study of the Relation of St. John's Gospel to the Ancient Jewish Lectionary System.* Oxford: Clarendon Press, 1960.

Gunstone, John. *Commentary on the New Lectionary.* Rev. ed., vol. 1. London: S.P.C.K., 1979.

―――. "Contemporary Problems of Liturgical Time: Calendar and Lectionary." *Studia Liturgica* 14, nos. 2, 3, 4 (1982): 74–89.

Hageman, Howard G. "A Brief Study of the British Lectionary." *Worship* 56, no. 4 (July 1982): 356–64.

Heinemann, Joseph. "The Triennial Lectionary Cycle." *Journal of Jewish Studies* 19 (1968): 41–48.

Heuser, Rick. "Case for a Study of Old Testament Lectionary Texts: Connections Between Ancient Hebrew History and Current Political Affairs in the Middle East." An unpublished paper by members of the Boston Presbytery of the Presbyterian Church (U.S.A.), 1989.

Huxtable, John, John Marsh, Romilly Micklem, and James Todd. "Lectionary," compiled for the use of Congregationalists. In *A Book of Public Worship*, pp. 212–22. London: Oxford University Press, 1959.

Inter-Lutheran Commission on Worship, "Propers," In *Lutheran Book of Worship*, Ministers Desk Edition, pp. 121–95. Minneapolis: Augsburg Publishing House; Philadelphia: Board of Publication, Lutheran Church in America, 1978.

Joint Liturgical Group. *A Four Year Lectionary*. Norwich, England: Canterbury Press, 1990.

———. *The Calendar and Lessons for the Church Year*. London: S.P.C.K., 1969.

———. Ronald C. D. Jasper, ed. *The Calendar and Lectionary: A Reconsideration*. London: Oxford University Press, 1967.

Jones, Cheslyn, Geoffrey Wainwright, and Edward Yarnold, eds. *The Study of Liturgy*. New York: Oxford University Press, 1978.

Lamb, J. A. "The Place of the Bible in the Liturgy." In *The Cambridge History of the Bible*, vol. 1, *From the Beginnings to Jerome*, pp. 572ff. New York: Cambridge University Press, 1970.

Lengling, E. J. "Pericopes." In *New Catholic Encyclopedia*, vol. 11, pp. 130–38. New York: McGraw-Hill Book Co., 1967.

Lowry, Eugene L. *Living with the Lectionary: Preaching the Revised Common Lectionary*. Nashville: Abingdon Press, 1992.

Mann, Jacob. *The Bible as Read and Preached in the Old Synagogue*. Vol. 1, *The Palestinian Triennial Cycle: Genesis and Exodus*. Cincinnati: Hebrew Union College–Jewish Institute of Religion, 1940. Reprinted in The Library of Biblical Studies (New York: KTAV Publishing House, 1971). Vol. 2 (with Isaiah Sonne), *Leviticus and Numbers to Seder 106*. Cincinnati: Hebrew Union College–Jewish Institute of Religion, 1966.

McArthur, A. Allan. *The Christian Year and Lectionary Reform*. London: SCM Press, 1958.

"Minutes of the Consultation on Common Texts." Washington, D.C., 29–31 March 1978.

Morris, Leon. *The New Testament and the Jewish Lectionaries*. London: Tyndale, 1964.

Nesper, Paul. *Biblical Texts* (A Collection of Lectionaries). Columbus, Ohio: Wartburg Press, 1952.

Nichols, James Hastings. *Corporate Worship in the Reformed Tradition*. Philadelphia: Westminster Press, 1968.

Old, Hughes Oliphant. "The Ministry of the Word." In *Worship: That Is Reformed According to Scripture*. Guides to the Reformed Tradition. Atlanta: John Knox Press, 1984: 57–85.

———. Review of *A Handbook for the Lectionary*, by Horace T. Allen, Jr. *Worship* 56, no. 1 (January 1982): 85–86.

———. *The Patristic Roots of Reformed Worship*. Zurich: Theologischer Verlag, 1975.

Porter, J. R. "The Pentateuch and the Triennial Lectionary Cycle: An Examination of a Recent Theory." In *Promise and Fulfillment: Essays Presented to Professor S. H. Hooke*, edited by F. F. Bruce, pp. 163–74. Edinburgh: T. & T. Clark, 1963.

Proctor-Smith, Marjorie. "Images of Women in the Lectionary." In *Women—Invisible in Theology and Church*, edited by Elisabeth Schüssler Fiorenza and Mary Collins, pp. 51–62. Edinburgh: T. & T. Clark, 1985.

———. "Reorganizing Victimization: The Intersection Between Liturgy and Domestic Violence." *Perkins Journal*, October 1987, pp. 17–27.

Reed, Luther D. *The Lutheran Liturgy*, rev. ed., pp. 460–62. Philadelphia: Muhlenberg Press, 1960.

Reumann, John. "A History of Lectionaries: From the Synagogue at Nazareth to Post-Vatican II." *Interpretation: A Journal of Bible and Theology* 31, no. 2 (April 1977): 116–30.

Revised Common Lectionary, The. The Consultation on Common Texts. Nashville: Abingdon Press, 1992.

Sacred Congregation for the Sacraments and Divine Worship. *Ordo Lectionum Missae*. Rome: Vatican Polyglot Press, 25 May 1969.

———. *Lectionary for Mass*, Introduction (Second Editio Typica, 1981), no. 4, translated by International Commission on English in the Liturgy, *Lectionary*, 1. London: Collins Liturgical Publications and Cassell Ltd.; Dublin: Veritas Publications; Sydney: E. J. Dwyer Ltd., 1981, and *Liturgy Documentary Series*, 1. Washington, D.C.: Office of Publishing Services, United States Catholic Conference, 1982.

Sanders, James A. "Canon and Calendar: An Alternative Lectionary Proposal." In *Social Themes of the Christian Year: A Commentary on the Lectionary*, edited by Dieter T. Hessel, pp. 257–63. Philadelphia: Geneva Press, 1983.

Section on Worship of the Board of Discipleship of The United Methodist Church. *Seasons of the Gospel: Resources for the Christian Year*. Nashville: Abingdon Press, 1979.

Schuller, Eileen. "Some Criteria for the Choice of Scripture Texts in the Roman Lectionary." In *Shaping English Liturgy: Studies in Honor of Archbishop Denis Hurley*, pp. 385–404. Edited by Peter C. Finn and James M. Schellman. Washington, D.C.: Pastoral Press, 1990.

Shepherd, Massey H., Jr. "The Lectionary." In *The Oxford American Prayer Book Commentary*, pp. xi–xlv. New York: Oxford University Press, 1963.

Skudlarek, William. "The Structure and Use of the Lectionary," and "The Pastoral Use of the Lectionary." In *The Word in Worship: Preaching in a Liturgical Context*, pp. 31–44, 45–64. Nashville: Abingdon Press, 1981.

Sloyan, Gerard S. *A Commentary on the New Lectionary*. New York: Paulist Press, 1975.

———. "Some Suggestions for a Biblical Three-Year Lectionary." *Worship* 63, no. 6 (November 1989): 521–35.

———. "The Lectionary as a Context for Interpretation." *Interpretation: A Journal of Bible and Theology* 31, no. 2 (April 1977): 131–38.

"Sunday Lectionary Systems." A series of essays in *Studia Liturgica* 21, no. 1 (1991).

Trotter, J. Irwin, "Are We Preaching a 'Subversive' Lectionary?" *School of Theology at Claremont Bulletin: Occasional Paper Number 7*, vol. 28, no. 2 (December 1985).

Vatican Council II, Constitution on the Liturgy. *Sacrosanctum Concilium*, 4 December 1963, translated by International Commission on English in the Liturgy. In *Documents on the Liturgy, 1963–1979: Conciliar, Papal, and Curial Texts*. Collegeville, Minn.: Liturgical Press, 1982.

Werner, Eric. *The Sacred Bridge: Liturgical Parallels in Synagogue and Early Church*. New York: Columbia University Press, 1959.

White, James F. *Christian Worship in Transition*. Nashville: Abingdon Press, 1976.

———. *Introduction to Christian Worship*. Nashville: Abingdon Press, 1980.

273

Wikgren, Allen P. "Chicago Studies in the Greek Lectionary of the New Testament." In *Biblical and Patristic Studies in Memory of Robert Pierce Casey,* edited by J. N. Birdsall and R. W. Thomson, pp. 96–121. Freiburg: Herder, 1963.

Willis, G. G. *St. Augustine's Lectionary,* Alcuin Club Collection, 44. London: S.P.C.K., 1962.

INDEX OF SCRIPTURE READINGS

....

Dates refer to Sundays in Ordinary Time (e.g., Sunday between October 2 and October 8). When a number is given for a Sunday in Ordinary Time, it will correspond to the bracketed number beside the title of that Sunday.

Genesis

1:1–2:4*a*	Trinity Sunday A
	Easter Vigil ABC
1:1-5	Baptism of the Lord B
2:15-17; 3:1-7	Lent 1 A
6:9-22; 7:24; 8:14-19	May 29–June 4 (Proper 4) A
7:1-5,11-18; 8:6-18; 9:8-13	Easter Vigil ABC
9:8-17	Lent 1 B
11:1-9 (alt.)	Pentecost C
12:1-4*a*	Lent 2 A
12:1-9	June 5–June 11 (Proper 5) A
15:1-12, 17-18	Lent 2 C
17:1-7, 15-16	Lent 2 B
18:1-15(21:1-17)	June 12–June 18 (Proper 6) A
21:8-21	June 19–June 25 (Proper 7) A
22:1-14	June 26–July 2 (Proper 8) A
22:1-18	Easter Vigil ABC
24:34-38,42-49,58-67	July 3–July 9 (Proper 9) A
25:19-34	July 10–July 16 (Proper 10) A
28:10-19*a*	July 17–July 23 (Proper 11) A
29:15-28	July 24–July 30 (Proper 12) A
32:22-32	July 31–Aug. 6 (Proper 13) A
37:1-4,12-28	Aug. 7–Aug. 13 (Proper 14) A
45:1-15	Aug. 14–Aug. 20 (Proper 15) A
45:3-11,15	7th Sunday in Ord. Time C

Exodus

1:8–2:10	Aug. 21–Aug. 27 (Proper 16) A
3:1-15	Aug. 28–Sept. 3 (Proper 17) A
12:1-14	Sept. 4–Sept. 10 (Proper 18) A
12:1-4(5-10),11-14	Maundy Thursday ABC
14:10-31; 15:20-21	Easter Vigil ABC
14:19-31	Sept. 11–Sept. 17 (Proper 19) A
15:1*b*-11,20-21 (alt. resp.)	Sept. 11–Sept. 17 (Proper 19) A
15:1*b*-13,17-18 (resp.)	Easter Vigil ABC
16:2-15	Sept. 18–Sept. 24 (Proper 20) A
17:1-7	Lent 3 A
	Sept. 25–Oct. 1 (Proper 21) A
20:1-4,7-9,12-20	Oct. 2–Oct. 8 (Proper 22) A

275

20:1-17	Lent 3 B
24:12-18	Transfiguration A
32:1-14	Oct. 9–Oct. 15 (Proper 23) A
33:12-23	Oct. 16–Oct. 22 (Proper 24) A
34:29-35	Transfiguration C

Leviticus

19:1-2,9-18	7th Sunday in Ord. Time A

Numbers

6:22-27	Holy Name ABC
11:24-30 (alt.)	Pentecost A
21:4-9	Lent 4 B
21:4*b*-9	Holy Cross ABC

Deuteronomy

8:7-18	Thanksgiving A
26:1-11	Thanksgiving C
	Lent 1 C
30:15-20	6th Sunday in Ord. Time A
	Sept. 4–Sept. 10 (Proper 18) C
34:1-12	Oct. 23–Oct. 29 (Proper 25) A

Joshua

3:7-17	Oct. 30–Nov. 5 (Proper 26) A
5:9-12	Lent 4 C
24:1-3*a*, 14-25	Nov. 6–Nov. 12 (Proper 27) A

Judges

4:1-7	Nov. 13–Nov. 19 (Proper 28) A

Ruth

1:1-18	Oct. 30–Nov. 5 (Proper 26) B
3:1-5; 4:13-17	Nov. 6–Nov. 12 (Proper 27) B

1 Samuel

1:4-20	Nov. 13–Nov. 19 (Proper 28) B
2:1-10	Visitation ABC
2:1-10 (resp.)	Nov. 13–Nov. 19 (Proper 28) B
2:18-20, 26	Christmas 1 C
3:1-10(11-20)	2nd Sunday in Ord. Time B
	May 29–June 4 (Proper 4) B
8:4-11(12-15),16-20	
(11:14-15)	June 5–June 11 (Proper 5) B
15:34–16:13	June 12–June 18 (Proper 6) B
16:1-13	Lent 4 A
17:(1*a*,4-11,19-23),	
32-49 (alt.)	June 19–June 25 (Proper 7) B
17:57–18:5,10-16 (alt.)	June 19–June 25 (Proper 7) B

2 Samuel

1:1,17-27	June 26–July 2 (Proper 8) B
5:1-5,9-10	July 3–July 9 (Proper 9) B
6:1-5,12*b*-19	July 10–July 16 (Proper 10) B
7:1-11,16	Advent 4 B

7:1-14a	July 17–July 23 (Proper 11) B
11:1-15	July 24–July 30 (Proper 12) B
11:26–12:13a	July 31–Aug. 6 (Proper 13) B
18:5-9,15,31-33	Aug. 7–Aug. 13 (Proper 14) B
23:1-7	Christ the King B

1 Kings

2:10-12; 3:3-14	Aug. 14–Aug. 20 (Proper 15) B
8:(1,6,10-11)22-30,41-43	Aug. 21–Aug. 27 (Proper 16) B
17:8-16(17-24)	June 5–June 11 (Proper 5) C
18:20-21(22-29),30-39	May 29–June 4 (Proper 4) C
19:1-4(5-7),8-15a	June 19–June 25 (Proper 7) C
21:1-10(11-14),15-21a	June 12–June 18 (Proper 6) C

2 Kings

2:1-12	Transfiguration B
2:1-2,6-14	June 26–July 2 (Proper 8) C
5:1-14	6th Sunday in Ord. Time B
	July 3–July 9 (Proper 9) C

Nehemiah

8:1-3,5-6,8-10	3rd Sunday in Ord. Time C

Esther

7:1-6,9-10; 9:20-22	Sept. 25–Oct. 1 (Proper 21) B

Job

1:1; 2:1-10	Oct. 2–Oct. 8 (Proper 22) B
14:1-14 (alt.)	Holy Saturday ABC
23:1-9,16-17	Oct. 9–Oct. 15 (Proper 23) B
38:1-7(34-41)	Oct. 16–Oct. 22 (Proper 24) B
42:1-6,10-17	Oct. 23–Oct. 29 (Proper 25) B

Psalms

1	6th Sunday in Ord. Time C
	Easter 7 B
	Sept. 18–Sept. 24 (Proper 20) B
	Sept. 4–Sept. 10 (Proper 18) C
2 (alt.)	Transfiguration A
4	Easter 3 B
5:1-8	June 12–June 18 (Proper 6) C
8	Holy Name ABC
	Trinity Sunday AC
	New Year ABC
9:9-20 (alt.)	June 19–June 25 (Proper 7) B
13	June 26–July 2 (Proper 8) A
14	July 24–July 30 (Proper 12) B
	Sept. 11-Sept. 17 (Proper 19) C
15	4th Sunday in Ord. Time A
16	Easter 2 A
	Easter Vigil ABC
17:1-7,15	July 31–Aug. 6 (Proper 13) A
19	Easter Vigil ABC
	Lent 3 B
	3rd Sunday in Ord. Time C

	Oct. 2–Oct. 8 (Proper 22) A
19 (alt.)	Sept. 11–Sept. 17 (Proper 19) B
20	June 12–June 18 (Proper 6) B
22	Good Friday ABC
22:1-15	Oct. 9–Oct. 15 (Proper 23) B
22:19-28	June 19–June 25 (Proper 7) C
22:23-31	Lent 2 B
22:25-31	Easter 5 B
23	Easter 4 ABC
	Lent 4 A
24	All Saints B
	July 10–July 16 (Proper 10) B
24:7-10 (alt.)	Presentation ABC
25:1-10	Lent 1 B
	Advent 1 C
26	Oct. 2–Oct. 8 (Proper 22) B
27	Lent 2 C
27:1,4-9	3rd Sunday in Ord. Time A
29	Baptism of the Lord ABC
	Trinity Sunday B
30	6th Sunday in Ord. Time B
	Easter 3 C
	July 3–July 9 (Proper 9) C
31:1-4,15-16	Holy Saturday ABC
31:9-16	Passion/Palm Sunday ABC
31:1-5,15-16	Easter 5 A
32	Lent 1 A
	Lent 4 C
33:1-12	June 5–June 11 (Proper 5) A
34:1-8(19-22)	Oct. 23–Oct. 29 (Proper 25) B
34:1-10, 22	All Saints A
36:5-10	2nd Sunday in Ord. Time C
36:5-11	Monday in Holy Week ABC
37:1-11,39-40	7th Sunday in Ord. Time C
40:1-11	2nd Sunday in Ord. Time A
40:5-10 (alt.)	Annunciation ABC
41	7th Sunday in Ord. Time B
42 and 43	June 19–June 25 (Proper 7) C
	Easter Vigil ABC
45:10-17	July 3–July 9 (Proper 9) A
45 (alt.)	Annunciation ABC
45:1-2,6-9	Aug. 28–Sept. 3 (Proper 17) B
46	Easter Vigil ABC
	May 29–June 4 (Proper 4) A
47	Ascension ABC
48	July 3–July 9 (Proper 9) B
50:1-6	Transfiguration B
50:1-8,22-23	Aug. 7–Aug. 13 (Proper 14) C
51:1-12	July 31–Aug. 6 (Proper 13) B
51:1-12 (alt.)	Lent 5 B
51:1-17	Ash Wednesday ABC
52	July 17–July 23 (Proper 11) C
62:5-12	3rd Sunday in Ord. Time B
63:1-8	Lent 3 C

Hosea
1:2-10   July 24–July 30 (Proper 12) C
2:14-20   8th Sunday in Ord. Time B
11:1-11   July 31–Aug. 6 (Proper 13) C

Joel
2:1-2,12-17 (alt.)   Ash Wednesday ABC
2:21-27   Thanksgiving B
2:23-32   Oct. 23–Oct. 29 (Proper 25) C

Amos
7:7-17   July 10–July 16 (Proper 10) C
8:1-12   July 17–July 23 (Proper 11) C

Jonah
3:1-5,10   3rd Sunday in Ord. Time B

Micah
5:2-5a   Advent 4 C
6:1-8   4th Sunday in Ord. Time A

Habakkuk
1:1-4; 2:1-4   Oct. 30–Nov. 5 (Proper 26) C

Zephaniah
3:14-20   Easter Vigil ABC
                Advent 3 C

Haggai
1:15b–2:9   Nov. 6–Nov. 12 (Proper 27) C

Malachi
3:1-4   Presentation ABC
3:1-4 (alt.)   Advent 2 C

Baruch
3:9-15, 32–4:4 (alt.)   Easter Vigil ABC

Matthew
1:18-25   Advent 4 A
2:1-12   Epiphany ABC
2:13-23   Christmas 1 A
3:1-12   Advent 2 A
3:13-17   Baptism of the Lord A
4:1-11   Lent 1 A
4:12-23   3rd Sunday in Ord. Time A
5:1-12   4th Sunday in Ord. Time A
                All Saints A
5:13-20   5th Sunday in Ord. Time A
5:21-37   6th Sunday in Ord. Time A
5:38-48   7th Sunday in Ord. Time A
6:1-6,16-21   Ash Wednesday ABC
6:24-34   8th Sunday in Ord. Time A
6:25-33   Thanksgiving B

7:21-29	May 29–June 4 (Proper 4) A
9:9-13,18-26	June 5–June 11 (Proper 5) A
9:35–10:8(9-23)	June 12–June 18 (Proper 6) A
10:24-39	June 19–June 25 (Proper 7) A
10:40-42	June 26–July 2 (Proper 8) A
11:2-11	Advent 3 A
11:16-19,25-30	July 3–July 9 (Proper 9) A
13:1-9,18-23	July 10–July 16 (Proper 10) A
13:24-30,36-43	July 17–July 23 (Proper 11) A
13:31-33,44-52	July 24–July 30 (Proper 12) A
14:13-21	July 31–Aug. 6 (Proper 13) A
14:22-33	Aug. 7–Aug. 13 (Proper 14) A
15:(10-20),21-28	Aug. 14–Aug. 20 (Proper 15) A
16:13-20	Aug. 21–Aug. 27 (Proper 16) A
16:21-28	Aug. 28–Sept. 3 (Proper 17) A
17:1-9	Transfiguration A
17:1-9 (alt.)	Lent 2 A
18:15-20	Sept. 4–Sept. 10 (Proper 18) A
18:21-35	Sept. 11–Sept. 17 (Proper 19) A
20:1-16	Sept. 18–Sept. 24 (Proper 20) A
21:1-11 (palms)	Passion/Palm Sunday A
21:23-32	Sept. 25–Oct. 1 (Proper 21) A
21:33-46	Oct. 2–Oct. 8 (Proper 22) A
22:1-14	Oct. 9–Oct. 15 (Proper 23) A
22:15-22	Oct. 16–Oct. 22 (Proper 24) A
22:34-46	Oct. 23–Oct. 29 (Proper 25) A
23:1-12	Oct. 30–Nov. 5 (Proper 26) A
24:36-44	Advent 1 A
25:1-13	Nov. 6–Nov. 12 (Proper 27) A
25:14-30	Nov. 13–Nov. 19 (Proper 28) A
25:31-46	New Year ABC
	Christ the King A
26:14–27:66 (alt.)	Passion/Palm Sunday A
27:11-54 (alt.)	Passion/Palm Sunday A
27:57-66 (alt.)	Holy Saturday ABC
28:1-10	Easter Vigil A
28:1-10 (alt.)	Easter A
28:16-20	Trinity Sunday A

Mark

1:1-8	Advent 2 B
1:4-11	Baptism of the Lord B
1:9-15	Lent 1 B
1:14-20	3rd Sunday in Ord. Time B
1:21-28	4th Sunday in Ord. Time B
1:29-39	5th Sunday in Ord. Time B
1:40-45	6th Sunday in Ord. Time B
2:1-12	7th Sunday in Ord. Time B
2:13-22	8th Sunday in Ord. Time B
2:23–3:6	May 29–June 4 (Proper 4) B
3:20-35	June 5–June 11 (Proper 5) B
4:26-34	June 12–June 18 (Proper 6) B
4:35-41	June 19–June 25 (Proper 7) B
5:21-43	June 26–July 2 (Proper 8) B

6:1-13	July 3–July 9 (Proper 9) B
6:14-29	July 10–July 16 (Proper 10) B
6:30-34,53-56	July 17–July 23 (Proper 11) B
7:1-8,14-15,21-23	Aug. 28–Sept. 3 (Proper 17) B
7:24-37	Sept. 4–Sept. 10 (Proper 18) B
8:27-38	Sept. 11–Sept. 17 (Proper 19) B
8:31-38 (alt.)	Lent 2 B
9:2-9	Transfiguration B
9:2-9 (alt.)	Lent 2 B
9:30-37	Sept. 18–Sept. 24 (Proper 20) B
9:38-50	Sept. 25–Oct. 1 (Proper 21) B
10:2-16	Oct. 2–Oct. 8 (Proper 22) B
10:17-31	Oct. 9–Oct. 15 (Proper 23) B
10:35-45	Oct. 16–Oct. 22 (Proper 24) B
10:46-52	Oct. 23–Oct. 29 (Proper 25) B
11:1-11 (alt.) (palms)	Passion/Palm Sunday B
12:28-34	Oct. 30–Nov. 5 (Proper 26) B
12:38-44	Nov. 6–Nov. 12 (Proper 27) B
13:1-8	Nov. 13–Nov. 19 (Proper 28) B
13:24-37	Advent 1 B
14:1–15:47 (alt.)	Passion/Palm Sunday B
15:1-39(40-47) (alt.)	Passion/Palm Sunday B
16:1-8	Easter Vigil B
16:1-8 (alt.)	Easter B

Luke

1:26-38	Annunciation ABC
	Advent 4 B
1:39-45(46-55)	Advent 4 C
1:39-57	Visitation ABC
1:47-55 (alt. resp.)	Advent 3 AB
	Advent 4 BC
1:68-79 (resp.)	Advent 2 C
	Christ the King C
2:(1-7), 8-20	Christmas Day 2 ABC
2:1-14(15-20)	Christmas Day 1 ABC
2:15-21	Holy Name ABC
2:22-40	Presentation ABC
	Christmas 1 B
2:41-52	Christmas 1 C
3:1-6	Advent 2 C
3:7-18	Advent 3 C
3:15-17,21-22	Baptism of the Lord C
4:1-13	Lent 1 C
4:14-21	3rd Sunday in Ord. Time C
4:21-30	4th Sunday in Ord. Time C
5:1-11	5th Sunday in Ord. Time C
6:17-26	6th Sunday in Ord. Time C
6:20-31	All Saints C
6:27-38	7th Sunday in Ord. Time C
6:39-49	8th Sunday in Ord. Time C
7:1-10	May 29–June 4 (Proper 4) C
7:11-17	June 5–June 11 (Proper 5) C
7:36–8:3	June 12–June 18 (Proper 6) C

8:26-39	June 19–June 25 (Proper 7) C
9:28-36 (alt.)	Lent 2 C
9:28-36(37-43)	Transfiguration C
9:51-62	June 26–July 2 (Proper 8) C
10:1-11,16-20	July 3–July 9 (Proper 9) C
10:25-37	July 10–July 16 (Proper 10) C
10:38-42	July 17–July 23 (Proper 11) C
11:1-13	July 24–July 30 (Proper 12) C
12:13-21	July 31–Aug. 6 (Proper 13) C
12:32-40	Aug. 7–Aug. 13 (Proper 14) C
12:49-56	Aug. 14–Aug. 20 (Proper 15) C
13:1-9	Lent 3 C
13:10-17	Aug. 21–Aug. 27 (Proper 16) C
13:31-35 (alt.)	Lent 2 C
14:1,7-14	Aug. 28–Sept. 3 (Proper 17) C
14:25-33	Sept. 4–Sept. 10 (Proper 18) C
15:1-3,11b-32	Lent 4 C
15:1-10	Sept. 11–Sept. 17 (Proper 19) C
16:1-13	Sept. 18–Sept. 24 (Proper 20) C
16:19-31	Sept. 25–Oct. 1 (Proper 21) C
17:5-10	Oct. 2–Oct. 8 (Proper 22) C
17:11-19	Thanksgiving A
	Oct. 9–Oct. 15 (Proper 23) C
18:1-8	Oct. 16–Oct. 22 (Proper 24) C
18:9-14	Oct. 23–Oct. 29 (Proper 25) C
19:1-10	Oct. 30–Nov. 5 (Proper 26) C
19:28-40 (palms)	Palm/Passion Sunday C
20:27-38	Nov. 6–Nov. 12 (Proper 27) C
21:5-19	Nov. 13–Nov. 19 (Proper 28) C
21:25-36	Advent 1 C
22:14–23:56 (alt.)	Palm/Passion Sunday C
23:1-49 (alt.)	Palm/Passion Sunday C
23:33-43	Christ the King C
24:1-12	Easter Vigil C
24:1-12 (alt.)	Easter C
24:13-35	Easter 3 A
24:13-49	Easter Evening ABC
24:36b-48	Easter 3 B
24:44-53	Ascension ABC

John

1:(1-9)10-18	Christmas 2 ABC
1:1-14	Christmas Day 3 ABC
1:6-8,19-28	Advent 3 B
1:29-42	2nd Sunday in Ord. Time A
1:43-51	2nd Sunday in Ord. Time B
2:1-11	2nd Sunday in Ord. Time C
2:13-22	Lent 3 B
3:1-17	Trinity Sunday B
3:1-17 (alt.)	Lent 2 A
3:13-17	Holy Cross ABC
3:14-21	Lent 4 B
4:5-42	Lent 3 A
5:1-9 (alt.)	Easter 6 C

6:1-21	July 24–July 30 (Proper 12) B
6:24-35	July 31–Aug. 6 (Proper 13) B
6:25-35	Thanksgiving C
6:35,41-51	Aug. 7–Aug. 13 (Proper 14) B
6:51-58	Aug. 14–Aug. 20 (Proper 15) B
6:56-69	Aug. 21–Aug. 27 (Proper 16) B
7:37-39 (alt.)	Pentecost A
9:1-41	Lent 4 A
10:1-10	Easter 4 A
10:11-18	Easter 4 B
10:22-30	Easter 4 C
11:1-45	Lent 5 A
11:32-44	All Saints B
12:1-8	Lent 5 C
12:1-11	Monday in Holy Week ABC
12:12-16 (alt.) (palms)	Palm/Passion Sunday B
12:20-33	Lent 5 B
12:20-36	Tuesday in Holy Week ABC
13:1-17,31b-35	Maundy Thursday ABC
13:21-32	Wednesday in Holy Week ABC
13:31-35	Easter 5 C
14:1-14	Easter 5 A
14:8-17(25-27)	Pentecost C
14:15-21	Easter 6 A
14:23-29 (alt.)	Easter 6 C
15:1-8	Easter 5 B
15:9-17	Easter 6 B
15:26-27; 16:4b-15	Pentecost B
16:12-15	Trinity Sunday C
17:1-11	Easter 7 A
17:6-19	Easter 7 B
17:20-26	Easter 7 C
18:1–19:42	Good Friday ABC
18:33-37	Christ the King B
19:38-42 (alt.)	Holy Saturday ABC
20:1-18 (alt.)	Easter ABC
20:19-23 (alt.)	Pentecost A
20:19-31	Easter 2 ABC
21:1-19	Easter 3 C

Acts

1:1-11	Ascension ABC
1:6-14	Easter 7 A
1:15-17,21-26	Easter 7 B
2:1-21 (alt.)	Pentecost ABC
2:1-14a, 36-41	Easter 3 A
2:14a,36-41	Easter 2 A
2:42-47	Easter 4 A
3:12-19	Easter 3 B
4:5-12	Easter 4 B
4:32-35	Easter 2 B
5:27-32	Easter 2 C
7:55-60	Easter 5 A
8:14-17	Baptism of the Lord C

8:26-40	Easter 5 B
9:1-6(7-20)	Easter 3 C
9:36-43	Easter 4 C
10:34-43	Baptism of the Lord A
10:34-43 (alt.)	Easter ABC
10:44-48	Easter 6 B
11:1-18	Easter 5 C
16:9-15	Easter 6 C
16:16-34	Easter 7 C
17:22-31	Easter 6 A
19:1-7	Baptism of the Lord B

Romans

1:1-7	Advent 4 A
1:16-17; 3:22b-28(29-31)	May 29–June 4 (Proper 4) A
4:1-5, 13-17	Lent 2 A
4:13-25	June 5–June 11 (Proper 5) A
	Lent 2 B
5:1-5	Trinity Sunday C
5:1-8	June 12–June 18 (Proper 6) A
5:1-11	Lent 3 A
5:12-19	Lent 1 A
6:1b-11	June 19–June 25 (Proper 7) A
6:3-11	Easter Vigil ABC
6:12-23	June 26–July 2 (Proper 8) A
7:15-25a	July 3–July 9 (Proper 9) A
8:1-11	July 10–July 16 (Proper 10) A
8:6-11	Lent 5 A
8:12-17	Trinity Sunday B
8:12-25	July 17–July 23 (Proper 11) A
8:14-17 (alt.)	Pentecost C
8:22-27 (alt.)	Pentecost B
8:26-39	July 24–July 30 (Proper 12) A
9:1-5	July 31–Aug. 6 (Proper 13) A
10:5-15	Aug. 7–Aug. 13 (Proper 14) A
10:8b-13	Lent 1 C
11:1-2a,29-32	Aug. 14–Aug. 20 (Proper 15) A
12:1-8	Aug. 21–Aug. 27 (Proper 16) A
12:9-16b	Visitation ABC
12:9-21	Aug. 28–Sept. 3 (Proper 17) A
13:8-14	Sept. 4–Sept. 10 (Proper 18) A
13:11-14	Advent 1 A
14:1-12	Sept. 11–Sept. 17 (Proper 19) A
15:4-13	Advent 2 A
16:25-27	Advent 4 B

1 Corinthians

1:1-9	2nd Sunday in Ord. Time A
1:3-9	Advent 1 B
1:10-18	3rd Sunday in Ord. Time A
1:18-24	Holy Cross ABC
1:18-25	Lent 3 B
1:18-31	Tuesday in Holy Week ABC
	4th Sunday in Ord. Time A

2:1-12(13-16)	5th Sunday in Ord. Time A
3:1-9	6th Sunday in Ord. Time A
3:10-11,16-23	7th Sunday in Ord. Time A
4:1-5	8th Sunday in Ord. Time A
5:6b-8	Easter Evening ABC
6:12-20	2nd Sunday in Ord. Time B
7:29-31	3rd Sunday in Ord. Time B
8:1-13	4th Sunday in Ord. Time B
9:16-23	5th Sunday in Ord. Time B
9:24-27	6th Sunday in Ord. Time B
10:1-13	Lent 3 C
11:23-26	Maundy Thursday ABC
12:1-11	2nd Sunday in Ord. Time C
12:3b-13 (alt.)	Pentecost A
12:12-31a	3rd Sunday in Ord. Time C
13:1-13	4th Sunday in Ord. Time C
15:1-11	5th Sunday in Ord. Time C
15:1-11 (alt.)	Easter B
15:12-20	6th Sunday in Ord. Time C
15:19-26 (alt.)	Easter C
15:35-38,42-50	7th Sunday in Ord. Time C
15:51-58	8th Sunday in Ord. Time C

2 Corinthians

1:18-22	7th Sunday in Ord. Time B
3:1-6	8th Sunday in Ord. Time B
3:12–4:2	Transfiguration C
4:3-6	Transfiguration B
4:5-12	May 29–June 4 (Proper 4) B
4:13–5:1	June 5–June 11 (Proper 5) B
5:6-10(11-13),14-17	June 12–June 18 (Proper 6) B
5:16-21	Lent 4 C
5:20b–6:10	Ash Wednesday ABC
6:1-13	June 19–June 25 (Proper 7) B
8:7-15	June 26–July 2 (Proper 8) B
9:6-15	Thanksgiving A
12:2-10	July 3–July 9 (Proper 9) B
13:11-13	Trinity Sunday A

Galatians

1:1-12	May 29–June 4 (Proper 4) C
1:11-24	June 5–June 11 (Proper 5) C
2:15-21	June 12–June 18 (Proper 6) C
3:23-29	June 19–June 25 (Proper 7) C
4:4-7	Christmas 1 B
4:4-7 (alt.)	Holy Name ABC
5:1, 13-25	June 26–July 2 (Proper 8) C
6:(1-6),7-16	July 3–July 9 (Proper 9) C

Ephesians

1:3-14	Christmas 2 ABC
	July 10–July 16 (Proper 10) B
1:11-23	All Saints C
1:15-23	Ascension ABC

2:8-15	Oct. 9–Oct. 15 (Proper 23) C
3:14–4:5	Oct. 16–Oct. 22 (Proper 24) C
4:6-8,16-18	Oct. 23–Oct. 29 (Proper 25) C

Titus

2:11-14	Christmas Day 1 ABC
3:4-7	Christmas Day 2 ABC

Philemon

1-21	Sept. 4–Sept. 10 (Proper 18) C

Hebrews

1:1-4(5-12)	Christmas Day 3 ABC
1:1-4; 2:5-12	Oct. 2–Oct. 8 (Proper 22) B
2:10-18	Christmas 1 A
2:14-18	Presentation ABC
4:12-16	Oct. 9–Oct. 15 (Proper 23) B
4:14-16; 5:7-9	Good Friday ABC
5:1-10	Oct. 16–Oct. 22 (Proper 24) B
5:5-10	Lent 5 B
7:23-28	Oct. 23–Oct. 29 (Proper 25) B
9:11-14	Oct. 30–Nov. 5 (Proper 26) B
9:11-15	Monday in Holy Week ABC
9:24-28	Nov. 6–Nov. 12 (Proper 27) B
10:4-10	Annunciation ABC
10:5-10	Advent 4 C
10:11-14(15-18),19-25	Nov. 13–Nov. 19 (Proper 28) B
10:16-25 (alt.)	Good Friday ABC
11:1-3,8-16	Aug. 7–Aug. 13 (Proper 14) C
11:29–12:2	Aug. 14–Aug. 20 (Proper 15) C
12:1-3	Wednesday in Holy Week ABC
12:18-29	Aug. 21–Aug. 27 (Proper 16) C
13:1-8,15-16	Aug. 28–Sept. 3 (Proper 17) C

James

1:17-27	Aug. 28–Sept. 3 (Proper 17) B
2:1-10(11-13),14-17	Sept. 4–Sept. 10 (Proper 18) B
3:1-12	Sept. 11–Sept. 17 (Proper 19) B
3:13–4:3,7-8*a*	Sept. 18–Sept. 24 (Proper 20) B
5:7-10	Advent 3 A
5:13-20	Sept. 25–Oct. 1 (Proper 21) B

1 Peter

1:3-9	Easter 2 A
1:17-23	Easter 3 A
2:2-10	Easter 4 A
2:19-25	Easter 5 A
3:13-22	Easter 6 A
3:18-22	Lent 1 B
4:1-8	Holy Saturday ABC
4:12-14; 5:6-11	Easter 7 A

2 Peter

1:16-21	Transfiguration A
3:8-15*a*	Advent 2 B

1 John

1:1–2:2	Easter 2 B
3:1-3	All Saints A
3:1-7	Easter 3 B
3:16-24	Easter 4 B
4:7-21	Easter 5 B
5:1-6	Easter 6 B
5:9-13	Easter 7 B

Revelation

1:4-8	Easter 2 C
1:4b-8	Christ the King B
5:11-14	Easter 3 C
7:9-17	All Saints A
	Easter 4 C
21:1-6	Easter 5 C
21:1-6a	New Year ABC
	All Saints B
21:10,22–22:5	Easter 6 C
22:12-14,16-17,20-21	Easter 7 C